PENGUIN BOOKS

MARTIN LUTHER

Eric Metaxas is the #1 *New York Times* bestselling author of *If You Can Keep It*, *Bonhoeffer*, *Amazing Grace*, and *Miracles*. His books have been translated into more than twenty-five languages. His writing has appeared in *The Wall Street Journal*, *The New York Times*, and *The New Yorker*, and Metaxas has appeared as a cultural commentator on CNN, the Fox News Channel, and MSNBC. He is the host of *The Eric Metaxas Show*, a nationally syndicated daily radio show. Metaxas is also the founder and host of *Socrates in the City*, the acclaimed series of conversations on "life, God, and other small topics," featuring Malcolm Gladwell, Dick Cavett, and Rabbi Lord Jonathan Sacks, among many others. He is a senior fellow and lecturer at large at the King's College in New York City, where he lives with his wife and daughter.

Praise for *Martin Luther*

"There is much here that is praiseworthy. The details of Luther's life and of his struggles against the status quo are related with verve, and with a genuine talent for rendering the intricacies of late medieval theology approachable to those who may have never encountered it before. Metaxas knows how to tell a story and how to develop characters, and this talent makes his narrative at once gripping and accessible. . . . An excellent glimpse of the whole of Luther's life."
—*The New York Times Book Review*

"A meticulously researched and detailed account of Luther's life and times . . . A very human portrait . . . Metaxas is a scrupulous chronicler and has an eye for a good story. The result is full, instructive, and pacey." —*The Washington Post*

"Mr. Metaxas has a knack for capturing the heart and mind of his subjects. . . . His conclusions about the sixteenth-century revolutionary are uniquely Metaxas, a deep and thoughtful writer with much to teach the world."
—*The Washington Times*

"A new magisterial biography . . . Another epic work [from Eric Metaxas] . . . Extensively researched . . . A beautifully balanced separation of fact from fiction."
—Hugh Hewitt

"A meaty autobiography of the Reformation leader. Metaxas brings his flair for epic biography that was on such impressive display in his 2010 book, *Bonhoeffer*. . . . Metaxas offers something different and special."

—*Kirkus Reviews* (starred review)

"A masterful portrait of a seminal figure." —*Booklist* (starred review)

"A highly readable, fast-paced biography." —*Publishers Weekly*

"Metaxas is the best storyteller among the Luther biographers."

—*WORLD* magazine

"A biography designed to peel back the myths and reveal Luther as the fascinating and influential man he was . . . A fast, easy read." —*Houston Chronicle*

"Outstanding . . . full of clever turns of phrase and humor that makes the incredible story of Luther all the more accessible." —ChristianHeadlines.com

"Metaxas offers something different and special. . . . The author's fast-paced style and attention to interesting details sets this 450-page book apart."

—Institute for Faith, Work & Economics

"Deeply researched and surprising." —*Tampa Bay Times*

"Metaxas's *Martin Luther* is a breathtaking achievement and a gripping read. Bold, fast-paced, and magisterial like its hero, yet always stylish and witty like its author, this account blows the cobwebs off long-settled expectations, and helps us to understand the man who shook the medieval world and helped to shape the modern world." —Os Guinness, author of *Impossible People*

"If you had to make a list of five people who shaped the modern West, Martin Luther would be on it. Yet almost everything you think you know about Luther is wrong, as Eric Metaxas shows in this brilliant biography. This is an amazing story, beautifully told. You'll emerge wiser."

—Tucker Carlson, host of *Tucker Carlson Tonight*

"When Martin Luther made it possible to read the Bible for yourself, he did more than anyone else to create the future. Read this book for yourself to understand the story we're all still living through."

—Peter Thiel, cofounder of PayPal, entrepreneur, and author of *Zero to One*

"A marvelous, brilliant book that is equal parts biography, theology, political philosophy, and cultural history. With a light and rapid touch that nonetheless is capable of conveying deep truths and insights, Metaxas deftly blends these many elements into a narrative that reads as compellingly as a novel. I imagine that Luther himself—not an easy man to please—would be deeply impressed by this master portraiture." —Mark Helprin, bestselling author of *Winter's Tale* and *A Soldier of the Great War*

"Eric Metaxas has blessed us with yet another indispensable biography. With his customary verve and elegance, profound reverence, and biting wit, Metaxas's *Martin Luther* is an education in the meaning of man's relation to God. It makes Luther's life come alive and illuminates how deeply that life has affected our own." —Bret Lott, bestselling author of *Jewel* and nonfiction editor of *Crazyhorse* magazine

"As with his seminal work on Bonhoeffer, Eric Metaxas, in this extraordinary work on Martin Luther, reveals those nuances that made Luther the force that he was. As the details gather in the book, you soon feel the presence of the man himself." —Dr. Gerald L. Schroeder, lecturer and teacher at College of Jewish Studies Aish HaTorah's Discovery Seminar

"This massive but eminently readable biography of Luther deserves no less an adjective than 'formidable.' Eric Metaxas is to religious biographers what Pixar is to cartoons." —Peter Kreeft, author of *Catholics and Protestants: What Can We Learn from Each Other?*

"Extraordinary. A tour de force." —Johnnie Moore, Jr., founder of The KAIROS Company

"If you wish to know why Martin Luther is remembered as one of the most consequential figures in history, and why Eric Metaxas has emerged as one of the most prominent storytellers of our generation, you'll find the answers in this book. Eric's skill as a writer and biographer are on full display here, even as he corrects the myths and secures the history of a monk who changed the world." —John Stonestreet, president of The Colson Center for Christian Worldview

"One of the most engaging, inspiring, and entertaining books on Luther I've ever read. Every page a joy." —J.D. Greear, pastor of The Summit Church in Raleigh-Durham, NC

Martin Luther

The Man Who Rediscovered God and Changed the World

ERIC METAXAS

PENGUIN BOOKS

PENGUIN BOOKS

An imprint of Penguin Random House LLC

375 Hudson Street

New York, New York 10014

penguinrandomhouse.com

First published in the United States of America by Viking Penguin,
an imprint of Penguin Random House LLC, 2017
Published in Penguin Books 2018

Map by Jeffrey L. Ward

Photograph and illustration credits appear on pages 479–480.

ISBN: 9781101980019 (hardcover)
ISBN: 9781101980026 (paperback)
ISBN: 9781101980033 (e-book)

Printed in the United States of America

1   3   5   7   9   10   8   6   4   2

Set in Adobe Jenson Pro and ITC Golden Cockerel
Designed by Amy Hill

This book is dedicated to my friends Markus Spieker
and Dr. Gregory Alan Thornbury

CONTENTS

CHRONOLOGY

1483 Luther is born in Eisleben on November 10 and baptized the following day. He is the eldest of what history believes to be eight children born to his parents, Johannes "Hans" Ludher and Margarethe Ludher née Lindemann.

1484 Luther's parents move to Mansfeld when he is around six months old. This is where they will raise all of their children and remain for the rest of their lives.

1490 Martin is sent to school in Eisenach.

1496–97 Martin attends school in Magdeburg for one year.

1501 Martin goes to the University at Erfurt.

1505 Martin begins his law studies at Erfurt.

1505 Martin vows to become a monk on July 2 while traveling through the village of Stotternheim. He enters the Augustinian monastery in Erfurt and takes holy orders.

1506 Martin meets Johannes von Staupitz.

1507 Martin is ordained and performs his first Mass with his parents and others in attendance.

1508 In the fall, Staupitz sends Luther to Wittenberg for a year.

1509 While at Wittenberg, Martin receives his bachelor's degree in the Bible.

1510–11 Martin makes walking pilgrimage to Rome.

1511 Staupitz transfers him to Wittenberg monastery, where he will remain throughout his life.

1512 Under a pear tree, Staupitz persuades Luther to study for his doctorate. Luther earns his doctorate.

1513–17 Luther lectures on Psalms, Romans, Galatians, and Hebrews, laying the exegetical foundation for all that lies ahead.

1517 Luther posts his Ninety-five Theses (traditionally on October 31) and mails a letter and the theses to Archbishop Albrecht at Magdeburg.

1518 Luther speaks at the Heidelberg disputation in April. Melanchthon arrives in Wittenberg.

1518 Luther travels to the diet at Augsburg in October and appears before the papal legate Cardinal Cajetan.

1519 Leipzig debate with Johannes Eck in July.

1520 Luther writes his three powerful works: *To the Christian Nobility of the German Nation; The Babylonian Captivity of the Church;* and *The Freedom of a Christian.*

1520 Leo X writes the papal bull *Exsurge Domine,* giving Luther sixty days to appear in Rome to answer the accusations of heresy.

1521 The sixty days expire, and Leo X officially excommunicates Luther. Luther burns the bull and other writings in Wittenberg.

1521 Luther appears at the Diet of Worms in April.

1521 In May, following Luther's imperial condemnation as a heretic and outlaw, Frederick arranges for him to be "kidnapped" and taken to his exile at the Wartburg Castle, where he remains incognito for ten months.

1521 In December, Luther travels incognito to Wittenberg for a short visit. Cranach paints a portrait of him as Junker George.

1522 Luther translates the New Testament into German in eleven weeks at the Wartburg. In March, he returns to Wittenberg and preaches his eight Invocavit Sermons, reversing the excesses that Karlstadt and Zwilling began in his absence, and resumes leadership of the Reformation at Wittenberg.

1523 In February, Luther's German translation of the New Testament is published.

1525 German Peasants' War. Müntzer is killed.

1525 In June, Luther marries Katharine von Bora. Karlstadt's family arrives in Wittenberg; Luther writes *On the Bondage of the Will.*

1526 Johannes "Hans" Luther is born.

1527 In December, a daughter, Elisabeth, is born.

1528 In August, Elisabeth dies, aged seven months.

1529 In May, a second daughter is born, named Magdalena (Lenchen); Marburg Colloquy in October.

1530 The Diet of Augsburg. Luther remains at the Coburg Castle during this time.

1531 In November, a son, Martin junior, is born.

1533 In January, a son, Paul, is born.

1542 Luther's thirteen-year-old daughter, Lenchen, falls ill. She dies in her father's arms on September 20.

1546 Luther travels to Eisleben with his three sons. Preaches his last sermon on February 14 or 15. Dies there on February 18. Buried at Wittenberg.

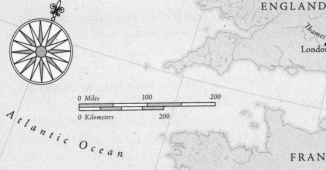

CENTRAL EUROPE IN 1517

at the Dawn of the Reformation

North

ENGLAND

Thames River
London

Atlantic Ocean

Seine River

FRANCE • Paris

0 Miles   100   200
0 Kilometers   200

• Where Martin Luther Lived •

0 Miles   50
0 Kilometers   50

Magdeburg •

Elbe River

BRANDENBURG

Wittenberg •

Dessau •

ELECTORAL SAXONY

Mansfeld •

Eisleben •   • Halle

Torgau •

Allstedt •

Leipzig •

Kyffhäuser Mountains

Saale River   SAXONY

Elbe River

Eisenach/
WARTBURG
CASTLE

Stotternheim •   • Naumburg

Erfurt •

Altenburg •

Mulde River

Dresden •
Pirna •

• Jena

DUCAL SAXONY

Orlamünde •

Schmalkalden •

• Zwickau

Werra River

THURINGIAN FOREST

BOHEMIA

• Coburg

Lyon

Rhône River

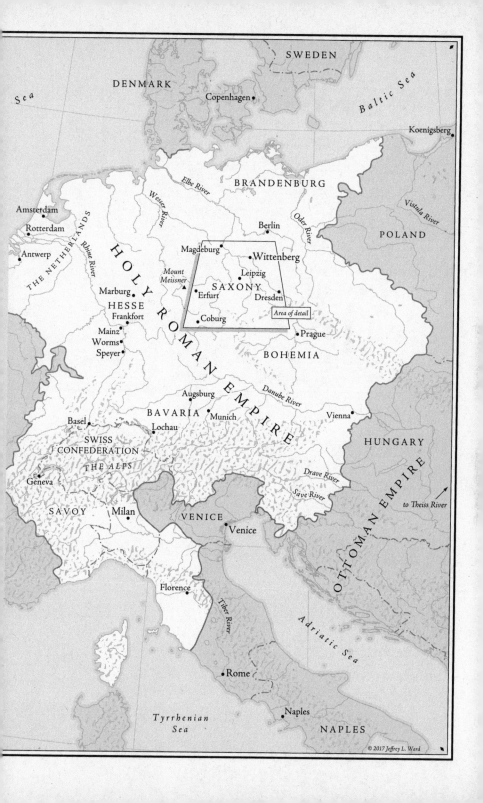

Pastor, Rebel, Prophet, Monk

I N 1934, AN African American pastor from Georgia made the trip of a lifetime, sailing across the Atlantic Ocean, through the gates of Gibraltar, and across the Mediterranean Sea to the Holy Land. After this pilgrimage, he traveled to Berlin, attending an international conference of Baptist pastors. While in Germany, this man—who was named Michael King—became so impressed with what he learned about the reformer Martin Luther that he decided to do something dramatic. He offered the ultimate tribute to the man's memory by changing his own name to Martin Luther King. His five-year-old son was also named Michael—and to the son's dying day his closest relatives would still call him Mike—but not long after the boy's father changed his own name, he decided to change his son's name too, and Michael King Jr. became known to the world as Martin Luther King Jr.

This father-and-son name change is just one dramatic measure of the influence of Martin Luther. Luther's writings and actions so altered the landscape of the modern world that much of what we now take for granted may be traced directly to him, the quirky genius of Wittenberg.

For example, the quintessentially modern idea of the individual—and of one's personal responsibility before one's self and God rather than before any institution, whether church or state—was as unthinkable before Luther as is color in a world of black and white; and the similarly modern idea of "the people," along with the democratic impulse that proceeds from it, was created—or at least given a voice—by Luther too. And the more recent ideas of pluralism, religious liberty, and self-government all entered history through the door that Luther opened to the future in which we now live.

Luther is principally known for two iconic events that precipitated all else. The first, in 1517, was his posting of the Ninety-five Theses on the great wooden doors of the Wittenberg Castle Church, criticizing the then wildly popular practice of indulgence. The second was his unyielding courage at the imperial diet that was held in the city of Worms in 1521. It was there, before the Holy Roman Emperor Charles V and an impressive array of German nobles—and perhaps most important, before the pope's representative, Thomas Cajetan—that Luther took his implacable stand and made the statement in which he immediately vaulted from the medieval cosmos into the modern. When he made it clear that he feared God's judgment more than the judgment of the powerful figures in that room, he electrified the world. How dare anyone, much less a mere monk, imply there could be any difference between them? Since time immemorial, such men had spoken for God and for the state. But Luther defied them, humbly but boldly, in a watershed moment in world history. Those of us in the West have lived on the far side of it ever since.

What followed ended up scrambling the landscape of Western culture so dramatically that it's hardly recognizable from what it was before. Luther was the unwitting harbinger of a new world in which the well-established boundaries of what was acceptable were exploded, never to be restored. Suddenly the individual had not only the freedom and possibility of thinking for himself but the weighty responsibility before God of doing so.

Perhaps the most remarkable aspect of Luther's story is that it need never have happened. Martin Luther was not a man born—or later inclined—to tilt at papal windmills. In fact, until about 1520 he was as vigorous a champion of the church as anyone who had ever lived. He desired desperately to help Rome elude the fate it ended up experiencing. In fact, in a case of extreme irony—so much so that one might think of Oedipus—he became the very man who brought about everything he had hoped to avoid. As his story illustrates, it was a sublime and ridiculous decoction of forces that created the perfect storm that burst over the European continent, creating what we now call the Reformation and the future. We can only wonder what might have been avoided had the distracted Pope Leo been sensitive to his role in history and taken the German monk's earnest suggestions to heart. It was Rome's mystifying inflexibility that drove Luther to bolder and bolder public positions, eventually putting him beyond rapprochement and setting him along a path that will forever be debated either as heretical and ignominious or as orthodox and glorious. But for good and for ill, Martin Luther was the midwife of the irrevocably divided world in which we now live.

Myth and Truth

During his lifetime, Luther's celebrity grew at such a pace that the momentum of it could not be slowed even by his death. In fact, the magma of his celebrity soon cooled into hagiographic stone, such that much of what the world has come to "know" about him is fiction. The most well-known "facts" of his life illustrate the point. First, he was born into a family of peasants, the poor son of a miner who was raised in a home humble and cramped; second, his hardscrabble upbringing was a brutal one in which his dour working-class father buffeted him so viciously that it warped his psyche, causing him to see God the Father as a similarly glowering and sadistic figure to be placated and assuaged in endlessly humiliating religious contortions—or to be avoided entirely. Third, it was a literal bolt of fire from the heavens that caused the jumpy twenty-one-year-old suddenly to blurt out a binding vow—one he had never previously considered but that in his abject fear he indeed spoke—and then felt duty bound to honor the rest of his born days, thus leading him to become a monk. Fourth, it was on a trip to Rome that he was so shocked at the blasphemous devilry of that vile city that he decided he must destroy the soft and decadent Italian church and remake it in his own uncompromising and upright German image. Fifth, he began this lifelong project by angrily and defiantly hammering his damning accusations against Rome onto the very door of the Castle Church in Wittenberg, thus putting the quivering pope on notice that his deeds had been weighed in the balance and found wanting. Sixth, after his great stand at the Diet of Worms—where he said, "Here I stand. I can do no other!"—he fled to the Wartburg, where in his overflowing umbrage he took on the devil personally and at least once punctuated his fury by hurling a pot of ink at the fiend who dared to trespass his quarters. Indeed, anyone who doubts this need only go to the Wartburg to see the swart blots themselves, still staining the wall of his cell these five centuries later. Seventh, the nun he married escaped from her nunnery by hiding inside a large barrel that had only just been emptied of herring. In fact, all of the twelve nuns hid in filthy herring barrels secured to the wagon that hurtled them away to freedom.

These important details have been recounted innumerable times and are being confidently recounted this minute, told in tours of Luther sites around Germany in many languages, being written and read in otherwise excellent books about Luther, and posted in online articles and blogs. But not a single one of these seven things is true. They are each sloppy glosses on the actual facts and have over time congealed and finally ossified into the marmoreal narrative that has existed for half a millennium. Parson Weems's pious legends of Washington chopping down cherry trees and casting silver dollars across the wide Potomac persisted for about 150 years, but these false details about Luther have persisted for more than three times as long. Their cultural roots are therefore that much deeper. It is my hope that what follows in this volume will do its humble part in uprooting them.

The Madness of Martin Luther

It is not just Luther's influence in history that is extraordinary. His demeanor and character and behavior—all of which led to these events that changed history—are themselves extraordinary. But these things were not so much innate attributes as ones that revealed themselves unannounced and by degrees at some point after 1517. So we must wonder what can account for the change in his personality in the years following the publishing of his theses. How can history reconcile the intense and dourly over-pious monk of his earlier years with the bold, courageous, and even sometimes raucous joke-and-insult-producing machine of later years? Whereas he had earlier been obsessively serious, he later became fun loving, sometimes rising to rarefied heights of gag-inducing scatology and buffoonery. Although the change in him did not have the speed of Paul's on the Damascus Road, it nonetheless is obvious and important. And whatever it was that happened, he eventually seemed born anew and became a kind of giddy pied piper for that newness and freedom and joy, so much so that many thought he must be demon possessed—or at least simply mad.

The short answer to this question, as well as the reason the story of Luther is unlike any other, is that he felt that after tremendous and agonized searching he finally—by God's grace—had found that thing for which every human since Eden had pined. He had found the hermeneutical lever with which the whole world could be raised to the height of heaven. This had been the principal problem of all humanity—how to bridge the infinite abyss between imperfect mankind and a perfect God, between earth and heaven, between death and life. And Luther's discovery was that this problem had been solved by the promised Messiah of the Jews fifteen hundred years before. In its way, the discovery was more a rediscovery. And it all amounted to only this: by simple faith one could accept God's diagnosis and solution to the otherwise insoluble problem, and at the moment one did this, the problem was instantly solved. After wandering in the wilderness for centuries, the people of God could be led by this new Moses into the Promised Land.

Luther further came to see that to do anything but accept this notion as itself utterly sufficient would be to whistle past the graveyard. It would be to behave as though we might in some way add to what God had already done, which would itself destroy our ability to benefit from it. So like some madman—and yet one who understood he had unaccountably been given the honor of great knowledge—he dedicated every subsequent second of his life and spent every calorie of energy available to spreading these world-changing tidings. He did it fearlessly, too, but not because he was traditionally brave; rather, because in this discovery, he had also come to see that death itself had been soundly and forever defeated and that this was in fact the central point of what he was saying. So taken together, Martin Luther's is as dramatic a tale from history as one can discover, and as one should expect, its ramifications in history and for us today are similarly dramatic. How it was that Martin Luther came to rediscover this greatest of good news and how he then spent his life publishing it abroad in the wide world is the story that follows.

CHAPTER ONE

Beyond the Myths

THERE IS NO beginning to the story of Martin Luther. This is because in telling the genuinely extraordinary story of a genuinely extraordinary human being, one immediately stumbles over two perfect conundrums, both of which make a clean beginning impossible. One is calendric, and the other is so odd that it can hardly help seeming more than coincidental.

The first and calendric conundrum is that—although we now know far more about Martin Luther than about anyone from his era and possess endless corroborative documentation about him—we cannot establish one of the simplest and most foundational facts of all: the year in which he was born. We are sure of the date of his birth, November 10, and we are even sure of the hour, which was just past midnight, according to his mother. But the year, alas, eludes us. Much for this reason, Luther would heap scorn upon astrological prognostications of any kind during his life—especially those of his future co-conspirator Melanchthon, a dedicated devotee of this art. Luther always maintained that he was probably born in 1484, but neither Luther nor even his own mother could be sure, and current reckoning puts it more likely at either 1482 or 1483, with the preponderance of evidence favoring the latter, so that in the course of this book we shall use that year.

The second conundrum is of another order entirely. We know that on November 11—the day following his birth—the infant was bundled and trundled a mere hundred yards away from his home to the awe-inspiring majesty of the Church of SS. Peter and Paul, there to be baptized and forever snatched from the gaping maw of everlasting fire and death. Because November 11 was St. Martin's Day—the feast day of Saint Martin of Tours—the child was given the saint's name, a common enough practice at that time. But unbeknownst to Luther's parents, there was a detail of this saint's life that would one day form an eerie and seemingly prophetic parallel with the career of the newborn that day named for him.

Saint Martin lived in the fourth century. He was born in what is to-day Hungary; grew up in what is today Pavia, Italy; and spent most of his adult life in what is today France, all three of which at that time were within the borders of the Roman Empire. He became a Christian at an early age, despite his father's disapproval, and was enlisted in the Roman army. One day while in the Gallic provinces—it was in the town of Bor-betomagus, in what is today central Germany—the future saint was or-dered to participate in a battle. But in the belief that shedding blood was not consonant with his deep Christian convictions, Martin bravely de-clared, "I am a soldier of Christ. I cannot fight."[1] For this shocking refusal to submit to this duty assigned him, he was imprisoned and charged with cowardice, but he turned this charge on its head by then volunteering to go to the front lines unarmed, because he did not fear for his life, only that he might take the life of another. In the end, the battle did not take place, and he was released from duty, shortly thereafter becoming a monk. The Roman city called Borbetomagus where this Martin took the death-defying stand for his faith that set him on his path of sainthood would in the future become known as the German city of Worms. Thus, eleven centuries from when this first Martin took his Christian stand against the Roman Empire, the second Martin would take his Christian stand against the Holy Roman Empire—in precisely the same place. So on the second day of his life, Martin Luther was linked with both the distant historic past and his own historic future.

The world into which Luther was born was the world that had existed unchanged for many centuries. It was a world separated by an infinite ocean from the vast continents we know now as the Americas. Christo-pher Columbus was during this time sailing and trading along the West African coast, with no idea that within a decade he would daringly set out across the Atlantic in three caravels. The printing press was in its earliest infancy, having been invented some forty years earlier by Jo-hannes Gutenberg, and although the great schism of 1054 had separated Eastern Christianity from Western, the idea that the vast seamless uni-verse of the Holy Catholic Church led by the pope might be challenged and then riven forever was perfectly nonexistent.

Martin Luther was born in the final year of the reign of Pope Sixtus IV, one of a series of six popes at once so comically bungling and tragi-cally scandalous that it was almost as though this sextet had deliberately placed their collective corruptions in a papier-mâché monster, hung it from a tree, and begged an Augustinian monk to take a dozen or so good whacks at it.* But for the name his parents had given him, there is nothing in the childhood or the upbringing—or even the early adulthood—of Martin Luther to suggest him as a candidate for the extraordinary life that followed.

Before we pluck Martin's woven basket from the cattails and proceed further, we should add that Luther's name was originally not Luther at all but Luder or Ludher. Luther changed it at some point later in life, although precisely when and why is unclear. His father and mother eventually incorporated the change to their own names, probably because of their son's increasing fame, and perhaps also because the word *Luder* had a number of unattractive associations they preferred to leave behind and thereby relegate to the squint-eyed netherworld of historical footnotes.†

One of the greatest challenges in telling the story of Martin Luther is in distancing him from the endless fables, myths, and tall tales told about him in the last five centuries. The first of these is that he was born into a family of peasants—that his father was but a humble miner and that his mother was of even humbler background and was probably a bathhouse attendant of low morals. It is only because of very recent archaeological discoveries that we can put the persistent untruth about Luther's humble background to sleep.

The fact is that Martin's father—his name was Johannes, so he was called Hans—was indeed a man of great intelligence and fire. Although it is often said he was a miner, he was certainly no day laborer, but was in fact an ambitious and ultimately successful entrepreneur in the mining business. He owned several smelting works and moved to Eisleben with his young wife, there to discover and exploit the rich veins of copper that spidered beneath the forested lands of that region. His young wife, Margarethe, was from the local Lindemann family, who were established, prominent, and quite well-to-do burghers in the Eisenach area. In fact, one of them became mayor of the town in 1497. Two of Martin's first cousins—the sons of his mother's eldest brother—made names for themselves: one became a doctor of law and an electoral councillor in

---

* The story of these six tragically unpapal pontiffs, which also included Pope Innocent VIII (1484–1492), Pope Alexander VI (1492–1503), Pope Pius III (1503), Pope Julius II (1503–1513), and Pope Leo X (1513–1521), is well told in Barbara Tuchman's *The March of Folly.*

† *Ludher* typically referred to a slovenly woman of deficient morals and is translated as "hussy"—or today would simply be translated as "bitch" (of the non-canine variety). Equally unhappily, the etymologically related root word *lude* signifies "pimp" and traces back to the word for a lure of some kind; in this application, it denotes a lure to sexual sin.

Saxony, and the other studied in Leipzig, Frankfurt, and Bologna, becoming a medical doctor who served as the personal physician to Elector Frederick the Wise and sometimes treated Luther. In the last years of his life, he taught medicine at the University of Wittenberg, while Luther lived there. The humble beginnings often attributed to Luther's parents, and especially to his mother, are part of the sometimes misleading hagiographic narrative that sprang into being after his death.

We may also assume that the well-to-do Lindemann family lent Hans Luther the substantial amount of money needed for him to get his start in the risky copper-smelting business. Luther's father knew that to make good on the serious investment his in-laws had made in him and his business would be difficult, and that it was. He worked very hard and clearly expected his son Martin to be a part of the larger plan. Because Martin was exceedingly bright, Hans planned an excellent education and a subsequent legal career for him.

We may also assume that the Ludhers were no more or less religious than most people of their time and social station, which is to say they took God and the church very seriously. They almost certainly had a shrine in their home to Saint Anne, which not the Bible but Christian tradition declared was the name of Mary's mother, who became the patron saint of miners. The reason for this is that her womb was said to have borne two inestimable jewels. From her own womb had come Mary, and then from Mary's womb had come Jesus. Anyone whose womb had produced these eternal treasures could hardly be improved upon as a patron saint for those making their livings searching for treasures themselves.[2]

Recent Archaeological Discoveries

A resounding boon to Luther studies arrived in very recent years via archaeological discoveries in the city of Mansfeld, where Luther lived from the age of six months until he went off to school in Magdeburg. Most remarkable, in an excavation begun in 2003, the small and humble house in Mansfeld where for centuries Luther was said to have been raised was demonstrated to be merely one-third of the actual house in which his family lived. Thus, as we have already stated, Luther's reference to himself in later years as the son of "peasants" and "poor miners" is proven to have been a typically Lutheran admixture of humility and hyperbole. Contrary to the five centuries of myths born of this self-characterization, he was raised in a well-appointed home. The measure of how well can be taken from another (2008) archaeological discovery on the site of that home. It was then that a "previously unknown brick-lined cellar room" from the time of Luther's childhood was discovered, and it was bursting with such a dazzling variety of household waste as to constitute a veritable King Tut's tomb of the late fifteenth-century quotidian. The forensic details that emerge illuminate the day-to-day life of the Luthers during this time. That Martin and his family handled these long-buried objects in the course of their lives five centuries ago is simply remarkable to consider, as is the scale and breadth of the find. The findings confirm the idea that this was not the home of poor or humble people but, on the contrary, the home of a very respectable and established leading family of the city.

Not less than seven thousand animal bones were analyzed, and from these it was determined that 60 percent of the Luther family diet was pork. The porcine fragments came principally from "young, fully grown" animals, whose meat was more expensive than that of older, less flavorful hogs. Thirty percent of the bones were from sheep and goats, and the remaining 10 percent from cattle. More than two thousand bones from domestic fowl were identified, most of them goose, also higher on the price scale than other options. Young chickens were also eaten regularly, "along with the occasional duck or pigeon." Some of the goose bones discovered had been turned into pipes with drilled stops, indicating they had been used as birdcalls, to lure smaller songbirds, which were commonly part of the menu in German homes for many centuries. Finally, the local fishes carefully plucked and identified included freshwater species such as "carp, bream, roach, asp, pike, pike-perch, perch, and eel." There was also a significant presence of imported saltwater fishes, including "herring, cod, and plaice," which would have arrived at the Luther house either dried or salted.[3]

But more revealing yet in this 2008 trove were the objects of kitchen life. A number of *Grapen* were found. These were the earthenware tripod pots put directly into the fire. Some fragments of much rarer metal *Grapen* pots were discovered too. These were so valuable they are often mentioned in wills from that era. The shards of whimsical *Igelgefässe* (hedgehog vessels) were also found, as well as the remnants of "stemmed glasses, knobbed glasses, and ribbed beakers." The knife handles and all else bespeak a household of upper-middle-class prosperity.

The archaeologists discovered many of the toys with which Martin and his three brothers likely played. Seven marbles of irregular sizes were recovered, indicating that they were probably made at home and fired in Frau Luther's hearth. The "phalanx bone" of a cow with a drilled hole was also found, and it is believed this hole would have been filled with molten lead and this and similarly weighted bones used as children's bowling pins. The background of Brueghel the Elder's famous painting *Children's Games* depicts just such an activity. There was also a *Pfeifvogel* (bird whistle) that "could be filled with water to produce a warbling song." There is even a curious little object that was identified as a miniature replica of the "nut"—part of the trigger mechanism—of a crossbow. It seems this was from a toy crossbow that belonged to Martin and his brothers, and so now, to the many images we have of Luther in our collective cultural memory, we must add this new one of him as a boy mischievously chasing and shooting his brothers with this toy crossbow. To be sure, the son of "poor peasants" would hardly have had access to something so fanciful and expensive.[4]

A potentially tantalizing mystery of this great trash heap, however, reveals itself in the variety of valuable objects that are scattered throughout those less valuable. We have no difficulty fathoming why someone would throw away a fishbone, but why brass aglets and buttons, an embroidered purse affixed to a belt, or even some silver coins? One current theory holds that about 1505, immediately after Luther had become a monk against his father's wishes, the plague struck Mansfeld, as it did many times during these centuries. It is believed that two of Martin's brothers perished.[5] According to the medical advice of that time, all of the clothes and bedclothes of someone who had died from the plague would have to be burned. As the rooms of those who had died were cleared out, some more valuable objects could have been mixed in with the others, thus accounting for this otherwise strange and highly revealing find.

Luther's Relationship with His Father

Another fable that has clung like a burr to Luther's story is the canard of Luther's father being so impossibly strict and perpetually glowering that it resulted in the boy's eventual rebellion against not just his earthly father but his heavenly father too. Whereas no one should doubt that Hans Luther would have clouted his son about the head when the situation demanded it—and what boy would not create situations along these lines from time to time?—such corporal discipline was de rigueur at that time, and not only then but throughout nearly all of the history and cultures of the world. So to attach some significance to it is to embrace an anachronism. If corporal punishment of this kind had anything like the effect so strongly suggested, the world would have been filled with nothing but Luthers throughout the centuries. Luther's upbringing, from all we know, was about as typical as can be, and the only thing that would be worth remarking on, given the ubiquitous practice of physical parental discipline, would be if we had information that Luther's father had indeed spared the rod. Martin's father once disciplined his son so severely that the young Martin withdrew from his father for some time, whether out of fear or anger. But again, this is hardly beyond what we might expect, nor was Herr Luther the only one to be at times severe. In later years, Luther would recall how his dear mother once beat him—"until the blood flowed"—for the terrible crime of having filched a single nut.

But the persistent fiction concerning Luther's father's harshness comes to us almost entirely from *Young Man Luther*, a widely read biography by the psychoanalyst Erik Erikson, who maintained that it was Luther's conflation of a grim, judging God with his own father that produced the predictable and involuntary Oedipal spasm that tore Western Christendom in two. Though Erikson's thesis would befog Luther scholarship for decades, there is no reason to accord this fatuous Viennese theory any validity except as a historical curiosity to be cataloged with Dr. Spock's books. That his 1958 book was published with encomia from Margaret Mead and Reinhold Niebuhr completes the embarrassingly mid-century cliché. It's a fact that because there is far more information available about Luther's emotional and intellectual life than about any of his contemporaries—whether Vasco da Gama or Henry VIII—anyone angling to impose a silly interpretation on him will find a prominent vein from which to mine nuggets and with them to erect another monument to dated pseudo-intellectual fiddle-faddle.

What is perhaps oddest about Erikson's theory is that it must not only arrange many facts rather precariously to fit its preconceived mold but also ignore many facts about Luther's relationship with his father that were not unknown at the time. So much passed between them over the years that Erikson's assertion comes across as dishonest cherry-picking in the service of a modish Freudian narrative. There is ample evidence that Luther loved his father and that Luther's father loved his son. Indeed, when Luther's school-yard chum Hans Reinecke wrote to him of his father's death, Luther wrote, "Seldom if ever have I despised death as much as I do now." He said that it "has plunged me into deep sadness not only because he was my father but also because he loved me very much." Even more, he says, "through him my creator has given me all that I am and have."[6]

School Days

Luther's recollections of his earliest years come to us almost exclusively from the much older Luther. From his marriage in 1525 until his death in 1546, Luther and his wife, Kathie, lived in the former Augustinian cloister—called the Black Cloister—where they took in a number of student boarders and had frequent guests. At some point, it became acceptable for some of these boarders and guests—the students especially—to record much of what Luther said. These notes filled many volumes and came to be known as *Tischreden*, or *Table Talk*, often containing several versions of the same anecdote or statement as recorded by more than one participant, so that it can be confusing to sort them out. Furthermore, Luther's mature recollections have more than a little editorial English on the ball and must be understood as an often irascible older man making a particularly sharp point about an event from decades earlier, rather than as a simple and placidly indifferent recounting of the facts. Given these caveats, we may nonetheless say that Luther's reminiscences of his school days are not at all fond ones. For example, he says that one morning during his earliest years at school he was thrashed fifteen times for failing to conjugate and decline a certain Latin verb. Luther explains it was a verb the class had not yet been taught—and was therefore not obliged to know—so the errors made that day were only the teacher's, in administering these now immortalized quindecimal hidings. But even in a treatise in 1524, he already spoke of having "learned less than nothing despite all the flogging, trembling, anguish, and misery." One gets the general impression that childhood for an exceedingly sensitive and intelligent boy such as the young Martin Luther must have been an endless, fear-filled trial from which he could hardly wait to escape.

The lingua franca in educated circles at that time was Latin, which all students were required to speak at all times. As a measure of his father Hans's social status, we may mark the fact that he did not himself speak Latin, so whatever schooling he got was far from the caliber of his son's. At Luther's first school, each day began with a Latin hymn and ended with another Latin hymn. Every morning the teacher would designate one of the students as *der Wolf* (the wolf), and it was this student's responsibility to tattle on any students who spoke German or who otherwise misbehaved. The worst perpetrator of that day would be designated *der Esel* (the jackass) and all the following day must bear the ignominy and humiliation of wearing around his neck a carved wooden jackass on a string. Luther's other remembrances are no less dour, but one reason it seems he is at least somewhat exaggerating is that the school maxim was decidedly positive toward education and students. It was "Neglecting a student is no less serious than deflowering a virgin."

Later in life, Luther described the general atmosphere of fear of authority at school as something that became chronic throughout all of life, so that even when someone meant him well, he could hardly conceive of it. Luther said that the irrational and ignorant fear of a good God that was perpetuated by the churches and theology of that time was connected to this, and it reminded him of a specific incident from childhood. He explained that it was the custom of that place and time for children to go begging in the streets for sausages. (This was not something poor children did, as some of the older biographies of Luther have averred, but something that all children did, so this is one more fable about Luther that must be peeled away from the true story.) One day a kindly man ran after Luther and his friends with sausages in his hands. His intention was to give them the sausages, but Luther and his friends ran away in fear, certain that this real-life *Hanswurst** somehow meant them harm. Luther used this as an illustration of how even when God reached out to us in love and grace, we are often so suffused with the idea of him as a stern judge bent on punishing us that we tragically shrink from his loving

* A clown character from that time who was depicted wearing a sausage necklace.

grasp, thus to our own sad detriment denying ourselves the very thing for which we long.

Magdeburg, *Aetatis* 13

In the fall of 1496—or possibly in the spring of 1497—Martin's parents sent him to a school in Magdeburg, forty miles north. He was then thirteen years old and went there with Hans Reinecke,* the son of a notably successful colleague of his father's. There can be little doubt that Hans Luther's plans for his son were ambitious, and being able to send him to schools where he could learn Latin and mix with the sons of distinguished figures must have been gratifying. Still, Hans Luther seems to have fought mightily hard his whole life long to pull himself up the social ladder, or at least to cling to the rung where he was fortunate enough to find himself. Having a genius son who could further the family's fortunes through education was clearly a part of the larger goal. Mixing with the "right" people was naturally part of this, and the opportunity to join Reinecke's son in faraway Magdeburg must have seemed an attractive opportunity and an important piece of the larger, long-term plan for his son. One of the officials in the Magdeburg archdiocese was Dr. Paul Mosshauer, who originally hailed from Mansfeld and who had relatives in the mining and smelting world of Mansfeld, which accounts for Luther and Reinecke's connection to the school.

Martin's time in Magdeburg had a profound effect on what would ultimately be an important turn in his life when he entered the monastery in 1505. While at Magdeburg, he was placed with the *Nullbrüder* (Brethren of the Common Life), who were not an official monastic order but who nonetheless had gathered together in a monastic-type community and took in student boarders. They lived in relative poverty but, unlike most actual monks, did not resort to begging, choosing instead to make a living by copying books, because printing presses had not yet become commonplace. Luther would here have for the first time been exposed to lives of serious piety, and it follows that any penchant he might have had for taking God more seriously than the average student would first have been encouraged during this time. Of course, had his father ever dreamed that his son might

---

* Luther would stay friends with Reinecke throughout his life.

end up moving in this direction, we cannot doubt that he wouldn't have sent him to live with the *Nullbrüder*. But there seems to have been no reason at all to believe that Martin was anything other than a dutiful son who would fulfill his father's good wishes for him, which at that time were for him to be a strong student who one day would bring honor to his family by becoming a lawyer.

During this year in Magdeburg, Luther was also taken with a local figure known as Prince Wilhelm of Anhalt, whose gaunt frame haunted the streets of the city. His family had been quite religious: both of his brothers became priests, and his one sister became a nun. But Wilhelm would outdo them all when he took orders as a Franciscan monk, formally dedicating himself to a life of poverty and renouncing all filial claims to his father's principality. Like the founder of his order, he set his worldly title and riches aside to follow Christ in the humblest way imaginable, as a public beggar.

Wilhelm's severe presence on the streets of Magdeburg at that time must have been affecting. In the mendicant Franciscan fashion, he went about with a sack on his back. He was also known to be assiduous in performing tasks in the monastery. And his endless vigils and fasts— along with the self-flagellation au courant at that time—ultimately reduced him to a walking skeleton. He died in 1504, while only in his mid-forties. Luther later wrote, "With my own eyes I saw him carrying the sack like a donkey. He had so worn himself down by fasting and vigil that he looked like a death's-head, mere bone and skin. No one could look upon him without feeling ashamed of his own life."[7] That Wilhelm had so utterly forsaken the trappings of this world, even those of a prince, could not have failed to captivate the sensitive young man, whose extraordinary introspection, as would be so powerfully evidenced in later years, would place a powerful check on the worldly ambitions his father had carefully planned for him.

Eisenach, *Aetatis* 14

Just one year after arriving in Magdeburg, Luther was sent seventy-five miles southwest of Mansfeld to the city of Eisenach. Here he would spend the next three to four years and put down roots, later referring to it as "Eisenach, my dear city." Luther had many relatives there, from both his mother's and his father's sides of the family. One of the most popular of the false legends that grew up around Luther was a certain story of him all alone in Eisenach, a poor boy many miles from home, having to sing in the streets as a way of begging for food. As the story went, a certain widow took pity on him and was so charmed by his singing voice that she took the forsaken child in to live with her. The problem with this story is that it's both wrong and misleading. The tradition of young people singing from door to door to receive food on certain holidays was all the rage during Luther's childhood. It was not much different from the modern American tradition of children trick-or-treating on Halloween or the Christmas tradition of going from house to house singing carols and then being invited in for eggnog and fruitcake. To do this was to be a *Partekenhengst*, which is to say a collector of *Parteken*, which were just pieces of bread.

Eisenach boasted three monasteries during this time: the Dominicans, Carthusians, and Franciscans were all represented. There were three corresponding parishes too: St. Nicholas, St. George, and the foundation of St. Mary. The capacious church of St. Mary had twenty altars and innumerable relics, the most remarkable of which was a bone fragment from Saint Mary herself. Pilgrims to that shrine believed they were gazing upon a sanctified chunk of the very arms that held the infant Jesus.[8] Luther later called the city of four thousand a "nest of priests and an emporium of clergy."[9]

While in Eisenach, Luther attended the parish school of St. George, where he grew quite close to one of his teachers, Wigand Güldenapf, with whom he stayed in touch throughout his life. He also had a relationship with his great-uncle Konrad Hutter, who was once the custodian of St. Nicholas's church there.

During this time, the teenage Luther through some connections became acquainted with the prominent Schalbe family and lived with them for some years. Heinrich Schalbe was mayor of the town during this period, first in 1495 and again in 1499. So once again, far from being the son of a horn-handed miner, Luther was already at the very young age of fourteen ensconced in the life of a wealthy, well-connected young man with tremendously bright prospects. The Schalbe family were not only prominent and affluent but also deeply pious and as such were leading patrons of the local Franciscan monastery. It was Heinrich Schalbe's wife who first planted in the young Luther's mind the notion that marriage could be something out of the ordinary. She sometimes quoted a verse Luther recalled decades later: "To whom it can be given, there is no dearer thing on earth than a woman's love."[10]

During his nearly four years in Eisenach, Luther also came under the influence of Father Johannes Braun, at that time vicar of the foundation of St. Mary there. Braun had a relationship with St. George's school and seems frequently to have entertained its students at his home, and it is there that Luther would have become acquainted with him. We gather from their later letters that Braun was a powerful spiritual influence on Luther and that the godly Braun early on saw in Luther a brilliant and sensitive soul upon whom God surely had particular designs, if only he would be open to them.

The Schalbe family not only taught Luther that God must be at the center of life in a way that far surpassed anything he would have learned at home in Mansfeld but also exposed him to the idea that there could be a dark side to the church and that there might be some daylight between God's idea of the church and the institution of the church itself. It was through the paterfamilias Heinrich Schalbe that Luther would first have heard of the elderly Franciscan monk Johannes Hilten, who was at that time imprisoned in the Eisenach monastery for his pronounced criticisms of the church.

Just as Saint Martin's stand at Worms (Borbetomagus) in the fourth century may be viewed as an odd augury of Luther's life a thousand years in the future, so Hilten's apocalyptic statements can be similarly prophetic and unsettling. Hilten predicted in his apocalyptic writings that a man would arise in the year 1516 who would fight to reform the church—and who would succeed—and who would end the centuries-long reign of the monks. We do not know whether Luther was aware of Hilten's writings at this time, but we do know that in the years ahead Luther would indeed identify himself as that figure Hilten had prophesied. This would certainly have strengthened him in his battle, bolstering the faith and courage that would become his greatest weapons in that battle. Hilten also prophesied that within a hundred years the Muslims would have overtaken Christendom, so for Luther in the decades ahead—given Hilten's accuracy in predicting Luther's own ascent and successes, if indeed he had done this—it must have been impossible not to feel that Hilten was right about the rest of it, that they were indeed all living in the Last Days of the world, and that the Antichrist was indeed abroad spreading destruction and in his final throes would wreak such unimaginable havoc that "even the elect" might be deceived.

Hilten died as a prisoner in the monastery in 1500, at the age of seventy-five, most likely of starvation, which might or might not have been self-imposed. But in his story we may again see that the idea of a holy man standing against the church was not at all a foreign one. We must not tolerate a simplistic view of church history, as though there had been no dissent until the Great Day of Martin Luther. Many others had done as much to bring the church back to its true and only roots and had failed. That the church was lacking in many ways and that many monks and priests and other ecclesiastics were greedy, hypocritical, and odious were hardly new ideas. And apart from what had been done about it or hadn't been done about it, the laypeople saw it and expressed their thoughts on the subject, both privately and not so privately. But in all of these things, they had lacked a champion who would fight and win.

It had indeed already been centuries since the church had first begun to manifest grave problems and therefore to lose its power and grip on the people's imaginations. So its corruption was by the time of Luther widely known. Indeed, not just the problems but the loud cry "Reform!" had been heard here and there for centuries before Luther. The earliest dramatic and well-known example comes from the thirteenth century when the nobleman's son who one day became Saint Francis heard God's voice say, "My house is in ruins. Restore it!"[11] Between Francis and Luther, there were numerous figures within the church who had tried to bring reform, although some of them, far from being lauded like Francis, had rather because of their efforts been denounced as heretics and excommunicated and gruesomely immolated.

John Wycliffe was born around 1328 in England, and in many truly remarkable ways he prefigured Luther and Luther's eventual reforms. Wycliffe agitated for a vernacular translation of the Bible so that the people could read God's Word, and he himself translated most of the New Testament into English—although of course in the fourteenth century it was not the so-yclept Modern English of our own time but the Middle English of Chaucer.* Thus John 3:16 was rendered as "For God

---

* The late sixteenth-century English of Shakespeare and all the English in the decades since then are categorized as Modern English. The language of Chaucer is known as Middle English, and the eleventh-century language of *Beowulf* is known as Old English.

louede so the world, that he 3af his oon bigetun sone, that ech man that bileueth in him perische not, but haue euerlastynge lijf."

Wycliffe also worked with others to translate the Old Testament and was as passionate in his day as Luther would be in his own that everyone should know the Gospels in his own spoken language. "Christ and his apostles taught the people in that tongue that was best known to them," he said. "Why should men not do so now?" Of course the printing press would not be invented until about 1450, and the first book printed would be the now famous Gutenberg Bible of 1455, in the Latin Vulgate edition. There is no question that Luther's future ability to have his own vernacular German translation of the Bible printed en masse would dramatically help him in the wider work of reformation that Wycliffe had hoped for in his own time.

Like Luther, Wycliffe spoke out against monasticism and against the special caste of the priests, even coming out against transubstantiation for much the same reason Luther would 150 years later. He spoke against the wealth of the church and even spoke harshly against the papacy itself; when the peasants of England revolted, Parliament and the English church both blamed Wycliffe for having fomented it by his teachings, just as Luther would in future years be blamed for the Peasants' War. Wycliffe died of a stroke in 1384 while in the very act of saying Mass, but at the Council of Constance in 1415 he was posthumously denounced as a heretic, and in 1428 his bones were exhumed from their "Christian burial" and burned. His ashes were then thrown into the river Swift, which flows through the English village of Lutterworth.*

Another reformer before Luther was the Bohemian Jan Hus, who was born in 1369 and became a theologian at Prague University. Hus was greatly influenced by Wycliffe and spoke strongly against indulgences and the papacy, specifically criticizing the pope for his use of military power, holding that the church could not wield the sword. Hus was condemned as a heretic at the Council of Constance and suffered burning at the stake in 1415. But his followers, known as Hussites, continued the movement long after his death.

But many inside the Vatican itself knew how corrupt the church had become and how badly reform was needed. Just after the death of Pius II

---

* In a world in which it was believed that one's body must be corporeally resurrected from officially hallowed ground, to have one's body exiled from such ground and forever destroyed via burning so that no actual bodily resurrection was ever possible was a horrifying fate.

in 1464, Bishop Domenico de' Domenichi wrote a blistering critique of the papacy, saying that the laypeople were calling the church "Babylon, the mother of all fornications and abominations of the earth!" He said that the "dignity of the Church must be reasserted, her authority revived, morals reformed, the Curia regulated, the course of justice secured, the faith propagated."[12] What's more, the devil's hordes in the shape of the Turks were on the march, and Domenico and many others knew that if things in Rome did not change dramatically, all of Christendom would be lost to the martial religion of Muhammad. But such prophetic cries were as wasted as though someone had been preaching to Nero or Caligula about Roman decadence and the looming threat of the Visigoths. The subsequent election in 1471 of Pope Sixtus would in fact catapult things dramatically in the wrong direction. Like his predecessors and successors, Sixtus saw the cry for reform only as a wearisome threat to his power, and thus with his ruby slippers kicked it away. Anyone crying out for reform must be shooed out of the room like a fly—or crushed like a beetle.

The moral septic field that was the Vatican of the Medici seems to have existed mainly to provide material for tawdry television miniseries *nel futuro*. For example, when the Florentine Pazzi family had drunk its fill of papal Medici malevolence, they plotted to murder Giuliano and Lorenzo de' Medici in a single fell swoop—during a church service. It may well have been purely practical, because it was during the church service that they were most likely to be unprotected. The high sign to the dagger-wielding *assassino* was when the bell was rung to mark that holiest of holy moments during the Mass, when the host is elevated. At that sacred signal, Giuliano was bloodied sufficiently to meet his Maker instantly, but Lorenzo survived to launch more mayhem.

During Luther's years as a teenage student at Eisenach, the pope in Rome was Alexander VI, perhaps the most depraved of all the many depraved pontiffs in that nadir of the institution, and his established excesses can scarcely be believed. When his predecessor Innocent VIII died, Alexander declined to lobby for the golden throne, which was the accepted corrupt practice of that time, but simply leaped ahead of his competitors by purchasing it outright with cash. As the story goes, four muscular mules bore the extraordinary weight of reinforced panniers laden with silver. They staggered from Rodrigo Borgia's spectacular palace to the palace of his chief rival, Ascanio Sforza, to deliver the gleaming argentine load. In his years as a cardinal, the virile pope-to-be fathered seven children, all of whom were understandably considered illegitimate. But now armed with the great powers of the papacy, he was able to officially "legitimize" whom he pleased. All that was required was his signature on the *bulla,* or papal bull.* Thus, with a flourish of Simon Peter's sacred pen, the *bastardi* were parthenogenetically reconceived into the fold of respectable citizens and more than that, into that particularly exclusive club constituted of legitimate children of the popes. Just prior to purchasing the papacy, Alexander at the age of fifty-nine ambitiously took as his mistress one Giulia Farnese, forty-three years his junior, who already at the age of sixteen was a celebrated beauty, most renowned for her cataract of golden tresses that tumbled to the marble floors of the Vatican. Some called her "the Pope's whore," while cleverer detractors referred to her as "the bride of Christ."

Erfurt, *Aetatis* 17

In 1501, when he was seventeen, it came time for Luther to enter the university. His father had by now prospered enough in his mining business to be able to afford to pay his son's way. So it must have been a moment of tremendous pride for Hans Luther to send his eldest off to the great university at Erfurt. "My dear father," Luther later recalled, "maintained me there with loyal affection, and by his labour and the sweat of his brow enabled me to go there." This was in many ways the culmination of all of his father's efforts. In a few years, when Luther could go on to take his law degree, it would further crown these achievements, for then Luther would be able to return to Mansfeld, take a suitable wife from among the respectable families of their region, and at last begin his practice of law, much of which would consist of aiding his father in his business affairs.

By our own standards, life at the university was quite regimented, with students arising at 4:00 a.m. for devotions and going to bed at 8:00 p.m. All students lived in a residential college called a *bursa,*† of which there were six in Erfurt. Students paid for room and board. Two meals per day were served, the first at 10:00 a.m., after four hours of exercises

---

* The term "bull" is the Anglicized form of the Italian *bulla,* which comes from the Latin *bulla* and refers to the seal placed on the important document itself. Documents with such large and official seals came to be themselves called *bullae,* or "bulls."

† *Bursa* is the Latin word for sack or purse; this term is still with us in modern universities, where the treasurer or business officer is called the bursar.

and lectures. After the first meal, there were more exercises and lectures until 5:00 p.m. Luther seems to have been in the Heaven's Gate *bursa*, where the entire Psalter was prayed through every fifteen days during the early morning devotions, so he would certainly have become closely familiar with the Psalms during his four years at Erfurt. Also, during both meals of the day the students listened quietly as someone read aloud passages from the Vulgate Bible. Sometimes the *Postillae* of Nicholas of Lyra were read aloud too. These were exegetical Bible commentaries of which Luther thought so well that he praised them highly many years later, and when he was writing on the book of Genesis, he used them extensively. It's therefore only logical to assume that Luther was at this early age deeply affected by what he heard. This must have been one important factor that impelled him to consider matters of God far more than the average Erfurt philosophy student, and we cannot doubt that even if he had never thought of it before then, he would during these years first have begun considering the idea of a life in holy orders.

Humanism

It was as a philosophy student at Erfurt that Luther first encountered the fashionable new intellectual movement called Humanism* and there met a number of professors and students devoted to it. Two of these professors were Bartholomaeus Arnoldi Usingen and Jodokus Trutfetter, with whom he would stay in touch for many years. And one of the students at Erfurt during this time was a young man named Georg Burkhardt, a tanner's son from the Bavarian village of Spalt. This Georg Burkhardt would in a few years do what most Humanists of the time did and take a Latin or Greek name. Burkhardt chose to Latinize the name of his village and was thenceforth known as Spalatinus, although the German form of this was Spalatin, and it was as Spalatin that he was known to Luther. He would one day become an extraordinarily close friend to Luther and as important à player in this story as anyone. But at this early point, the two were simply acquaintances.

The school of thought that had previously and for centuries held sway in medieval Europe was known as Scholasticism. Its principal figures

---

* Throughout this book when we speak of Humanism, we mean what is today called Renaissance Humanism, as opposed to the more modern and distinctly secular version of humanism.

were Duns Scotus, William of Ockham—of eponymous "razor" fame—
and Thomas Aquinas. Today most regard Scholasticism as a fussy, over-
formalized way of instruction that was fatally removed from practical
life issues. The idea of ivory-tower academics wrangling and perspiring
over outré philosophical riddles—as the marauding Turks lay siege to
Constantinople and Christendom—is memorably summed up in the
classic question "How many angels can dance on the head of a pin?" This
was no hyperbolic joke but something that the Scholastics earnestly
debated. Also, instead of reading the Bible itself, students during the
Scholastic period read Peter Lombard's *Sentences*, which were his commentaries on portions of Scripture—or even read Duns Scotus's gloss on
Lombard's *Sentences*. Thus students were enticed to gambol on the loose
tiles of the roof, unable to see or know anything of the house and foundation below them.

Ironically, then, it was the 1453 fall of Constantinople to the Muslim
aggressors that spawned what came to be the definitive response to Scholasticism. Innumerable Byzantine Greek scholars fled the region to settle
in Europe, and as a result Greek and Latin studies enjoyed a great revival,
leading to what we now call Renaissance Humanism, whose great cry
was *ad fontes!* Back to the sources! This suddenly presented fascinating
and tantalizing possibilities in the realization that one might for the first
time in so many centuries uncover what lay at the root of what everyone
believed. One might also uncover things that threw into question or entirely disproved conventional teachings. "Renaissance" means "rebirth,"
and so it was not just a return to the original sources of antiquity but a
new birth of all of these sources that would allow scholars to apply their
newfound knowledge to these old texts. These things had been hidden
and even believed lost forever, but now suddenly the doors were opened
and everyone could go picking through what had been untouched for
many centuries. Who knew what they might find?

The Bible was of course central to all of these new developments. For
one thing, the world of Scholasticism had put it at a significant remove
from even monks themselves, and even when they were able to read portions of it, it was always in the sometimes obscuring Latin of the Vulgate.* But because the Old Testament was actually written in Hebrew

---

* The Vulgate was the fourth-century Latin translation of the Bible that by the sixteenth century had
become the official version used by the Catholic church. It was chiefly the work of Saint Jerome. The
word "vulgar" derives from the Latin *vulgaris*, which means "common" or "commonly used."

and the New Testament in Greek, there were numerous passages in which the Latin translation did a disservice to the original meanings, and these errors had been passed down through the centuries. Erasmus of Rotterdam would play the central role in restoring the New Testament to its original Greek, making the raw and original words of the first Christians available to a new generation. Most notable among those eager to delve into these long hidden depths was Luther himself, who would use Erasmus's own restored Greek New Testament when he translated the New Testament into German many years later. But for now it was all still just an exciting possibility. It's impossible to think that Luther didn't wonder what treasures lay as yet undiscovered in the original texts and whether there in the original sources he might somehow find succor for his restless soul.

It was as a student at Erfurt that Luther's genius first began to shine. Before this, nothing very remarkable is said of him, at least nothing that has survived. After only three semesters at Erfurt, Luther attained his baccalaureate degree, passing the examination on September 29 (Michaelmas Day), 1502. But the more serious studies now began as he aimed for the master's degree. Many years later, his future colleague Melanchthon reported that according to a number of Luther's fellow students from that time Luther's talent was then "the wonder of the whole university." He was ready to take the master's exam as early as December 1504, but to receive a master's, one must be at least twenty-two years old. Because Luther did not know his exact year of birth, this rule was probably waived for him. If he was born in 1483, as we have surmised, he would have turned twenty-one the previous month. Luther took these exams in January 1505, just after Epiphany.[13]

When Luther was awarded the master of liberal arts (*magister artium*) degree, he was ranked second among the seventeen that day receiving it. He was given a master's ring, along with the coveted red-brown biretta. Achieving the master's degree was a spectacular achievement for the son of a hardworking smelter. In fact, this degree now placed Luther in a special category within his own family, for his own father had certainly not attended a university, nor had any of the forebears on his father's side. But now this son of Hans Ludher had achieved academic distinction in one of the finest universities in the world. On a more personal note, because of his new status, Luther's own father would no longer use the informal *du* when addressing his son but would henceforth use the formal *ihr*.

"What a moment of majesty and splendor was that," Luther recalled years later, "when one took the degree of Master, and torches were carried before, and honor was paid one. I consider that no temporal or worldly joy can equal it." It made a lifelong impression on him, the blazing fire of the torches and the procession of horses, the grandness and pomp of it all. It was an august yet genuinely joy-filled memorial to all that had been achieved, and still many years later he said, "That is how we should still be able to celebrate!"[14]

Before Lightning Strikes

After taking his master's degree, Luther was prepared to begin the study of law. Until this juncture in his life, he had been precisely fulfilling his father's expectations, and now, by entering the study of law, he would take the final step toward becoming a lawyer. But perhaps something about having arrived at this point gave him pause. Perhaps the finality of it struck him. But whether the idea to enter a monastery had ever been in his head, as we guess it must have been, it must have been jarred loose to swim into his ken at this juncture. In any case, the mythic notion that his idea of entering the monastery was exclusively delivered by a lightning bolt from the sky near Stotternheim can hardly be the whole story. Like much else in the more fanciful and idealized versions of his life, it is far more folk legend than fact. That one day he was fear stricken and blurted a vow, and by some powerful sense of obligation decided to see it through, can hardly be the whole truth.

Luther had been planning on studying the law and becoming a lawyer and had now at last stepped through this final door. He had purchased his *Corpus Juris*—the expensive book every law student must have to study—and was now seemingly incorrigibly on his way. But in addition to Luther's apprehending the finality of his life's course at this time, we may imagine that other things affected him now too. It is easy for the modern mind to forget that at all times in history before our own the imminence of sudden death loomed heavily, especially for anyone thoughtful or sensitive, and Luther was both. Already at Erfurt the *Anfechtungen** that would famously affect him as a monk began to rear its hopeless head, causing him to wonder disturbingly about his own eternal

---

* A German word that Luther used to describe his depression and anxiety.

fate and whether, were he to die suddenly, he would be welcomed into the loving arms of God or, more likely, be condemned to fall everlastingly into the taloned clutches of grotesque devils.

Once again, in considering the life of a late medieval man, we must set our modern, materialistic prejudices aside, and not only those prejudices but the equally anachronistic idea that if God is to be considered, it is always as a benevolent and loving figure. In Luther's day, far more emphasis was put on God as an eternal judge, one whose holiness was almost always offended by us, so that if we were especially lucky, we might find ourselves in purgatory instead of hell. But even if we found ourselves in purgatory, we might face a steep and painful climb of literally thousands or perhaps even millions of years until we were properly purged of our deep-rooted sinfulness. Who knew what steep and half-infinite climb one might face? We know that Luther was too smart not to consider these things deeply and soberly and too sensitive not to have been bothered by them, often to the point of debilitating depression, which he called *Anfechtungen*. In fact, the word *Anfechtung* really has no English equivalent. It has as its root the verb *fechten*, which means "to fence with" or "to duel with." *Fecht* is also obviously etymologically related to the word "fight." So Luther's *Anfechtungen* meant to do battle with one's own thoughts and with the devil. But for him this was something so horrible that it's difficult for us to fully comprehend.

Anyone who has experienced depression may have an idea. For Luther, it seems to have manifested itself as a widening hole of sheerest hopelessness, an increasing cacophony of devils' voices accusing him of a thousand things, and all of them true or true enough—and no way out of it. This is the very thing that has driven people to suicide through the centuries. It is hopelessness made real, or to use Milton's famous phrase, it is "darkness visible,"[15] a description that the author William Styron used as a title for his own poignant memoir on depression.[16] We may also think of the words graven on the gate of Dante's Inferno, "Abandon All Hope, Ye Who Enter Here."[17] So for Luther, this *Anfechtungen* was a vivid picture of the nightmare of hell itself, a place in which one had indeed been utterly forsaken by God, with no end to the hopelessness. And perhaps it was even something worse than that. Perhaps it was not merely a vivid and horrifying picture of hell but the actual beginning of hell itself, a black tendril that would in time put him down to Sheol itself. It was not something Luther could easily ignore. He was somehow determined to understand it all, to get solid answers. Whether it was already in the back of his mind now, or would simply arise in the next few years, we don't know, but at some point the idea must have struck him that the Bible itself—apart from the obscuring glosses and the bad translations—might hold the key to this puzzle, if it was a puzzle that could ever actually be solved. But he was not able to study the Bible as such. For him, it was the law he must now study. But we can hardly doubt that the profound agony of this depression, this *Anfechtungen*, would have driven him in fits and starts at first and then in a kind of wild, single-minded quest to find the problem and slay it. That much he believed was possible. His faith made it possible. And if we wonder in the future chapters of his life and this book what it was that made Luther more than anyone else persist and persist where others had failed, it is this despair that must be our answer. He had no patience for theological bromides and had no fear of being burned at the stake. That would have been less painful than the deep soul agony of his *Anfechtungen*, and the inescapable tortures of hell itself, so he rode on and on and would get where he meant to go or would die riding.

Only one year before he began his legal studies, in 1504,* Martin had been traveling home to Mansfeld for Easter when the student's sword that he carried—and that many students carried in those days— somehow badly cut his leg, severing a main artery. The bleeding was clearly life threatening, and so Luther's traveling companion quickly ran to the nearby town to summon a doctor. During this time, Luther lay alone in the field, desperately applying pressure with his hand to stanch the bleeding, wondering whether he would survive the afternoon. He well knew that he could die there and then, so he cried out to Saint Mary in prayer, begging her to spare his life. Finally, a doctor appeared and sewed up the wound. But the doctor seems not to have done his job very well, because that night as Luther lay in bed sleeping, the wound reopened and he bled copiously once more. Luther feared for his life, again crying out to Mary to spare him. And again he survived, but not without a long time to think about what might have been. The injury was severe enough that it was some time before he could walk. He clearly had much time to rest and think about twice leaning over the pit of death.†

Luther's thoughts about death during this time must also have been

---

* This accident might actually have happened as early as 1503.
† On a less grim note, it was during this time of recuperation that Luther resourcefully taught himself to play the lute.

exacerbated by the deaths of several people he knew. In April 1505 and then later in that year, two young Erfurt lawyers were swept from this life by the plague, which had freshened its attacks in that region. To see two young men die who had taken the same path Luther was now taking could not help but cause him to wonder whether he had made the right choice, whether if he too were suddenly to leave this world he would be prepared as he should be for what lay ahead. In fact, Luther later said that the last words of both of these lawyers had been "O, that I had become a monk!"[18] The idea was that they knew that their eternal salvation was at stake, and in the nightmarish light of the eternity that yawned before them, they both piteously remonstrated against the worldly paths they had chosen. Luther surely participated in the requiem masses for both men. If these deaths were not enough, there would be two more from the plague, and both still closer to home. Two of his own fellow students during this time were struck down by death's scythe. One was Hieronymus Buntz, who took part in Luther's own master's examination.

So it was in this doubtful frame of mind that Luther returned home to Mansfeld in June 1505. Exactly what he was thinking and hoping for during this time, we cannot know. He might simply have wanted time away from his studies and from the thoughts that had been affecting him. Or he might have been hoping to screw up the courage necessary to tell his father he had been thinking better of his life's course. Or perhaps his father had been the one to initiate the trip, summoning his son home for a reason we do not know. Some have speculated that now that Luther was on the way to getting his law degree, it was time to plan a marriage to a suitable woman from Mansfeld, perhaps the daughter of one of his father's business acquaintances. Of these things, we do not know, but we do know that Luther's fifty-three-mile trip back to Erfurt would not be completed until his life had changed forever.

CHAPTER TWO

Lightning Strikes

I saw Satan fall like lightning from heaven.[1]

—Jesus of Nazareth

H ARD BY SOME fields outside the village of Stotternheim, there is a humble red monolith set on end, standing as a memorial to what happened at that spot on the second day of July, 1505. It was on that humid summer day that Martin Luther, fatigued from the very long journey and only six miles from Erfurt, found himself overwhelmed by a sudden, tremendous thunderstorm. He had been riding a horse, but it seems that at this juncture he dismounted. The falling rivers of water and the moaning wind—and the deafening cracks of thunder and lightning around his head—caused him to tremble with the realization that at any moment, like so many others caught in storms like this, he might instantly be summoned from this life. In those moments, death and hell were suddenly horribly palpable, and the twenty-one-year-old Martin Luther did not meet these grim possibilities with equanimity. The raging electrical storm so frightened him that all of the worst phantasms of his demise and damnation were before him, as real as and more frightening than the raging storm, and the great weight of it all simply became unbearable. When an impossibly close blast of lightning struck, Luther collapsed to the wet ground in abject terror and cried out to Saint Anne. *"Hilf du, Sankt Anna!"* he shouted. "Help me, Saint Anne!" And then into the rain and wind he shrieked the words that would change his life and the future of the world, words none heard but him. *"Ich will ein Mönch werden!"* he shouted. "I will become a monk!" He shrieked them as a solemn vow, meaning that if Saint Anne helped him now, helped him to survive this terror, he would repay her great mercy by devoting the rest of his born days to being a man of God, to taking holy orders and forever leaving the world he had lived in until that time.

Luther did not die that day outside Stotternheim. He arose from the soaked ground to stagger his final miles to Erfurt and his law studies. But what had happened there would not be forgotten. He was a serious and pious young man, and he had vowed to the Holy Mother of the Holy Mother of a Holy God—and therefore to God himself—that he would become a monk. And so become a monk he must and certainly would do.

What can have gone through his mind during that last hour as he continued the six miles to the University of Erfurt and the life he had just vowed to leave forever? Was he exhilarated at what had just taken place? Was he frightened by what he had just done, something he knew that, as a solemn vow, was irrevocable? Did his mind now range over the possibilities of a loophole in the vow he had just uttered? We can never know. What we do know is that once he returned to the university, he told his fellow students about it, and they did all they could to talk him out of it. But the young man was immovable. To make the decision more final, he even sold his *Corpus Juris*.

But there can be no question whatsoever that the most difficult part of what he had promised to do concerned his father, who would be shocked and outraged, who would feel betrayed and disappointed and horrified, and who would certainly rage against it and do all he could to force his son to change his mind. Hans Luther had worked tremendously hard to get his son to where he was now. So to see him stand on the verge of achieving his goal—a goal that concerned not only him but his whole family, and one in which they had invested sacrificially—and then take leave of his senses to throw away everything by becoming a monk—a monk!— would undo his father. So Luther shrank from the dreaded task. He would simply enter the monastery and inform his father afterward.

On July 16, precisely two weeks after the Stotternheim storm, Luther invited some fellow students to a grand farewell dinner. Even at this event they tried to dissuade him from taking the outrageously fateful step. But what he had vowed, he had vowed and must do. "Tonight you see me!" he announced to them, with all the drama of the young man that he was, "but never again!" He would the next day launch himself upon a course that would take him far from the world his father had hoped for him; indeed, it would take him far beyond the world itself, in its way, for that was the point. And the course upon which he would launch would inevitably take him far past anything he himself imagined at that bold moment. It would take him where he himself did not wish to go and would cause the rising and falling of many. It would beget violence and would even reshape nations and empires, and would paint the panorama of the future in as yet unimaginable colors. But first, Luther had to become a monk.

The following morning, accompanied by a number of his friends, who even now persisted in entreating him to change his mind, the young man made his way to the door of the Augustinian cloister of Erfurt and presented himself there to take holy orders. Precisely why he chose the Augustinian order, and not the Dominicans or the Franciscans or the Benedictines, we do not know. It has been said that the Augustinians in Erfurt were known to be a strict order and that that would have appealed to him. They were also known for their devotion to theology, which also might have appealed to him. But these must remain speculations. We do not have the information firsthand, but we can assume that the porter of the monastery, having asked what Luther wished, would have then gone inside to inform the prior of the monastery, while Luther waited. The prior, Winand von Diedenhofen, would have then appeared and led Luther inside to the monastery's chapter room, where he could inquire in some depth about the young man's intentions and then hear his full confession. Once the prior had established that Luther was sincere and of sound mind, he would have let him stay in the monastery's guesthouse, which still stands in Erfurt today.*

At this early point, Luther was what is called a supplicant. Before he could become an actual novice monk, there was a significant waiting period that included extensive confession. But after some time, this first trial period ended, and the great day came. Luther was again brought into the chapter room, this time with all of the monks of the order present to witness the great moment. The twenty-two-year-old before them now did what they had once done, some recently and others many decades before. Luther on this day officially left the world outside the monastery behind him irrevocably and forever and became a novice monk, just as he had vowed that July afternoon on the blasted heath in Stotternheim.

During this ceremony, Luther as the supplicant abased himself before the prior and before the altar, prostrating himself upon the tile floor, which remains there to this day. Only a few feet away from the young

---

* Built in 1277, it is the city's oldest building.

Luther lay the bones of Andreas Zacharias, the most renowned of the monastery's monks, whose remains had the principal place of honor in the monastery. A hundred years earlier, at the Council of Constance, it was Zacharias who had most vigorously attacked the theology of the Bohemian Jan Hus, who was soon thereafter burned at the stake for heresy, most say as a direct result of Zacharias's zealous efforts. Hus's principal concerns were with the institution of the papacy, for Hus said Christians were to follow not any man but Christ himself. He also said that the Eucharist should be proffered as bread and wine both, just as Jesus did in the Gospels, and also because proffering both bread and wine only to priests created a false distinction between priests and laypeople. Hus was strongly against this division between laity and clergy, which he held simply could not be found in the New Testament. Luther would in time follow in the footsteps of this famous martyr, advocating for almost precisely the same things that Hus did, so his prostration for holy orders only a few feet away from the hallowed bones of the man who had kindled the fire to burn Hus was a strange beginning to his life as a monk.

The prior Diedenhofen asked the supplicant Luther whether he was indeed willing to take on the difficult demands of the life of a monk, and outlined something of the great privations and trials that lay ahead. Luther heard these things and solemnly assented. And lest Luther believe he had now achieved his salvation by entering the monastery, Diedenhofen would have gravely intoned, "Not he that hath begun, but he that endureth to the end shall be saved."² In other words, the twenty-two-year-old had only now just arrived at the base of the great seven storey mountain that must "now be climbed."*

Luther would endeavor with all of his considerable might to achieve salvation, would follow as best he could all of the prescribed rules, neglecting neither jot nor tittle, and he would fail. He would climb the Tower of Babel toward the blue vault of the heavens, aching to touch it with his hand, and when he had reached the top, exhausted from his efforts, he would see that it was every bit as far from him as it was before he had begun. And he would then realize that either there was no way for man to touch God—or there must be another way than the one they had been following. Either salvation was universally impossible or the whole current system—including the fearsome God behind it—was a diaboli-

---

* In Dante's *Divine Comedy*, purgatory is pictured as a "seven storey mountain." That phrase is also the title for the autobiography of Thomas Merton, the twentieth-century Trappist monk.

cal hoax. It was that simple. But the endless writhings he would go through before he could see this! In his famous 1950 Luther biography, *Here I Stand*, Roland Bainton writes, "The meaning of Luther's entry into the monastery is simply this, that the great revolt against the medieval church arose from a desperate attempt to follow the way by her prescribed."[3]

Martin's year as a supplicant and monk-to-be followed the same path as that of all monks at the monastery. With them, he was awakened by a bell at 2:00 a.m., making the sign of the cross and then quickly putting on his white robe and scapular* before hustling out of his cell to the chapel, where he prayed at the high altar and took his place in the choir stalls to sing and pray Matins, the first of the seven "hours" prayed in monasteries throughout the world. Matins consisted of singing hymns and psalms antiphonally and lasted about forty-five minutes. At the end of Matins, the monks prayed the *Salve Regina* (Latin for "Save us, O Queen") to Mary: "Save O Queen, Our Mother of Mercy, our delight, and our hope. To thee we exiled Sons of Eve lift up our cry. To thee we sigh as we languish in this vale of tears. Be Thou our advocate, sweet Virgin Mary, pray for us, Thou holy Mother of God." After singing the *Salve Regina*, the monks sang the *Ave Maria* ("Hail Mary") and *Pater Noster* ("Our Father"). Then they rose and filed out of the chapel.[4]

Part of the difficulty that Luther would find as he trod this well-worn path was that God the Father and Jesus the Son were both principally thought of as fierce judges. So the role of comforter fell to Mary, the human one who understood us and our trials, the soft mother full of grace who could protect her beloved child from harsh and unyielding men. Although Christian doctrine had always clearly taught that Jesus himself had been fully human, and could therefore understand and sympathize with our trials and sufferings and temptations, the reality of church life at this point in history was that this part of Jesus had mostly been ignored, so that he was now thought of as every bit as distant and remote and terrible as God the Father ever had been. So only Mary, his entirely human mother, could comfort us. And not only that, but she could appeal to her harsh and perhaps indifferent son as only a dear mother could. Similarly, the faithful frequently appealed to the saints to understand human difficulties, again feeling that by dint of their humanity,

---

* A scapular is the sleeveless garment that hangs from the shoulders and takes its name from the Latin for shoulder, *scapula*.

they were closer to us than Jesus, who might technically have been human but who we knew was actually God. The saints would therefore be more patient with us and more desirous of helping us, and perhaps the implication was also that they had more time on their hands than God himself, who was far too busy running the vast universe to be bothered with our insignificant concerns. This way of thinking was in fact as heretical as saying that God was the devil, but it was not seen as such at the time. This infinitely significant error was simply glossed over and ignored.

Luther Becomes a Priest, *Aetatis* 23

At last, the day came when Luther had passed the period of suppliance and could become a full-fledged monk. At this time, early in 1506, there were fifty-eight monks in the monastery. Eleven of them were lay monks, while the rest were priests. Luther's superiors rightly saw in him someone with special gifts, and early on determined that he should be ordained as a priest, and soon. For this, however, the vicar-general of the order must also approve. The vicar-general of the Augustinians at that time was an especially gifted man named Johannes von Staupitz. He had accepted that post three years earlier, and the year before that—in 1502—had become dean of the theology department at the brand-new university at Wittenberg. This Staupitz would become extremely important in Luther's life in the years following, and although he would never leave the church as Luther did, his relationship with Luther would have much to do with Luther's own path. On April 3, 1506, Staupitz—then forty-six years old—spent the night in the Erfurt monastery, so it is presumed that it was during this time that he spoke with Luther and agreed that Brother Martinus should be ordained a priest. Thus it was precisely one year to the day after this that was fixed for Luther's ordination: April 4, 1507. After that looming milestone, Luther would be able to celebrate Mass.

The first Mass for a priest was a festive occasion. In its way, it was as important as a baptism or a marriage or a funeral. It was an epochal moment that, like these other events, was a door through which one passed irrevocably. Therefore, much was made of the first Mass. Relatives and friends would be invited to attend, probably to spend a night or two in the monastery, and immediately following the Mass a celebratory dinner would be held. By this time, relations with Luther's father had improved enough that Luther invited him. It seems that for the previous two years they had not communicated, and there could be no question Hans Luther felt betrayed and furious over his son's dramatic change in plans, which Luther had surely known were against his father's wishes. Doing something against one's father's wishes was at that time almost unthinkable. But as it happened, Hans Luther's feelings had by this time changed enough that he was invited and would come. He was unable to come to Erfurt until May 2, however, but it was so important to Luther that he insisted on planning things around his father's schedule. We can imagine that it would have meant a great deal to see his father and after nearly two years it would present the opportunity for a reconciliation between them—or so Luther hoped—and so May 2 was settled as the date.

Once this date had been fixed, Luther could invite others. One of the first letters we have from him is the invitation he extended to his old Eisenach friend Johannes Braun. Luther's tone in the first paragraph is one of such excessive humility that one can only imagine what Braun thought:

> Greetings in Christ Jesus, our Lord. I would fear, kindest sir, to disturb your love with my burdensome letters and wishes, if I did not consider (on the basis of your gracious heart which is so generously inclined toward me) the sincere friendship I have experienced in so many ways and favors. Therefore I do not hesitate to write this little letter to you, trusting that in the closeness of our mutual friendship you will listen, and that it might find you easily approachable.

What ghastly horror was Luther worming his way forward to reveal? Perhaps he needed money or was in some kind of trouble with the law? Much to Braun's relief, the whole thing was only an invitation, and to a very happy event indeed. But still, the excessive humility continued:

> God, who is glorious and holy in all his works, has deigned to exalt me magnificently—a miserable and totally unworthy sinner—by calling me into this supreme ministry, solely on the basis of his bounteous mercy. Therefore I have to fulfill completely the office entrusted to me so that I may be acceptable (as much as dust can be acceptable to God) to such great splendor of divine goodness.

When one considers the tone of many of Luther's future writings, the tone of this particular letter seems nearly impossible. It is true that

Luther was always deeply respectful of authority, but this letter gives us a measure of his mind-set at this time. He had been at the monastery for more than a year and was doubtless consumed with his own unworthiness. A postscript to the letter concerning the Schalbe family, with whom he had stayed while in Eisenach, reads,

> I do not dare to importune or burden those excellent people of the Schalbe Foundation, who certainly have done so much for me. I am sure that it would not befit their social position and prestige to be invited to such an unimportant and humble affair, or to be bothered by the wishes of a monk who is now dead to the world. In addition I am uncertain and somewhat dubious whether an invitation would please or annoy them. Therefore I have decided to be silent; but if there should be an opportunity, I wish you would express my gratitude to them. Farewell.[5]

Luther's general sense of his own unworthiness before God was not necessarily theologically out of line, but it would nonetheless lead to a significant problem at the event to which he was inviting Braun and so many others. This is because on that day Luther would do something he had never done before: he would bring himself face-to-face with God. Every priest knew that to handle the host and pour the wine was not something to take lightly, as though one were merely handling bread and pouring the fermented juice of grapes. In the transformation that the priest would himself oversee, the bread would in his sinful but sanctified hands miraculously become the very body of God incarnate, the body of the King who had been cruelly broken for mankind. And at the sound of his human words, the wine would be transformed into the very blood of the one who in his sacrifice of extreme agony had bled for us, and died. Luther would take this responsibility as seriously as any priest ever had.

Luther well knew that in the ceremony he would, for the first time in his life, be talking directly to the ineffable Almighty. Luther was thunderstruck at the tremendous prospect of it all. To see the vast distance between himself and the God on high whom he dared approach was to reel with dizziness. Who was he to do such a thing? He was more sensitive than most priests to the number and depth of his sins, and he was never sure he had genuinely confessed all of them, although he certainly tried. But Luther knew that if he had any unconfessed sin in him as he performed the holy rite of Mass, he might well be struck dead in that moment. Because many monks would not have understood this as Luther did, those in authority over them would have made the awesomeness of it all terribly clear. But Luther was the last person to need this clarified and underscored, and as the day approached, the prospect of what he faced tore him apart. How dare he, the sinful Martin Luther, approach an infinitely holy and all-powerful God?

If Luther thought his father might not come or might come only as a grudging pro forma gesture, he was mistaken. When the great day came, Hans Luther arrived, and did so in almost regal fashion, with no fewer than twenty guests, and all on horses too. It would not do for someone of his stature to have any of his guests riding the many miles to Erfurt on unyielding wooden carts. And if this entourage weren't enough to impress his son and his son's new circle, the prosperous father took the occasion to make a considerable financial gift of twenty gulden to the monastery. The whole thing might even have verged on ostentation, but the point was made. Hans Luther was himself not insensitive to the moment of what he had come to see. Whether he was sincerely reconciled to the idea that his eldest son had become a poor monk, however, is another question.

Why he had come and had brought so many guests and had made an impressive contribution to the monastery all remains something of a mystery. Some have speculated that the recent deaths of two relatives close to him from the plague had caused him to fear God more than previously.[6] The most recent scholarship suggests it was two of his younger sons who had died during this period—for the plague struck Mansfeld hard in 1505, the year of Luther's entrance into the monastery—so it might well have been the horror of losing two of his boys that brought Hans Luther to some kind of repentance, or perhaps simply to a deeper appreciation of his eldest living son. In fact, it seems that during his time being out of communication with Martin, Hans received word that Martin too had died in the plague. So perhaps this journey and gift were his way of thanking God for his son's life and of repenting of his earlier ire toward Martin for the shocking decision to abandon his father's well-intentioned plans for him. What was in his father's mind was not quite clear, but Martin was glad he had come.

But at the very moment when Martin would celebrate Mass for the first time, the twenty-three-year-old novice balked. All of these witnesses from his earlier life looking on with pride might have underscored what was for this young monk a giddy realization: that he was about to do the very thing that would separate him from all mankind forever, that he was about to handle the body and blood of the incarnate God, that he was about to address the Holy One in whose presence he should tremble or die. He knew that to do what he was doing now in a state of uncon-fessed sin was tantamount to stepping off a cliff. Priests had a genuinely godlike role in the medieval church. They were separated from every other human being on earth in that they had the right to perform the most sacred of all acts on the planet. Luther was well aware of this and felt unworthy of this honor.

Luther would have been familiar with the annual practice described in the Old Testament, in which on the Day of Atonement (Yom Kippur) the high priest entered the so-called holy of holies, the heavily curtained-off sacred center of the temple. That holiest of all things in this world, the magnificently carved ark of the covenant, containing the very tablets given to Moses on Mount Sinai, was there, and it was firmly believed that God's presence was there, too. The high priest would enter wearing a special garment with bells attached, and the idea was that while the bells could be heard as he moved about, he was known still to be alive. Some traditions held that a rope was tied around his ankle so that if, in the presence of the living God, he were struck dead, he might be pulled out. To look upon the living God, to stand in his presence, was something that was so awesome as to be terrifying. And this is what Luther now felt.

So here, at the very threshold of entering into that presence via the sacramental offering, he flinched. "We offer unto thee," he said, "the liv-ing, the true, the eternal God." Years later, he said,

> At these words I was utterly stupefied and terror-stricken. I thought to myself, "With what tongue shall I address such Majesty, seeing that all men ought to tremble in the presence of even an earthly prince? Who am I, that I should lift up mine eyes or raise my hands to the divine Majesty? The angels surround him. At his nod the earth trembles. And shall I, a miserable little pygmy, say 'I want this, I ask for that'? For I am dust and ashes and full of sin and I am speaking to the living, eternal, and the true God."[7]

When it came time to lift the host, he was frozen, unable to do that very thing for which he had prepared nearly two years, and for which everyone in the room had traveled so many miles. There was another priest with Luther during this ceremony, as there always would have been when a priest was performing his first Mass. Luther was in this moment so paralyzed with what he had to do that he whispered to this priest that he wanted to run from the altar. But the elder priest had stood at this precipice once himself, and he now ordered the young monk to continue, and Luther obeyed. No one knows whether Luther's celebration of the Mass came across as halting to those there as witnesses, nor whether any of them noticed his uncomfortableness and anxiety. But there were in attendance people from every part of his life. Although it is not known whether his mother and sister and a sister-in-law were there, we may assume that they were, because women were allowed into the all-male world of monasteries on important occasions like this. A brother and brother-in-law were there, as was Luther's elderly great-uncle Konrad Hutter, from Eisenach, and the Eisenach teacher to whom he was close, Wigand Güldenapf. And of course Johannes Braun. Nonetheless somehow Luther got through it. But what would happen next, at the festive dinner with all of the guests, was just as momentous and would be just as memorable for Luther for the rest of his life.

Because it was at the dinner celebration that Luther dared to say publicly, "Dear Father, why were you so contrary to my becoming a monk?" We cannot know the tone in which this remark was made, but given the father's deep antipathy toward his son's decision it seems a daring, if not a downright cheeky, question. Was Luther teasing his father good-naturedly, or was he somehow challenging him? Even after this bold question, there was more. "And perhaps you are not quite satisfied even now," he said. "[This monastic] life is so quiet and godly."

His father's response to this was a shocking one. "You learned scholar," he said, "have you never read in the Bible that you should honor your father and your mother? And here you have left me and your dear mother to look after ourselves in our old age." Most biographies present this as a deadly and stinging rebuke, the all-too-public and uncomfortable eruption caused by powerful, subconscious Freudian plate tectonics. Here at the very moment that Luther sought comfort and conciliation and fatherly blessing for the decision he had made during the thunderstorm in Stotternheim, he was instead rudely smote by paternal thunder. But was he?

Is it not also possible that the event was so festive and such a palpable relief from two years of unspoken tension that Luther's question was asked half in jest? And that his father's response was less a withering public rebuke, made awkwardly in front of the gathered assemblage, than a "you should talk" *tu quoque* riposte, made in the same semi-jesting spirit? We know that later in life Luther's taste for japery knew no bounds, and we know that the Thuringian/Saxon world was famously fond of just this kind of playful persiflage, so it's impossible to say.

"But Father," replied the son, "I could do you more good by prayers than if I had stayed in the world." And then to cinch things nicely, he reminded his father that it was God speaking to him through the thunder that had brought him to where he was. Surely no good father would wish to overrule God himself. But Luther's father was as clever as his son, replying, "God grant it was not an apparition of the Devil!"

What we do know is that no matter how it came across at the time, these final words of this exchange somehow struck Luther and haunted him for many years. This was of course because Luther in later years often wondered about what really had happened to him that day amid the cracking thunder and lightning. Had it been God or the devil? The thin twenty-three-year-old was years from thinking of monkery as nonsense, but the seeds were planted that day that would in time germinate and inadvertently soar up into a beanstalk of such power that it would split the monolith of European Christendom, something which at that time was as shocking as if it had cracked the very sky itself.

Trying to Get to Heaven

In 1507, Luther was a monk and an ordained priest. But it wasn't enough simply to be a monk. Now he had to do what monks did: be scrupulous in his prayers and his thoughts and constantly confess the slightest unscrupulousness that he could see in these areas. Whereas it would be wrong to suggest other monks didn't take all of this seriously, one gets the impression that Martin Luther took it about as seriously as anyone ever could, and because of this he bumped hard into the limitations of this life in a way that few ever did, which in turn is precisely what caused him to think about the whole religious system in a way that few ever did.

Although the theology of the Christian faith had always been that God saved us from our sins—that Jesus was the Savior, not we—and that in his mercy and love God rescued us who could not rescue ourselves, there had nonetheless crept into the reality of Christian life another idea altogether, one that was dramatically opposed to this first idea. There was in medieval Christian life the strong implication that if one could not earn one's own salvation outright, one could certainly go a long way toward earning it, and one had better do what one could. Had not others distinguished themselves in holy living? Had not the saints shown that it was possible to live holy lives? Had not even Saint Paul said we were to "work out our salvation with fear and trembling"?[8] So the theology of the church had strayed very far from the pure idea that God saved us, and strongly implied that, on the contrary, we must save ourselves.

Luther had no quibbles with this, and once inside the monastery, where he had time and space to study the Bible, he searched painstakingly for a path to heaven as few had ever done before. The reason it was all so pernicious was that there were clear implications it really was up to the sinner to redeem himself, that this was indeed achievable, and that whether with the help of God's grace or not, others had done it and so could you. Luther, who was never cynical and who was sometimes innocent to the point of naïveté, took this all at face value and began to work the program, as it were, with all his will.

But precisely because he was so scrupulous and honest and clear thinking, it didn't work. Luther's overactive mind was constantly finding ways in which he had fallen short, and so every time he went to confession, he confessed all of his sins, as he was supposed to do, but then, knowing that even one unconfessed sin would be enough to drag him down to hell, he racked his brain for more sins and found more. There was no end to them if one was honest about one's thoughts, and Luther was entirely honest. What if he left confession but had forgotten to confess one errant foul thought from three days before? If one died before one had one's last rites, one died "in one's sins." So Luther would drive himself and his confessor half-mad with his endless confessions, which seemed to make him feel no better, because he would torture himself afterward, feeling that surely he must have forgotten something.

The penal system that the church had worked out over the centuries was a bit complicated, but what was clear was that the priest had the authority of the church, and the church had the authority of God, to determine what one must do to be forgiven, to clear one's slate of sins. First of all, one must go to confession. This was not optional but absolutely required. Indeed, it was a sacrament "of the Church." So one must go to confession, and when one went to confession, one must confess every sin one could possibly recall. Once the priest had heard one's confession, he would then assign penance. For example, he might say that one was obliged to say twenty Hail Marys and forty Our Fathers or to pray the rosary so many times. Our knee-jerk modern view of this tends to be dismissive, as though these assignments were always mere rote exercises. But they were not originally intended as such. To pray the Our Father forty times over a certain period was meant to be done in a thoughtful and focused way, in which the prayer helped one to focus on God. So if the person praying did the prayers in a rote manner—simply mumbling the words to get past them and be done with the tedious assignment—that was hardly the fault of the priest who had assigned them.

The effect of all of this was to give the faithful the idea that they could via confession and penance wipe their slates clean and get back to zero, as it were. Their sins would be repented of and forgiven and forgotten, and they could start anew. But beyond this concept was another concept that the church has called the "treasury of merit." The church taught that some special people, such as the saints and Jesus, had been not merely able to get back to zero but had in their lives sinned so little and had done so many good works that they had in fact amassed a surplus of merit. So by the time they went to heaven, they had put these merits in the heavenly bank, so to speak, and, far from being in the red, were in the black. They had achieved not just the bare minimum to get them to heaven but an impressive positive balance—not of money, but of merits. So the collected merits of all the holy people in church history amounted to this tremendous treasury of merit. Who could ever imagine how vast it was? Who could say how much merit had been amassed by Jesus alone? And by Mary? And Peter and Paul and all the hundreds of saints who had ever lived? And who controlled that vast treasury of merit but the church itself? In fact, it was also called the "treasury of the church." The church believed that Jesus had given "the keys of the kingdom" to Peter, whom it believed to be the first pope, and that those keys had been transferred from pope to pope, down through the ages, so that the church and the pope had these keys, which gave them access and authority to dip into that treasury of merits and make a withdrawal whenever they deemed it necessary. Which of course brings us to the thorny subject of indulgences.

The idea of indulgences comes from the treasury of merit. In order to see how it works, we must imagine someone in confession, telling the priest he had done this and that and another thing. The priest might assign him twenty Our Fathers and suggest that he do some good work for the church too. But at some point, the church came up with the idea of indulgences, and if someone bought an indulgence from the church, it was just like doing a good work and could be counted toward one's penance. And of course giving money to the church was a good work. So if I decided to give money to the church to build a cathedral—by buying an indulgence set up for this purpose—it only made sense that the church could count this as a good work I had done that would go into the "merit" category. And if I were able to give ten times as much money, I should therefore be able to get ten times as many "merits." But those merits didn't go into a heavenly treasury. They were mine to keep and "spend" as I saw fit. So with my money I could buy an indulgence that granted me forgiveness for a certain sin. So if I were to sin and the priest assigned me certain prayers and good deeds as penance, I could pull out my indulgence certificate and show him that I had already paid my penance for that particular sin.

Of course once the church had established this idea, we can see how it might very easily have been abused and led to trouble. Because what had in effect happened was that a market had been created, and the spiritual world of sins and good works had been linked to the monetary world of debts and surpluses. It should be no surprise that once something enters the financial market as a commodity, unpredictable behavior may follow. For one thing, the church had put itself in the troubling position of being tempted to use indulgences to raise money. After all, the medieval church was as much like a vast corporation or a nation as anything, and it needed funds to pay for buildings and salaries. There is hardly anything surprising in that. But if money got especially tight because the pope happened to be a spendthrift, it was only too easy to turn to indulgences to solve the problem. And this is of course precisely what happened. Indulgences became a surefire income stream that in time became an absolute necessity. It became so important that looking the other way when abuses occurred, as they must, was very easy to do.

This tremendous problem and temptation got much worse in 1476, when Pope Sixtus IV realized that the market for indulgences needn't be confined to those millions who were alive and sinning but could extend to those multiplied millions who had already left the land of the living and were languishing in purgatory. We can only imagine the moment when Sixtus realized that as pope he was able to decree that the infinite treasury of merits could be sold not just for sins committed by people living but to people who wanted to use them to alleviate the sufferings of their relatives in purgatory. It was as if Sixtus had discovered a gleaming vein of gold as long and wide as the Tiber. He had discovered a monstrously large untapped market—the suffering dead. So suddenly the market for indulgences was dramatically increased. Every deceased parent and grandparent and brother and uncle was now someone for whom an indulgence could be purchased. And of course not only did this mean that the market had been expanded, but because these poor souls were suffering the torments of purgatory, one might dwell upon this pointedly in one's marketing pitch too, and the indulgence preachers certainly did. What son did not want to relieve his old mother and father of the agonies they suffered on the other side? One might well skimp on oneself when money was tight, but who could deny a beloved deceased relative relief from the pain he was undergoing that very moment, while one sat there, twiddling one's thumbs?

The medieval church's penal system led people to believe that they could earn their way to heaven, and that they therefore must try as hard as possible to do so. Most people weren't especially successful at it. But Martin Luther had entered the life of a monk precisely because he wished to be successful at it. So he prayed the monastic hours every day as every monk must do, arising extremely early and praying all through the day. And he went to confession at every opportunity. So why did he feel he was making no progress? He confessed and confessed, and yet he knew that if he was honest, there were always some bad thoughts that he had forgotten to confess. Or perhaps if he had been thorough in confession, he would have experienced a sinful pride over that thoroughness, and now he was obliged to confess that pride. The bottom line was that he knew he wasn't getting anywhere and it was all torturing him. Here he was, having forsaken all, having forsaken even the plans his dear father had worked so hard to make possible, and still he did not feel an iota of comfort that he had really made any spiritual progress. He seemed to be swimming against a riptide, growing more and more tired the harder he tried, to be going backward with every stroke, backward to death and perdition. Would all of these great efforts end with his going to hell after all?

Luther Tries to Earn Heaven, Fails

Luther was obsessive about confession. In fact, it eventually got to the point that his confessor—who ended up being Staupitz—began to get fed up with his maddeningly overscrupulous confessee. Once, Luther actually continued confessing for six consecutive hours, probing every nook and cranny of every conceivable sin and then every nook and cranny within each nook and cranny, until Staupitz must have been cross-eyed and perspiring just listening. When would it end? But Luther didn't care. He was simply determined to keep digging until he got to the bottom of it all. But he never did. He did not yet understand that there really was no bottom, that we were sinful all the way down. All Luther knew was that as soon as he left confession, there likely lurked sins he had not ferreted out, despite his digging like a terrier after a rat. He knew that according to all he understood of church doctrine, a sin must be recalled and confessed before it could be repented of and forgiven. But hadn't he tried as hard as possible to find and confess every one? How did the others do it? Was he more sinful than they? He concluded that he must be and must therefore try harder yet.

Staupitz's frustration with Luther grew. Luther seemed some kind of unprecedented moral madman on a never-ending treadmill of confession. Instead of looking upward and outward toward the God who loved him, he zealously and furiously fixated on himself and his own troubling thoughts. Staupitz, on more than one occasion, tried to shock Luther out of his downward spiral of navel-gazing. "God is not angry with you!" he once said. "You are angry with God! Don't you know that God commands you to hope?" Another time he said, "Look here. If you expect Christ to forgive you, come in with something to forgive—parricide, blasphemy, adultery— instead of all these peccadilloes." Luther would confess negative thoughts about one of his brethren, or his impatience with something that morning, or his poor attitude toward prayer. And if he had not had any such sins to confess, he would confess his pride at not having had any such sins. Staupitz was an important and busy man, and he didn't have time for this niggling ridiculousness. Give him a big fat juicy sin, one that anyone could see was a sin, and then repent of it and be gone! But Luther brought him gnat after gnat, with nary a camel to be seen. The taxonomy of Luther's sins seemed never to tend toward anything sizable that Staupitz might grab with both hands. He could see that Luther was chasing his own tail, making both of them winded and dizzy.

It is clear that Luther's struggles had little to do with concupiscence. There are many things he said as a young man and later in life that suggest he didn't struggle particularly in this area. His struggles instead usually had to do with his own doubts that he could ever be good, no matter how he tried, that he could ever be worthy of God's mercy, grace, and salvation. He knew that the life of a monk was designed to free one from temptation, to keep one so busy with praying and singing and doing that there was no room for the sorts of things he might have been able to do if he had continued as a lawyer. But for Luther, the more he tried to be holy, the more he saw that he couldn't be. The more he cleaned, the more furniture he moved, the more dirt he saw. He was leagues past fretting over sexual temptations. Such things were small beer compared with what he called the "real knots."

He didn't know what to do to untangle them, and this led to tremendous problems for him, but he was determined to wrestle and wrestle with them until at last he had an answer. Nonetheless, any real answer still lay years in the future. Meanwhile the agonies of *Anfechtungen* he experienced as a result of this hopeless quest persisted.

But here is what Luther wrote about these experiences some years later, in 1518:*

> I myself knew a man who claimed that he had often suffered these punishments, and in fact over a very brief period of time. Yet they were so great and so much like hell that no tongue could adequately express them, no pen could describe them, and one who had not himself experienced them could not believe them. And so great were they that, if they had been sustained or had lasted for half an hour, even for one-tenth of an hour, he would have perished completely and all of his bones would have been reduced to ashes. At such a time God seems so terribly angry, and with him the whole creation. At such a time there is no flight, no comfort, within or without, but all things accuse. . . . In this moment, it is strange to say, the soul cannot believe that it can ever be redeemed.[9]

Here was the central difficulty of late medieval Catholic theology: that one was brought to the place of understanding one's sinfulness and

---

* He is obviously writing about himself as the apostle Paul does in 2 Corinthians 12:2–4, and the biblically literate readers of his time would have understood this immediately.

one's unworthiness before God but was not told what to do at that moment of understanding except to lie paralyzed with hopelessness, to confess and try harder. At some point, the sinner—and Luther chief among them—came to feel that he wholly deserved God's fierce anger. For Staupitz, who had a remarkably healthy view of God for that time and place, God was someone who loved us and had mercy on us, but for Luther, God was still and only the harsh judge whose righteousness condemned us with withering fierceness. Staupitz saw Luther's agonies and took a personal and fatherly interest in him. His importance in the life of Martin Luther cannot be exaggerated. He early on saw the genius and potential in Luther and wanted to do all he could to help him find his way. Staupitz—and his connections and relationships, most important with Frederick the elector and with the university at Wittenberg—would play such a significant role in Luther's life that we cannot imagine Luther without him. And yet where he seemingly and ultimately helped Luther to go, he would never himself end up following, which is another curious detail in a story composed almost exclusively of them.

*A portrait of
Johannes von Staupitz.*

CHAPTER THREE

The Great Change

What if it's not true?

—Martin Luther

T HE JOURNEY THAT Luther made from being a devoted son of the church toward becoming the face of the Reformation that broke away from that church took place over many years and was a gradual transformation. It was not as though a second thunderbolt caused him to leap from the Middle Ages right into the Reformation, as though the two epochs were separated by a prostrate broomstick. Nonetheless, in 1517 something happened during which he would find himself on the far side of a great theological divide.

Part of that process began with understanding his role as a seeker of truth and how that role could conceivably lead him to question what was thought of as received and therefore unquestionable truth. At what point did loving the church mean questioning the church? At what point did one have an obligation to boldly and forthrightly—albeit lovingly—help it see its errors? And at what point could one move from being shown one's own errors by the church to oneself showing the church its errors? If the church was the repository of all truth, what should one do if one found a splinter of truth outside the church? Or if one found a splinter of untruth inside the church? At what point could one even admit that these two things were possibilities, and on what basis? These were the questions.

Many of these questions arose as a result of Luther's reading of Aristotle. Having lived in the fourth century B.C., Aristotle was obviously not a Christian. But the medieval Scholastics deeply valued Aristotle and his writings and believed that his teachings on reason could be incorporated into church theology. This was at the heart of Scholasticism itself, and Thomas Aquinas's writings in the thirteenth century were its culmination. But at some point between the writings of Aristotle and the writings of Saint Augustine, Luther saw a small thread sticking out, and he decided to pull at it.

Problems with Aristotle

In the years 1889 and 1890, at the Ratsschul Library in Zwickau, about seventy-five miles east of Erfurt, someone came upon what turned out to be early fifteenth-century volumes that Luther had held and studied as a young monk. It was a spectacular find. Several of these books were works by Augustine. The marginal notes and other writing were confirmed as Luther's own handwriting, so suddenly historians could know what he had underlined as he was reading. His youthful jottings make it clear that as early as the fall of 1509—when Luther was twenty-five—he was noticing disturbing discrepancies between Aristotle and Augustine. In one of the margins he had written, "Augustine can even use reason to prove that the whole of philosophy is foolishness. Imagine what that means!" His copies of Augustine's *Trinity* and *City of God* are also annotated. In one of them, Luther wrote, "I find it more than astonishing that our scholars can so brazenly claim that Aristotle does not contradict Catholic truth."[1] So here we have manuscript proof that it was the great Augustine—who was as foundational and revered a church thinker as any who ever lived—who first helped Luther begin to see things that would lead him to challenge the church of his own day. And one of these things was the idea that human truth had limits and that by itself it could never reach heaven.

In fact, Luther came to believe that the very idea that mere human reason could do so was not merely wrong but was a hubristic folly. How with human words and thoughts could we bridge the infinite distance between man and God, between earth and heaven? Was this not by definition impossible? Wasn't the attempt to do so—to build an impossibly high ladder of dead men's bones stretching toward the pearly gates—by definition a fool's errand and even a diabolical enterprise? Was this project not simply the Tower of Babel in another guise? It was true that Aristotle and philosophy and reason could take us to the top of a very high mountain. But what then? They could not fashion wings for us, with which we could fly the rest of the way to God. They would leave us stranded on the top of the mountain. We could stretch and strain all we liked, but we would never touch the blueness of the sky itself. God must bring the sky to us, and therefore it must be divine revelation initiated by God to bridge this most unbridgeable of all gulfs.

So Luther was puzzled. Why had the church swallowed Aristotle's thinking along these lines for so many centuries and baptized human philosophy as though it could do what it plainly could not? Answering this very important question would occupy Luther for some time to come.

The Bible

In a world in which we nearly always associate the Bible with churches—and churches with the Bible—it is difficult to imagine a time when the two had almost no connection. That this changed so dramatically is yet another measure of Luther's immense impact on history. But what Luther himself said many times was that the study of the Bible per se was simply unheard of in his early years as a monk. Of course there were no Bibles in pews and average laymen had almost no idea whatever of what it contained, nor even that it was a book. They heard bits and pieces of it read aloud in Latin during the masses they attended, but the idea that there was a book containing all of these things was foreign to them, even in the decades after Gutenberg published his celebrated first Bibles. This did not mean that monks were unacquainted with much of what the Bible taught and said, but even for them biblical material was filtered by and parsed via the institution of the church, so one caught snippets here and there, but to think of them collected in the Bible itself was still rather a rare idea. For example, monks and theological students read the commentaries of Duns Scotus and the *Sentences* of Peter Lombard, both of which were mainly about what was in the Bible. But in a way these things obscured the Bible itself as a whole text. It was a plain fact that no one was really entrusted with reading the Bible by itself, so that monks and even priests and theologians were typically kept at one or more removes from it. But the new intellectual movement of Humanism—with its emphasis on reading the actual Greek and Latin and Hebrew texts of the Bible and other books of antiquity—was beginning to challenge Scholasticism and this view of the Bible that had held for many centuries.

So it is not any particular wonder, given the atmosphere that had been maintained for centuries, and given the high cost of books of such length, that there were very few Bibles to be had. Still, as it happened, by the time Luther entered the monastic life, the one book that novices were allowed to read was in fact the Bible. We know that immediately upon entering the monastery, Luther was lent one that was bound in red leather, for he recollected this often in his later years. It seems that Luther did not receive the book lightly, for he not only read it but almost devoured it. He read it over and over until he was inordinately and perhaps even peculiarly familiar with it. This would of course have everything to do with the events of his future and the future itself. What propelled him in this intensive reading, we cannot know for sure, but it seems undeniable that his personal struggles—his *Anfechtungen*—formed the lion's share of his obsession. In a word—and of course in the Word—Luther was desperately searching for the answer to his bitter difficulties, to the problems that surely had sent him to the monastery in the first place. Because he had been so powerfully influenced by Humanist thinking at the university as a student of philosophy, he had a strong idea that if he went to the source itself, he might at last find the unobscured answers to his questions, if such answers existed. So he was desperate, a man on a mission to locate the things that might be there, or perhaps that must be there, somewhere. So he now at last had in his hands the urtext itself, and like a scientist at a microscope looking for a cure to a fatal epidemic—one with which he is himself afflicted—Luther hardly took his eyes from the eyepiece. What lay there was more important to him than anything that lay outside it.

In contrast with his frenetic and passionate Bible reading, Luther said that the other monks did not read their Bibles very much or at all, and it is extremely likely that Luther's obsession with and mastery of the book attracted the attention of Staupitz during this time.[2] This is because as odd as Luther was among the monks of his monastery in wanting to read and understand the Bible, Staupitz was nearly equally odd among the theologians of that era.

Strangely enough, once a novice actually became a monk, he was no longer allowed to keep his Bible. At that point, he must limit himself to only reading scholarly books, and those while in his cell. It seems that only in Luther's private time in the library of the monastery did he have access to the Bible after his novitiate. We get the clear impression that Luther felt he must read the thing itself, must pull from it the answers to his questions and problems, and we get the idea that for him the scholarly books and commentaries were not helping. If anything, they were making his problems worse and were more obscuring than enlightening.

In Luther's time, Bible interpretation was hopelessly mired in an odd and hidebound fourfold academic approach that must have been mind-numbing and depressing to someone like Luther, who was impatiently searching for truth itself. Nonetheless, it was the custom at this time for every biblical passage to be duly laid out on this Procrustean dissecting table and mutilated accordingly. As Mark Twain said of jokes, one must first kill a joke to look inside it. According to this entrenched academic approach, the four ways of seeing the text were: first in its literal sense; second in its topological; third in its allegorical; and fourth in its anagogic. For the Psalms, for example—which Luther read and sang every day in his prayers—the literal sense of the text was always interpreted as the Christological. The topological sense was seen as the text's significance for humanity and was mainly a moral interpretation. The allegorical sense had to do with the church, and the anagogic had to do with the text's relation with the biblical "End Times." How this odd way of reading the Bible had arisen is beside the point, but what is not beside the point is that it surely forced students to invent interpretations that were downright wrong, that it was pedantic and tedious, and that most important it was not much use helping Luther—or anyone else—find God in or behind the words. But it was how the Bible had been read for years, and as a young monk Luther was in no position to bloody himself in kicking against these goads. But one can understand that Luther's frustration with this formed a significant element in his theological journey.

But there were other things that made him wonder whether he—or the church—was missing something important. For example, during his time in the Erfurt monastery, Luther once happened upon the sermons of Jan Hus. It is curious to think the sermons of this infamous heretic were available for monks to read, but apparently they were and Luther read them. We also know that in reading them, Luther was mystified and disturbed as to why Hus had been denounced as a heretic and burned. But he was not yet ready to speak of this or discuss it with anyone. He was still at this time willing simply to be obedient and to trust the judgment of the church, to assume that he himself had missed something that he would eventually see.

Luther began his studies at the monastery in the summer of 1507; but already by the fall of 1508, Staupitz had sent him to Wittenberg. It was fully expected that he would spend his life in Erfurt, but Staupitz was the vicar-general of the order and had the authority to send monks wherever he needed them, and he needed Luther in Wittenberg for a short period. Luther was never meant to stay there indefinitely. In fact, he stayed only for a year. We know that he would return to Wittenberg in due time and never leave again, but when Staupitz sent him there in 1508, that was not the plan. We suspect that Staupitz sent Luther there because he saw Luther was not making any real progress in his own struggles with sin, so perhaps he felt that a change of environment would help. Or we may guess that Staupitz indeed had a secret master plan to bring Luther to Wittenberg for good eventually. Perhaps because he was the dean of the theological department there, he hoped Luther might be a spectacular addition to it.

During his year at Wittenberg, Luther's progress was swift. Already on March 9, 1509, Luther earned his first theological degree, bachelor of the Bible, and that autumn he took the examination for a second theological degree, which was a bachelor's in Peter Lombard's *Sentences*, universally reckoned the most important theology textbook of the Middle Ages. Of course Luther also studied Duns Scotus and Thomas Aquinas, and judged the latter guilty of "rambling long-windedness."[3] During this year in Wittenberg, Luther participated in an academic debate—a disputation, as they were called—on dogmatic principles. Luther argued against the established idea that theological ideas must simply be accepted and advocated instead for proofs. This, in its small way, is an augury of what was to come. Luther was hardly bold in condemning the way things were, but it is clear in retrospect that he was unsatisfied with what he was finding. His view of the truth was far too high for him to let confusing things or errant things slip by the wayside. He wanted real answers, and he wanted to read the Bible in such a way that he could get those answers, and he now began to suspect that some of the official answers being peddled might be as much obfuscation as anything else.

When they heard of how quickly their temporarily uprooted brother was progressing in Wittenberg, a number of his colleagues at Erfurt were resentful. In any case, after a year at Wittenberg, Luther was called back to his home monastery. But he was never required to take the standard oath at Erfurt saying that those who got their bachelor's degrees there must get their doctorate degrees at Erfurt too. Why this is, we do not know. But it would cause trouble for him later. In any event, Luther had not been back at Erfurt for very long when his studies were interrupted by a call to travel to Rome.

Trip to Rome, *Aetatis* 27

It was Staupitz who elected Luther to make the trip to Rome. The official reason he sent Luther (and presumably his fellow Erfurt brother Nathin, who was his senior in the order) was that there was at that time a certain controversy among the Augustinians that needed resolution. One branch of the Augustinian monks was called the Observant Augustinians, who held very strictly to the rule of the order, whereas the rest of the Augustinian monasteries were generally more lax. The Erfurt monastery was among the Observant group. As vicar-general of the entire order, Staupitz insisted that the Erfurt monastery—and the eighteen other Observant monasteries—should come under his authority and lose its relative independence. It was Staupitz's intention—and the desire of his superior in Rome—to bring all Observant monasteries under his jurisdiction so that he could then bring the more lax monasteries closer to the higher standard of the Observant monasteries. But the Erfurt brethren strongly opposed the idea of losing their independence. Luther attended an initial meeting that fall in Nuremberg, and the Observant monasteries flatly refused to submit to Staupitz's idea. In fact, they felt so strongly about this that they chose to appeal directly to Rome, which was their right. Staupitz acceded to this and thought that sending Luther to Rome to appeal the judgment would help the situation.

But again, we must assume there were other reasons Staupitz chose Luther to make this significant and long journey. For one thing, Staupitz surely believed that a break from the monastic routine would have been a good idea for his intense protégé. Surely a sixteen-hundred-mile round-trip journey on foot to Rome and back would be helpful in distracting young Martin from his excruciating confessional navel-gazing.

Luther's journey to Rome commenced in November 1510. Amazingly, this would be the only trip in his lifetime that strayed beyond the borders of his small world, for after the Diet of Worms, in 1521, when he was branded a heretic and outlaw in the empire, his movements would necessarily be limited to Saxony. Luther and his colleague Nathin would have walked the entire journey.

One of Luther's first stops on the long journey was the city of Nuremberg, 140 miles south of Erfurt. There Luther beheld the recently completed *Männleinlaufen*, an impressive mechanical clock at the top of the fourteenth-century Frauenkirche. Luther must have been stunned to look at this darling and marvel of the clockmaker's art. At the center of the clock face is seated the Holy Roman emperor, resplendently painted in golden costume. At noon each day, the bells sound and the two trumpeters hoist their long trumpets up, followed by bell ringers ringing their bells and drummers banging their drums, all to herald the awaited entrance from a door of the seven electors, whose figures deferentially process around the emperor before disappearing into the left door. They make this circuit three times before the magical movements cease until twenty-four hours later.*

Three or so days later, he and his companion came to Ulm, where they goggled at the monumental Ulm Minster, whose 530-foot steeple made it the tallest church in the world. Five hundred years later, it still holds the title. The interior of the church is 400 feet long and 160 feet wide, and the central nave soars to a height of 136 feet, making it something incomprehensibly vast for that time. Before pews were introduced, it was able to accommodate twenty thousand people. Luther had certainly never seen anything that approached it. But he later remarked that the immensity of this church, as well as of the Cologne Cathedral and St. Peter's in Rome, rendered them appallingly unsuited to preaching, which for him, of course, was more than a mere pity; it was a fatal flaw and a monumental tragedy. Luther felt that the impressiveness of the structure sacrificed the spiritual lives of the people who would come there. If feeding the Word of God to hungry flocks was the point of it all, and not mere shock-and-awe splendor, then these cavernous interiors would never do. What was the point?

Luther's journey then took him through Swabia and Bavaria and then on through the majestic silence of the snowy Alps. When they at last arrived in the great city of Milan, Luther discovered that he was unable to say Mass, although this time the difficulty had nothing to do with his own sense of worthiness. It was because of something that had happened

---

* One may still see this magnificent clock go through these motions today.

more than one thousand years before, when in the fourth century Saint Ambrose was the bishop of that city. All through those eleven centuries the so-called Ambrosian rite held sway there, as it still does today. Like most priests outside the Milanese region, Luther was familiar only with the Roman rite. From Milan they continued to Bologna, home to the world's oldest university, founded more than four centuries earlier, in 1088, and there in this extremely cold December they encountered what one rarely finds in that venerable city: snow.

From snowy Bologna, Luther and his companion continued southward through Florence. There, only twelve years earlier, Savonarola had been condemned as a heretic and burned at the stake. Undoubtedly, Luther here took in the astonishing *David* of Michelangelo, completed just seven years before. The mammoth, nearly eighteen-foot-high masterpiece then stood outside the Palazzo della Signoria,* but somehow Luther made no mention of it in his commentary. It has been said that Luther went right through Italy in the middle of the Renaissance but somehow missed it.

After Florence, Luther and his companion journeyed through Siena, and then, sometime at the end of December, they arrived at that certain spot on the ancient Via Cassia when their eyes at last fell upon their journey's end: the great and fabled city of the popes, the Eternal City, the city of the Seven Hills, and, most notably for Luther, the city where untold thousands had been cruelly murdered for their Christian faith, Saints Peter and Paul most famously among them. And in a few days with his Saxon eyes he would see their ancient bones. At this moment, Luther fell to his knees, prostrated himself on the cold ground, and said, "Be greeted, thou holy Rome, truly holy because of the holy martyrs, dripping with their blood."[4]

Luther would stay in Rome for a month, lodging either at the residence of the head of the papal representatives whom they had come to see or nearby in the monastery of Santa Maria del Popolo. History does not tell us which. We do know, however, that their only reason for making this round-trip journey of sixteen hundred miles on foot produced a veritable goose egg of results. Egidio of Viterbo, who was Staupitz's superior and who had ordered that the monasteries be combined in the first place, flatly refused to hear the case. So officially speaking, Luther

---

* Today a replica stands in the same place, while the original stands in the Uffizi Gallery nearby.

and his companion had walked eight hundred miles for nothing. In any case, Luther makes no mention of this crucial aspect of the journey.

But the spiritual opportunities in Rome were something else altogether, and of these he would speak throughout his life. Access to such eternal riches was without parallel in this world. Inasmuch as it was the very seat of the faith, Rome presented untold opportunities for spiritual advancement, which was of course why so many made the arduous trek. Once there, one would hardly know where to begin and what to do first. Positively required for any ambitious pilgrim was a single-day marathon in which one did not imbibe a morsel of food while visiting all seven of the city's principal churches, the final of which was of course St. Peter's, where one would attend Mass. Luther was terribly excited at the many possibilities. Perhaps, here in Rome, God had opened the door for him at last to advance in his quest for holiness, to move past the crippling *Anfechtungen* that kept him perpetually mired at the place of hopelessness where he had begun.

To be clear, the Rome of 1510 to which Luther and other faithful pilgrims came was a shrunken ghost of its quondam glory under the Caesars. The twelve miles of the third century's Aurelian Walls—soaring fifty-two feet high and punctuated with nearly four hundred towers—now absurdly enclosed a vast, pitted wasteland populated principally by wandering goats, cows, and stray dogs that, surprisingly, remained largely unmolested by the prostitutes and roving bands of brigands who frequented the city. It was also a far cry from the Renaissance Rome on the verge of being built, the Rome of Michelangelo and the "new" St. Peter's.

In fact, the "new" St. Peter's, which would soon become the marvel of the world, was during this time a mere architectural bud, not least because heaping mountains of the faithful's money were still required for it to be built. Little did Luther reckon that this building project would poke uncomfortably into his future and into the futures of the papacy and the church in a way that would change the world. At this point, he was just a young monk with no idea of what lay ahead, nor how this city and its religious failings would become an obsession with him. He was a twenty-seven-year-old who was happy to have walked across the Alps to see the fabled city where Peter and Paul had died their martyrs' deaths. He came as a Christian pilgrim whose soul needed improving, and here he would scour through the treasury of merits available to him.

One way a humble Christian could get ahead and earn indulgences was not only in paying money when an indulgence preacher came by but in traveling to a place exhibiting relics. One paid a small amount to view the relics, of course, but once one had viewed them, one was awarded an indulgence, and some of these indulgences could be quite significant. For example, here in Rome lay the fabled Crypt of Callixtus, which was said to hold the bones of forty popes and seventy-six thousand martyrs!* If one journeyed through a certain one of these catacombs five times while Mass was being celebrated, one earned an indulgence allowing a single soul to be freed from purgatory. Considering it was believed that one might spend thousands or even millions of years suffering in purgatory, this was a bargain that would be nearly impossible to pass up. Still, who knew how this had all been calculated? On the other hand, who would have time to care? It was an endless buffet of eternal riches, a veritable groaning board of everlasting goodies, and anyone wasting time thinking about them and not taking advantage of them while one had the opportunity must be reckoned worse than a fool!

Here in Rome, one could goggle at a preserved piece of the original burning bush, a branch of the very one Moses himself beheld in the Sinai desert three millennia before. It was one of the very branches that, though engulfed in flames, had failed to be consumed, and here was proof! And although everyone knew Judas had been paid thirty pieces of silver to betray Jesus, how must it feel to feast one's eyes on one of those pieces; but here it was, the fabled filthy lucre itself. For beholding this singular abomination, one was awarded an indulgence shortening one's time in purgatory by fourteen hundred years, almost the very number of years as had passed since this most miserable of all financial transactions.

Though it is not mentioned in the Bible, it was believed that before being exiled to the isle of Patmos, the apostle John had been summoned to Rome by Emperor Domitian, who in an effort to humiliate the holy man ordered that all of his hair be cut off. If any of the pilgrims to Rome doubted this, behold! Here they were, the very scissors that—*snip-snap-snip!*—had done the fabled barbering. The bodies of Saints Peter and Paul were in Rome too, albeit cloven in twain so that twice as many churches might share in the happy bounty. In fact, to stretch these treasures still further, the saints' heads had been removed from

* Today we know that these numbers are considerably inflated. It is more like six popes and fifty martyrs.

their bodies and now rested comfortably in the Archbasilica of St. John Lateran.

But because of the vast throngs, Luther was not able to avail himself of the special grace of viewing these celebrated icons. He was also unable to say Mass in St. John Lateran, which was more than a pity, because it had been stipulated that a priest saying Mass there could obtain his own mother's salvation. The very idea of it must have been disturbing and confusing: that because of the gabbling crowds Luther's dear mother might suffer the horrors of purgatory, or worse. What sense did it all make? But the church was full of such mysteries, and who was this Martin, a mere sinful monk, to question any of it?

While in Rome, Luther climbed the fabled Scala Sancta (Holy Stairs) that were purported to be the marble stairs of Pilate's first-century palace in Jerusalem, which stairs Jesus himself had mounted and at the top of which he heard his fate from the assembled rabble: "Crucify him!"[5] It is believed that Saint Helen, the mother of the fourth-century emperor Constantine, had brought them back from the Holy Land on a relic-hunting trip in which she also somehow managed to locate and bring back the "True Cross." Although the purportedly Tyrian marble of the Scala Sancta is now protected with a wood overlay, pilgrims can still today climb them on their knees, praying all the while, just as Luther did five hundred years ago. It was stipulated in Luther's time that the pilgrim ascending these stairs must upon each step recite the *Pater Noster* (Our Father).[6] Doing this would count toward decreasing the suffering of any deceased relatives in purgatory, and at the time Luther seriously lamented that his parents were still alive. What a terrible conundrum it presented! How he dearly wished his time in Rome might count toward relieving the suffering in purgatory that likely yawned ahead of them, but the fact that they yet breathed terrestrial air cut off any hope of his helping them. But happily, Luther's grandpa Heine had departed this world in time to benefit from his grandson's ardent piety. Luther earnestly said the *Pater Noster* twenty-eight times, but when at last he reached the top of this holy ziggurat, a terrible thought entered his mind. Years later, he said that as he knelt at the top of those twenty-eight steps, with his knees still registering the coolness of their marble, he suddenly wondered whether all he had just done so obediently would have the effect that the church so authoritatively and specifically and confidently said it would. The doctrine that the church possessed the authority to make these decisions about who suffered in purgatory and for precisely how long was believed to be absolutely clear. After all, had Jesus given the keys to Peter or hadn't he? Still, after Luther had done his twenty-eight kneeling *Pater Nosters*, the question somehow arose in his head whether it was all in fact as had been told him. "What if it's not true?" he wondered. He knew at the time that this thought had come into his mind, but had it come from the devil, who caused Eve to doubt God's promise in Eden, or was it a question provoked by a genuine desire to know the truth, which is to say, from God himself? Luther didn't know the answer, nor could he know it, but soon enough he would endeavor to find out.

Another disturbing aspect of his time in Rome was the astonishing incompetence and cynicism of many of the priests there. Luther had never seen anything that began to approach it. It was one thing to have questions about God and the religious life, but what to make of these priests who seemed to go through the motions with a contemptuous indifference, or in some cases even a mocking blasphemy? It was positively diabolical. On the first score, Luther noted that Mass was said with such breathless speed that even he, who was exceedingly familiar with every word, found it utterly unintelligible. It was mystifying, as though the priests had secretly been replaced with fast-talking auctioneers. For Luther, who had revered the Mass to the point of awe and even terror, this cavalier attitude toward this holiest of privileges must have been a horror to behold. If ever one needed a picture of "dead religion" and "dead works," here it was in all of its most legalistic ghastliness. Luther saw that these priests hadn't the slightest reverence for the holy act in which they were participating but wished only to tick off the appropriate box and gallop off to something less demanding. The shortest time officially allowed in which a priest could hurry through the Mass was twelve minutes, but Luther recalled that at the basilica of St. Sebastian seven masses were said in an hour—in other words, in something less than nine minutes each. And when Luther himself said Mass, the next priest—fidgety with impatience—almost literally breathed down his neck. "Quick, quick!" he said to Luther, sarcastically adding, "And send our Lady back her Son!"—obviously a joke about the transubstantiated host. At St. Sebastian, Luther also recalled the freakish oddity of two masses being said simultaneously at the same altar, the priests merely separated by a painting.

Luther also heard scandalous stories from other monks that boggled his innocent and pious mind. He recalled at one meal a group of monks screaming with laughter about how when they were saying Mass, they sometimes blasphemously said, "*Panis es et panis manebis, vinum es et vinum manebis*"—"bread thou art and bread shalt thou remain, wine thou art and wine shalt thou remain." For someone to whom the Mass was ineffable and numinous—indeed it was something for which he would give his very life, as others had and many would in centuries hence—Luther hardly knew how to react. The monks making these jokes obviously never considered that there was someone at the table who didn't share their jaundiced views. Everywhere Luther looked, he was horrified. Later he referred to "the chaos, the filth, and the practice of locals who urinated in public and openly patronized prostitutes."

But lest we wonder if all of this was Luther's perspective alone, we should remember that even the great Erasmus of Rotterdam had visited Rome five years earlier and experienced similar horrors. "With my own ears," Erasmus said, "I heard the most loathsome blasphemies against Christ and His apostles. Many acquaintances of mine have heard priests of the curia uttering disgusting words so loudly, even during mass, that all around them could hear it."[7]

The Curious Case of Anna Laminit

Eventually, it was time for Luther and his companion to walk the eight hundred miles back to Erfurt. We know little of their return journey, but we do know that once they had reentered the boundaries of Germany, they made a stop in Augsburg, where Luther paid a call on Anna (a.k.a. Ursula) Laminit, a famous ascetic whose tragic story can scarcely be believed. When Luther met her, this extraordinary holy woman was renowned far and wide for having nibbled nary a single crumb of food for fourteen years. She subsisted only—it was said—on the Holy Sacrament itself. And added to this celebrated feat was the homologous boon of not having dropped a single stool or even a drop of urine during all this time. The name Laminit was a shortening of *Lass mir nicht* (Leave me not), though the meaning of it remains unclear. Luther was no stranger to asceticism, but surely he was unfamiliar with anything approaching this decidedly extreme case. To be so otherworldly as this woman was, to eschew not only the emoluments of life but food and drink themselves and all of their attendant effects, certainly spoke of a nearness to heaven, which accorded perfectly with the idea that one could via "holy works" earn one's own way to paradise. Never to eat and drink, and neither to urinate nor defecate, was to have transcended this world in a very palpable way, to have eschewed the simplest physical necessities of human existence so thoroughly that one was, as it were, on par with the angels. Because this achievement represented the ne plus ultra of monastic and holy life, Luther could not pass up the opportunity to see the woman himself, for she had achieved precisely the kind of perfection he longed for.

Luther hoped to discover whatever he could from her, and so, when at last they met, the young monk asked this celebrated woman whether she longed to go to heaven—to die and leave this world. Of course that seemed to be the very point of all of her activities, and as far as anyone could tell, she was already halfway there. But her answer to the question shocked Luther. "Oh no!" she answered. And then, by way of explaining herself, said, "Here I know how things work, but there I don't know what will happen."[8] Luther's bafflement now increased. How could someone so extraordinarily holy say such a thing? But today we know how she was able to say this, because the woman who styled herself Anna Laminit, the dedicated ascetic, was a thoroughgoing fraud. The details of her life are worth dilating upon briefly, because they illustrate the absurd end of the very kind of otherworldly asceticism that Luther sought but that he would in the end reject with everything in him.

The woman who came to call herself Anna Laminit was born in 1480 into humble circumstances in Augsburg, where she was raised. But because of "loose living" while still in her teen years, she was publicly thrashed on the pillory and then driven from the city. But she nonetheless returned in 1497 and was taken in by some Christians who ran a poorhouse, and here she was evidently exposed to the things of God. Thus inspired, she betook herself to reemerge as a "hunger martyr" and visionary, wearing austere black and regaling her visitors with visions of angels and Saint Anne. She soon became renowned as a living saint and was visited by the emperor himself, along with his naive and curiously childlike second wife, both of whom were thoroughly taken in by the mystical woman.

This naturally provided her with an excellent reference, and thus her fame grew, such that the rich and famous suddenly beat a path to her door, seeking her counsel on matters large and small. Her influence became so great that she would often lead large religious processions of repentance through the city in which all of the local clergy, including monks and nuns, participated. A particular highlight came in June 1503, when Emperor Maximilian's queen participated, along with her entire entourage. The queen was herself dressed in black sackcloth, holding a candle at the center of the holy spectacle. Anna's wealthy and powerful friends showered her with gifts that because of her special religious disposition were not taxed, and the ascetic soon amassed a tidy fortune.

But the emperor's sister Kunigunde, Duchess of Bavaria, was not so gullible. Herself a woman of considerable Christian piety, she smelled something amiss in all the holy rigmarole and thought she should investigate further. So the duchess somehow contrived to invite the unsuspecting sibyl to visit with her at a Munich cloister, where she would be deliberately situated in a certain guest room. For it was into this carefully selected chamber, via a peephole, that Duchess Kunigunde could observe all of Anna's doings, hoping to perhaps unmask the real truth behind all the pious foofaraw. So Anna accepted the invitation and soon clambered into the duchess's trap, for once alone in her guest room this "hunger martyr" was observed to unpack—and then tuck into—a fabulous stash of dainties and delicacies, including juicy pears and pepper cakes. And as far as her inevitable stools were concerned, once they had found egress, she was to be observed coolly flinging them from the window. When the duchess had the hard facts, she and some others confronted Anna with the foul evidence and, to ensure the ascetic chicanery would end once and for all, forced her to eat and drink in front of the assemblage. They charged her with reforming her ways, to which she solemnly agreed, and then let her return to Augsburg. But once there, she resumed the well-worn "hunger martyr" act just as sincerely as before.

By this time, it had been widely rumored that she had had sexual relations with several men of the city, most notably the vicar of a local church, as well as the tremendously wealthy and powerful merchant Anton Welser. There can be no doubt of the latter, because she bore him a son, for whose support Welser would pay the handsome sum of thirty gulden each year. The child soon died, but in order to continue receiving the annual payments, Anna kept the news from Welser for many years.

When the duchess discovered that Anna had returned to Augsburg only to continue the holy charade, she had had enough. She informed her brother, the emperor, who now decreed that Anna be expelled from

Augsburg. But because she agreed to leave her considerable assets with the city, she was allowed to depart with dignity, and did so, in a luxurious carriage provided by Welser.

Anna now traveled to a nunnery in Kempten, sixty miles south, where she once more plied her "hunger martyr" arts, but the sanctified fakery was exposed there too, so she fled north to Kaufbeuren, there taking up with a widowed crossbow maker named Hans Bachman. The couple moved to Fribourg, Switzerland, where they were married in November 1514. But a few years later, in 1518, her lifetime of crimes at last caught up with her. Welser had decided to send his son, whom he had never seen, to school, and he wrote to Anna, asking her to send the boy to him. Because her son with Welser had been dead for many years, she contrived in an act of desperation to send her husband's son instead. He was about the same age as her son with Welser would have been, had the child lived. But somehow Welser discovered this ruse, as well as the equally humiliating fact that he had been defrauded out of thirty gulden a year for many years. Furious, he sought justice and Anna was soon arrested in Fribourg and charged. After confessing to everything (without torture), she was sentenced by the court to death by burning, although the judgment was "mercifully" reduced to death by drowning. She was to be put in a sack and held under water at a certain spot in the river Saane "until the soul left her body." This grim sentence was carried out as scheduled on May 5, 1518.

So Luther's experience with what was undeniably a celebrated and— to him—rather suspicious example of the asceticism of that time would have been one more early indication that something was rotten with the state of the medieval church.

CHAPTER FOUR

A Monk at Wittenberg

W HEN LUTHER RETURNED from Rome, his brothers in the Erfurt monastery decided that despite hearing nothing encouraging from Staupitz's superior there, they still would not submit to Staupitz's authority. Luther was in a quandary. As he reckoned the situation, Staupitz was his superior, and he had taken a vow of obedience. So Luther refused to have anything further to do with the Erfurt rebellion against Staupitz, but this caused a deep rift between him and most of the other brethren in the monastery, one that would follow him for many years. Staupitz saw that Luther was in a difficult situation, and so he transferred him back to Wittenberg, along with Luther's dear friend Johannes Lang, who had sided with Luther in the controversy. As far as the bitter Erfurters were concerned, it was good riddance to the pair of them. In any case, compared with Erfurt, Wittenberg was a pathetic, hickish backwater. If Luther and Lang loved Staupitz that much, they could now be near him full-time.

What Luther thought of his posting to Wittenberg, we don't know, but he hardly had any choice in the matter. As for Staupitz, he was undoubtedly thrilled. This was in part because as vicar-general of the order, he very often traveled to the many other monasteries he oversaw. Practically speaking, he needed someone to replace him at Wittenberg, and there is little doubt he thought Luther the perfect choice. But in order for Luther to do what Staupitz was now doing at Wittenberg, he would need to obtain his doctorate, something Luther certainly never intended. What impressed Staupitz about Luther was not merely his impressive intelligence and abilities as a scholar but his relationship with the Bible itself. This was in that time and place not only rare but unique. As Luther often said, no one at that time read the Bible.

In later years, when talking about how no one was able to read the Bible at that time, Luther sometimes referred to his friend and colleague at Wittenberg Andreas Bodenstein von Karlstadt. He had been raised in the town of Karlstadt in Bavaria and in the fashionable Humanist manner of that time simply took to calling himself Karlstadt, dropping the Bodenstein entirely. He was on the theology faculty at Wittenberg and was greatly respected there but hardly knew the Bible at all. Karlstadt, however, deeply respected Luther for his knowledge of the Bible, although no one seemed to think this was something to which other theologians should aspire. Only those who felt a special affinity with the book spent time with it, and at Wittenberg the only one besides Luther who did so was Staupitz himself. Staupitz saw that for Luther the Bible was not a book like Aristotle's *Ethics* or like a volume of Livy or Cicero. It was something entirely apart from every book in the world. It was the living Word of God and therefore could not be read like any other book. It was inspired by God, and when one read it, one must do so in such a way— with such closeness and intimacy—that one fully intended to feel and smell the breezes of heaven. If one missed this aspect, one missed the whole point. For Staupitz, to read any other book like this was to be a fool, but to read the Bible in any other way than this was to be twice the fool. So he obviously hoped that he might persuade Luther to help him in this.

Under the Pear Tree, *Aetatis* 28

Because Staupitz had heard so many of Luther's confessions, he understood that Luther clung tightly to the Scriptures for spiritual succor and that in them he sought God and the answers that only God could provide. This was the sort of man he knew could ably replace him at Wittenberg, so one day in October 1512, Staupitz broached the subject as they sat together under a pear tree in the monastery's courtyard. In the course of the conversation, Staupitz made himself clear: Luther must commence studies for the doctorate.

Decades later, Luther would regale his students with the story of how Staupitz argued with him that day and would point to the old pear tree, saying that it was just there under that very same tree—before many of his students were born—that Luther and Staupitz had had their conversation. In that conversation, the young monk made it clear to his beloved and respected mentor that he was opposed to studying for his doctorate, and his reasons against it were several. For one thing, he didn't think himself up to the significant physical and mental toll of teaching and preaching. In fact, he confided in Staupitz that he didn't think he would live very long, which seems to have been an odd—and ultimately false— but sincere belief on Luther's part. The six years he had already spent mortifying his flesh with fasting and other monastic hardships had likely taken their toll. Now, nearly twenty-nine, he was a far cry from the stout figure we see in Cranach's later paintings. Though it may be hard for us to imagine Martin Luther as bony and frail, at this time in his life he was indisputably more ibex than ox. In fact, fully seven years after this conversation—at the 1519 Leipzig disputation—he was described by an observer as being so thin one could almost see his bones through his skin. So during this time with Staupitz, Luther was not imagining things when he described himself as someone whose health was less than robust. Still, whatever Luther meant by this, Staupitz knew Luther himself all too well. In their endless confessions, Staupitz had been parrying with the gloomy, dramatically self-effacing monk for years, and he was now ready with a jocose answer. "Even if you die soon," he said, "God has need of clever advisors in heaven, too. In fact, I'm sure he needs more doctors!"[1]

Luther took the point, probably with a smile, but he had a score of other objections and brought them before Staupitz. One was that he felt he was simply too young, that it was unseemly for someone of his age to bear the august title of doctor. He had been a monk only for a few years. Who was he to preach and teach? Besides, it was clear that many of the Erfurt brethren had resented his rapid rise, and Luther was sensitive to such things. But Staupitz explained that if Luther were to take up his offer, Luther would be teaching the Bible, which must surely have held great appeal for him. Then Staupitz sweetened the pot further. He told Luther that not only would he be teaching the Bible; he would be teaching the Bible *only*. For into the bargain Staupitz now threw the promise that Luther needn't teach Aristotle ever again, and because Luther had by now in fact come to loathe Aristotle, he must suddenly have found the offer unfailingly appealing.

Once Luther officially acceded to Staupitz's wishes, the brilliant monk qualified for his doctoral studies very quickly and very soon thereafter was awarded his degree. At the doctoral ceremony, he also was given a Bible, a golden doctor's ring—bearing three interlinked rings that symbolized the Trinity—and the special doctoral biretta. The ceremony took place on October 18 and 19, 1513, and Luther had invited many to be there, including everyone from the Erfurt monastery, which was a generous gesture on his part. Many of the Erfurt brethren were still bitter toward him over his behavior after returning from Rome, when he had sided with Staupitz, but their fresher outrage was that Luther had dared to study for his doctorate in Wittenberg and not in Erfurt. So they refused the invitation. In fact, so miffed were they at the whole affair that they attempted to have his degree revoked. Luther's Wittenberg doctorate was for them a rank betrayal of the oath all Erfurt monks had taken, vowing to continue their studies at Erfurt. But Luther had never taken such an oath, although why he did not is not clear. Still, it pained Luther greatly that even his former teachers at Erfurt would take such a stand against him. Nathin, in particular, became his lifelong enemy over this.

Nonetheless, from this point on, Luther's course at Wittenberg was set. He began teaching on August 1, 1513, two months before the actual doctoral ceremony. His lectures were held at 6:00 a.m. and in the winter at 7:00 a.m. For the first two years at Wittenberg, Luther would teach on the Psalms. Two years later, he would teach on Paul's Epistle to the Romans, and two years after that he would teach on the book of Galatians.

Luther's dream had now come true; he could spend infinite hours digging into the Bible in a way he had never been able to do before. He could find out what it really was saying on certain issues that had always eluded him, and he could perhaps even find the fabled golden ticket—the deeper meaning that was the key to the whole—that lay buried someplace deep beneath the Latin strata. Luther was hunting for the truth itself about who we are and who God is and what he really expects of us and how we can reconcile the infinite breach between heaven and earth, between God and man, between peace and agony. For this he would look and look very hard, because if he found it he would at last have a way out of the miserable doubt and agony that had plagued him since long before the thunderstorm in Stotternheim.

Wittenberg

In the tale of Luther's life, there are many important players, but the town of Wittenberg played as vital a role as any. In fact, it's quite impossible to divorce Wittenberg itself from several of those players, among them

Staupitz and Frederick, the Duke of Saxony. Frederick was also known as Frederick the elector, and later as Frederick the Wise, and there would hardly be any Wittenberg per se if not for him. Later, the great painter Lucas Cranach becomes another Wittenberg figure whose role in Luther's story cannot be exaggerated. Our present-day grand view of Wittenberg—as a respected name in the pantheon of those places where history has been lived and made—is dramatically different from the view people would have had of it when Luther went to live there. In fact, compared to the many truly great cities of Germany at that time, Wittenberg was then decidedly pathetic. A number of the German cities—the so-called imperial free cities—were so powerful that they were able to flout the authority of any nearby prince and be truly independent. Among these were Augsburg, Nuremberg, Hamburg, Cologne, Strasbourg, and Basel. In 1512, when Luther arrived to stay, Wittenberg was a far cry from any of these. But what made Wittenberg into the city it would become and was already becoming—in part as the staging ground for the Reformation to come—had begun as the pure ambition that was born of a bitter sibling rivalry.

It all began in 1485, when the former lands of the Wettin-Saxon dukes were divided between Frederick's father, Ernest, and Ernest's brother Albert. According to Saxon custom, Albert, as the youngest, was able to choose which of the territories he wished to take, and he naturally chose the best ones available, with Saxony's prize city, Leipzig, among them. This division of Saxony into what became known as "Albertine Saxony" and "Ernestine Saxony" created a rivalry that would be played out in numerous ways with many important ramifications in the decades ahead.

Thus, after his brother had taken the better part of the lands, what remained for Ernest was an inelegant, positively scrawny strip of territory, too long and thin to have any actual center—and most annoyingly lacking Leipzig. In fact, the only town it had worth bothering about was Wittenberg, a jerkwater burg that was nothing more than a humiliating embarrassment. Still, despite getting the short end of the geographical stick, Ernest cannily obtained something else that was of enormous potential value.

The Holy Roman Empire at that time was a lumpy quilt of three hundred territories, of which seven were ruled by nobles, called electors. They were called electors* because it was they alone who held the privilege of

* In 1356, the emperor created an "electoral college" consisting of seven princes, who were thenceforth called electors. Four of them were secular, and three were ecclesiastical. (See Ozment, *The Serpent and the Lamb*.)

Albrecht Dürer's portrait of Frederick the Wise, elector of Saxony.

choosing the Holy Roman emperor. So apart from the emperor himself, these seven electors were by a great margin the most powerful figures in the empire. And as a sop for receiving the awkward, gerrymandered strip of territory, Ernest now became one of them. With the political power he would have in this role came a great opportunity for amassing yet more power. Who knew what an ambitious man might make of it? History would soon find out, but that ambitious man would be not Ernest himself but his son Frederick. That's because in 1486, just a year after all of this had been settled, Ernest died as a result of a fall from his horse; he was forty-five. So it was to his son Frederick that the responsibilities of this new and important position now fell.

Frederick was only twenty-three years old at that time, but he seemed to know what to do to make the most of the opportunity that presented itself, and he immediately took his new role as elector very seriously. Whenever there was an assembly—called an imperial diet—of the various rulers in the empire, Frederick assiduously attended and learned the political ropes as quickly and as well as anyone could have hoped to do.

In a few years, all of this would pay off handsomely, as we shall see. He also decided that he would transform Wittenberg into a place fully worthy of its important status as an electoral capital, and here he succeeded too. His fierce ambition in all these things would end up playing a crucial role in his decision to protect Luther in the years to come.

So in 1490, the young Frederick began in earnest to lift Wittenberg to the height he thought it deserved. To start, the old Ascanian fortress was razed, and a handsome double-winged new palace began to rise in its place, though this would take twenty years before it was finished. Immediately next to Frederick's palace, the Castle Church* was now built, and of course this too must be nothing less than magnificent. For one thing, it must be large enough to hold—and at certain times properly display—the impossibly large collection of relics that Frederick would soon be amassing. And it was this new church whose massive wooden doors in just a few years would display the ninety-five incendiary theses that sparked the Reformation. The church's tower rose nearly three hundred feet and can still be seen for many miles.

Frederick knew that to create a palace and a church worthy of serious attention, he must expend great sums on art, which he did, attracting the immortal talents of Albrecht Dürer and Lucas Cranach, among many others. It would be a particular feather in Frederick's crown when Cranach himself decided to move to Wittenberg. His home would be the most well-appointed in the town, and his business the most thriving. Frederick would even make him his official court painter—and give him the title *pictor ducalis* (the duke's painter).

Frederick also knew that an electoral capital must have a university. His uncle Albert's domain included Leipzig, with its already venerable university (founded in 1409). So Frederick would make up for lost time in 1502; he founded the University of Wittenberg, and immediately invited his old friend Johannes von Staupitz to teach theology there. They had known each other for many years, probably having met in Grimma, where Staupitz attended school in an Augustinian cloister. Staupitz had come from an upper-class family as well, as one may surmise from the "von" in his name. He had gotten his doctorate in theology from Tübingen two years earlier and a year after coming to Wittenberg was made dean of the theology faculty. In May 1507, he was also elected vicar-general of the Observant branch of the Augustinian order. It was

---

* The German for "Castle Church" is *Schlosskirche*.

because of his duties as vicar-general over several monasteries that he would eventually decide to replace himself at the University of Wittenberg with the rising genius Martin Luther. Frederick's relationship with Staupitz enabled him to attract to the university not only Martin Luther—whose spellbinding lectures would swell the numbers of students—but a certain Greek-language savant called Philip Schwartzerdt, later to be known as Melanchthon, because the Humanistic tradition of Latinizing or Grecizing one's name would turn the German words *Schwarz* (black) and *Erde* (earth) into the Greek Melanchthon. In keeping with the Humanistic style, the university was itself called Leucorea, combining the Greek words for "white" and "mountain." Four hundred sixteen students matriculated in the first year, and another 258 in the second. For a town of a mere 2,000 inhabitants, this was a dramatic boost, not only in sheer population, but more important for Frederick's plans in terms of intellectual and cultural capital too.[2]

But the university was at this point a mere side project when compared with Frederick's outsized penchant for collecting relics. This would obsess him for decades, and he knew his relic collection would greatly bolster the income and influence of the Wittenberg Castle Church, and therefore Wittenberg itself. The relic bug first bit Frederick in 1493, when he made a pilgrimage to the Holy Land and there found himself mesmerized by all manner of ancient and pious objects. The trip from Saxony to Jerusalem was of course a long one in those days and bespoke the sincere piety of Frederick in making it. At some point on the trip, his ship dropped anchor off the Greek island of Rhodes, and it was on his visit to its shores that Frederick discovered and obtained an extremely important relic. It was the thumb of Jesus's reputed grandmother, Saint Anne, which had some years before hitched a ride from Jerusalem to this Greek island and which would now hitch a second ride to its final destination at Frederick's *Schlosskirche* in Wittenberg.

Frederick the Wise's Relics

Whenever one discusses relics, as we have already said about those one could find in Rome, one must assume that while some of them are indeed what they are purported to be, most of them probably are not. For example, in the dazzlingly vast collection that Frederick amassed, there was said to be yet another twig from the burning bush itself. Perhaps even less plausibly, the centerpiece of the collection was said to be a thorn from the crown of thorns worn by Jesus, although somehow this thorn was not merely from the fabled crown of thorns but one that was actually known— and even somehow officially certified—to have pierced the Savior's brow. This had been a gift to an earlier Saxon elector, Rudolf, given to him by King Philip VI of France two centuries earlier. And of course among these treasures was the aforementioned thumb that had belonged to the very woman to whom Luther had made his vow during the Stotternheim storm, whom the Savior likely called Grandma.

Thanks to Frederick's ambitions for Wittenberg, the relics here rivaled even those ancient treasures at Rome. A tooth of Saint Jerome was in the collection as well, as were several fragments of the bodies of other saints: four each from Saint Augustine and Saint Chrysostom. There were six from Saint Bernard. The purported relics from the life of Christ included a swatch of his swaddling clothes, a piece of the very gold brought to him by the Magi, and three precious fragments of the funereal myrrh they had prophetically included. There were also thirteen lucky fragments said to be from Jesus's childhood crib, doubtless made by Joseph's own hands (no precious bone fragments of which, alas, had found their way to Wittenberg). But, lo, here was a strand of hair from the beard of Jesus and four hairs from the head of his dear mother. Mary was also represented by three holy fragments from her cloak and four from her girdle. There were also seven fragments taken from the veil that had been sprinkled with the blood of Jesus. If it was desiccated food that fueled one's devotional fires, there was a preserved piece of the very bread served at the Last Supper in the Upper Room fifteen centuries earlier, as well as a vial containing drops of milk from the breast of the Virgin Mary. How and why they had not been consumed by the infant Jesus but had instead found their way into this vial is lost to history. There was even a piece of John the Baptist's cloak and a portion of the very rock upon which the Savior had stood as he wept over Jerusalem. There was the complete skeleton of one of the infants killed by Herod in Bethlehem, as well as an additional 204 bones from some others in that tragic category. And there were precisely thirty-five splinters from the True Cross! And last and certainly most ethereal of all was the pinnate stunner of the collection, the very feather of an angel! Its provenance is not recorded.

Frederick's collection grew and grew as the years passed, becoming the magnet that attracted innumerable pilgrims and their money to this city so far off the beaten track. Already in 1509, Lucas Cranach created 124 woodcut illustrations for a catalog of the relics that pilgrims could purchase to guide them through the endless maze of these curiosities and treasures. Masses were constantly being said in the Castle Church so that people could view these relics, which were also a healthy source of income. The number of masses recorded for 1517 was about nine thousand. The records also indicate that during these masses 40,932 candles were burned, amounting to some 7,000 pounds of wax. By 1520, there were 19,013 relics in Frederick's collection, and it had been carefully calculated that those who visited these relics on the day appointed—and made whatever contributions were required—were able to shorten their own time in purgatory, or the time of a loved one, by nearly two million years. The exact number tabulated was 1,902,202 years and 270 days.[3]

Wittenberg Professor

Luther was now in Wittenberg for good. In 1513, it was a town of 384 houses, and compared with Luther's previous home cities of Eisleben, Mansfeld, Eisenach, and Erfurt, Wittenberg was by far the humblest and least populous place Luther had ever lived. Despite the elector's ambitious plans for its future, it was at this time still a geographical cipher in the middle of nowhere. But in a way, the smallness of it would in time prove a boon to Luther, because the people of Wittenberg would come to identify with him and stand by him in a way they might not have in a larger, more sophisticated place.

So here in this Saxon backwater, Luther began teaching and generally kept extremely busy. Some have speculated that Staupitz knew that being busy was one way for Luther to deal with the *Anfechtungen*, that in dealing with others he would be forced to take his mind off himself. And because Luther was brilliant and capable, he was given more and more to do. His duties became staggering. In 1514, he was made the preacher in the Wittenberg City Church. He was already the vicar of the Wittenberg monastery, and in 1515 Staupitz promoted him to become the vicar-general of eleven monasteries, which he was obliged to oversee and visit. In a letter to his friend Lang in the fall of 1516, Luther explained just how busy he was during this time:

I could almost occupy two scribes or secretaries. All day long I do nothing but write letters. . . . I preach at the monastery, I am a lector during mealtimes, I am asked daily to preach in the city church, I have to supervise the program of study, and I am vicar, i.e., prior of eleven cloisters. Plus: I am warden of the fish-pond at Leitzkau, and at Torgau. I am involved in a dispute with the Herzbergers. . . . I lecture on Paul and I am still collecting material on the Psalms. . . . I have little uninterrupted time for the daily [monastic] hours or for celebrating mass. Besides, I have my own struggles with the flesh, the world, and the devil. See what a lazy man I am![4]

Perhaps Luther's most important insight of the two-year period in which he taught the Psalms (1513–15) was that the only way to read the Word of God properly involved seeing beyond the mere words. To read legalistically and simplistically was to miss God himself. Therefore, one must not merely see what the devil could see, which is to say the words on a page, but see what only God could see and would reveal to those who desired it, which was in the words and around them too. This superrational element gave the words their vital context and deeper meaning. So Pharisees and other legalists could get stuck on the letter of the law, but to truly read the Word of God and not merely the words of God, one required revelation and the anointing of God himself, which itself previously required a prayerful and contrite attitude. To read the Word of God in any other way was to miss the spiritual truth and therefore to miss the main point of reading it at all.

In making these observations, Luther was no doubt thinking of the innumerable hours that he and other monks had prayed the Psalms in their daily offices, sometimes reciting them with little more heartfelt understanding than a mynah bird or parrot might have done. To do that, Luther felt, not only was wrong, but actually hardened the heart against the deeper meaning. It was, in some way, blasphemous to read God's Word in this superficial way. One must bring one's heart and one's whole person into it. Even Satan in the wilderness flawlessly quoted the words of God to Jesus, which of course had been blasphemy of the highest order. So without entering into God's presence and asking for God's understanding of the words, one was doing no better than the devil himself had done.

During this time, Luther also put forward the idea that to truly be a part of the church of Jesus Christ was inevitably to enter into a spiritual battle. He was keenly aware that before Emperor Constantine made the Roman Empire officially Christian in the fourth century, the Roman state had murdered men and women for their faith; but he believed that suffering and battling nonetheless continued throughout the ages, until the day of Christ's return. And he believed that now this battle must be fought within the church against those who would pervert God's doctrines and the deeper meaning of God's Word. Such enemies had formerly been outside the church, but now they were inside it and had gained leading positions in it. Luther later referred to them as "impious prelates."[5] So to battle against them, one would suffer too, and to suffer for this was a noble honor. Anyone wishing to follow Christ must not shrink from suffering for his sake, however that suffering should manifest itself. So the idea that one could advance as a Christian merely by amassing a head full of intellectual knowledge was not only wrong but evil and perverse; it was the very reason for which Christ had railed against the Pharisees, who clearly knew the Torah backward and forward but whose lives were often at odds with what it taught. The Christian faith was an affair of the heart and of the whole person. To relegate it to the attic of mere learning was to miss the point. Luther understood this and stressed it in teaching his students.

Already in 1513, Luther was convinced that the church of Christ was in an advanced state of decrepitude that had been prophesied in the Bible, one in which the Antichrist would reveal himself and do battle with the saints of God. Luther had picked up much of his thinking along these lines from Saint Augustine, but Bernard of Clairvaux had also been an influence. Bernard had been canonized only twenty years after his 1153 death and while alive held that there were three ages of the church. The first had been the epoch of martyrs, in which Christians were persecuted and killed for their faith; the second had been the era of heretics, in which Christians perverted church teaching; and the third and most terrible would be the third epoch, the Last Days, in which the church itself would be so corrupt that the Antichrist himself would arise from within it. Luther believed the church had entered this third and final stage. He had been sickened by the sales of indulgences and even spoke about it to his students. He was convinced that this abuse was a clear sign of having entered the end-time spoken of by Christ. "The way I see it," he had said, "the Gospel of St. Matthew counts such perversions as the selling of indulgences among the signs of the Last Days."[6]

As Luther taught the Bible from 1513 on, he often said things that were critical of how the Bible had previously been read or how the church was doing things that were not in accordance with what the Bible taught, but he never did so as someone who was itching for a larger battle. Like Erasmus and other critics of the church, he did so humbly hoping to help others see what he saw. Perhaps another reason Luther's fire to speak out did not flare up before 1517 was that he had not until that year found the smoking gun, theologically speaking, that he needed for an open-and-shut case, and that gun he found during what he later termed the "cloaca" experience. It was only then that the light from heaven shone upon him and helped him to see everything differently forever.

Spalatin

In 1512, another crucially important figure would make his entrance to Wittenberg. This was Georg Burkhardt, known as Spalatin, who was part of the Humanist circle at the University of Erfurt when Luther was there.

Spalatin was so bright and so personable that he was recommended to Frederick the Wise as a tutor for Frederick's nephew John in 1509. Frederick's brother Duke John (also known as John the Constant and John the Steadfast) would succeed Frederick as elector when Frederick died, and when John died in 1532, his son John Frederick I (also called John the Magnanimous) would succeed him; all three electors would play important roles in Luther's life. As for Spalatin, he quickly found favor with Frederick, soon gaining his deepest confidence. In 1512, Frederick made him his librarian and tasked him with the centrally important job of building up the new university's library. In time, Frederick elevated him to be his chaplain and secretary too, so that, in the end, virtually everything concerning Frederick was handled by Spalatin.

But Spalatin's relationship with Luther grew quickly too. Luther was one or two years his senior, and he became the man that Spalatin entrusted as his own spiritual and theological guide, as the many letters between them make clear. So Spalatin became the single and vital point at which Luther and Frederick communicated, and without Frederick, Luther's story would be very different. It is a truly strange fact that Frederick and Luther never met but only and always communicated through Spalatin.

Lucas Cranach

Lucas von Kronach was born in the town of Kronach, from which he of course took his name. It was Cranach who would single-handedly turn the unknown monk named Martin Luther into a household name throughout Germany, spreading his image in various forms over much of Europe. But as with Staupitz and so many other of the principal figures without whom the story is unimaginable, Cranach's presence in Wittenberg is owed to Frederick the Wise.

It was because Frederick would spare no expense in his rivalry with his uncle Albert the Brave—and then, on his uncle's death in 1500, with his first cousin Duke George the Bearded, who would become a dedicated foe of Luther's—that he sought to decorate Wittenberg in the spectacular style befitting the capital city of an electoral territory. Of course this must involve the finest fine art available. On a trip to Nuremberg in April 1496, Frederick met the fabulously talented Albrecht Dürer, who already had his own workshop and had begun his spectacular rise to international prominence. During this time, Dürer painted Frederick's portrait, and Frederick was so impressed that he lost no time in commissioning something far more ambitious from the genius. It was to be a work of eight panels that became known as the *Seven Sorrows Polyptych*. A few years later, when Frederick decided it was time to have an official court painter, he consulted innumerable friends and acquaintances, Dürer certainly among them. Only after being reassured that Cranach was the closest thing to Dürer did he settle on him. So in 1505, the thirty-three-year-old bachelor moved to Wittenberg. For this post, he received not only a handsome stipend but all the artistic materials he needed, as well as a well-appointed apartment in the elector's castle and a horse.

But what he must do in return for this august position and compensation beggars description. Being the official court painter involved far more than creating the occasional masterpiece in oils, which he did, some of them even being favorably compared to the acclaimed altarpieces of Matthias Grünewald. The job also required a stunning artistic versatility, which Cranach certainly had. This is easily seen by juxtaposing any of his spiritually powerful altarpieces with the later shockingly vulgar woodcuts featuring demons and defecating popes and cardinals, which were of course created in concert with his future literary collaborator

Martin Luther. But beyond his artistic range, Cranach was possessed of astonishing skills as a businessman and as the leader of a vast workshop of other painters and craftsmen.

In 1508, at the imperial diet, as a signal tribute to his court painter, Frederick bestowed upon Cranach the tremendous honor of a coat of arms created especially for him, although by whom is unknown. It pictured a pair of winged serpents wearing golden crowns, each with a ruby ring in its mouth. In contemporary German folklore, both crowns and rings connoted magical powers, which Frederick obviously meant to say Cranach possessed as an artist. The serpent's wings seem to spread and flutter upward delicately, like flowers or flames. The first serpent undulates on the background of a bright yellow shield, with the second one above the shield itself. They are separated by a blue and gold knight's helmet and some green thorns. According to the Cranach scholar Steven Ozment, even in "a world of novel coats-of-arms Cranach's shield was truly enigmatic and bizarre."[7]

Cranach was renowned for his speed in painting and therefore given the Latin appellation *pictor celerrimus* (the swiftest of all painters), so one must assume the winged serpent was somehow meant to convey this too. Cranach also went along with the Humanist fashion of taking a Greek version of his name, so Cranach became Chronos, which is the Greek word for "time" and was obviously meant to reinforce this notion of speed. History can never know whether Cranach truly liked what he saw when Frederick presented the gift to him in 1508. Of course he had little choice in the matter, and the prestige of receiving a coat of arms must have outweighed the immediate shock of seeing something he might have thought aesthetically unfortunate—and which he must invariably be saddled with, and pretend to like, for the rest of his days. Dürer had been the first to "sign" his artworks with the famous glyph of his initials, and Cranach began to do the same in his early years as Frederick's court painter, but as time passed, he eventually began to use the serpentine coat of arms as his official signature, so one assumes he either actually did like it or at least grew to accept it. In any case, already by 1514 he was proudly using it almost everywhere.

Apart from that of Frederick himself, Cranach's wealth and prestige in Wittenberg were unparalleled. In 1512, the year Luther arrived for good in Wittenberg, Cranach had decided he had had enough of living in the somewhat cramped apartment in the elector's castle. He wanted to get married and have a family and would obviously need more space. So that year he married Barbara Brengbier of Gotha, who bore him five children in seven years. To prepare for his new and expanding family, and also to construct the huge workshop that would be the hub of his various businesses, Cranach purchased two significant properties on Wittenberg's main street. One of them was the most impressive piece of real estate in the town, and over a period of five years he would remodel it extensively. Records reveal that in 1512 alone Cranach purchased a whopping 11,500 bricks and 6,000 roof tiles. In the five years that he created his mansion at 1 Schlossstrasse, he and his family lived in his second house, less than two hundred feet down the street, which he also remodeled extensively. By the time the mansion was finished in 1518, it boasted a staggering eighty-four rooms—all with heating capacity, which was itself remarkable at the time—plus sixteen kitchens. It was so impressive that in 1523, when the king of Denmark had to flee his country, having failed to establish the Lutheran Reformation there, he came to Wittenberg and took up refuge in Cranach's capacious and luxurious home. Cranach also owned numerous other properties throughout Wittenberg, many of which he rented, and his holdings and presence in the city increased steadily through the decades.[8]

Even though Cranach would do all he could to promote the Luther brand and goose Luther's reformative efforts, he also managed to stay in the good graces of Archbishop Albrecht of Mainz, for whom he did much work, and of the Catholic church of Rome generally. Cranach was a canny fellow who knew which side his bread was buttered on, as they say, and in his case it happened to be buttered on both sides.

Reform from Within the Church

The portrait of the Roman Catholic Church as a gold and marble edifice that Luther shattered with the thunderous hammer blows upon the Wittenberg *Schlosskirche* door on October 31, 1517, is a caricature of the actual story in several ways. For one thing, it perpetuates the false idea that the church was utterly inflexible to change and opposed to criticism. There were a number of reform movements, each with its own story, but of course none of them ended as Luther's would, in tearing away from the church itself and beginning a new church. How one properly expressed criticism or dissent of any kind varied. To be sure, the wrong way might end in a horrific death by fire or drowning. But there were many who dissented in various ways, including Reuchlin and Erasmus, who did so around this time, and both of whose respective dissents Luther tracked closely.

Reuchlin

Reuchlin was a brilliant and feted Humanist scholar of Hebrew, Greek, and Latin whose famous grandnephew Melanchthon will leap into our story shortly. In 1478, Reuchlin produced a Latin dictionary, but it was his affinity with and devotion to Hebrew texts that drew him into a great controversy that finally led to his appearance before the Inquisition at Rome.

The affair began when one Johannes Pfefferkorn—a Jew who had converted to the Christian faith—advocated to Emperor Maximilian that the Hebrew books of the Jews be confiscated and destroyed. He felt that they were among the chief reasons Jews did not convert to the Christian faith, as he himself had done, and he enlisted the Dominican friars of Cologne in his efforts to find and destroy all Jewish literature they could. But when he tried to enlist Reuchlin's help, Reuchlin demurred, preferring to remain safely on the sidelines of the controversy. But then, in 1510, the emperor himself appointed Reuchlin to a commission to look into the matter, and he was forced to speak his mind. In the end, Reuchlin was the only one on the commission who disagreed that all Hebrew books should be confiscated and destroyed. Pfefferkorn and the Cologne theologians were furious with him, and they attacked him for his views.

The whole Reuchlin affair became a fight that pitted the new Humanism against the old Scholasticism, and in both circles it became a grand cause célèbre. Of course the Humanists valued all literature, especially ancient literature, so the idea of destroying these Hebrew texts was repulsive. And the Scholastics, such as Pfefferkorn and the Dominicans, evinced not a little anti-Semitism. But Reuchlin's position was also compromised, because he was promoting not just Hebrew texts but the Kabbalah, which promoted not a typically biblical view of the Old Testament but a kind of Jewish mysticism bordering on the occultic practices forbidden by the God of the Old Testament. Still, this was not the principal difficulty that Rome and the Scholastics had with Reuchlin. Nor was the battle with him waged on a purely academic level. In fact, things got dirty almost immediately, when Pfefferkorn circulated a pamphlet claiming Reuchlin had been bribed. Reuchlin in turn wrote a pamphlet defending himself, which the Cologne theologians then worked to suppress. They finally succeeded, and the inquisitor officially ordered that the pamphlets be confiscated.

In 1513, as things escalated, Reuchlin was ordered to appear before a court of the Inquisition, where he refused to recant what he had said. But still, things were not clearly resolved, so in 1514 the case was sent to Rome. Luther had been following it closely from the beginning and clearly took Reuchlin's side. When he heard the case would go to Rome, he was pleased and wrote to Spalatin about it. The viciousness of the Cologne theologians had become impossible to ignore, especially the grating sarcasm of Ortwin Gratius, who had mocked Reuchlin in a poem. Luther's letter to Spalatin is dated August 5. When he wrote to his dearest friends, Luther's energy and humor were sometimes irrepressible:

> Greetings. Up to this point, most learned Spalatin, I considered Ortwin, that little "poet" in Cologne, to be an ass. But as you can see he has [now] become a dog, even more, a ravenous wolf in sheep's clothing, if not even a crocodile, as you sense so keenly. I assume that finally he himself "caught on" to his asininity (if I may use Greek in Latin), since our John Reuchlin pushed his nose in it. But since Ortwin has considered stripping off [his donkey skin] and clothing himself with the majesty of the lion, he has now instead ended up as a wolf or a crocodile due to an unfortunate leap, since he exceeded his ability in trying to accomplish this metamorphosis. Good Lord, what can I say?

Then Luther expressed his satisfaction that the case had come to Rome at last. He was obviously a long way from the views he would hold of the papacy and the cardinals in a few years.

> One thing, however, pleases me: namely, that this matter reached Rome and the Apostolic See rather than that permission of far-reaching consequence would be granted to these jealous people of Cologne to pass judgment. Since Rome has the most learned people among the cardinals, Reuchlin's case will at least be considered more favorably there than those jealous people of Cologne—those beginners in grammar!—would ever allow.[9]

The Reuchlin affair affected how things proceeded when Luther stepped into his own controversy with Rome in 1517. As a result of it, many church officials in Rome were inclined to see Luther as yet one more troublemaking German with damnable Humanist sympathies. And many in Germany as a result of the Reuchlin controversy became deeply skeptical and even hostile to Rome. Reuchlin never left the church, but the attacks against him did not die down until the end of 1517, when Luther nailed his ninety-five theses to the Wittenberg Castle Church door. That controversy would consume all the oxygen in European Christendom for decades, and Reuchlin would himself declare, "God be praised that now the monks have found someone else who will give them more to do than I."[10]

Erasmus

The story of Erasmus and his criticisms and troubles with the church is a much larger story than that of Reuchlin, and because he had a relationship with Luther that had significant ups and downs, it's worth introducing him here.

Born in Holland in 1466, Desiderius Erasmus—or Erasmus of Rotterdam, as he came to be known—was a towering figure of his time. Known far and wide as the Prince of the Humanists and more recently as "the crowning glory of the Christian humanists," he exemplified more than anyone else the Humanist cry of *ad fontes!*—meaning "back to the sources!"[11] The Latin Vulgate was at that time the primary Bible text, but it was Erasmus who led the way in changing this, and in restoring the original Greek first-century texts of the New Testament. He also restored the Greek texts of the ancient Greek fathers of the church. His joy over the original Greek of all these writings was quite unbounded:

> For we have in Latin only a few small streams and muddy puddles, while they have pure springs and rivers flowing in gold. I see that it is utter madness even to touch with the little finger that branch of theology which deals chiefly with the divine mysteries unless one is also provided with the equipment of Greek.[12]

Erasmus was an independent scholar who was nonetheless deeply faithful to the church. He had been ordained a priest at age twenty-five and was then at Queens' College, Cambridge from 1510 to 1515. Erasmus taught himself Greek and by 1516 had published his definitive edition of the Greek New Testament, dedicating it to Pope Leo X, perhaps just to be safe. In a few years, while marooned in the Wartburg, Luther would use Erasmus's Greek New Testament to create his own German translation. But Erasmus is particularly important to our story at this point because although he was a critic of the church, he managed somehow to keep himself from being embroiled in the way that Luther eventually would be. Erasmus was a very popular writer and one way he stayed out of trouble was by using humor, which somehow softened his otherwise pointed criticisms of the church.

In 1504, Erasmus published a severe criticism of the religious piety of that time. It was titled *Enchiridion; or, Manual of the Christian Soldier* and became a great bestseller. Many of his criticisms also centered on the preposterous religious formalism of that time. Erasmus said that simply going through the motions was not real worship. It was phony religiosity, which in its way was worse than nothing. In 1511, Erasmus published *The Praise of Folly*, which was even more popular. In it, he lampooned many of the superstitions that had crept into Roman Catholic practice, including overstressing the veneration of the saints to the point that it had become worship of them. In his writings, Erasmus scorned many of the same things Luther eventually would rail against, including the widespread immorality of the clergy and the legalism he saw in much of monasticism. And just as Reuchlin had done, Erasmus lifted up Humanism, with its desire to get at the roots beneath things, and he sneered at Scholasticism. In all of this, however, Erasmus somehow managed to position himself as a faithful Christian, always lifting up what he thought of as pure church doctrine over and against the debased forms he saw everywhere around him. In 1514, he even published a satire whose butt was the pope himself, titled *Julius Excluded from Heaven*, and some how managed to get away with this too. Erasmus harshly criticized the trafficking in relics, many of which he averred were not the real thing. For him, the most ridiculous of all were the innumerable fragments of what was vouched to be the True Cross. "If all of the fragments were joined together," he quipped, "they'd seem a full load for a freighter."[13]

So Erasmus and Luther had a great deal in common, but their paths would end up diverging dramatically. For one thing, the spirit versus body dualism that so appealed to Erasmus would be the very thing

Luther felt was the problem with the church's understanding of grace and would be at the heart of the larger misunderstandings. Another difference between them was that Luther, while aware of the problems with the church, never thought that they could be fixed by dealing with the problems directly. Even in his theses on indulgences, it was not the indulgences that needed fixing but the deeper theological errors that had led to the practice of indulgences. The reason Luther wrote much of what he wrote in his Ninety-five Theses was to pry up the theological problems that lay beneath them. So whereas Erasmus never directly dealt with the theology and doctrines behind or beneath the problems he saw, Luther, as an exegete savant, was always trying to dig into the kernels of the text, knowing that if the church's understanding of things was made plumb at its foundation, the rickety structure above it would inevitably be able to correct itself,

But all of them—Reuchlin, Erasmus, and later Luther—sincerely hoped to awaken Rome to the problems they saw. If only the pope himself would take an interest in them, what might be accomplished! But the popes of that time were not only not interested in these things but also very generously contributing to them. So having touched upon two of those who got crosswise of Rome, before we come to Luther's battles with the Holy See, we should form a picture in our minds of what that Holy See was like during this period. We have already seen Rome from the perspective of Luther, during his trip in 1510–11, but the view of a young monk looking at things with an outsider's perspective can hardly begin to give us a view of the truly bizarre inner workings of Rome and the papacy at the time.

Rome

In 1513, just as Luther was beginning to teach the Bible at Wittenberg, there ascended to the throne of Peter the former Giovanni di Lorenzo de' Medici. The papacy itself during this period was the very picture of corruption, so to compare any one of the most egregious six popes of that period—that murderers' row of troublemakers stretching from Sixtus VI to Leo X—to any pope of more recent years is to compare a gorgon to a milkmaid. These popes and the papacy were at that time as much worldly principalities as anything else, and the spiritual and ecclesiastical element was often merely an addition or overlay to this fundamental reality. So power was the inevitable coin of the papal realm during this time, and as the historian Barbara Tuchman explains in her book *The March of Folly*, "the process of gaining power employs means that degrade or brutalize the seeker, who wakes to find that power has been possessed at the price of virtue—or moral purpose—lost."[14] The pope who reigned during the time of Luther's approach to writing his Ninety-five Theses—and up through his subsequent appearance at the Diet of Worms in 1521—was Leo X, whose story is more something like a tale out of Baron Münchhausen than the papal chronicles.

Born Giovanni di Lorenzo de' Medici, the child who would one day rise to become Leo X was set apart for the church at a very early age by his father, although what was meant by that in those days is a far cry from what it would mean to us today. Little Giovanni was tonsured* at the age of seven and through his father's impertinent wheedling was given an archbishopric just a year later. The idea of an eight-year-old archbishop can and should be curious, but it further reveals how the papacy had become as much like a secular government as imaginable. One might imagine an eight-year-old prince or an eight-year-old duke, so in thinking of the ecclesiastical titles of that day, we must understand we are essentially and practically talking about titles that correspond to aristocratic secular titles. That said, Giovanni was made a cardinal at age thirteen. As some kind of concession to the idea of what a cardinal is supposed to be, this was awarded only *in pectore* (literally, in the bosom, which is to say, hidden), and three years later, when he was a seasoned and mature sixteen-year-old, it was made *flagrante*, at which point Giovanni could blaze publicly in his full red-hatted splendor as a teen-aged prince of the church.

At the tender age of thirty-seven, he would become pope. On hearing the news of the death of his predecessor, Julius II, Giovanni hied himself with no delay to Rome but all along the journey was bedeviled by a painful anal fistula. When he got to the Vatican for the conclave—which of course in terms of secrecy and exclusivity is unparalleled in the world—he nonetheless was afforded the tremendous and welcome privilege of keeping his anal surgeon close to hand. Already at this relatively young

---

* Traditionally, a tonsure—derived from the Latin "to shear"—involves shaving a circle on the top of the head of someone who is being dedicated to God. Because some of the early apostles had their heads shaved by Roman rulers as a way of humiliating them, being tonsured means that one chooses to identify with these early Christians in that humiliation.

age, the future Leo X was a nearsighted and corpulent fellow whose girth and gout made walking difficult. As we know, the conclave indeed chose him to fill the fabled Shoes of the Fisherman. But rather bizarrely, this pope-elect was not yet an ordained priest. In fact, he was the last non-priest to be elected pope. So before he could officially take the papal mantle, Giovanni first must be ordained a priest, which he quickly was. Then, three days after becoming a priest, he was consecrated a bishop. And only then could he officially become Pope Leo X.

In reviewing the life of Leo and the popes of that era, one is obliged by comparison to think of Asiatic despots or Roman emperors. Pope Leo X differed from some of his genuinely wicked confreres in being mostly harmless, but his appetite for amusements and buffoonery lifted to impossible heights was infamous. One outrageous and illustrative story along these lines may help us understand what Luther was dealing with in the Rome of his era, although thankfully Luther himself would have had no idea of it. It took place in 1514. At this juncture in his own life, Luther was routinely waking at 4:00 a.m. to lecture on the Psalms and generally busying himself in innumerable ways to draw closer to God and his fellow man. But eight hundred miles south, the Holy Father Leo X was focused on something that anyone would reckon quite different: He was planning a lavish event to publicly mock a mentally unstable person. The kooky spectacle involved Giacomo Baraballo, a preposterously self-regarding courtier whose penchant for witty verse and japery eventually eclipsed all else in his life. Like so many who operated in this fashionable Florentine mode, Baraballo held an ecclesiastical title that was essentially meaningless. He was at that time the abbot of Gaeta, a self-styled "arch-poet" whose extemporaneous verses had brought endless amusement to the mirth-addicted Leo but who had somehow flipped his wig—according to a contemporary account he from a "good courtier ha[d] become mad"—and he became far more the butt of jests than jester. Baraballo sincerely thought his verses were superior to those of the venerable Petrarch, and Leo thought this outrageous misconception on Baraballo's part would provide the occasion for his friends—and indeed for all of Rome—to have some great fun.

So Leo one day decided that on the feast day of the Medici's patron saints an almost inconceivably elaborate festivity called the Cosmalia should be arranged, and the grand celebration would culminate in the "burlesque coronation" of Baraballo as arch poet.[15] What could be better? It would be celebrated with an impossibly grand triumphal procession that began at the Apostolic Palace off St. Peter's Piazza, where the pontiffs have lived since it was built in 1450. It seems that everyone in Rome and far beyond was in on the sadistic prank. Baraballo's family begged him not to participate and tried to explain to him that the elaborate ceremony was not on the level, but he madly waved them off. As far as he was concerned they were all bitterly jealous. And as though managing this baroque super gag were the principal duty of the Vicar of Christ, Leo personally oversaw every petty detail. So it was Leo's idea that his own beloved elephant Hanno—an exotic gift from the king of Portugal—would carry Baraballo in the procession! Leo adored this short-lived pachyderm more than life itself, so the giddy notion that Hanno could participate made the childish pontiff nearly levitate for joy.

The secret plan was that Hanno would carry Baraballo all the way to the Tiber and thence on into Rome proper via the Ponte Sant'Angelo (then the Ponte Adriano), with thousands cheering and choking with laughter from the sidelines, as they surely must. Leo knew that he would writhe with ecstasy at finally being acknowledged as among the greatest poets who had ever lived, though it was all of course a cruel joke at silly Baraballo's expense. *Ma come buffa!*

Because he loved drawing everyone into his swamp of low buffoonery, the actual physical act of "coronation" was awarded to Cardinal Matthäus Lang, a dour German who was also the bishop of Gurk. But the humorless Lang, who doubtless felt this outsized farce far beneath his dignity, could hardly refuse the pope's indecorously loopy request. He was charged with hefting the chapeau aloft and mock-seriously setting it atop the harebrained abbot's *testa vuota!* On the day it finally took place, the well-turned-out Roman elites who were invited to see this ceremony up close convulsed themselves with hysteria. But Baraballo was convinced that he was finally being honored as he deserved. Once the crown was on his head, beaming as only a fool can beam, he began his journey toward the waiting elephant, with pipers piping and trumpeters heralding his self-conscious steps. Shouts went up as he neared the great beast, which he was obliged to mount. For a fleshly man of his age to accomplish this was no small thing, and after a number of clumsy attempts accompanied by more cackling from the sidelines, he was indecorously boosted aloft and onto his precarious perch—on a carved throne within a turret of sorts—atop the celebrated animal's back. Baraballo was then handed a laurel branch, and the great procession could begin. Baraballo and Hanno now

The self-deluded poet Baraballo making his way through Rome atop Pope Leo's pet pachyderm. The elephant Hanno was a gift from the king of Portugal. Hanno perished not long after this episode, despite being given a powerful laxative that contained pure gold.

commenced the long, awkward journey toward the river. The distance from the palace to the bridge was three thousand yards, with crowds holding their sides and slapping their knees at every step, as Hanno—with the Moorish mahout straddling the beast's head—and the crackers arch poet "with wand'ring steps and slow"[16] made their hilarious way. But as the clown poet and the exotic beast approached the Tiber, the ribald cacophony of the crowds, now fairly gagging on their uncontrollable laughter, must have seemed confusing to the animal. With the skirl of the pipes, the thundering of the drums, and the ceremonial blasting of trumpets, it all combined to ratchet the docile Hanno's anxiety to a point of imminent fracture. So at the very threshold of the Ponte Adriano, the massy beast suddenly ceased all forward movement and refused to budge, as the perspiring and exotic mahout berated him in a foreign language, all to the further delight of the crowds. By this time, Leo had hauled his considerable frame from the papal palace to the Castle Sant'Angelo, where through his perpetual looking glass he could get a closer look at the epic tomfoolery he had orchestrated. As Hanno refused to move at all, the crowds increased their howling until, in a great and terrible spasm, the animal flung from its laden back the turret, the throne, and the arch poet himself, who was cast onto the muddy banks of the river below. Baraballo was greatly shaken and covered in filth but uninjured, and the moment he hoisted himself to his feet, he scampered off like a madman, disappearing through the vast crowds and into historical ignominy.

But what became of Hanno, that most exotic of the fabled city's inhabitants since Romulus and Remus were suckled by a she-wolf on the banks of the Tiber? In the early summer of 1516, he was taken ill with a disease none of the papal physicians could fathom. They did what they could to make the beast comfortable and Leo himself was perpetually and devotedly at Hanno's side, but the great beast did not rise from his sickbed to delightfully blast water as he had once done, to the squeals of drenched onlookers. Then one of the physicians had a suggestion: when all else was lost, a dynamic purgative might sometimes find its mark. But all of them could only pull at their chins, for they had ever and only plumbed the bowels of daintier constitutions. In the end, they employed a rare and peerless laxative, being an admixture containing a significant amount of actual gold—after all, for what reason did the papal coffers overflow with it, if not this? After taking this fabulously expensive medicine, Hanno nonetheless wheezed his last and was eventually buried with great honors beneath the Cortile del Belvedere. Leo was so bereft at the loss of his enormous sidekick that he composed a long poetic epitaph and, with the faithful's money, commissioned none less than Raphael himself to paint a memorial fresco portrait, which, alas, has not survived. But another portrait of Hanno has survived and can today be seen in the Ashmolean Museum at Oxford.

CHAPTER FIVE

The "Cloaca" Experience

If our Lord God in this life—in das Sheisshaus*—
has given us such noble gifts, what will happen
in that eternal life, where everything will
be perfect and delightful?

—Martin Luther

T HERE CAN BE little question that October 31, 1517, looms as the most significant date in Luther's story. Following the trail of bread crumbs that lead us to that date is not so easy, but there are happily a few that the birds have missed, so we may have some idea of what path Luther took to arrive on that date with his Ninety-five Theses. Throughout the years leading up to this date, Luther was sometimes given to making observations in his lectures that in retrospect look like the comments of someone who might one day cause some controversy. For example, by the time he was lecturing on the book of Romans in 1516, he even spoke directly against the Holy Father himself:

> The pope and the priests who are so generous in granting indulgences for the temporal support of churches are cruel above all cruelty if they are not even more generous or at least equally so in their concern for God and the salvation of souls.[1]

In early February 1517, Luther wrote to his friend Johannes Lang, enclosing a letter he hoped Lang would give to their former teacher Jodokus Trutfetter. That letter and the letter to Lang touch upon something that would figure prominently in what lay ahead for Luther, because it

---

* Meaning "in this toilet," but literally "in this shit house."

concerned nothing less than upending the entire medieval system of education:

> We are to believe everything, always obediently to listen and not even once, by way of a mild introduction, wrangle or mutter against Aristotle and the *Sentences*. What will they not believe who have taken for granted everything which Aristotle, this chief of all charlatans, insinuates and imposes on others, things which are so absurd that not even an ass or a stone could remain silent about them! . . . I wish nothing more fervently than to disclose to many the true face of that actor who has fooled the church so tremendously with the Greek mask, and to show to them all his ignominy, had I only time! . . . He is the most subtle seducer of gifted people, so that if Aristotle had not been flesh, I would not hesitate to claim that he was really a devil.[2]

These are strong words. Luther's volcano was not quite on the verge of blowing, but it was not dormant either. The pieces of the bigger picture were coming together, and one of them of course concerned what Luther clearly saw as a church that was no longer in love with the truth and the pursuit of same, that answered good and honest questions with an imperious "Be silent and do as we say, or else." Luther knew instinctively that this was wrong, that it went against the essence of the God of the Bible, and in his letter to Lang and Trutfetter anyone with eyes to see may discern hairline cracks in his previously immaculate alabaster exterior.

On May 18, he wrote to Lang again:

> Our theology and St. Augustine are progressing well, and with God's help rule at our university. Aristotle is gradually falling from his throne, and the final doom is only a matter of time. It is amazing how the students disdain the lectures on the *Sentences*. Indeed, no one can expect to have any students if he does not want to teach this theology, that is, lecture on the Bible or on St. Augustine, or another teacher of ecclesiastical eminence.[3]

So all of these things were slowly leading Luther in a certain direction, theologically and otherwise. But there was a moment in 1517, it seems, long before he posted his Ninety-five Theses, when it all came together, when the signal issue of God's grace shone over everything he had been thinking and worrying over, when the clouds parted and he could see clearly that for which he had been so diligently searching.

The Reformation "Breakthrough," *Aetatis* 33

Just a year before his death, Luther wrote a preface to his collected Latin works. In it he tells how on the path to his great breakthrough, he had actually come to despise God:

> Though I lived as a monk without reproach, I felt that I was a sinner before God with an extremely disturbed conscience. I could not believe that he was placated by my satisfaction. I did not love . . . yes, I hated the righteous God who punishes sinners, and secretly, if not blasphemously, certainly murmuring greatly, I was angry with God. . . . Thus I raged with a fierce and troubled conscience. Nevertheless I beat importunately upon St. Paul at that place [Romans 1:17] most ardently desiring to know what St. Paul wanted.[4]

One of the iconic moments from Luther's life has come to be called "the tower experience." As the story comes to us, it was during this world-changing year of 1517 that Luther's struggles with that verse in the book of Romans came to fruition. But as with so much else with Luther's story, it is the Luther legend that obscures our view of the actual events of his life—and the legend almost always comes to us via Luther's later recollections of what took place decades earlier.

Nonetheless, the moment in which the Middle Ages buckled under their own weight and thus gave way to the Reformation and the future seems to have occurred when a single tremendous insight came to Luther, who was at that moment in the so-called Cloaca Tower at the Black Cloister in Wittenberg. In 1532 and then again in 1545, Luther mentioned what happened at that point, sometime in early 1517.

The 1532 comments mentioning this illuminating and life-changing moment are much briefer than his own commentary of it is. In fact, they are just a single sentence, recorded from his *Table Talk* by Johannes Schlaginhaufen. The German is simply "*Diese Kunst hat mir der Spiritus Sanctus auf diss Cloaca eingeben.*"* The meaning of this famous phrase is

---

* Luther and those around him were usually fluent or at least conversant in Latin, and we can see from this sentence that Luther often spoke macaronically, which is to say in a language that combined two other languages, in his case German and Latin.

"The Holy Spirit gave me this art in [or upon] the cloaca." But the word "cloaca" presents the difficulty. This is because Luther—who couldn't resist making a joke and who often made terribly serious points while joking—was implying that God had given him this insight while he was sitting on the toilet. *Cloaca* was the ancient Latin term for "sewer" and at the time of Luther had come to mean "outhouse." Not only this, but whereas many English writers incorrectly translate "*auf*" as "in," most Germans would take "*auf*" to mean "on" or "upon"—which in concert with "outhouse" or "toilet" makes perfect sense. But we now know that the heated room that was Luther's study for decades—and where he therefore did his biblical exegesis—was in that part of the monastery located in the tower. It so happened, however, that in the base of this tower there was an outhouse. Thus this tower was always referred to as the Cloaca Tower, probably by the many monks who went there only when that particular duty summoned them. So even if Luther got the tremendous insight not precisely while indisposed upon the commode but upstairs in his heated study, he nonetheless would have said the "cloaca," as was the general habit. But in this 1532 comment, Luther was deliberately playing upon the ambiguity by using "*auf*"—which is to say "upon." He clearly meant half in jest to convey something along the lines of "while on the john."

But here is the longer version of that moment, which Luther wrote in 1545, the year before his death, and which tells us precisely what he meant by "this art" when he said "*diese Kunst*" in that 1532 sentence:

At last, by the mercy of God, meditating day and night, I gave heed to the context of the words, namely, "In it the righteousness of God is revealed," as it is written, "He who through faith is righteous shall live." There I began to understand that the righteousness of God is that by which the righteous lives by a gift of God, namely by faith. And this is the meaning: the righteousness of God is revealed by the gospel, namely, the passive righteousness with which the merciful God justifies us by faith, as it is written, "He who through faith is righteous shall live." Here I felt that I was altogether born again and had entered paradise itself through open gates. Thus a totally other face of the entire Scripture showed itself to me. Hereupon I ran through the Scriptures from memory. I also found in other terms an analogy, as the work of God, that is, what God does in us, the power of God, with which he makes us strong, the wisdom of

God, with which he makes us wise, the strength of God, the salvation of God, the glory of God.

And I extolled my sweetest word with a love as great as the hatred with which I had before hated the word "Righteousness of God." Thus that place in Paul was for me truly the gate to paradise.[5]

This is the earthshaking insight that gave Luther the solidest of all foundations in Scripture upon which to base what may well be reckoned the greatest revolution in human history. But by jesting in 1532 that it happened in that most humbling and humiliating of places—"upon the toilet"—Luther made it a perfect illustration of his theological foundation. That is because it is in keeping with everything he knew about the incarnated God of the Bible. The specific point here is that the infinite and omniscient and omnipotent creator God of heaven did not descend to earth on a golden cloud. He came to us through screaming pain, through the bloody agony of a maiden's vagina, in a cattle stall filthy with and stinking of dung. This is how humans enter the world, and if God would enter the world as a human being, he must enter it that way. It was the only way to reach us *where we are* and *as we are*, and because of his love for us he did not shrink from this approach, vile and difficult as it must be.

Luther saw in this the very essence of Christian theology. God reached down not halfway to meet us in our vileness but all the way down, to the foul dregs of our broken humanity. And this holy and loving God dared to touch our lifeless and rotting essence and in doing so underscored that this is the truth about us. In fact, we are not sick and in need of healing. We are dead and in need of resurrecting. We are not dusty and in need of a good dusting; we are fatally befouled with death and fatally toxic filth and require total redemption. If we do not recognize that we need eternal life from the hand of God, we remain in our sins and are eternally dead. So because God respects us, he can reach us only if we are honest about our condition. So it fit well with Luther's thinking that if God were to bestow upon him—the unworthy sinner Luther—such a divine blessing, it must needs be done as he sat grunting in the "cloaca." This was the ultimate antithesis to the gold and bejeweled splendor of papal Rome. There all was gilt, but here in Wittenberg it was all *Scheisse*. But the shit in its honesty *as shit* was very golden when compared to the pretense and artifice of Roman gold, which itself was indeed as shit when compared to the infinite worth of God's grace. That was cheap grace, which was to say it was a truly satanic counterfeit. True grace was concealed in the honesty—in the unadorned shit—of this broken world, and the devil's own shit was concealed in the pope's glittering gold.

The Luther scholar Volker Leppin says that there are a number of reasons to accept the idea that Luther was referring to the cloaca itself specifically. But Leppin's principal argument comes to us via another *Table Talk* comment, in which Luther was talking about the wonder of music. The German is "*So unser Herr Gott in diesem Leben in das Scheisshaus solche Edle gaben gegeben hat, was wird in jhenem ewigen Leben geschehen.*" Leppin's translation of this is "If the Lord in this life has provided the shithouse with such noble gifts, what will happen in that eternal life [where everything will be perfect and delightful]?" But by separating "in this life" and "the shithouse" with the verb "has provided," Leppin has blunted his point. Luther's sentence can better be translated as "If our Lord God in this life—in this shit house—has given us such noble gifts, what will happen in that eternal life, where everything will be perfect and delightful?" So "in this life" is clarified as "in this shithouse," meaning in this execrable, this abominably shitty, life.[6]

So the point is made. C. S. Lewis more elegantly said that life in this world was merely "the Shadowlands," but Luther predictably phrases it much more bluntly and earthily. This life is "a shit house" compared to the glories of heaven, and Luther was marveling at God's extravagant generosity in bestowing upon us such glorious and heavenly things as music here, where we shouldn't expect them, where they were but foretastes of what was to come. So Leppin's point, that Luther thought of this life in such terms, means that when he referred to the cloaca, he was speaking tongue in cheek and seriously at the same time, as he so often did. The cloaca was not only literally that place in the tower where he went to the bathroom but also the essence of this world, a world not merely begrimed with but filled with and consisting of sin and shit and misery and death. For God to come into this foulest world is for him already to come most of the way into hell. This world is the antechamber to hell and eternal death, and unless we allow the God of life to come here, we do not allow him to redeem us. He cannot redeem and resurrect what is not foul and dead, but we are both.

The power of this insight—this "Reformation breakthrough" or "tower experience" or "cloaca experience"—is profound. It is indeed as though every medieval mountain were uprooted and the whole Potemkin range of them cast into the heart of the sea. The hypocrisy of works and human righteousness was forevermore revealed. The curtain was whisked back and the papal Oz exposed as a fraud, frantically pulling his ecclesiastical levers. There would never be any going back. If ever there was a moment when the future as we have come to know it was born, this was it.

According to this Reformation breakthrough, all the marmoreal and golden splendor of the Vatican was nothing more or less than a monument to mankind's efforts to be as God—indeed was a monument to the very devil of hell. It was our attempt to be good without God, to impress God and be like him without his help. It was all far worse than excrement could ever be, for it pretended to be good and beautiful and true and holy, and in reality it was not just *not* these things but the very bitterest enemy of them.

So much followed from this single insight. For example, if we appeal to Mary and the other saints before we appeal to Jesus himself, are we not effectively denying the Incarnation itself? Are we not saying that God incarnate never really came into this filthy world to be among us and to love us and suffer for us? For Luther, any appeal to Mary and the saints instead of to Jesus himself became a satanic twisting of the holiest and highest truth in the universe. It was therefore anti-Christ, and he knew that to expose it as such was the most important thing imaginable. In the end, he came to believe that the very devil had taken over the holy church and that somehow he, the lowly monk from Wittenberg, had been entrusted by God with the task of declaring this to the world.

So these coals from the very throne room of heaven had been given to Luther in his "cloaca" experience, but what would they light on fire? Where was the fuel for this heavenly fire? It would arrive now, as if on cue, in a literal wagon bearing an indulgence preacher named Johannes Tetzel.

The Indulgence Controversy

Johannes Tetzel was a Dominican friar. Though he was bald, pleasantly plump, and pushing sixty, his powers of persuasion with a crowd were nonetheless entirely unparalleled. It was for this reason that Pope Leo, increasingly desperate for cash, had bestowed upon Tetzel the title of commissioner of indulgences in Germany—specifically in Magdeburg and

Halberstadt. If you needed to raise what was then the equivalent of billions of dollars from the back of a wagon, Tetzel was your man. It is true that he would often say things that were technically not true—which is to say, doctrinally false—but if he could gin up the generosity of the faithful in doing so, the powers that be would look the other way. After all, what was good for business was good for business. The financial needs of Rome were so pressing, so especially urgent, and the powers

The Dominican priest Johannes Tetzel, whose vigorous preaching of indulgences prompted Luther's Ninety-five Theses.

that be had become so inured to this way of raising funds, or perhaps even so addicted to it, that it would take a very special person to stand athwart this juggernaut and shout, "Halt!"

And so Tetzel now arrived in Jüterbog, just twenty-five miles from Wittenberg, to set up his papally sanctioned medicine show. What he was selling now made snake oil cure-all potions seem like fresh fruits and vegetables. Indeed it was so fabulous and so extraordinary that people hauled themselves from many miles around to hear him, and not just to hear him but to throw money at him, that they might get something of what he was offering, which, to cut to the chase, was heaven itself. And who would not trade money for eternal paradise, if one really believed it was? And no one could doubt that it was, for the pope himself was behind this and the papal insignia were displayed and intentionally clearly visible wherever Tetzel preached.

This special indulgence that the pope had sanctioned and that Tetzel was preaching was through Archbishop Albrecht of Mainz, whose own bishopric needed the funds. He would split them evenly with Rome, as was the usual practice. The main reason Tetzel did not come directly into Wittenberg itself was that the Saxon elector Frederick saw the raising of moneys via indulgences as being in direct competition with people coming to visit his relic collection. This indulgence was therefore a threat to that source of income for him and electoral Saxony. There were other reasons too. But many of the faithful in Wittenberg had nonetheless heard about this tremendous opportunity to have their sins forgiven for a simple cash payment, so when Tetzel set up his operations in nearby Jüterbog and Zerbst—each equidistant from Wittenberg and just beyond the electoral border—many Wittenberg citizens scurried thither, for who but a fool would remain home when heaven was for sale?

But as a local priest and pastor, Luther heard all too plainly what was going on and was more than anything concerned for the souls of his flock. He knew that Rome was playing on the ignorance and foolishness of the faithful with this indulgence business, and while this had been going on for many decades, it had never come quite so close to him, so the cynicism of it had never been quite so obvious and awful. It all came even closer to home when some of Luther's own parishioners showed up in the confession booth and beamed with ignorant pride as they showed Father Martinus the precious certificates they had purchased from Tetzel; they clearly expected a much less harsh penance from Luther because, in their

'ALBERTVS· MI·DI·SA·SANC·
ROMANE·ECCLAE·TI·SAN·
CHRYSOGONI·PBR·CARDINA·
MAGVN·AC·MAGDE·ARCHI·
EPS·ELECTOR·IMPE·PRIMAS·
ADMINI·HALBER·MARCHI·
BRANDENBVRGENSIS·

Cardinal Albrecht of Brandenberg. Wishing to add another
archbishopric to his résumé, Albrecht incurred a staggering debt
to the Vatican that led him to invite Johannes Tetzel to preach
the papal indulgence, which kicked off the Reformation.

minds, they had already paid in advance for the sins they were there to
confess. If anyone doubted as much, here was the receipt. They were themselves unsure what the certificate they had purchased was worth, but
surely Father Martinus would know and could redeem it for them now,
couldn't he?

Here was where the theological rubber met the road, because the church
could officially say what it liked, but this was the local and particular

reality of the whole indulgence business, in all its ugliness. Luther saw and heard with his own eyes and ears the effect this was having on simple people, trying to live out their Christian lives. They had no idea they were being used by the church for its own distant ends, to build buildings they would never see and far worse than that, as we shall see. Luther was certainly bothered that money was being sucked away from those who had so little, but it bothered him more that the church via this practice of indulgences was actually leading the faithful away from Christ. That was the far greater scandal, and someone must speak out. Luther did not imagine doing so in any grand way. He was a priest with a pulpit, and that was the forum God had given him. So in February 1517, Luther preached on the subject of indulgences, and then in March he did so again. He was far from the first priest to do so, and he explained to his flock that the paper they purchased meant nothing if they were not genuinely contrite for any sins they had committed. And if they were genuinely contrite, the paper still meant nothing, because God forgave their sins anyway.

But to be sure, the most diabolical and cynical aspect of indulgences had to do with those that could be purchased to alleviate the suffering of one's relatives in purgatory. Who could allow one's loved ones to suffer the tortures of the damned when one had only to pay some money? What price could one put on that? Tetzel's pitch along these lines was recorded, and it's clear he spared none of his skills to pinch every pfennig possible from his rapt listeners:

> Listen now, God and St. Peter call you. Consider the salvation of your souls and those of your loved ones departed. You priest, you noble, you merchant, you virgin, you matron, you youth, you old man, enter now into your church, which is the Church of St. Peter. Visit the most holy cross erected before you and ever imploring you. Have you considered that you are lashed in a furious tempest amid the temptations and dangers of the world, and that you do not know whether you can reach the haven, not of your mortal body, but of your immortal soul? Consider that all who are contrite and have confessed and made contribution will receive complete remission of all their sins. Listen to the voices of your dear dead relatives and friends, beseeching you and saying, "Pity us, pity us. We are in dire torment from which you can redeem us for a pittance." Do you not wish to? Open your ears. Hear the father saying to his son, the

mother to her daughter, "We bore you, nourished you, brought you up, left you our fortunes, and you are so cruel and hard that now you are not willing for so little to set us free. Will you let us lie here in flames? Will you delay our promised glory?"

Remember that you are able to release them, for *As soon as the coin in the coffer rings, The soul from purgatory springs.**

   Will you not then for a quarter of a florin receive these letters of indulgence through which you are able to lead a divine and immortal soul into the fatherland of praise?[7]

Over the centuries, the church bureaucracy had swelled to become something like a vast corporation or government whose distant leaders were out of touch with its various outposts. It had grown more and more powerful, and the rules and laws of the church had become less and less in tune with anything that would have been recognizable to the first-century Christians; so if Paul or Peter were to stumble upon the church of 1517, he could hardly recognize it as something that had grown out of what he had begun.

The practice of selling indulgences, which had started as something consonant with the church's teachings, had by Luther's time slipped the surly bonds of all reasonableness. Thus does the "invisible hand of the market" unmoored from virtue fly troubleward. In his excellent book *Brand Luther*, Andrew Pettegree calls Cardinal Raymond Peraudi "the great impresario of the indulgence trade," who brought

> to the economy of salvation both logistical brilliance and a real sense of theater. The campaigns were planned like the military operations they were ostensibly intended to fund. Towns that Peraudi proposed to visit on his preaching tour were contacted in advance, and detailed contracts agreed for the division of the sums raised (generally one third to the local church and two thirds to Peraudi and his team).[8]

Many others besides Luther had spoken against indulgences, but their booming popularity drowned out any niggling cries of dissent. In 1489, there was one distinguished theologian from Würzburg who had

---

* The German phrase is *"Sobald der Gülden im Becken klingt im huy die Seel im Himmel springt."*

An illustration of indulgence selling from 1521.

spoken out against indulgences rather forcefully. In his sermons at the cathedral church there, Dr. Dietrich Morung spoke against the preposterous notion that anyone, even the pope, could sell a reduction of one's years in purgatory. It was madness. But the church—in the shape of Cardinal Peraudi—would not suffer this idealistic priest gladly. For his troubles, Morung was promptly excommunicated and then thrown into prison, where he languished for a decade. But after Peraudi's death in 1505, others began to speak out. Even Staupitz spoke against indulgences in a sermon series that he preached at Nuremberg in 1516. And these sermons were published early in 1517 in both Latin and German. So we cannot help but think that Luther was encouraged by the example of his beloved superior and friend. Nor was the blowback in all of this limited to Germany. At the Sorbonne in Paris, theologians spoke out against indulgences. It was a widely recognized problem that needed fixing, but who was listening, and who would do anything about it?

There was one more reason that many German leaders did not like the practice of indulgences. This was because they were paid for with coins, and the great popularity of indulgences with the faithful meant that vast amounts of German currency were being carried out of the country to Rome. Emperor Maximilian himself had confronted Peraudi on this score and at one point was able to keep significant moneys from being taken out of Germany.

A contemporary of Luther's named Myconius recounted the following hilarious incident regarding Tetzel:

After Tetzel had received a substantial amount of money at Leipzig, a nobleman asked him if it were possible to receive a letter of indulgence for a future sin. Tetzel quickly answered in the affirmative, insisting, however, that the payment had to be made at once. This the nobleman did, receiving thereupon letter and seal from Tetzel. When Tetzel left Leipzig the nobleman attacked him along the way, gave him a thorough beating, and sent him back empty-handed to Leipzig with the comment that this was the future sin which he had in mind. Duke George at first was quite furious about this incident, but when he heard the whole story he let it go without punishing the nobleman.

CHAPTER SIX

The Theses Are Posted

T HE DATE ALWAYS given as the beginning of the Reformation is October 31, 1517, and the reason for that date is invariably the assertion that on that date the Augustinian monk Martin Luther nailed his Ninety-five Theses to the door of the Castle Church in Wittenberg. That iconic moment ranks with other dramatic moments of almost violent masculine action, as in the image of Columbus's planting Spain's flag into the previously inviolate soil of a virgin continent. The difficulty with this ideal is that in Luther's case it never happened in this way. The images that crowd collective cultural memory are distillations of something that is, in fact, far less visually stirring.

In his unsurpassable 1981 volume on Luther, Martin Brecht explains that while the theses had been written before that celebrated day, they were perhaps not actually posted on the fabled cathedral doors until roughly two weeks after that date.[1] It is only because of the decades-later recollection of Melanchthon that this image and date so stubbornly persist. But Melanchthon was not in Wittenberg in 1517 and was basing his own statement on what he had heard over the years. Why, then, is the Reformation's beginning always given as that date? For several reasons, but mainly because it was on that day that Luther did what was truly significant in the story of all that was to follow: he posted a letter.

It is self-evident that the image of someone mailing a letter lacks sufficient oomph to catapult it into the empyrean realm of "Great Moments in World History." Indeed, one can hardly put one's finger on any specific moment at all where mailing a letter is concerned, especially if one lives in a world without postboxes, as Luther surely did. What image should be presented? Luther docilely handing a courier a letter? Luther thoughtfully folding the finished document? It is obvious that none of these quiet transactions can compare with the thunderous *ba-zazz* of a hammer pounding a document of truth into fixed and plain sight for all to see.

The boldness of it as an act bears metaphorical power too, inviting the observer to imagine a man doing something defiant and public and noisy. "Here!" it seems to say. And "thus!" and "look!" and other monosyllabic declarations that refuse to compromise their effect with the effeminate delicacy of a second syllable. Nor have we mentioned that the point of posting these theses on the Castle Church doors was not to alert the world to what he was saying but simply to let the academic community of Wittenberg know that he was proposing a scholarly debate—or disputation, as they were called—on the subject of these theses. So it was a declaration not to the world—most of whom could not read the Latin in which the theses were written anyway—nor even to Rome or to the pope. It was but a declaration to other theologians, all of whom read Latin, and it meant to say that this was a very important subject worthy of debate. But surely posting this ultimately incendiary document on the very doors of the Wittenberg Castle Church was itself a bold and dramatic act, was it not? Luther was after all posting theses denouncing indulgences on the door of the very church that his own prince, Frederick the Wise, had built to house his almost innumerable relics, whose viewing entitled the viewer to indulgences! Surely his posting them on these very doors was this upstart monk's none-too-subtle way of commenting on the hypocrisy of what went on inside those doors, was it not? Could there be any other way of seeing it? Alas, for those invested in seeing great drama in this action, there certainly could be. For it so happens that because the Castle Church was very much at the center of life in the community of Wittenberg, the huge wooden doors through which everyone entered the church were the best place to post anything of any community interest, making them the all-purpose bulletin board for the small city. Innumerable other things were posted there of which history has taken no notice, but once we realize that Luther's theses were posted in that context, we see their posting in a very different light. They were simply put on the bulletin board of that day, as anything posted must be. Even less dramatic is the entirely plausible notion that it was not Luther himself who posted the theses, but the church custodian, who was typically responsible for posting important notices on the doors of the church.[2] Finally, it is even possible that a number of copies were posted on the doors of several churches in Wittenberg, as during this time there were as many as six churches in the town, the doors of which were all used for this same purpose. Of course this extraordinarily and even shockingly reduces the import and drama that history has for five centuries invested in this remembered act, but one must revise one's understanding in accord with the facts of the situation, and these are indisputable.

And there is still one more detail to be touched upon regarding the posting. Even if Luther did post the theses on the church doors on the day it is said that he did, or on any subsequent day, he might well have done it not with a hammer and nails at all but with a sloppy jar or bucket of paste. So even on the subject of how they were affixed, the hoary stock image we all have from Western cultural memory seems that much more fanciful. How, then, did that now iconic image take root in the cultural imagination?

The facts are simply this: On October 31, 1517, Martin Luther addressed an important letter to Archbishop Albrecht of Mainz, for, as we have said, it was in Albrecht's name that indulgences were being peddled far and wide, and Luther wanted to let the honorable archbishop know of it, lest the faithful under his care continue to be torn away from the faith. Luther naturally supposed this was something with which an archbishop should be concerned, unless he was an archbishop in name only, in which case there would be other problems. But there was nothing especially bold about writing this letter to the archbishop. Luther was very humbly bringing something important to the attention of someone who ought to care and who ought to be in a position to do something to correct it. Nor was there anything defiant about the letter. On the contrary, it was deeply and appropriately respectful. In fact, it was more than merely respectful, for the tone of the letter's opening may well be seen as a model of cringing sycophancy:

> Most Reverend Father in Christ, Most Illustrious Sovereign: Forgive me that I, the least of all men, have the temerity to consider writing to Your Highness. The Lord Jesus is my witness that I have long hesitated doing this on account of my insignificance and unworthiness, of which I am well aware. I do it now impudently, and I am motivated solely by the obligation of my loyalty, which I know I owe you, Most Reverend Father in Christ. May Your Highness therefore deign to glance at what is but a grain of dust, and for the sake of your episcopal kindness, listen to my request.

But now, having established himself as someone appropriately respectful of his ecclesiastical superior, Luther came to the difficult and painful point:

Under your most distinguished name, papal indulgences are offered all across the land for the construction of St. Peter. Now, I do not so much complain about the quacking of the preachers, which I haven't heard;* but I bewail the gross misunderstanding among the people which comes from these preachers and which they spread everywhere among common men. Evidently the poor souls believe that when they have bought indulgence letters they are then assured of their salvation. They are likewise convinced that souls escape from purgatory as soon as they have placed a contribution into the chest.

Further, they assume that the grace obtained through these indulgences is so completely effective that there is no sin of such magnitude that it cannot be forgiven—even if (as they say) someone should rape the mother of God, were this possible. Finally they also believe that man is free from every penalty and guilt by these indulgences.

O great God! The souls committed to your care, excellent Father, are thus directed to death. For all these souls you have the heaviest and a constantly increasing responsibility. Therefore I can no longer be silent on this subject. No man can be assured of his salvation by any episcopal function. He is not even assured of his salvation by the infusion of God's grace, because the Apostle [Paul] orders us to work out our salvation constantly "in fear and trembling."

. . . How can the [indulgence agents] then make the people feel secure and without fear [concerning salvation] by means of those false stories and promises of pardon? After all, the indulgences contribute absolutely nothing to the salvation and holiness of souls; they only compensate for the external punishment which—on the basis of Canon Law—once used to be imposed.[3]

Of course what Luther had no idea about when he wrote and sent this letter—and what his correspondent had no idea about either—was that Luther had now put his finger on an issue that was but the uppermost excrescence of something else, something that was at least enormous, something with a root system so very deep and exceedingly vast that it stretched to the nethermost blind crevasses of hell itself. So excising this unpleasant blot was not something that would merely require a local anesthetic, as it were. It would, in the end, entail uprooting the very

---

* Because Luther was twenty-five miles away from where Tetzel had set up shop in Jüterbog, he had not been there himself, but was getting his information from those who had.

structure of European reality, one that had been growing and thriving these many centuries. But who could see that now, at this early juncture?

So the image in our collective minds of Luther audaciously pounding the truth onto that door for the world and the devil to see is a fiction. It implies that the man doing this heroically understood that it could lead to his excommunication and probable horrific death by fire and that it was the first shot in a war to upend this devilish system that was as deeply entrenched as a mountain range. But this is very far from the truth. Luther hadn't the slightest inkling of these things when he wrote and posted his theses, nor when he wrote and sent his letter to Albrecht of Mainz. So the venerable image of Luther posting truth onto the front-page of history is one that can come into focus only retroactively. Apart from what was to happen as a result of these things in the years and decades and centuries to come, that image can make no sense. In fact, it began to make sense only decades later, when Melanchthon recalled it, although, as we have said, he was not yet in Wittenberg when it happened, and was really only recounting the recollections of others who had been there. So when he did, he was speaking in the way so many of us do when remembering things: we aren't telling an untruth but conflating things in a way that is not perfectly and literally accurate, specifically to make a larger point, and, as good fiction does, to tell a greater truth.

To be sure, in doing what he did, Luther hoped to effect change and be thanked by the powers that were. Most of all, he wanted to be recognized by God for doing what any responsible teacher of God's truth would have done. Indeed, in the years to come, Luther often said that he was a "doctor" who was "sworn" to teach the truth, so there was no other course for him. He felt that he was doing something good, something that the pope and others would surely recognize as such. They were not his adversaries—not yet—and he was a faithful monk in the only church in Western Christendom. And he could not himself conceive of things snowballing as they would soon do. So, on the day he posted his letter and on the day he posted his theses, he had no idea what dark forces he would rouse from their slumbers.

One major reason for not knowing what he had awakened in his "teaching moment" with the Ninety-five Theses was that he had no idea how personally invested Archbishop Albrecht was in the success of Tetzel's indulgence campaign. As it happened, the archbishop had a dirty dog in this fight about which almost no one knew besides him and the pope. But it is this particularly sordid detail that frames the controversy perfectly, that underscores just how far the greasy bandwagon had traveled by the time of Luther's theses. The truly extraordinary detail of which Luther was unaware was that the Archbishop Albrecht was not merely overseeing the papal indulgence in his territory to raise money for the building of St. Peter's in Rome. There was a second extremely personal and deeply secret reason for allowing indulgences to be preached and sold in his territory.

The story begins in 1513, when Albrecht first became the archbishop of Magdeburg at the tender age of twenty-three. Then just one year later, he also became the elector of Mainz, a plum political position. But now came the rub: Albrecht's territorial and ecclesiastical ambitions were still not sated. The ambitious Albrecht also wished to become the archbishop of Mainz. But alas, by the time this ambition had bloomed, the Vatican had put in place a new rule that said holding several archbishoprics simultaneously was strictly verboten. This practice had been terribly abused over the years, so some cadre of scrupulous Vatican officials had stepped in and passed this new prohibition, just in time to frustrate Albrecht. It was a prohibition that could not be relaxed; after all, what was the point of a prohibition or a rule if it could easily be relaxed? No, this was not something that could be undone—unless of course one was willing to pay a genuinely exorbitant sum of money. It was understood that the Vatican was always in dire need of money, because Leo's habits as a spendthrift made all others look like sober landlubbers. So if someone was able to get his hands on an especially impressive amount of money—which he was somehow inclined to give as a gift to the Vatican treasury—that could always cover a multitude of sins.

In fact, the young Albrecht so desperately desired the Mainz archbishopric that he was willing to get his hands on the necessary funds, if that was possible. And in the end, despite strong misgivings, the pope suggested that Albrecht cough up the mighty sum of twenty-three thousand ducats in order to have the unpleasant rule waived. It was a staggering figure, and truth be told, Albrecht didn't have anything close to it to hand. What, then, was to be done? There was one possible solution: he could simply borrow it from Jakob Fugger of the dizzyingly wealthy Fugger banking family. But how could Albrecht ever pay it back? Where there was a will, there was a way, and Pope Leo happened to come up with a way that was ingenious. What if Albrecht was willing to sponsor an indulgence crusade in his territory—ostensibly to help build the new St. Peter's in Rome? But what if the pope would officially allow him to retain half of all he raised for himself and with that money pay back the greedy Fuggers? No one need know the details, and everyone might come out ahead. And so it happened.

This dirty secret was about as dirty as the business of indulgences could get. It therefore seems fitting that this particular excess would be the last straw that broke the back of medieval Christendom. That the humble faithful would hurl their coins into an iron coffer believing they really would pay for their sins—and simultaneously build St. Peter's— was bad enough. But that half of what they paid was actually going to pay an exorbitant debt so that a papal rule might be ignored—and the ambitious archbishop could collect a second impressive bishopric—took the cake. And ate it too.

Luther knew nothing at all of these details. But he knew enough of what was happening that he wished to tell the archbishop of his concern and to provoke an academic debate on the subject among the church theologians at Wittenberg. That was the only point of posting the theses on the church doors. Our ideas about the import of the theses have been twisted in hindsight. Luther was only posting the theses he wished to debate with his fellow academics. And following his posting them, an academic debate on the subject was scheduled. But not a soul showed up for this debate. Why students did not show up, we don't know. But because the theses were written in Latin, the non-Latin-speaking citizens of Wittenberg were at a disadvantage and did not show up either. Except for the actions of Archbishop Albrecht and Tetzel, the whole thing might have fizzled like an errant spark landing on damp ground.

Tetzel was so outraged when he read Luther's theses that a few weeks afterward, as he was peddling heaven's treasures near Berlin, he is reported to have said, "In three weeks I will throw the heretic into the fire!" And as the customary garb for heretics burned at the stake was something resembling a bathing cap, Tetzel added, "And he will go to heaven in a bathing cap!"[4]

So that we are clear on what it was that launched this Revolution of Revolutions, here are the theses that Luther posted, with his brief introduction:

Amore et studio elucidande veritatis:hec subscripta disputabuntur Wittenberge. Presidente R. P. Martino Luther:Artiu et S. Theologie Magistro:eiusdemq̄ ibidem lectore Ordinario. Quare petit: ut qui non possunt verbis presentes nobiscū disceptare:agant id literis absentes. In noīe dn̄i nostri Iesu chr̄i. Amē.

1. Dominus et magister noster Iesus chr̄s dicendo. Penitentiam agite. xc̄. omnē vitam fidelium penitentiam esse voluit.

2. Q̄d verbū de penitētia sacramentali:(id est confessionis et satisfactionis que sacerdotum ministerio celebratur)non pōt intelligi.

3. Nō tn̄ solam intendit interiorē:immo interior nulla est.nisi foris operetur varias carnis mortificationes.

4. Manet itaq̄ pena donec manet odium sui (id est penitentia vera intus) scz vsq̄ ad introitum regni celoꝝ.

5. Papa nō vult nec pōt vllas penas remittere. ꝓter eas:quas arbitrio vel suo vel canonum imposuit.

6. Papa nō pōt remittere vllā culpā nisi declarando et approbando remissam a deo. Aut certe remittendo casus reseruatos sibi:quib⁹ ꝓtēptis culpa prorsus remaneret.

7. Nulli prorsus remittit deus culpā:quin simul eū subijciat:humiliatū in oīnibus:sacerdoti suo vicario.

8. Canones penitentiales solū viuētibus sunt impositi. nihilq̄ morituris sm̄ eosdē sm̄ debet imponi.

9. Inde bn̄ nobis facit sp̄ssctūs in papa. excipiendo in suis decretis sp̄ articulū mortis et necessitatis.

10. Indocte et male faciunt sacerdotes ij:qui morituris p̄nias canonicas in purgatorium reseruant.

11. Zizania illa de mutanda pena Canonica in penam purgatorij. vident certe dormientibus episcopis seminata.

12. Olim pene canonice nō post:sed ante absolutionem imponebantur: tanq̄ tentamenta vere contritionis.

13. Morituri ꝑ mortē omnia soluunt.et legibus canonū mortui iam sunt habentes iure earum relaxationem.

14. Imperfecta sanitas seu charitas morituri:necessario secum fert magnū timorem:tantoq̄ maiorem:quāto minor fuerit ipsa.

15. Hic timor et horror satis est:se solo (vt alia taceā) facere penā purgatorij:cum sit proximus desperationis horrori.

16. Videntur infernus:purgatorium:celum differre:sicut desperatio. ꝓpe desperatio:securitas differunt.

17. Necessariū videt aīab⁹ in purgatorio:sicut minui horror: ita augeri charitatem.

18. Nec ꝓbatū videt vllis:aut rōnibus aut scripturis. q̄ sint extra statū meriti seu augende charitatis.

19. Nec hoc ꝓbatū esse videt:q̄ sint de sua beatitudine certe et secure saltē oēs.licz nos certissimi simus.

20. Igitur papa ꝑ remissionē plenariā oīm penaꝝ.nō simpliciter oīm.intelligit earū que a se sunt impositae.

21. Errant itaq̄ indulgētiarū p̄dicatores:ij:qui dicūt per pape indulgētias:hoīem ab oīi pena solui et saluari.

22. Q̄m nulli remittit aīabus in purgatorio:quā in hac vita debuissent sm̄ Canones soluere.

23. Si remissio vlla oīno penaꝝ:pōt alicui dari.certū est eā nō nisi ꝑfectissimis.i.paucissimis dari.

24. Falli ob id necesse est:maiorē partē populi:ꝑ indifferentē illā et magnificam pene solute ꝓmissionem.

25. Qualē pōtestatē hz papa in purgatoriū gn̄aliter:talem hz quilibet Episcopus et Curatus in sua diocesi et parochia specialiter.

1. Optime predicat. qui statim vt iactus nummus in cistam tinnierit: euolare dicunt animā.

2. Certū est:nūmo in cistā tinniente:augeri questū et auariciā posse. suffragium aūt ecclesie:in arbitrio dei soli⁹ est.

3. Quis scit:si oēs aīe in purgatorio velint redimi. sicut de s. Seuerino et paschali factū narratur.

4. Nullus est securus de veritate sue contritionis.multominus de cōsecutione plenarie remissionis.

5. Q̄ rar⁹ est vere penitēs:tā rar⁹ est vere indulgētias redimēs.i.rarissim⁹.

6. Damnantur in eternū cū suis magistris:qui ꝑ literas veniarum securos sese credunt de sua salute.

7. Cauendi sunt nimis:qui dicūt venias illas Pape:donū esse illud dei inestimabilem:quo reconciliat homo deo.

8. Gratie enim ille veniales:respiciunt penas satisfactionis sacramētalis ab homīe constitutas.

9. Non christiana predicant:qui docent: q̄ redemptionis aīas vel cōfessionalis:nō sit necessaria contritio.

10. Quilibet christianus vere cōpunctus: hz remissionē plenariā:a pena et culpa.etiam sine litris veniarū sibi debita.

11. Quilibet verus christianus:siue viuus siue mortu⁹:hz participationē oīm bonoꝝ Chr̄i et Ecclesie.etiam sine litris veniarū a deo sibi datam.

12. Remissio tn̄ et participatio Pape:nullo mō est cōtemnēda. q̄:(vt dixi) est declaratio remissionis diuine.

13. Difficillimū est:etiā doctissimis Theologz simul extollere veniaꝝ largitatem:et contritionis veritatē coram populo.

14. Contritionis veritas penas querit et amat.Veniaꝝ aūt largitas relaxat:et odisse facit saltem occasione.

15. Caute sunt venie apl̄ice p̄dicande.ne populus false intelligat.eas p̄ferri ceteris bonis op̄ibus charitatis.

16. Docendi sunt christiani:q̄ Pape mens nō est:redemptionē veniaꝝ vlla ex parte cōparandā esse op̄ibus misericordie.

17. Docendi sunt christiani:q̄ dans paup̄i:aut mutuans egenti:meli⁹ facit q̄ si venias redimeret.

18. Quia q̄ opus charitatis crescit charitas: et fit hō melior.sed ꝑ venias nō fit melior:sed immodo a pena liberior.

19. Docendi sunt christiani:q̄ qui videt egenū:et neglecto eo.dat ꝑ venijs:nō indulgētias Pape:sed indignationē dei sibi vendicat.

20. Docendi sunt christiani:q̄ nisi superflua abundent:necessaria tenent domui sue retinere:et nequaquā ꝓpter venias effundere.

21. Docē di sunt christiani:q̄ redemptio veniarū est libera:nō precepta.

22. Docēdi sunt christiani:q̄ Papa sicut magis eget:ita magis optat in ve nijs dandis ꝓ se deuotam orationem:q̄ ꝓmptam pecuniam.

24. Docēdi sunt christiani.q̄ venie Pape sunt vtiles:si non in eas confidant.Sed nocentissime:si timorem dei per eas amittant.

25. Docēdi sunt christiani.q̄ si papa nosset exactiones venialiū p̄dicatorum mallet Basilicā.s.petri in cineres ire.q̄ edificari.cute carne et ossibus ouium suaꝝ.

1. Docēdi sunt chr̄iani.q̄ Papa sicut debet ita vellet.etiam vendita (si opus sit) Basilica.s.petri de suis pecunijs dare illis:a quorū plurimis quidā cōcionatores venias pecuniam eliciunt.

2. Vana est fiducia salutis ꝑ literas veniaꝝ.etiā si Cōmissarius:immo Papa ipse suā aīam ꝓ illis impigneraret.

3. Hostes chr̄i et Pape sunt illi:qui ꝓpter venias p̄dicandas verbū dei in alijs ecclesijs penitus silere iubent.

4. Iniuria fit verbo dei:dū in eodē sermone: equale vel longius tēpus impenditur venijs q̄ illi.

5. Mens Pape necessario est.q̄ si venie (q̄ minimum est) vna cāpana: vnis pompis:et ceremonijs celebrant. Euangelium (q̄ maximū est) centū campanis:centū pompis:centū ceremonijs predicet.

6. Thesauri ecclie vn̄ Papa dat indulgētias:neq̄ satis nolati sunt:neq̄ cogniti apud pp̄m chr̄iū.

7. Temporales certe nō esse patet. q̄ nō tā facile eos ꝓfundūt:sz tm̄mo colligunt multi cōcionatores.

8. Nec sunt merita Chr̄i et sctōꝝ. q̄ hec sp̄ sine Papa op̄ent̄ gr̄am hoīs interioris:et cruce:mortē:infernūq̄ exterioris.

9. Thesauros ecclie.s.Laurēti⁹ dixit esse:paupes ecclie.sz locutus est vsu vocabuli suo tpe.

10. Sine temeritate dicim⁹ clauce ecclie (merito Chr̄i donatae) esse thesaurum istum.

11. Clarū est eni.q̄ ad remissionē penaꝝ et casuū sola sufficit p̄tas Pape.

12. Verus thesaurus ecclie.est sacrosctū euāgeliū glorie et gratie dei.

13. Hic aūt est merito odiosissimus. q̄ ex primis facit nouissimos.

14. Thesaurus aūt indulgentiaꝝ merito est gratissimus. q̄ ex nouissimis facit primos.

15. Igitur thesauri Euangelici rhetia sunt:quibus olim piscabant̄ viros diuitiarum.

16. Thesauri indulgentiaꝝ rhetia sunt:q̄bus nūc piscant̄ diuitias viroꝝ.

17. Indulgētie:quas cōcionatores vociferant efficacissimas:intelligunt̄ vere tales:quoad questum ꝓmouendum.

18. Sunt tamen re vera minime ad gr̄am dei et crucis pietatē compate͏̄.

19. Tenent tn̄ et Curati venias apl̄icaꝝ Cōmissarios q̄ oīm reuerentia suscipi.

20. Sed magis tenent oībus oculis intendere:oībus aurib⁹ aduertere: ne p̄ cōmissione Pape sua illis somnia p̄dicent.

21. Cōtra venias apl̄icaꝝ veritatē q̄ loquit̄.sit ille anathema et maledict⁹.

22. Qui vero contra libidinē ac licentiā verborū Cōcionatorū veniarū curam agit:sit ille benedictus.

23. Sicut Papa iuste fulminat eos:qui in fraudem negocij veniarum quacunq̄ arte machinantur.

24. Multomagis fulminare intendit eos:qui ꝑ veniarū pretextū in fraudem fidei charitatis et veritatis machinant̄.

25. Opinari venias papales tātas esse:vt soluere possint hoīes.etiā si qui impossibile dei genitricē violasset.Est insanire.

1. Dicimus contra.q̄ venie papales:nec minimū venialium pōt:q̄ tollere possint quo ad culpam.

2. Q̄ dr̄.nec si.f.Petrus modo Papa esset: maiores gr̄as donare poss̄e est blasphemia in sctm̄ Petrum et Papam.

3. Dicimus contra.q̄ etsi iste et quilibet papa maiores hz.scz Euangelium:virtutes:gr̄as curationū.xc̄.vt.i.Co.xij.

4. Dicere.Cruce armis papalibus insigniter erectā:cruci christi equualere:blasphemia est.

5. Rationē reddent Ep̄i:Curati:et Theologi:qui tales sermones in populum licere sinunt.

6. Facit hec licētiosa venias p̄dicatio.vt nec reuerentiā Pape facile sit: etiā doctis viris redimere a calūnijs aut certe argut̄ q̄stiōib⁹ laicoꝝ.

7. Scz.Cur Papa nō euacuat purgatoriū ꝓpter sctissimā charitatē et summā aīarū necessitatē:vt cām oīm iustissimā. Si infinitas aīas redimit ꝓpter pecuniā funestissimā ad structurā Basilice:vt cām leuissimā.

8. Itē.Cur ꝑmanent exequie et anniuersaria defunctoꝝ:et nō reddit aut recipi ꝑmittit pecunias ꝓ illis instituta.cū iā sit iniuria ꝓ redempt⁹ orare.

9. Itē.Quid illa noua pietas Dei et Pape.q̄ impio et inimico ꝑ ꝑ pecuniā concedūt aīam pie et dei amicā redimere. Et tn̄ ꝓpter necessitatē ipsius met pie et dilecte aīae nō redimunt eā gratuita charitate.

10. Itē.Cur Canones penitētiales re ipsa et nō vsu iā dudū in semet abrogati et mortui:adhuc tn̄ pecunijs redimunt̄ ꝑ concessione indulgētiaꝝ:tanq̄ viuacissimi.

11. Itē.Cur Papa cui⁹ opes hodie sunt opulētissimis crassis crassiores: nō de suis pecunijs magis q̄ pauperū fidelium struit vnā tm̄mo Basilicā sancti petri.

12. Itē.Quid remittit aut participat Papa iis:qui ꝑ cōtritionē ꝑfectam ius habet plenarie remissionis et participationis.

13. Itē.Quid adderet ecclie boni maioris.Si Papa sicut semel facit: ita cētico in die cuilibz fidelium has remissiones et participationes tribuet.

14. Ex quo Papa salutē querit aīaꝝ ꝑ venias magis q̄ pecunias. Cur suspendit literas et venias iam olim cōcessas:cū sint eque efficaces.

15. Hec scrupulosissima laicoꝝ argumēta:sola p̄tate cōp̄cere:nec reddita ratione diluere.est ecclesiā et Papā hostib⁹ ridendos exponere:et infelices christianos facere.

16. Si ergo venie iam spiritū et mentē Pape p̄dicarent̄.facile illa omnia solueret̄:immo nō essent.

17. Valeat itaq̄ oēs illi ꝓph̄e:q̄ dicūt pp̄lo Chr̄i. Pax pax.et nō est pax.

18. Bn̄ agāt oēs illi ꝓph̄e:q̄ dicūt pp̄lo Chr̄i. Crux crux. et nō est crux.

19. Exhortandi sunt Christiani:vt caput suū Chr̄m per penas:mortes:inc̄: infernosq̄ sequi studeant.

20. Ac si magis p̄ multas tribulatiōes intrare celū:q̄ ꝑ securitatē pacis confidant.

M.D.Xvij.

The original 1517 printing of Luther's Ninety-five Theses.

Out of love for the truth and from desire to elucidate it, the Reverend Father Martin Luther, Master of Arts and Sacred Theology, and ordinary lecturer therein at Wittenberg, intends to defend the following statements and to dispute on them in that place. Therefore he asks that those who cannot be present and dispute with him orally shall do so in their absence by letter. In the name of our Lord Jesus Christ, Amen.

1 When our Lord and Master Jesus Christ said, "Repent" (Mt 4:17), he willed the entire life of believers to be one of repentance.*

2 This word cannot be understood as referring to the sacrament of penance, that is, confession and satisfaction, as administered by the clergy.†

3 Yet it does not mean solely inner repentance; such inner repentance is worthless unless it produces various outward mortification of the flesh.‡

4 The penalty of sin remains as long as the hatred of self (that is, true inner repentance), namely till our entrance into the kingdom of heaven.

5 The pope neither desires nor is able to remit any penalties except those imposed by his own authority or that of the canons.§

6 The pope cannot remit any guilt, except by declaring and showing that it has been remitted by God; or, to be sure, by remitting guilt in cases reserved to his judgment. If his right to grant remission in these cases were disregarded, the guilt would certainly remain unforgiven.¶

7 God remits guilt to no one unless at the same time he humbles him in all things and makes him submissive to the vicar, the priest.**

---

* This first thesis, of course, frames the subject. The idea that a Christian believer is to be engaged in a kind of game with something like points is a mockery of God's will for our lives. We ought always to want to repent of anything that pushes us away from fellowship with the God who loves us. So Luther's first and most important thesis makes this clear: that the game of losing and gaining points in a system invented by the church—and made more complicated by practitioners like Tetzel—was itself anathema.

† Like many of these theses, this brought up other central issues that struck at the heart of the church system of that time, that priests must administer everything and that Christians cannot access God directly. Already here Luther is portending much of the debate to come regarding what authority the church had as a mediator between God and man.

‡ Luther is careful to say that our faith—and therefore our repentance—must be manifested in our outward behavior.

§ The pope does not have God's authority or a capricious authority based on his own human will; in other words, he himself is under God's authority and the authority of the historical church.

¶ For example, if someone as penance was assigned to do work for the church, the pope would have authority to revoke that assignment, but anything beyond that does not fall within his scope of authority.

** Luther is again stressing that the idea of penance is not a game. If our hearts are not humbled— toward God and his servants—then we are not genuinely forgiven of our guilt.

8 The penitential canons are imposed only on the living, and, according to the canons themselves, nothing should be imposed on the dying.*

9 Therefore the Holy Spirit through the pope is kind to us insofar as the pope in his decrees always makes exception of the article of death and of necessity.

10 Those priests act ignorantly and wickedly who, in the case of the dying, reserve canonical penalties for purgatory.

11 Those tares of changing the canonical penalty to the penalty of purgatory were evidently sown while the bishops slept (Mt 13:25).

12 In former times canonical penalties were imposed, not after, but before absolution, as tests of true contrition.

13 The dying are freed by death from all penalties, are already dead as far as the canon laws are concerned, and have a right to be released from them.

14 Imperfect piety or love on the part of the dying person necessarily brings with it great fear; and the smaller the love, the greater the fear.

15 This fear or horror is sufficient in itself, to say nothing of other things, to constitute the penalty of purgatory, since it is very near to the horror of despair.

16 Hell, purgatory, and heaven seem to differ the same as despair, fear, and assurance of salvation.

17 It seems as though for the souls in purgatory fear should necessarily decrease and love increase.

18 Furthermore, it does not seem proved, either by reason or by Scripture, that souls in purgatory are outside the state of merit, that is, unable to grow in love.

19 Nor does it seem proved that souls in purgatory, at least not all of them, are certain and assured of their own salvation, even if we ourselves may be entirely certain of it.†

20 Therefore the pope, when he uses the words "plenary remission of all penalties," does not actually mean "all penalties," but only those imposed by himself.

21 Thus those indulgence preachers are in error who say that a man is absolved from every penalty and saved by papal indulgences.

---

* Luther is here asserting that the church and the pope can have nothing to say regarding what occurs in purgatory. That is the precinct of God alone.
† Luther is for the first time calling into question the church's doctrine of purgatory itself, which holds that all souls not in heaven or hell are guaranteed eventually to progress to heaven.

22 As a matter of fact, the pope remits to souls in purgatory no penalty which, according to canon law, they should have paid in this life.

23 If remission of all penalties whatsoever could be granted to anyone at all, certainly it would be granted only to the most perfect, that is, to very few.

24 For this reason most people are necessarily deceived by that indiscriminate and high-sounding promise of release from penalty.

25 That power which the pope has in general over purgatory corresponds to the power which any bishop or curate has in a particular way in his own diocese and parish.

26 The pope does very well when he grants remission to souls in purgatory, not by the power of the keys, which he does not have, but by way of intercession for them.*

27 They preach only human doctrines who say that as soon as the money clinks into the money chest, the soul flies out of purgatory.†

28 It is certain that when money clinks in the money chest, greed and avarice can be increased; but when the church intercedes, the result is in the hands of God alone.

29 Who knows whether all souls in purgatory wish to be redeemed, since we have exceptions in St. Severinus and St. Paschal, as related in a legend.

30 No one is sure of the integrity of his own contrition, much less of having received plenary remission.

31 The man who actually buys indulgences is as rare as he who is really penitent; indeed, he is exceedingly rare.

32 Those who believe that they can be certain of their salvation because they have indulgence letters will be eternally damned, together with their teachers.

33 Men must especially be on guard against those who say that the pope's pardons are that inestimable gift of God by which man is reconciled to him.

34 For the graces of indulgences are concerned only with the penalties of sacramental satisfaction established by man.‡

---

* Luther is here saying that the pope does not have the so-called power of the keys to make withdrawals from the treasury of merits in heaven, but he does have the power of prayer to help those souls struggling in purgatory.
† In other words, Tetzel and other indulgence preachers are lying, misrepresenting the church, and misleading the faithful.
‡ Once again, Luther is making the incendiary theological point that the church in fact has no rights regarding purgatory, and cannot effect anything there except through prayers.

35 They who teach that contrition is not necessary on the part of those who intend to buy souls out of purgatory or to buy confessional privileges preach unchristian doctrine.

36 Any truly repentant Christian has a right to full remission of penalty and guilt, even without indulgence letters.

37 Any true Christian, whether living or dead, participates in all the blessings of Christ and the church; and this is granted him by God, even without indulgence letters.

38 Nevertheless, papal remission and blessing are by no means to be disregarded, for they are, as I have said (Thesis 6), the proclamation of the divine remission.

39 It is very difficult, even for the most learned theologians, at one and the same time to commend to the people the bounty of indulgences and the need of true contrition.

40 A Christian who is truly contrite seeks and loves to pay penalties for his sins; the bounty of indulgences, however, relaxes penalties and causes men to hate them—at least it furnishes occasion for hating them.*

41 Papal indulgences must be preached with caution, lest people erroneously think that they are preferable to other good works of love.

42 Christians are to be taught that the pope does not intend that the buying of indulgences should in any way be compared with works of mercy.

43 Christians are to be taught that he who gives to the poor or lends to the needy does a better deed than he who buys indulgences.

44 Because love grows by works of love, man thereby becomes better. Man does not, however, become better by means of indulgences but is merely freed from penalties.

45 Christians are to be taught that he who sees a needy man and passes him by, yet gives his money for indulgences, does not buy papal indulgences but God's wrath.

46 Christians are to be taught that, unless they have more than they need, they must reserve enough for their family needs and by no means squander it on indulgences.

47 Christians are to be taught that the buying of indulgences is a matter of free choice, not commanded.

* Preaching indulgences has the active effect of leading people away from the love of God, and makes them cynical toward the church.

48 Christians are to be taught that the pope, in granting indulgences, needs and thus desires their devout prayer more than their money.

49 Christians are to be taught that papal indulgences are useful only if they do not put their trust in them, but very harmful if they lose their fear of God because of them.

50 Christians are to be taught that if the pope knew the exactions of the indulgence preachers, he would rather that the basilica of St. Peter were burned to ashes than built up with the skin, flesh, and bones of his sheep.

51 Christians are to be taught that the pope would and should wish to give of his own money, even though he had to sell the basilica of St. Peter, to many of those from whom certain hawkers of indulgences cajole money.

52 It is vain to trust in salvation by indulgence letters, even though the indulgence commissary, or even the pope, were to offer his soul as security.

53 They are the enemies of Christ and the pope who forbid altogether the preaching of the Word of God in some churches in order that indulgences may be preached in others.

54 Injury is done to the Word of God when, in the same sermon, an equal or larger amount of time is devoted to indulgences than to the Word.

55 It is certainly the pope's sentiment that if indulgences, which are a very insignificant thing, are celebrated with one bell, one procession, and one ceremony, then the gospel, which is the very greatest thing, should be preached with a hundred bells, a hundred processions, a hundred ceremonies.

56 The true treasures of the church, out of which the pope distributes indulgences, are not sufficiently discussed or known among the people of Christ.

57 That indulgences are not temporal treasures is certainly clear, for many indulgence sellers do not distribute them freely but only gather them.

58 Nor are they the merits of Christ and the saints, for, even without the pope, the latter always work grace for the inner man, and the cross, death, and hell for the outer man.

59 St. Lawrence said that the poor of the church were the treasures of the church, but he spoke according to the usage of the word in his own time.

60 Without want of consideration we say that the keys of the church, given by the merits of Christ, are that treasure.

61 For it is clear that the pope's power is of itself sufficient for the remission of penalties and cases reserved by himself.

62 The true treasure of the church is the most holy gospel of the glory and grace of God.

63 But this treasure is naturally most odious, for it makes the first to be last (Mt 20:16).

64 On the other hand, the treasure of indulgences is naturally most acceptable, for it makes the last to be first.

65 Therefore the treasures of the gospel are nets with which one formerly fished for men of wealth.

66 The treasures of indulgences are nets with which one now fishes for the wealth of men.*

67 The indulgences which the demagogues acclaim as the greatest graces are actually understood to be such only insofar as they promote gain.

68 They are nevertheless in truth the most insignificant graces when compared with the grace of God and the piety of the cross.

69 Bishops and curates are bound to admit the commissaries of papal indulgences with all reverence.

70 But they are much more bound to strain their eyes and ears lest these men preach their own dreams instead of what the pope has commissioned.†

71 Let him who speaks against the truth concerning papal indulgences be anathema and accursed.‡

72 But let him who guards against the lust and license of the indulgence preachers be blessed.

73 Just as the pope justly thunders against those who by any means whatever contrive harm to the sale of indulgences.

74 Much more does he intend to thunder against those who use indulgences as a pretext to contrive harm to holy love and truth.

75 To consider papal indulgences so great that they could absolve a man even if he had done the impossible and had violated the mother of God is madness.

76 We say on the contrary that papal indulgences cannot remove the very least of venial sins as far as guilt is concerned.

---

* Luther is directly addressing the idea that human greed is behind much of the indulgence efforts.
† We see here that Luther is careful not to attack the pope or the papacy but to attack those indulgence preachers who have deviated from official church doctrine.
‡ Luther is implicating Tetzel and others, who have twisted the official church doctrine on the teaching of indulgences.

77 To say that even St. Peter if he were now pope could not grant greater graces is blasphemy against St. Peter and the pope.

78 We say on the contrary that even the present pope, or any pope whatsoever, has greater graces at his disposal, that is, the gospel, spiritual powers, gifts of healing, etc., as it is written. (1 Co 12[:28])

79 To say that the cross emblazoned with the papal coat of arms, and set up by the indulgence preachers, is equal in worth to the cross of Christ is blasphemy.

80 The bishops, curates, and theologians who permit such talk to be spread among the people will have to answer for this.

81 This unbridled preaching of indulgences makes it difficult even for learned men to rescue the reverence which is due the pope from slander or from the shrewd questions of the laity.*

82 Such as: "Why does not the pope empty purgatory for the sake of holy love and the dire need of the souls that are there if he redeems an infinite number of souls for the sake of miserable money with which to build a church?" The former reason would be most just; the latter is most trivial.

83 Again, "Why are funeral and anniversary masses for the dead continued and why does he not return or permit the withdrawal of the endowments founded for them, since it is wrong to pray for the redeemed?"

84 Again, "What is this new piety of God and the pope that for a consideration of money they permit a man who is impious and their enemy to buy out of purgatory the pious soul of a friend of God and do not rather, because of the need of that pious and beloved soul, free it for pure love's sake?"†

85 Again, "Why are the penitential canons, long since abrogated and dead in actual fact and through disuse, now satisfied by the granting of indulgences as though they were still alive and in force?"

86 Again, "Why does not the pope, whose wealth is today greater than the wealth of the richest Croesus, build this one basilica of

---

* Luther's genius is to put the following provocative questions in the mouths of the laity and to say that they demand answers because the laity's faith in the authority of the church has been compromised.
† Luther is pointing out one of the contradictory ideas behind indulgences, asking how the church would allow "dirty" money given by someone whose heart is not right with God to bail out someone who already loves God and is working out the details of his own salvation in purgatory.

St. Peter with his own money rather than with the money of poor
believers?"*

87 Again, "What does the pope remit or grant to those who by perfect
contrition already have a right to full remission and blessings?"

88 Again, "What greater blessing could come to the church than if the
pope were to bestow these remissions and blessings on every
believer a hundred times a day, as he now does but once?"

89 "Since the pope seeks the salvation of souls rather than money by
his indulgences, why does he suspend the indulgences and
pardons previously granted when they have equal efficacy?"

90 To repress these very sharp arguments of the laity by force alone,
and not to resolve them by giving reasons, is to expose the church
and the pope to the ridicule of their enemies and to make
Christians unhappy.†

91 If, therefore, indulgences were preached according to the spirit and
intention of the pope, all these doubts would be readily resolved.
Indeed, they would not exist.‡

92 Away, then, with all those prophets who say to the people of Christ,
"Peace, peace," and there is no peace! (Jer 6:14)

93 Blessed be all those prophets who say to the people of Christ,
"Cross, cross," and there is no cross!

94 Christians should be exhorted to be diligent in following Christ,
their Head, through penalties, death and hell.

95 And thus be confident of entering into heaven through many
tribulations rather than through the false security of peace (Acts 14:22).[5]

The letter that Luther sent to Archbishop Albrecht included a copy of
these Ninety-five Theses. The letter and the theses were first sent to
Magdeburg and forwarded to Albrecht. He did not even open the letter
until November 17, and when he did open it, he was not in any mood to

---

* Croesus was a Greek king of Lydia in the sixth century B.C. who was widely renowned for his extraordinary wealth.
† Again, Luther's genius is in putting these criticisms in the mouths of the laity and asking why the
church doesn't deal honestly with these questions, but rather uses force to stop the questions, thus
leading to a decrease in respect for the church by its foes and friends alike.
‡ Luther cannily but not cynically puts the pope on the side of those who have been done a disservice
by the indulgence preachers.

take its contents very well. The main reason for this was that he was in a great financial difficulty owing to the fact that Tetzel's usual rain dance wasn't bringing in nearly the amounts Albrecht had been counting on. A related reason for his pique was that his elector rival Frederick had declined to allow this indulgence to be preached in Saxony. That would have helped dramatically. And now this theological fussbudget from Frederick's own university was writing to say that preaching indulgences was profoundly wrong and must be stopped as soon as possible. In fact, one reason the indulgences were not raising what had been predicted had to do with fatigue on the part of many of the faithful, who had been approached by other indulgence preachers not long before Tetzel. This was one of the reasons Frederick had given for not wishing to reintroduce indulgence preaching into his own territory at that time.

Albrecht hardly knew what to do with the letter, but he knew that it required some sort of response. He certainly could not throw it away, because the monk who had written it was the head of the theological faculty at Wittenberg, not to mention the vicar-general of eleven monasteries. So two weeks after reading the letter, Albrecht handed it over to the theological faculty at his own university in Mainz, hoping they might make something of it and advise him how to proceed. Albrecht was not a nefarious man and was not entirely dismissive of what Luther had to say, but this was hardly the best time for him to deal with the problem of indulgences. The Mainz theologians who got the letter and theses were slow in responding to Albrecht. No doubt they too realized what thorny issues the letter raised. When they finally did respond, their response was perfectly mealymouthed: they said that professors in Wittenberg were within their rights to have academic disputations—who would have disputed that?—and they said that the questions raised in the letter were probably something the pope should decide. One thing seemed quite clear: for them to say anything one way or another could only get them in trouble, so they opted simply to pass the buck to Rome. And this is what Albrecht now did. And that is how the warehouse of fireworks was finally lit.

Because he knew that it might be some time until he heard back from Albrecht, Luther also sent the theses to his friend Johannes Lang in Erfurt and some others. These were academic allies and friends he respected, and Luther doubtless thought sending the theses to them would help stir a debate and would lead toward dealing with the issues at hand more generally. The Nuremberg Humanist and printer Christopher Scheurl was impressed with what he read and thought that the theses should be reprinted, and without the fussy legality of needing to obtain copyright permissions, he simply printed them himself, right there in his own town of Nuremberg, instantly ensuring that they would have a dramatically wider reading. In this way, the horse snuck out of the barn, because once the theses were circulating, the whole controversy would take on a life of its own. But Luther did not realize this at the time, having never lived through anything like this before—and who had? After Scheurl had the theses reprinted in Nuremberg, other editions were soon printed in Basel and Leipzig too. In fact, the Basel edition was produced in an elegant pamphlet form, which promptly catapulted it into the intellectual jet stream and guaranteed it a far speedier and wider circulation. Where the theses went after that, no one can say. They were like milkweed seeds borne aloft by the wind, and they floated far beyond the borders of Saxony and Germany and settled everywhere. In January, they were translated into German, which infinitely multiplied their reach and started even non-academics jabbering with conviction and fire. By March 1518, even Erasmus himself had gotten his hands on a copy. And he sent it along to his friend Thomas More in England, which is how it fell under the wandering eyes of King Henry VIII, who would have something to say about it in due time, and nothing very nice.

The speed with which Luther's theses spread was simply unprecedented in the history of the world. The advent of printing had changed everything, but no one understood that yet, so what happened now stunned everyone, and it certainly concerned Luther. That March, he wrote to Scheurl:

> Greetings. I received both your German and Latin letters, good and learned Scheurl, together with the distinguished Albrecht Dürer's gift, and my Theses in the original and in the vernacular. As you are surprised that I did not send them to you, I reply that my purpose was not to publish them, but first to consult a few of my neighbors about them, that thus I might either destroy them if condemned or edit them with the approbation of others. But now that they are printed and circulated far beyond my expectation, I feel anxious about what they may bring forth: not that I am unfavorable to spreading known truth abroad—rather this is what I seek—but because this method is not that best adapted to instruct the public. I have certain doubts about them myself, and should have spoken far differently and more distinctly had I known what was going to happen.[6]

It was as though a hastily written e-mail to a friend were inadvertently forwarded to a major news organization or as though an ill-considered thought were captured on a "hot mic" and thenceforth broadcast to the world. Luther had no choice but to do his best with the events that had run far ahead of his control. In chasing them, he would end up in places he had never dreamed.

Tetzel Strikes Back

But what about the quacking preacher Tetzel, who had started all the hubbub in the first place? After making his initial death threats, Tetzel suddenly double-backed on himself and decided that the best way of countering Luther was to be mild and intellectual. He had recently matriculated at the Brandenburg University in Frankfurt and now thought he should fight academic fire with academic fire. So he would write his own countering theses on indulgences, and of course planned to debate them. Tetzel did post theses of his own, although in the end they were written not by him but by the renowned Frankfurt theologian Konrad Koch, whose birth in the city of Wimpfen led him to take the unfortunate Humanist appellation Wimpina.* On January 20, 1518, Tetzel did debate these theses, albeit with no one whom history remembers and to no particular fanfare. His theses rather preposterously put forward the same idea of indulgences that Luther himself would have agreed with. Thus his theses utterly—and whether cannily or idiotically we cannot know—neglected Luther's genuine concerns on what indulgences had effectively become under the fire-breathing preaching of such as Tetzel himself.

Sometime that spring, Tetzel sent a bookseller from Halle to Wittenberg, laboring under the bright notion that he might sell some printed copies of his theses there and that way fight back against Luther's ideas. After all, the debate hadn't accomplished much. But the Wittenberg students were by this time fully on the side of Luther and in no time had confronted the bookseller for bringing what they viewed as worse than trash into their fine city. One thing led to another, and before long an invitation went out far and wide in Wittenberg declaring that at the stroke of noon in the marketplace these ignorant theses would meet the fate they deserved.

* Half a millennium later, these Humanist names invariably come across oddly. For some in our own era, "Wimpina" will sound like a John Epperson creation.

Some eight hundred copies—which is to say the seller's entire shipment, which they had ignobly seized—were at that hour gracelessly dumped into the flames of a crackling bonfire. Luther was horrified when he learned of this shameful episode, because he knew the blame would fall at his feet, and he soon railed against it in a sermon. But the damage was done, and it was obvious that this was but another round in what had now become an unavoidably ongoing battle with Johannes Tetzel.

Meanwhile, in an attempt to rein in the situation, which was quickly swerving out of anyone's control, Luther began drafting a more fulsome explanation of his theses and sent a draft of it to the bishop of Brandenburg. The Ninety-five Theses had never been intended for public consumption. After all, they were academic theses; they were nothing like an essay in which Luther could explore all that needed saying. The theses were intended to be provocative—indeed to provoke debate on the subject and all that related to it—but now these pamphlets were flying all over creation, and they had been translated into German too! So they were certainly provoking debate, but precious little of it was fruitful. Luther's more measured and fuller treatment of the subject would be published under the title *Resolutions*. At this point, Luther still had every expectation that things could have an orderly way forward. So when the Brandenburg bishop told Luther not to publish his new document just yet, Luther happily complied. He wasn't trying to stir up trouble, only to help the church see what was occurring so that it might be corrected, and who could doubt that it would thank him for his efforts in time and make the important corrections?

So Luther held back on publishing what would become *Resolutions*, although he had already written a sermon on the subject (titled *Sermon on Indulgences and Grace*). In fact, he had already delivered this sermon and had even had it printed. Not all of his sermons were printed, only those he thought particularly important, as this one certainly was. When Luther heard from the bishop, he even agreed to curtail the distribution of the printed copies of the sermon, although not before some of them had slipped away and begun wreaking their own special havoc. Of course in this new era of printing, before there were copyright laws, a single copy could quickly beget others—which begat others, which begat others— and before anyone knew it, they would be fanning out across the landscape like Abraham's descendants and would become as numerous as the stars in the heavens. To be clear, Luther never received so much as a groat in royalties from anything he wrote, and in the Wild West that was the world of publishing at that time, printers simply printed what they thought would sell—and sold it. And it was a fact that Luther's writings sold very well indeed and would continue to do so for decades.

It is in this *Sermon on Indulgences and Grace* that we have Luther's first clear explanation of the issue in a form other than the Ninety-five Theses themselves. He made clear in the sermon that the idea that the church has any right (via indulgences) to remit the punishment that God would impose for sins is simply mistaken, being both unbiblical and theologically confused. He also explained that the idea that someone could by paying a few coins get out of what God in his infinite wisdom has ordained—such as suffering for a sin for the good of one's soul—is blasphemous and contrary to common sense. He was clearly saying that this erroneous view of indulgences constituted the church's usurpation of God's role, and was therefore implying the very thing that would get him in so much trouble in the years ahead—that the church and the pope were wrong to imply this and must be confronted with their error. In the sermon, he also made clear that it was a good thing to give to the building of St. Peter's Basilica, but to do so only as a way of avoiding the suffering that God has ordained for one's moral improvement was deeply misguided.

Because this sermon was out of the blocks and picking up speed far beyond Wittenberg, Tetzel predictably decided to pounce with his own publication. This was probably toward the end of April 1518. In his own writing, he slapped away the niceties of theological debate and leaped forward to pure ad hominem frontal assault, quickly placing Luther in the incendiary heretical category of Jan Hus and John Wycliffe. Here for the first time we see what will be the tragic way forward in the larger debate. In lieu of trying to actually wrestle with what Luther is humbly and genuinely saying, Tetzel—in his zeal to protect the honor of Mother Church—had chosen to stoke the fires of heresy, to dishonestly pit Luther against pope and church, when it was a plain fact that at this point Luther himself genuinely wished only to help the pope and the church. The gravamen of Tetzel's argument in this document is a bitterly sad one, one that again prefigures all that lay ahead. It is "Be silent and revoke all you have said. Unless you do so, the Church will crush you. Amen." Tetzel is selfishly and cynically trying to head off any actual consideration of Luther's arguments, and of course we know that in the end he mostly succeeded. By framing the debate as Luther standing against the pope himself, Tetzel had bet everything on the vanity and distracted narcissism of Leo X and those around him. If he was right that they wouldn't bother to consider this more carefully—perhaps even prayerfully—but would instead lazily decide to swat the renegade German monk into silence, all would be well as far as he was concerned.

For Tetzel, it came down to the simplest of all things. Let the arguments and the Bible be damned. The pope cannot err. To say that he can or that the church has erred is to be a heretic, and that is the end of it. Tetzel was a Dominican, and there was also a hot rivalry between the Dominicans and the Augustinians, which certainly played into this initial clash and much that would follow too. The Dominicans were founded by Saint Dominic de Guzmán early in the thirteenth century, and one of their main reasons for existing was to stamp out heresy, so when an Augustinian like Luther opposed a Dominican who was doing what Rome had instructed him to do, it could lead only to trouble. Although the Dominicans were obviously named for their founder, the Augustinians sneeringly called them "the dogs of the Lord"—from the Latin pun *Domini canes*—although a more charitable interpretation of this would be "the hounds of heaven."[7]

In June, Luther decided to reply to Tetzel, but it's clear that he didn't take Tetzel seriously. Luther's vintage sarcasm at last reared its head. Tetzel's ignorance, as evidenced by what he had written, made him patently unequal to any substantive debate. Luther knew he himself stood on as firm theological ground as existed and cheerily waved away Tetzel's childish threats of burning and drowning with "fire and water." Instead, Luther suggested that Tetzel stick "with wine and the fire that smokes from a roasting goose, with which he is better acquainted."[8] Here, we can detect the first coarse notes of a melody that would soon swell to become a virtuoso symphony of invective such as the world had never heard. Luther was thumbing his nose at Tetzel and blowing raspberries too, as though to say, "Excuse me, my good Herr Fatso, but please don't step away from your fine meal to debate me on these difficult issues! Hold fast to what you value most and keep shoveling food and drink down your gullet!" Luther also accused Tetzel of being a self-serving money-grubber. On the other hand, he taunted, if you are foolish enough to wish to debate me, I am here in Wittenberg, waiting: "And if there is an inquisitor anywhere who thinks he can eat iron and crack rocks, be it known that here he shall have safe conduct, open doors, free room and board."[9] In other words, Frederick the elector will happily provide these things if you like, because you have dared to suggest that he is harboring a heretic in Wittenberg.

That same month, Archbishop Albrecht, who was doubtless worried about where this back-and-forth teeth-baring might lead, suggested to the theological faculty at Leipzig University that they make a clarifying statement on the new controversy. But like the Mainz theologians, they demurred, knowing this was growing into a conflagration that could only cause them trouble with Rome. It was far better to lie low and watch the fire from across the street.

Obelisks and Asterisks

Another of the characters who must now come into our story is the theologian Johannes Eck, whom Luther considered a friend until the unfortunate months of early 1518. The two had been introduced by the leading Humanist Christopher Scheurl when Scheurl was the rector at Wittenberg, but when Eck read Luther's theses that January, he promptly let it be known that he desperately wished to debate Luther. In fact, he said he would gladly walk ten miles to do so. Eck then wrote and published a rebuttal of Luther's theses, titled *Obelisks*. The typographic term "obelisk"— which referred to the four-sided monolithic stone monuments that taper upward and date back to ancient Egypt—denoted the small daggers that were even then used in the margins of manuscripts, indicating that the text nearby was perhaps of spurious origin. So Eck's title must have seemed to Luther like the very thing itself, a poniard in the back of a friend. That a friend Luther considered a reasonable and educated man would attack him like this was certainly deeply hurtful. Nor was the attack measured, but vicious. In it Eck hurled boulders of invective Lutherward, calling him simpleminded, impudent, and Bohemian (which is to say, a heretic deserving of death, like the Bohemian Jan Hus) and a despiser of the pope, among other things. To Luther, it was a cruel betrayal.

What might have sparked Eck's emotion is hard to say, but surely part of it had to do with the fact that Luther was accusing the indulgence sellers of being greedy, and thereby somehow undermining the authority of the church itself. Even if there was truth to this, or if there was error to be reported, it seems Eck took greatest offense at Luther's naked appeal to the anticlericalism so rampant at that time, which served only to make matters worse by undermining the church's authority.

In any case, Luther was wounded and disinclined to reply, but his friends insisted that he must. So he wrote *Asterisks*. Thus touché. The word "asterisk" is from the Greek for "little star," and so asterisks were those marks in the margins of manuscripts that were the precise opposite of the pejorative downward-facing daggers.[10] Asterisks were put next to text that was considered particularly valuable. So only six decades after the invention of movable type, Luther and Eck treated the world to its first typographic battle, waged with pre-Zapf dingbats.

With the publication of *Obelisks* and then *Asterisks*, the theological war was now out in the open for all to see, and this was a war, more than anything, about authority. On the one side was the idea that the Scholastics and Aristotle and of course mainly the church, which had accepted and promulgated these ideas, could not be gainsaid in any way, that they were the final authority. On the other side was the idea that everything must be tested against the Scriptures. On the one side was the pope's unquestioned and illimitable authority. On the other was the authority of the Scriptures. Luther was abundantly clear that although his respect for the church and the pope was genuine and very deep, the truth of the Gospel itself must take precedence. The idea that the church had the unchecked authority to dispense the treasury of merits as it had been doing he regarded as "a drunken carnival prank."[11]

That June, Scheurl would make one more attempt to bring reconciliation between Luther and Eck. In the meantime, however, the overzealous Karlstadt—who would play the role of fly in the ointment many times in the years ahead—had written his own response to Eck and had failed to inform Luther of it. Karlstadt's response in turn required a response from Eck, ginning things up still further. Luther hoped to get Eck's response to be moderate, so they might indeed proceed in a measured way, as Scheurl was hoping. Luther wrote, "May both sides regret this argument begun by the devil."[12] In this statement alone, we see that there was a side to Luther that grieved deeply at what was happening, that he still very much hoped the sheer rancor could be avoided and that it might all have a happy ending. But it was too late.

The Heidelberg Disputation, *Aetatis* 34

In 1518, Luther was scheduled to travel to Heidelberg for the meeting of the Augustinian Reformed congregations. As district vicar, Luther must attend, and because the meeting was scheduled for April 25 and he would be walking the roughly three hundred miles, he was obliged to depart around April 9. But there was already such a widespread furor over the indulgence controversy that Luther was warned not to travel on foot. He might be arrested en route and snatched away to Rome, where he could be swiftly denounced as a heretic and consigned to the flames. But Duke Frederick had already made it clear to Luther—always via Staupitz— that he would not allow this. If Luther would not protect himself, Frederick would do it for him. It is interesting to see that when church and state are not separate—as they were not then and would not be anywhere in the world for nearly three centuries—the theological and ecclesiastical quickly became political. The pope didn't want to do anything untoward to raise the ire of the powerful Frederick, and for several reasons. This hesitation would become dramatically pronounced in a year, when the Holy Roman Emperor Maximilian died. This was because Pope Leo X would very much want Frederick on his side in choosing Maximilian's successor, and this political consideration crucially moderated the pope's response in the Luther affair.

So Frederick provided official letters of safe-conduct for the journey, and Luther left on April 9 with two companions. When he reached Judenbach, Luther learned from Pfeffinger—an electoral councillor who had just returned from the imperial court at Innsbruck—that Emperor Maximilian himself had asked after the monk from Wittenberg whose formidable theses had far and wide caused such trembling. On April 18, Luther reached Würzburg, where he bumped into his old Erfurt friends Johannes Lang and Bartholomaeus Usingen. They offered him a ride the rest of the way in their cart.

What took place at the meeting on April 25 is little known and dealt with the typical mundane issues of the order. For example, Staupitz was reelected vicar-general, and Luther was replaced as district vicar by Lang. But it was the disputation that took place the following day, on April 26, that concerns us and history.

That day Luther presented his "Theology of the Cross," which stipulated the fundamental idea that we cannot reason our way to God. The passage in Paul's first letter to the Corinthians 1:23 sums it up: "But we preach Christ crucified, to the Jews a stumbling block, and to the Greeks foolishness."[13] Luther might well have specified that the Greek he had in mind most of all was that fatiguing jackanapes Aristotle. But the point was that we can reason only so far. At some point, we come to an end and are stuck.

It is at this point that we must stand and wait for God's revelation to come to us. God must condescend to speak to us. If he does not, we have no hope. We are alone at the end of all human capability and logic, looking up. This view of course presented a challenge to the proponents of Scholasticism who were present, but what was most significant that day was that some of the younger participants seemed to understand it. Martin Bucer and Johannes Brenz were two young men who that day would become deeply enamored of Luther and his new theology and who would do their part in carrying it and its implications into their parts of the empire.

Luther saw that his own colleagues and elders had a much more difficult time seeing what he was trying to communicate, deeply entrenched as they were in Scholasticism. "My theology is a pain in the neck for the Erfurters," he said.[14] He tried hard to bring his former professors Trutfetter and Usingen around to his thinking but failed. There was no invective whatever in his communications with them. He was moderate and sincere and respectful. Still, he never seemed to get anywhere in his dialogue with them.

Prierias Takes the Case

Meanwhile, all of the dust that had been kicked up in Germany during these months had finally blown south to Rome, where there was much coughing, choking, and gagging. Who was this upstart German monk, and how had he dared to say such outrageous things against the pope and the church? Of course Luther hadn't said a third of what he was purported to have said, but whatever he had said, he must in any case be called to give a full accounting of himself and his outrageous statements. Archbishop Albrecht had sent the theses to Rome about two months after he had received them, but news traveled more quickly in those days than we can suppose, and because the theses had been published in a number of cities and were making their way around Europe, we cannot know when the first copies got to the Vatican, nor just what perversions of the originals the rumor mill had been grinding.

But we do know that at some point the Vatican put the whole matter in the hands of a Dominican named Sylvester Mazzolini. The Dominican order, as we have said, had come into being to protect church doctrine. Mazzolini hailed from the town of Priero, in northwestern Italy, so he took the name Prierias. At the Vatican, Prierias held the title "commissioner of the Sacred Palace," and it now fell to him to examine the theses and then determine and explain whether they constituted heresy, at which point Luther must appear before the Inquisition in Rome. So at last someone was charged with responding to Luther's words. And so Prierias did. It was hardly a measured response. Prierias bragged that he had written his stinging answer to the arrogant German monk in only three days! But what had been his findings? For the Wittenberg monk, the title of the work, *Dialogue Against the Presumptuous Conclusions of Martin Luther Concerning the Power of the Pope,* did not bode well.

In the hastily written publication, Prierias did not tunnel to any particular theological depths. For him, the matter was quite simple:

> As I intend to sift your doctrine thoroughly, my Martin, it is necessary for me to establish a basis of norms and foundations. . . .
>
> Third foundation:
>
> He who does not accept the doctrine of the Church of Rome and pontiff of Rome, as an infallible rule of faith, from which the Holy Scriptures, too, draw their strength and authority, is a heretic.
>
> Fourth foundation:
>
> The Church of Rome can make decisions both in word and deed concerning faith and morals. And there is no difference except that words are better suited. In this sense habit acquires the force of law, for the will of a prince expresses itself in deeds which he allows or himself arranges to have done. Consequently: as he who thinks incorrectly concerning the truth of Scriptures is a heretic, so too he who thinks incorrectly concerning the doctrines and deeds of the Church in matters of faith and morals is a heretic.

The work had many frothy put-downs, such as "Just as the Devil smells of his pride in all his works, so you smell of your own malevolence" and a description of Luther as "a leper with a brain of brass and a nose of iron."*[15] The conclusion to this peppery opus was a swift kick to the point: "Whoever says that the Church of Rome may not do what it is actually doing in the matter of indulgences is a heretic."[16] There it was. Luther must therefore now travel to Rome and face the Inquisition.

But Prierias had made such breathtaking leaps in what passed for his

---

* The phrase "nose of iron" was intended to summon the image of an obstinate bull.

theology that Luther was himself dumbfounded and, it seems, even amused. Prierias had simplistically declared things that the church had never before declared. Thorny issues that had been debated and contradicted and even deliberately glossed over were presented by Prierias as well-established facts. It was so ridiculous that Luther almost couldn't believe it, and just as someone will sometimes retweet a vicious tweet of especial idiocy to highlight and underscore that idiocy, Luther now made his point by simply reprinting Prierias's work, as though to say, "You've got to read this!"

But then Luther did write a reply to Prierias and gloated that it had taken him but *two* days. Perhaps most tellingly of all, he did what Prierias did not. He quoted Scripture. First there was 1 Thessalonians 5:21: "Prove all things; hold fast that which is good." And then Galatians 1:8: "Even if an angel descend from heaven and preach a gospel contrary to that you have received, let him be accursed." Luther might have stopped there. After all, what else was there to say? But he would find something:

> I am sorry now that I despised Tetzel. Ridiculous as he was, he was more acute than you. You cite no Scripture. You give no reasons. Like an insidious devil you pervert the Scriptures. You say that the Church consists virtually in the pope. What nominations will you not have to regard as the deeds of the Church? Look at the ghastly shedding of blood by Julius II. Look at the outrageous tyranny of Boniface VIII, who, as the proverb declares, "came in as a wolf, reigned as a lion, and died as a dog." . . . You call me a leper because I mingle truth with error. I am glad you admit there is some truth. You make the pope into an emperor in power and violence. The Emperor Maximilian and the Germans will not tolerate this.[17]

The final line was a canny, cocky shot across Rome's bow, underscoring the prickly nationalistic issues that would come into play if Rome wasn't more careful. We assume that Luther received Prierias's work on August 7, the day he received official word that he must appear in Rome within sixty days. Luther well knew that the Dominicans, led by Prierias, had it out for him and that he could never get a fair trial in Rome—which he dubbed a "Lernaean* swamp full of hydras and other monsters"—so he immediately wrote to Spalatin, hoping he could persuade Frederick to push for the trial to be conducted in Germany.[18] In fact, Luther wondered not only whether

---

* Luther's reference is to the swamp at Lerna (near Argos) in which Hercules and Iolaus were said to have killed the mythical Hydra.

he would get a fair hearing in Rome but whether he would be found guilty of heresy and executed by fire.

In his letter to Spalatin, he wrote that he was already (having probably received it the day before) responding to Prierias's work and that it is "exactly like a wild, entangled jungle."*

The previous April the bishop had finally released Luther from his earlier promise to hold back from publishing his longer explanation of the theses—titled *Resolutions*—but after Luther had returned from Heidelberg, he needed time to polish this essay, so it was not until well into August that it appeared in print. Luther sent the publication to the bishop and with tremendous and obviously earnest humility said that it was entirely up to the bishop to delete whatever he wished or to destroy the whole piece of writing altogether. He was still confidently expecting that the church would know that he was a humble monk trying only to serve God's purposes and help Mother Church. He even wrote that if what he had written was not in the spirit of Christ, it should be destroyed.

Luther then mailed a copy of *Resolutions* to Staupitz with a long letter asking him—as the head of the Augustinian order—to forward the document to the pope in Rome. Indeed, the entirety of *Resolutions* was Luther's way of trying to make the case directly to the pope, over the heads of his parochially minded—and now he saw nasty and fanged—opponents. He made clear that he in no way wished to undermine the authority of the pope and the church. On the contrary, it was because he feared that the abuses of the indulgence preachers were doing that very thing that he was acting as he was. Luther then went at least one extra mile and dedicated the work to Pope Leo X himself. He made it clear that he knew his own name had been much sullied in the pope's hearing but said that he trusted Christ would lead the pope in understanding the vital matter before him. He also explained that it was never his wish that the Ninety-five Theses be widely distributed as they were, but because that had happened and because of all that had transpired as a result, he felt an obligation to speak out—"as a goose among swans"—and now he was doing so.

So here, in the late summer of 1518, ten months after posting the Ninety-five Theses, Luther was still hopeful of a happy reception of all he had to say. He had at last made his case directly to the Holy Father, and

---

* In the letter, which like so much of Luther's correspondence was written in Latin, he called Prierias's dialogue "Sylvester's dialogue," because Prierias's actual first name was Sylvester, and making a pun on the word *silvester*, which in Latin means "overgrown thicket."

whereas he was deeply humble, he made no concessions about what was quite clear to him. He knew that reform must happen in the church, and as far as he was concerned, he was doing his solemn duty as a doctor of the church in presenting his findings. His faith and courage to stand as he did at this juncture—somehow combining both deep humility and an almost arrogant boldness—were something to behold.

On August 28, he wrote to Spalatin,

> In all this I fear nothing, as you know, my Spalatin. Even if their flattery and power should succeed in making me hated by all people, enough remains of my heart and conscience to know and confess that all for which I stand and which they attack, I have from God, to whom I gladly and of my own accord entrust and offer all of this. If he takes it away, it is taken away; if he preserves it, it is preserved. Hallowed and praised be his name forever. Amen.[19]

The Advent of Melanchthon

Luther's many other duties in Wittenberg did not evaporate in the midst of the great controversy he had aroused. He remained bent on attracting the best faculty possible for the university, and at the tail end of that summer of 1518 he had attracted the best of all, in the shape of a very young man named Philip Schwartzerdt, whom history remembers by the Humanist sobriquet Melanchthon. He was escorted into Wittenberg by Spalatin, and with him came tremendous expectations.

Melanchthon was born on February 16, 1497. From the earliest age, he had distinguished himself as a linguistic prodigy and soon established himself as a brilliant Greek scholar. He was also the grandnephew of the great Humanist scholar Johannes Reuchlin. When young Philip's father and grandfather both died in a ten-day period, the eleven-year-old boy was sent to Pforzheim to live with his maternal grandmother, who was Reuchlin's sister. It is said that Reuchlin soon thought of the boy almost as his own son. It was Reuchlin who persuaded Philip to change his German surname Schwartzerdt to the Greek equivalent, Melanchthon, in the Humanist fashion of that time, in which all true Humanists reckoned themselves also to be citizens of ancient Greece and Rome, and therefore chose a Greek or Roman name.

Already at thirteen, he had entered the university at Heidelberg and published his first poem; at the age of fourteen, he tutored the local count's two sons. He took his bachelor's degree at fourteen as well and not much more than a year later applied for his master's—so that he could begin officially teaching at the university—but was denied this well-deserved opportunity "on account of his youth and his boyish appearance." Melanchthon was deeply hurt by this and therefore left for Tübingen. There he fell under the influence of the noted professor Johannes Agricola, a devoted Humanist.

But at Tübingen, Melanchthon often found himself bored by fabulistic sermons. One priest piously spoke of how the wooden soles of the Dominican monks' shoes were made from the actual Tree of Knowledge in Eden. For just such painful moments, Melanchthon carried with him a Latin Bible, which his great-uncle Reuchlin had given him. A number of times during especially sappy sermons he found himself thirsty for something from the Word of God and, finding none being poured from the pulpit, opened his own Bible and drank a goodly draught therefrom. Several times he was seen to do this, however, and was gravely scolded. After all, who did this saucy fellow think he was to read a Bible in church?

Things at Tübingen proved less than ideal in other ways, so when his great-uncle Reuchlin learned that Wittenberg was looking for a Greek scholar, he promptly and heartily recommended his young nephew for the post. When the call came from Frederick and Spalatin, Reuchlin wrote to Philip with the happy news:

> Lo! A letter has arrived from our gracious Prince, signed with his own hand, in which he promises you pay and favor. I will not now address you in the language of poetry, but will quote the faithful promise of God to Abraham: "Get thee out of thy country, and from thy kindred, and from the house of thy father, and go unto a land that I will show thee; and I will make thee into a great nation, and I will bless thee, and magnify thy name, and thou shalt be a blessing." So the Spirit tells me, and so I hope the future will be for you, my Philip, my work and my consolation.[20]

When he arrived at Wittenberg late in August, Melanchthon was a mere lad of twenty-one. He was already so renowned and sought after at that young age that when he stopped in Leipzig on his way to Wittenberg, the Leipzig faculty tripped over themselves to entice him to take a position with them. Even Erasmus in Rotterdam had raved about him. Not only was Melanchthon young, but he was also physically very slight and even now looked far more like a shy fifteen-year-old than what one might have expected in a university professor. Some weren't at all sure about him, having far preferred the Leipzig Humanist Peter Mosselanus for the job. On his arrival, Melanchthon was on the receiving end of a few snubs and heard some rascally students making fun of him. Perhaps they noticed one shoulder was lower than the other or had heard he was a stutterer. In any case, when he gave his inaugural address at Wittenberg four days later, he soon put all worries to rest and then some. His subject was the decline of learning under Scholasticism and how Humanism brought the promise of a new resurgence. Luther was mightily impressed. In his letter to Spalatin, he wrote,

> Four days after he had arrived, he delivered an extremely learned and absolutely faultless address. All esteemed and admired him greatly . . . [so w]e very quickly turned our minds and eyes from his appearance and person to the man himself. We congratulate ourselves on having this man and marvel at what he has in him. . . . I certainly do not wish to have a different Greek instructor as long as he is alive. I only fear that perhaps his constitution is not sturdy enough for the rough way of life in our region.[21]

The paintings of Melanchthon by Cranach make him look like an extremely frail, almost ethereal fellow, someone whom a strong gust of wind might handily blow clean to the horizon. In some of Cranach's later depictions, Melanchthon's overcoat seems four sizes too large, which, along with his unshaven and distracted look, gives him the grizzled appearance of an old rummy on the bum. His juxtaposition with Luther, who was fourteen years his senior, must seem comical, with Melanchthon playing the role of Leo Bloom to Luther's Max Bialystock. One is bookish, slim, and diffident; the other stout, brash, and folksy. Later in life, Luther took on the familiar ox-like physical appearance that suited his personality, and the two of them would make a spectacularly effective odd couple in the years ahead.

For now, however, Melanchthon's job was simply to teach the Wittenberg students Greek, and this he did, with a passion and brightness that drew them by the hundreds. He quickly became so popular that no

Lucas Cranach the Elder's portrait of Melanchthon lost in thought—and in a dramatically oversized coat—underscores both his scholarly detachment from the world as well as his ethereal frame. (Note Cranach's signature flying serpent glyph beneath the date.)

fewer than four hundred students—two-thirds of the entire student body at that time—were enrolled in his Greek class, but many more who were not in the classes would come too. Luther crowed about Wittenberg's victory to Spalatin: "His classroom is jammed with students. He especially makes all theologians zealous to study Greek—the most outstanding ones, as well as the average and the weak."[22]

CHAPTER SEVEN

The Diet at Augsburg

Now I must die. What a disgrace
I shall be to my parents!

—Martin Luther

L UTHER KNEW THAT if he was forced to go to Rome, he would face death. This was why he had appealed to Spalatin to see whether Frederick could be persuaded to push for having Luther's trial held in Germany. Once more we see how very clearly and almost exclusively political the papacy then was. Whereas today the pope is a religious figure and only the titular head of the Vatican state, the pope was at the time far more a prince—and at this time a prince in the worldly Florentine Medici mold—than anything else, so that his life's focus and that of those around him consisted principally of manipulating worldly power. The elegant evil of the Medici popes sometimes makes Machiavelli himself come across like a gap-toothed rube.

Frederick was already displeased with the way Rome was spending German money. The indulgence sellers were yet another way that German money was leaving Germany. So Rome was partly troubled by Luther's spicy attacks on indulgences because they fed into the larger narrative that already existed in the minds of many Germans regarding the church. Of course another way that Rome put a financial burden on Germans—and on Frederick—was via taxes. An imperial diet had already been scheduled that fall at Augsburg, for example, and at the top of the agenda was a so-called Turkish tax, which was supposed to help pay for the considerable military efforts against the Muslim armies, who had been expanding ever westward for many decades. Emperor Maximilian was hoping this would be approved, but it was mainly the pope who was pushing for it, and he planned to send one of his legates—the highly esteemed cardinal Cajetan—to the diet.

Another ingredient in this unpleasant stew was the election of the next emperor. Maximilian I was at this time in his late fifties, but he was in ill health and constant pain due to a particularly unpleasant fall from his horse. He additionally seemed to possess a strong morbid streak, as evidenced by the fact that he had for the previous four years traveled everywhere with his own coffin. Maximilian was also obsessed with ensuring that when he died, he would be succeeded by his grandson Charles I of Spain. His own son Philip the Handsome, who was Charles's father, had died in 1506. Maximilian wanted at all costs to prevent Francis I of France from becoming the next emperor, and he enlisted the help of the immeasurably wealthy Fugger family to bribe the seven electors in this direction. Frederick the Wise was also on the list of those who might well be the next emperor. But for his own reasons, Pope Leo X did not want Charles I to be the next emperor, so he felt obliged to remain on Frederick's good side.

In the middle of August 1518, Frederick assented to keeping Luther in Germany. He had Spalatin write to the emperor's counselor Renner, asking that Maximilian approve the idea, and therefore cancel the order that Luther travel the eight hundred miles to Rome. The emperor was betwixt and between in all of this, because the foul rumors about this troublemaker Luther had by now come to his ears, and from all he had heard, he knew that he wanted Luther to be stopped from promulgating these horrific heresies. What good could come of it? The nationalistic and territorial side of things was at issue too. The Italians must be held at bay in their obvious zeal to take over the empire and must be given periodic demonstrations of the limits of their power. So in the end, Maximilian decided that Luther should be tried not in Rome but in Germany. It was on decisions like this—which had little to do with what was right or wrong, but everything to do with what was politically expedient—that the future of the Reformation and Europe, and the world, would hinge.

The diet at Augsburg would begin at the end of September. The papal representative at the diet—Cajetan—was already planning to be in Augsburg to represent the Vatican on a host of other issues. Why not have him stay a bit longer and conduct this important trial between the monk Luther and the Holy Church at that time? Thus Luther was summoned to appear at Augsburg in early October. After the regular business of the diet had been concluded, the papal legate could meet with him and do with him as Rome liked.

The emperor himself had made his feelings known about Luther, vowing "to set a stop to the most perilous attack of Martin Luther on indulgences lest not only the people but even the prince be seduced."[1] He had to play this just right, to show himself as on the side of the church, but to assert his authority against the church politically, which is why he required the meeting to be under his jurisdiction and the watchful eye of his people at Augsburg, but in no way was he thought—or did he wish to be seen—to be protecting Luther and his rebellion.

Appearance at Augsburg, 1518, *Aetatis* 34

Luther was grateful not to be on his way to Rome, but the threat of what might happen to him in Augsburg was no less grave. It was every bit as important as any meeting in Rome could be, because at Augsburg Luther would at last face the very representative of the Holy Father himself, a cardinal who had all of the power of the pope in his hands to do what he liked with this monk who had brought shame to the church far and wide. Luther well knew that he might in a few days be condemned to death. His faith was strong, but from time to time deeply troubling thoughts coursed through his mind too. Years later he recalled his thoughts as he walked on the road to what might have been his own execution. "Now I must die," he had thought. "What a disgrace I shall be to my parents!"[2]

Cardinal Cajetan, who represented the pope at the diet, was a brilliant and illustrious theologian of that time. He was born Jacopo de Vio in the then-Neapolitan city of Gaeta, but as so often is the case with figures from this period, the nomenclature referring to him is complicated. When at the age of fifteen he took holy orders, Jacopo took the name Tommaso and was thenceforth known as Tommaso de Vio. But because people were often referred to by their place of origin, he was also known as Gaetanus—or by a version of that, Cajetan. So he is now mainly remembered as Thomas Cajetan or Cardinal Cajetan. What makes him particularly interesting as the figure chosen to deal with Luther at Augsburg is that during the Fifth Lateran Council (1512–17), Cajetan played a leading role and was the one to bring about a decree claiming that the pope's authority was indeed superior to that of church councils. After this, Pope Leo X made him a cardinal, and he remained a powerful and important figure in the church for many years.

At the diet in Augsburg, it was especially important that Cajetan succeed in persuading the German estates to agree to pay the Turkish tax. The Vatican desperately needed help in fighting the encroaching Islamic forces, and indeed desperately needed money in general. But from the beginning of the diet, the German princes were quite clear about their displeasure with the church's endless demands for money. Here again one sees the political and nationalistic forces that were never far from the surface of these events. So at this diet the German estates resoundingly chose not to pay the new Turkish tax. They declared they had had enough of these Crusades and fighting the infidels. As far as they were concerned, the church had taken advantage of their generosity in this, and in case there was any doubt, they put their grievances on this and other subjects in a document. In it they even went so far as to accuse the church of corruption, declaring that in "cases before the ecclesiastical courts the Roman Church smiles on both sides for a little palm grease." They also protested at how "German money in violation of nature flies over the Alps." And they complained about the poor quality of the priests sent to them in Germany, saying many of them were "shepherds in name only." On and on the grievances mounted as the humiliated Cajetan stood listening. It all ended with a simple plea: "Let the Holy Pope stop these abuses."[3]

But the only abuses the pope and Cajetan were eager to stop were the heresies being spouted by that "son of perdition" from Wittenberg named Martin Luther. So Leo had written a letter to Frederick, who as one of the seven electors was one of the most important figures at the diet. Leo hoped to use his papal powers of persuasion to turn Frederick—and with him the whole of the diet—in Rome's favor:

> Beloved son, the apostolic benediction be upon you. We recall that the chief ornament of your most noble family has been devotion to the faith of God and to the honor and dignity of the Holy See. Now we hear that a son of iniquity, Brother Martin Luther of the Augustinian eremites, hurling himself upon the Church of God, has your support. Even though we know it to be false, we must urge you to clear the reputation of your noble family from such calumny. Having been advised by the Master of the Sacred Palace that Luther's teaching contains heresy, we have cited him to appear before Cardinal Cajetan. We call upon you to see that Luther is placed in the hands and under the jurisdiction of this Holy See lest future generations reproach you with having fostered the rise of a most pernicious heresy against the Church of God.[4]

As we know, the main objectives for which Cajetan had come to Augsburg had eluded him, and the diet had officially ended. But now Cajetan must pivot to deal with Luther, the "weed in the Lord's vineyard." Frederick had succeeded in getting a private meeting between Luther and Cajetan, but he was afraid—and rightly so—that the emperor and Cajetan might conspire to seize Luther, put him in chains, and bundle him off to Rome. Therefore he did not agree to let Luther appear until the emperor promised "safe passage." But no sooner was the diet over than the emperor slipped away to go hunting. So now he must be tracked down and his promise given. Cajetan too had to promise and was offended at having been asked. But in the end both men gave their word. The private meeting between Cajetan and Luther was to take place at Cajetan's quarters, which were at the opulent Augsburg home of the fabulously wealthy Fuggers.

Luther left Wittenberg on September 25 and walked for twelve days, but on October 7, with only three miles to go before he reached Augsburg, he was stricken with such intense stomach pains that he could walk no farther. The physical ailments that struck him throughout his life were doubtless related to the stresses he faced, and we cannot wonder that as he came within a few miles of the site of what might be his condemnation to death, he suffered these difficulties. As it happened, the wagon of his friend Wenceslas Linck approached at the precise instant of his internal distress. Luther knew Linck well from Wittenberg, where they had been faculty colleagues, and of course Linck offered to carry his ailing friend the rest of the way. When Luther arrived in Augsburg, he felt somewhat better. There was no Augustinian monastery in Augsburg at that time, so it was arranged that he would stay at the Carmelite cloister. Luther knew the prior, John Frosch, who had studied in Wittenberg.

Spalatin had arranged things for Luther in advance of his arrival so that he was greeted and welcomed by a number of ecclesiastical luminaries, all of whom were interested in meeting this courageous monk who had dared to poke Rome in the eye with a sharp stick. As protocol demanded, Luther immediately informed Cardinal Cajetan that he had arrived in Augsburg, although the cardinal was not prepared to summon him quite yet. First Luther was asked to meet with Urban de Serralonga, who was an ambassador of the Margrave of Montferrat and a confidant of Cajetan's. Cajetan thought that perhaps Serralonga could soften Luther up and prepare him for what was expected of him in the meeting with the cardinal. Serralonga put himself forward to Luther as a kind-hearted mediator between Cajetan and him, but somehow Luther sniffed a cloying "Italian" odor in the whole affair. The son of Hans Ludher was not some uncouth bumpkin who would be so easily outfoxed by some unctuous ambassador.

Nonetheless, Serralonga would try. He first made it clear that Luther must do nothing at all but recant. It was all precisely that simple, and nothing must deviate from this simplest of courses. By no means whatever should Luther attempt to "joust" with the cardinal. After all, this would be unseemly. But Luther's harsh and blunt German character did not take well to Serralonga's sickly sweet—and perhaps he thought oily—advice. He told Serralonga that he was not interested in "recanting," unless he first be shown exactly where it was that he had erred—if he had erred—and of course someone must have thought he had erred, or the curia in Rome would not have gone to these rather extraordinary lengths. So Luther said that he must be shown where and how he had failed in his thinking, because someone must have a definite opinion on this, and then and only then could he proceed to the "recanting" part. But until then, there was obviously nothing for him to recant. As we shall see, this is a refrain that will be sung again and again in the course of this opera.

Serralonga had certainly not expected such stiff resistance. Were all Germans like this? He continued to play the role of friendly and moderate mediator, but the strain to do so began to show. He now made it very clear to Luther that the only issue to be concerned with was the pope's authority. If the pope had declared indulgences to be doctrinally sound, they were then by definition doctrinally sound. So Luther must simply recant that he had not accepted the pope's unquestioned authority. This was the heresy, of course, and any fool could see that. But Luther was no fool. For good measure, Serralonga now felt free to add that Frederick the elector would not be able to protect Luther any further if he did not give a full recantation, which might well have been untrue and which Luther likely suspected to be untrue. But Serralonga was insistent on this point. "Then where will you be?" he asked. Luther was rarely caught without a reply. "Under heaven," he cracked, with typical Saxon wit. With this remark, Luther at last discovered the elusive and bitter end of Serralonga's patience. The silken ambassador now made a contemptuous gesture revealing as much and whisked himself away.

Rather than mollifying him, Serralonga had only tempered Luther's steely spine. Luther was now the more determined to have his say with the cardinal, come what may. And if the cardinal wished to use the threat of papal power, Luther had an ecclesiastical card up his monk's sleeve: he would call for a church council. That ought to blow them out of their cassocks. Whether Luther knew that Cajetan had been the one to put forward the decree claiming the pope's power was superior to that of any council is another story. But he knew that the pope and Rome indeed claimed that the pope had more authority than any council, so Luther's calling for a church council would have been intentionally incendiary. But Luther knew how to throw bombs when bombs were called for, and if he should throw this one, the explosion would singe the very mane of Leo himself.

So on October 12, Luther traveled to the Fuggers' fabulous palatial residence, accompanied by three monks from the Carmelite monastery and by Wenceslas Linck. To look a bit more presentable than his usual academic, monkish self, he had borrowed Linck's more elegant cowl for the occasion.

Luther had been carefully instructed by Serralonga to abase himself in the cardinal's presence—literally to first prostrate himself, and then to rise to his knees, which he did. The cardinal graciously asked him to stand and then spoke. He said that he hoped to keep things short and simple. Of course this was not to be, and far from it. Cajetan was fourteen years Luther's senior, and in this meeting he intended to come across as fatherly and calm. He repeatedly called Luther "dear son," which probably only irked Luther. After Luther rose, the cardinal made his opening statement, doubtless delivered as though speaking to a wayward child. "You shook Germany with your theses on indulgences," he said. "If you wish to be an obedient son and please the pope, then recant. Nothing bad will happen to you, for I hear that you are a doctor of theology with many disciples."[5]

So despite the fatherly tone, the threat of torture and death was palpable, and Cajetan knew it. He had no reason to believe this should take very long to resolve. But here is another one of the rubs in the story, for Luther was certainly not about to recant, as we know from what he said to Serralonga, but as much as Serralonga and Cajetan had been instructed to tell Luther he could not have a dialogue with Cajetan, Cajetan himself had been instructed that he was not at liberty to have a dialogue either. So even if things shifted such that he wished to have some kind of meaningful discourse with Luther, he was really not free to do so. He had been given but one task, and that was to get this unbridled monk back in his bridle. Only that and nothing more. So Luther had no wiggle room, and neither did Cajetan. The Latin word for "recant," *revoco*, was all that was necessary. Luther would say this word, or he would be brought to Rome and presumably fed to the flames and, far worse, would be consigned to those infinitely more horrible flames that are eternal and that are reserved for the devil and his angels.

But Luther had not the dimmest idea of recanting. Instead, he shot immediately off script and did what he told Serralonga he would do: he asked Cajetan to show him his errors. How could he recant unless he knew what it was that he had said that required recanting? Show me the errors. It appears that Cajetan felt he had the freedom to go this far, so he rather quickly produced two that he thought should suffice. First, Luther had denied that the "treasury of the church" contained the "merits of Christ and the saints." And second, he had said that faith brought certainty of forgiveness, even before someone had officially received absolution from a priest of the church. Both were clearly contrary to church teaching. So Cajetan had shown him the two principal errors—and now what about that revocation we have been waiting for?

But Luther was not at all moved by the cardinal's words. There was much more to these things, and surely the cardinal knew it. The first issue, that Luther had denied that the "treasury of the church" contained the "merits of Christ and the saints," dealt with the idea that the good works of Christ and the saints not only had been sufficient to earn them their own salvation but had risen far beyond that, so that all of the "extra" merits their many good works had earned were put in the good keeping of the church's "treasury." Thus the church—which had been given the keys to that treasury, per Matthew 16:19—could open the vault at any time and give portions of this treasure to whomever it pleased. According to the church, this was its solemn prerogative. So when someone paid for an indulgence, the church was deputized by Christ to trade that payment for a bit of "heavenly treasure." Someone's money could be taken by the church in payment to forgive sins and could cancel moral debts.

Luther admitted that yes, he had indeed denied this, and then he asked the cardinal to show him where in the Bible this idea could be found. Luther meant not the idea that the church had been given the keys to the Kingdom of Heaven but more specifically the idea that the church was allowed to do as it had been doing with indulgences. What Scripture, he wondered, proved that Christ's merits were this treasury of merits that the church assumed they were? But at this point Cajetan did not turn to the Bible. Instead, he flourished a papal bull authored in 1343 by Pope Clement VI, hoping this authoritative decree would guide Luther toward a speedy revocation. Cajetan certainly did not expect to wrestle with the details of the antique bull. Here was the bull for all to see. It was canon law; therefore it was official and it was binding. Perhaps now that the questions had been answered, they might proceed to that revocation everyone had been so patiently awaiting. The cardinal was not about to be drawn into a debate, and he pushed Luther with every atom of his authority for a simple answer. "Do you believe this or don't you?" he asked over and over, and now with increasing volume.

But for Luther it was not at all simple. Luther's penchant for exactness on these matters was immovable to the point of marmoreal. He would never fudge a distinction or elide a point, because he knew that souls were at stake and he knew that his own soul was at stake because he had such an important position as a doctor of theology. He was himself responsible for those other souls. So the cardinal never got the simple yes or no, nor the "I revoke these things," he had been hoping for. At some stage in the pointless and escalating back-and-forth, Luther asked for a recess, and the meeting with the cardinal ended for the day.

Sometime that evening, Staupitz arrived from Nuremberg. He had come to assist Luther, and it seems he had arrived just in time. During this evening, he and Frederick's imperial advisers put their heads together with Luther, trying to decide what to do next. They determined that Luther should make a written defense. This would give clarity and form to the issues at hand. So the next day Luther and this group returned to Cajetan at the Fuggers' and requested that Cajetan allow Luther to provide something in writing. Surely something in writing on these two vital sticking points would spell things out more clearly. But Cajetan was firmly opposed to the idea. He was certainly not excited about another day passing without the precious revocation for which he had come. His brief was only to acquire it from Luther, in writing, and then to skip away back to Rome with it; end of story. The idea of prolonging the fatiguing bickering with this impudent monk for another day—and then the inevitable nightmare of wading into the slimy weeds of that defense—was hardly attractive. But in the end, Cajetan had no choice. Luther would not recant. So Cajetan must do what he could to move things along, agonizing as it surely was, and he reluctantly agreed to accept a written explanation.

On the third day, October 14, Luther returned to Cajetan's quarters with his retinue, now including Philip von Feilitzsch, one of Frederick's counselors who had come to Augsburg specifically to help Luther. Luther presented his written defense to Cajetan, and now Feilitzsch soberly repeated to Cajetan—"in the Sovereign's name"—what the emperor Maximilian had requested for Luther in the original bargain with Rome: fairness and lenience. But by now the cardinal had exhausted his reserves of decorum; so he blew up. Whatever ability he had to be calm and "fatherly" had been exceeded, and emotional shouting was the new order of the hour. Luther wrote his own account in a letter to Spalatin:

> In the end the Legate disdainfully flung back my little sheet of
> paper and yelled again for me to recant. He considered me
> defeated and refuted by a verbose and long speech which he drew
> from the stories of St. Thomas.* Almost ten times I started to
> say something and each time he thundered back and took over
> the conversation. Finally I started to shout too, saying, "If I
> can be shown that the [papal bull, *Unigenitus dei filius*] teaches
> that Christ's merits are the treasury of indulgences, then I will
> recant, as you wish." O God, how much gesticulation and
> laughter that caused!

The cardinal and those around him obviously thought Luther some straw-headed hick who had no idea with whom he was fencing. The papal decree of 1343 that Cajetan had produced the day before was a relatively obscure one, not always included in canon law, so Cajetan and his crew likely thought Luther would be unfamiliar with it and that he would perhaps gulp to see it and bug his eyes out, realizing that what he had denied was indeed clearly supported in a papal bull. And that would be the end of his confident posturing. But Martin Luther had not spent the last fifteen years shucking corn. He knew the bull very well indeed, and

---

* The cardinal, being a Dominican, was a fierce proponent of Scholasticism and Aquinas, but of course Luther had no love for Aquinas and would hardly have considered anything from his works to be dispositive.

countered brilliantly by informing the cardinal that the bull of 1343 said no such thing as the cardinal was maintaining that it said. Luther's account continues,

> Here I interrupted, "See, Most Revered Father, and consider carefully the word, 'He has acquired.' If Christ has acquired the treasury by his merits, then the merits are not the treasury; rather, the treasury is that which the merits earned, namely the keys of the church; therefore my thesis is correct."

Luther knew the Latin verb tenses of the papal decree and could hardly be bamboozled so easily. What it said was quite different from what the cardinal was implying it said. Luther continued his account, positively gloating:

> Here [Cajetan] was all of a sudden confused, and since he did not want to appear confused, he pushed on to other things and shrewdly wanted to bypass this subject. I, however, was excited and interrupted (I am sure quite irreverently), "Most Reverend Father, you should not believe that we Germans are ignorant even in grammar! There is a difference between 'there is' a treasury and 'to acquire' a treasury."

So Luther had bested Cajetan and somehow could not resist a witty nationalistic dig for good measure. But he was more interested in showing how the papal bull itself did not comport with Scripture. And yet in all of this, Luther's greatest fears were realized. He saw that the cardinal cared not a fig for the Holy Scriptures, and quite seriously maintained that church decrees superseded them. The theological foolishness of this, and the disturbing evidence of it, were horrifying to Luther. He saw now what he had deep down feared but had desperately hoped could not be true: that the greatest minds of the church were genuinely unaware of having become unmoored from the rock of the Scriptures and were even indifferent to this. They were blithely floating down the river toward a great cataract and didn't seem to notice that they had ever moved. Luther sincerely hoped that somehow he might waken them from their reveries and get them to see their danger so they might paddle to shore before it was too late.

The second "problem" that Cajetan had raised concerning Luther's claims was the idea that it was one's faith that produced God's forgiveness. Church teaching clearly implied that it was not the person's faith but the priest's act that followed the person's declaration of faith. The moment a priest granted absolution, the person asking forgiveness was forgiven. The church held the power of God to forgive, and this forgiveness could not exist outside the church exercising that power. It must be mediated through the church and could not happen without the church and the church's priest. It was the church, after all, that had been given the keys. But Luther said that this was not possible, because even if the priest were granting absolution, the person must in his heart have faith, else the priest's absolution was an empty religious act. It was the faith that mattered more than the priest's actions. Luther backed up his position with several scriptural references, the most notable being the one with which he has come to be most closely associated, Romans 1:17, which states, "For in the gospel the righteousness of God is revealed—a righteousness that is by faith from first to last, just as it is written: 'The righteous will live by faith.'"[6] It did not say or imply that the church must somehow be involved in this, nor did the other scriptural examples imply that. On the contrary. Luther was implying that the priest was really only ratifying what had already taken place between the believer and God by faith.

As these conversations proceeded, Cajetan became increasingly and impossibly furious. Eventually, it only remained for smoke to blast from his ears. Lest this happen, he contained his anger no longer and erupted, demanding that this presumptuous German monk leave his presence immediately, adding, "And do not return to me again unless you want to recant!"[7]

And so Luther left, along with Staupitz and the others, and then Luther and Staupitz had lunch. Meanwhile, Cajetan was fumbling with this frustrating puzzle before him. How could he get this monk to give him what he wanted? Having failed to get the German estates to agree to pay the Turkish tax, he might at least have this smaller victory in hand when he slunk back to Rome. But how to get it? After lunch, Cajetan summoned Linck and Staupitz to meet with him. Surely they would be more reasonable than this smart aleck Luther. Serralonga was there too, and both Cajetan and Serralonga labored for many hours to persuade Staupitz and Linck to persuade Luther to recant. They even together helpfully drafted a possible recantation that he might sign. Cajetan was mostly focused on the issue of papal authority—on the issue of the keys—and he said that he would not insist on the other theological points. But Staupitz and Linck could not bring themselves to trust Cajetan, so in the end nothing came of this meeting.

During this time, a rumor arose that the leaders of the Augustinian order would step in. After all, they were under the authority of Rome and could not have this lone wolf sullying their name across Christendom. Some even said the Augustinian leaders from Rome were on their way to Augsburg to seize both Linck and Staupitz. And presumably Luther too. It was at this point that Staupitz did something extraordinary: He summoned Luther and absolved him of his vow of obedience to him. This way they could now operate independently of each other. Luther therefore could no longer be guilty of disobeying Staupitz, and Staupitz could no longer be held responsible for Luther's actions. It was a brilliant and genuinely dramatic solution. After he did this, Staupitz—and Linck with him—departed Augsburg with almost comical haste. It was odd that they did so, for Luther was now alone, unsure of what exactly was to follow. Days passed with Luther cooling his heels in the Carmelite monastery, wondering what would come next.

Finally, Luther decided to do what Staupitz and the Saxon counselors had advised. He would make a formal appeal directly to the pope, and this he did. In it he made clear that he had expected a genuine hearing in Augsburg in which he could explain himself thoroughly and then be fairly judged, but this had never taken place. So he asked in this written appeal to the pope that he be given a new hearing and that the final decision on that hearing be made by the pope himself. Luther realized that no matter what happened, this appeal would at least give him further breathing room. But his remaining friends in Augsburg knew that at any moment he might be arrested and taken to Rome, so they urged him to flee their city as soon as possible. Luther agreed. But to cover his tracks, he sent a very humble letter to Cajetan, informing him of his leaving. His excuses for leaving were that the church had not condemned him with the clarity necessary for a recantation, and so of course a recantation was currently out of the question. On a much more practical note, he said that he was fresh out of money and was therefore now taxing the limited resources of the Carmelite brethren who were hosting him. He also told the cardinal the big news: that he had officially appealed to Rome. And having delivered himself of these things, he waited for a response from

Cajetan. But two days passed, and none came. The tension for him became unbearable. Was the silence because the cardinal was now secretly fixing to abduct Luther and bundle him south to Rome? Luther wasn't about to wait to find out. So he decided to make a run for it.

It was the evening of October 20. The city gates were all shut and locked, presumably to keep Luther from doing exactly what he was now doing. It seemed that they really were making plans to seize him soon. But Luther was not inclined to give them the opportunity. We cannot say for certain how he breached Augsburg's walled perimeter. He seems to have either slipped out via a small gate in the city's northern wall or perhaps somehow scrambled over the wall itself and found the appointed horse waiting for him on the other side. In any case, he somehow escaped the confines of the city, and then a sullen guard, appointed to the task, led him on his frantic ride through the night. The horse that had been lent to him—presumably at the behest of his Saxon friends—turned out to be a frisky nag, and the taciturn guide maintained a blistering pace, perhaps literally for his novice companion. Luther was far from accustomed to such travel and would be saddle sore for days afterward. They traveled a bone-rattling forty miles that night. When Luther dismounted, he was unable to stand. The next day they logged another forty-five miles. When Luther at last reached Gräfenthal, which was about halfway to Wittenberg, he was met by Count Albrecht of Mansfeld, who howled with laughter at Luther's disheveled appearance. On October 31, Luther at last reached Wittenberg and safety. But now what?

If he thought his letter of departure to Cajetan had solved anything, Luther was mistaken. On October 24, Cajetan wrote Frederick a letter demanding that Luther be turned over to Rome. Who did he think he was giving a cardinal the slip? For Cajetan, there was nothing else to be done. Luther had not recanted his heretical statements, and so he maintained and dearly believed that he must be turned over to the Vatican for justice. He had had his chance and had refused. One part of Luther's argument before Cajetan was that the church had never dealt with the subject of indulgences definitively and so he was doing his duty as a doctor of the church in bringing his hard questions on this subject, forcing the church to see the theological gaps that existed and that must be closed before they led to further grievous errors. He hoped that by demanding the church show him where he had erred, he would provoke the disputation he had been hoping for all along, and at last the church would plainly see that it had been allowing theologically erroneous practices to continue, practices that were leading the faithful astray—and that the church would be grateful to him for showing this to it, and that it would of course fix it. But for reasons history will never understand, Cajetan and the church could not perceive the situation along these lines at all. They were oddly stubborn, and for this reason the Reformation, which might well have been averted, went forward.

One clear example of this willful obstinacy was what Cajetan now did. Luther had argued that the church had never dealt definitively with indulgences, and as proof of this, he pointed out that there was no definitive papal document on the subject. Writing such a document would of course require the church to deal with the theology first, and in dealing with the theology, it would see the problems at hand. Again, this was the principal impetus for his Ninety-five Theses, to bring about a disputation and a reckoning with the theological problems. Furthermore, because no such document existed, how could the church accuse Luther of heresy? What papal document was there to point to that differed from what Luther had said?

So Cajetan, eager to shut the mouth of this German heretic as quickly as possible, rather perversely decided to produce such a document himself. He drafted it hastily and on November 9 sent it to Rome. But Cajetan's document did not in the least deal with Luther's sincere questions and objections and with the sincerely thorny issues that needed facing. Instead, it high-handedly—and theologically ex nihilo—invoked papal authority. In effect, it was a document that said, "You must now be silent and do as you are told. There will be no questions here. You have heard all you will hear. The great and mighty pope hath spoken."

Of course Luther was not fooled. He heard these attempts to shut him up not as the true voice of God but as a great and mighty hoax, as a machine belching smoke and fire. The smoke and fire came not from the holy mountain of a holy God but were produced by a group of small and fearful men pulling ecclesiastical and legalistic levers from behind red and gold curtains. They did not really have the power they were invoking at all—which is to say, the power and authority of God and truth—and Luther, like a certain small dog, had sensed this and was trying to tell the world, was barking and barking, and would not stop barking, and would in fact eventually pull back the curtain and to the wide world reveal the imperious and worldly chicanery at the black heart of it all.

Cardinal Cajetan found himself buffaloed by Luther's confidence. But Luther's confidence was no act. He had little doubt there really was a God who should be feared and to whose authority he and everyone should submit. To that God—and to truth and plain reason—Luther would listen. But unless Cajetan and the rest of them pointed to that God through his Scriptures and plainly showed Luther his error, he was quite immovable. Along these lines between Luther's position and the church's lay the great fault in the tectonic plates beneath history, and every day the pressure between them increased, which would soon enough lead to the seismic cataclysm ahead. Luther understood why he could not give an inch, but why could the papal powers not see things as he did so that they could solve the situation? What had he missed in all of this? But they could not or would not, and so now, over and over, with an obstinacy that cannot be fathomed, they single-mindedly continued to insist on nothing from this well-meaning monk beyond a single Latin word. One little word from him would end all the trouble. One little word would quell them. And the word was *revoco!*

The pressure on Frederick to turn over Luther was now increased, but for some reason he did not do so; rather he chose to protect him. Precisely why this is, we can never fully know. And of course we know that Frederick had himself invested much of his life and treasure in the idea of indulgences. But probably because of the advice of many Wittenberg theologians—and principally because of Spalatin, whom he trusted utterly—he chose to protect Luther from Rome. Still, Luther knew that by staying in Wittenberg, he was doing harm to Frederick's reputation. The situation had become yet more political. Rome understood that it had a full-blown public relations disaster on its hands and it must do everything possible to stem this rising tide of questions and scandal, which was reducing the power and authority of the church by the day and would have dramatic consequences in every direction. Perhaps most disturbingly, it would affect the upcoming election of the new emperor. As we have said it was vital to Rome that the young Charles I of Spain— who was the grandson of Ferdinand and Isabella of Spain—not be elected. His power if elected would be so considerable that Rome worried it would be overwhelmed. This was so important that Rome clearly put the politics of this situation above "truth" and theological clarity. There was an imperial election coming up, and that now must take precedence over all else, and did.

So Rome made the fatal decision to put all of its chips on this political line. The past and the future be damned. The present now throbbed for attention. So the church needed Luther to come to Rome so that it could get him to recant—or face the fiery consequences. To this end, it put as much pressure as possible on Frederick to distance himself from Luther and turn the troublesome renegade over to Rome. But just what could Rome do to convince Frederick?

Meanwhile, Luther saw this was happening, but to his inestimable credit he put Frederick above himself. He resolved that to get Frederick out of the line of fire, he would leave Wittenberg and Saxony. He knew he would be putting himself in tremendous danger, but out of respect for his sovereign, and with full faith in the God whose truth he desperately meant to uphold, he would go. It is another example of Luther's faith that despite having no idea what lay ahead for him, he would do the noble thing and trust in God. In a letter to Spalatin on November 25, he wrote,

> I daily expect the condemnation from the city of Rome; therefore I
> am setting things in order and arranging everything so that if it
> comes I am prepared and girded to go, as Abraham, not knowing
> where, yet most sure of my way, because God is everywhere. But I
> will of course leave a farewell letter; see to it that you have the courage
> to read the letter of a man who is condemned and excommunicated.
> Farewell for now, and pray for me.[8]

Staupitz was by this time in Salzburg, Austria, and in an extraordinary letter he invited the reprobate Luther to take refuge with him there:

> The world hates the truth. By such hate Christ was crucified, and what
> there is in store for you today if not the cross I do not know. You have few
> friends, and would that they were not hidden for fear of the adversary.
> Leave Wittenberg and come to me that we may live and die together. The
> prince is in accord. Deserted, let us follow the deserted Christ.[9]

That this man who had so early seen the genius and promise of Luther would now encourage him in this fashion, by equating the papal power of Rome with the "world" that hated and killed the Savior—and with the Pharisees who had conspired to execute Jesus, and with the Roman mob that called for Barabbas—is simply astonishing. He seems very clearly to have made the distinction in his mind between the true church of God and that vast bureaucratic political entity centered in Rome called the church. But what is more astonishing still is that despite this perfect clarity about the situation Staupitz never followed Luther out of the church but faithfully remained there until his death. This must at least convince any objective observer of this history that there were deeply principled and godly men on both sides of the great and coming divide.

As for Luther, he had no idea what the future held, for him or for the church he loved and for which he wept. But he knew that what was happening in Rome was a horror and a disgrace. There had always been corruption, but this was the end. How could it writhe away from something so simple, something that would doubtless help it in the long run? That December, he wrote to his friend Wenceslas Linck, "I think I can demonstrate that today Rome is worse than the Turk."[10] For an Augustinian monk to see that things had moved to where the center of Western Christendom was doing more harm to the name of Christ than the Islamic warriors making their way west with frightening force and violence said much. But Luther was finally sensing that Rome was simply not inclined to do what it must.

And he was right, for as he wrote this, the Roman church had already made its decision not to accept Luther's pleas for change and openness, but rather to do whatever was necessary to stanch the widening and harmful scandal, and quickly. Nothing mattered as much. Still, what could Rome do to get the elector of Saxony to comply? There was one thing it might do—dangle in front of Frederick, that ardent lover of relics, something nearly irresistible to him. It could hold before him the prospect of receiving an inimitable and unique and fabled honor of honors. It might offer to give him the Golden Rose of Virtue.

The Golden Rose of Virtue

Inasmuch as the Vatican operated like a political power, we should not be shocked that it occasionally dangled and proffered such allurements as it might. It would be vulgar to call them bribes. One such allurement that the Vatican from time to time awarded to especially loyal "friends" was something called the Golden Rose of Virtue. In the hierarchy of Rome's arsenal, the Golden Rose was the daisy cutter, the Blessed Mother of All Dangled Allurements.

And because Rome decided that it desperately needed to get on the good side of Frederick the Wise of Saxony for several reasons—to gain his favor with regard to the selection of the next emperor, to get his approval of the so-called Turkish tax, and, almost certainly the most important of all at this time, to get him to turn over that rascal in a monk's habit who had turned the world upside down over indulgences—it was decided to confer upon this most loyal son of the church this exceedingly gracious favor. Thus was a papal nuncio named Karl von Miltitz now deputized to deliver this fragrant object.[11]

The pope's letter to Frederick read,

> Beloved son, the most holy golden rose was consecrated by us on
> the fourteenth day of the holy fast. It was anointed with holy oil
> and sprinkled with fragrant incense with the papal benediction. It
> will be presented to you by our most beloved son, Carl von Miltitz,
> of noble blood and noble manners. This rose is the symbol of the
> most precious blood of our Saviour, by which we are redeemed.
> The rose is a flower among flowers, the fairest and most fragrant
> on earth. Therefore, dear son, permit the divine fragrance to enter
> the innermost heart of Your Excellency, that you may fulfill
> whatever the aforementioned Carl von Miltitz shall show you.[12]

Whether there has ever been a more shameless, flowery, and "fragrant" bribe in the history of the world, we leave to others. But in truth, it was likely more a carrot than a bribe, because the rose was never quite delivered with the hopeful expectation that Frederick would get in line but was rather held before him as a promise, with the implication that it would come into his possession if he should finally come to his senses and cooperate. Frederick himself said this: "Miltitz may refuse to give me the golden rose unless I banish the monk and pronounce him a heretic."[13] Meanwhile, the *objet* would be held safely in the Fuggers' palace in Augsburg.

On his way to this assignment, Miltitz was loaded for bear. He had with him letters speaking very clearly and harshly about Luther, calling him a "child of Satan, son of perdition, scrofulous sheep, and tare in the vineyard," and so on.[14] But a strange thing happened as Miltitz made his way to Saxony with his arsenal of papal *brèves* and the fabled Golden Rose. Everywhere he stopped along the way, he saw that the public sentiment in Germany was disturbingly, was overwhelmingly for Luther. When he arrived in Nuremberg on December 18, Miltitz met with Scheurl, who confirmed this unpleasant development, and Scheurl used this information to influence Miltitz to take a somehow more conciliatory approach. Scheurl then put himself forth as a mediator, informing Spalatin that Luther should accept Miltitz's requests in a friendly way. Scheurl clearly felt this was the only way forward that could avoid the disaster of Luther's being sent to Rome and branded a heretic, while at the same time it would not require Luther to recant, which anyone who understood him knew he clearly would never do.

We see in Scheurl's meeting with Miltitz how much more complicated the situation was than we might be inclined to believe. Miltitz explained to Scheurl that Rome was in fact highly displeased with Tetzel's indulgence sermons, which had caused the whole mess. Miltitz went so far as to declare Tetzel a *Schweinehund* (literally "pig dog"). Miltitz even said that the highly vaunted Prierias had himself been dressed down by Rome for his hastily written response to Luther's writing. And he explained that it was mostly Luther's widely disseminated *Sermon on Indulgences and Grace* that had everyone up in arms, for it had been widely circulated in German, and had therefore greatly damaged the church in the eyes of the faithful.

In this, we observe how this thing that would come to be called the Reformation progressed due to forces beyond the control of the principal players. The new technology of printing and the subsequent hunger for printed works catapulted many of Luther's writings to distances and into places he had no intention of their going. When he had his *Sermon on Indulgences and Grace* printed, he had no idea it would get the traction that it did and spread his ideas far and wide without any context, and end up injuring the church. We can never know if the way such things happened harmed the cause of reformation or whether without such things happening the Reformation itself would ever have taken place at all.

Miltitz met with Luther on January 5, 1519, in Altenburg, presumably at the castle. He was shocked at how young Luther seemed. Luther was at that time thirty-five, but Miltitz was himself only twenty-eight. Our account of how things went at this early and extremely important meeting comes from Luther himself. In a letter to Spalatin, written February 20, Luther explained that Miltitz was sent to do everything he could to fix the situation. In what was clearly a very friendly fashion, Miltitz entertained Luther at dinner, and as they departed, Miltitz had affectionately kissed him. But it is an interesting early snapshot of Luther's personality that Luther did not go for this, saying he saw through "this Italian act and insincerity." We don't know whether this was because of his more emotionally restrained German constitution and training, or Luther's own fundamental distrust of anything outside the strict adherence to the theological matters at hand—which obviously were of such paramount importance to him that they were not worthy of being confused with glad-handing and getting-to-know-you nonsense.

At the end of 1518, Rome had been playing hardball with Frederick, demanding Luther be sent to Rome, where it would hold his feet and the rest of him to the literal fire. But now that the election of the new emperor was imminent, Rome suddenly chose to soften its approach. Let us not be too hasty, it seemed to say. After all, mayn't we come to some sort of amicable agreement? So it sent Miltitz to Saxony to see what was possible. On the one hand, he would graciously dangle the Golden Rose before Frederick, and while he was in the neighborhood, he would meet with that incorrigible nuisance Luther, whom he would push as hard as possible to do whatever was necessary, short of a public revocation. Luther could avoid Rome and the flames, but Miltitz would demand a number of things from him.

In a letter to Frederick after the meeting, Luther explained what Miltitz had required of him. First, Luther must agree to be silent about indulgences if his opponents (Tetzel and Archbishop Albrecht) also agreed to stop attacking him on that subject. The ongoing harm that had been done to the church's authority and reputation via Luther's writings, which had been dispersed extremely widely, must cease. Second, Luther must humble himself to the pope's authority and write the pope a letter toward this end. Third, Luther must write "a little book" that would "admonish everyone to follow the Roman church, to be obedient and respect it, and to understand my writings as having been intended to bring not dishonor but honor to the holy Roman Church."[15] Fourth, he would not insist that his case be adjudicated by the pope himself, as he had requested in his appeal to the pope, but would accept the archbishop of Salzburg as the one to make the final decision. Feilitzsch and Spalatin had been behind suggesting this, and it is believed that the archbishop to whom they were referring was Matthäus Lang of Augsburg, whom they trusted and whom we remember from Baraballo's "coronation."

Somewhat amazingly Luther agreed to all these terms and wrote his letter to Pope Leo from the Altenburg castle on either January 5 or January 6. It is an extraordinary document:

Most Holy Father:

Necessity again forces me, the lowest of all men and dust of the earth, to address myself to Your Holiness and August majesty. May Your Holiness therefore be most gracious and deign to lend your ears in a fatherly fashion for a short time, and willingly listen to the bleating of this, your little sheep, for you truly stand in the place of Christ.

The honorable Sir Charles Miltitz, chamber secretary to Your Holiness, has been with us. In the presence of the Most Illustrious Sovereign Frederick, he very harshly accused me in the name of Your Holiness of lacking respect for and being rash toward the Roman church and Your Holiness, and demanded satisfaction for this. Hearing this, I was deeply grieved that my most loyal service has had such an unhappy outcome and that what I had undertaken—to guard the honor of the Roman church—had resulted in disgrace and was suspected of all wickedness, even so far as the head of the church was concerned. But what am I to do, Most Holy Father? I do not know what to do further: I cannot bear the power of your wrath, and I do not know of any means to escape it. The demand is made that I recant my theses. If such a revocation could accomplish what I was attempting to do with my theses, I would issue it without hesitation. Now, however, through the antagonism and pressure of enemies, my writings are spread farther than I ever had expected and are so deeply rooted in the hearts of so many people that I am not in the position to revoke them. In addition since our Germany prospers wonderfully today with men of talent, learning, and judgement, I realize that I cannot under any circumstances recant anything if I want to honor the Roman church—and this has to be my primary concern. Such a recanting would accomplish nothing but to defile the Roman church more and more and bring it into the mouths of the people as something that should be accused. See, Father, those whom I have opposed have inflicted this injury and virtual ignominy on the Roman church among us. With their most insipid sermons, preached in the name of Your Holiness, they have cultivated only the most shameful avarice. . . .

Most Holy Father, before God and all his creation, I testify that I have never wanted, nor do I today want, to touch in any way the authority of the Roman church and of Your Holiness or demolish it by any craftiness. On the contrary I confess the authority of this church to be supreme over all, and that nothing, be it in heaven or earth, is to be preferred to it, save the one Jesus Christ who is Lord of all—nor should Your Holiness believe the schemers who claim otherwise, plotting evil against this Martin.

Since in this case I can do only one thing, I shall most willingly promise Your Holiness that in the future I shall leave this matter of indulgences alone, and will be completely silent concerning it (if [my enemies] also stop their vain and bombastic speeches). In addition I shall publish something for the people soon to make them understand that they should truly honor the Roman church, and influence them to do so. [I shall tell them] not to blame the church for the rashness of [those indulgence preachers], nor to imitate my sharp words against the Roman church, which I have used—or rather misused—against those clowns, and with which I have gone too far. Perhaps by the grace of God the discord which has arisen may finally be quieted by such an effort. I strive for only one thing: that the Roman church, our mother, be not polluted by the filth of unsuitable avarice, and that the people be not led astray into error and taught to prefer indulgences to works of love. All the other things I consider of less importance, since they are matters of indifference. If I can do anything else, or if I discover that there is something else I can do, I will certainly be most ready to do it.[16]

Rather tragically, Luther's letter to Pope Leo was never sent by Miltitz, who instead offered to write to the pope himself. But it is nonetheless a staggering and remarkable document for several reasons, not least that it shows that even at this late date, more than a year after what many now celebrate as the beginning of the Reformation, the Reformation seems to have still been eminently avoidable. Luther was obviously very sincerely attached to the church and had not at all been threatened into making these conciliatory and humble remarks, but hoped to do as little damage to the church as possible. He believed this possible at this juncture. But this pacific denouement was not to be.

We also see in this letter that in the line in which Luther asserts that nothing is to be preferred to the authority of the church—"save the one Jesus Christ who is Lord of all"—he is still rather clearly implying that these two are not the same thing, that daylight might shine between them. It was Luther's sly and theologically correct maintenance here of the existence of this crack, however slight, betwixt the church itself and the Lord himself, that would cause all the trouble ahead. Because to suggest that the church did not automatically speak with the voice of God was to suggest that the church could err. This would always be the sticking point and Luther would not even in this otherwise deeply humble letter remove that point.

But Luther now expected that he would at long last get the fair hearing he had been seeking, and he reckoned that the archbishop of Salzburg would probably be the judge. But what happened in the meantime would affect that too. And then, on January 12, the news came that the emperor had died. Years later, Luther recalled that with the earthshaking news of Maximilian's death "the storm ceased to rage a bit."[17]

CHAPTER EIGHT

The Leipzig Debate

A simple layman armed with Scripture is to be
believed above a pope or a council without it.

—Martin Luther

A plague on it!

—Duke George the Bearded

A s progress on Luther's case had slowed down in Rome and
the Vatican, things again heated up in Germany. Luther had
written his response to Eck's *Obelisks*, titled *Asterisks*, but he
had intended this to be rather private, along with their larger disagreement. And it had been, until Luther's somewhat bumbling Wittenberg
colleague Andreas Karlstadt had on his own accord—and without telling Luther—replied to Eck publicly, with his own 406 (*sic*) Theses.
Karlstadt sometimes seems to have been angling to upstage Luther, but
whatever his reasons for doing this, it was now unhelpful in the extreme, and the banked fires of the disagreement with Eck once more
flared up. This was because Eck now felt compelled to respond publicly. Eck's response to Karlstadt—titled *Response*—appeared in mid-
August 1518.

But Eck now escalated things dramatically. For some reason, he no
longer was interested in a quiet academic dispute in writing between the
universities of Wittenberg and Ingolstadt but rather in something more
like a colossal public spectacle. On the title page of his *Response*, he called
for a debate that should be decided by no less a person than the pope
himself, which should be held at the university of Paris or Cologne—or
Rome! He thought early April of the following year, 1519, would be about

*A portrait of Andreas
Bodenstein von Karlstadt.*

right for the date but said he would allow Karlstadt to decide the venue. The Wittenbergers thought that something closer to home would be far less expensive, not to mention theologically friendlier, so they suggested either of the universities at Erfurt or Leipzig. Eck chose Leipzig and immediately asked Duke George of Saxony for permission.

Duke George (also known as George the Bearded) was the son of Albert the Brave, who was the brother of Frederick's father, Ernest. George and Frederick were therefore cousins who continued the often acrimonious rivalry of their fathers. So for George the debate was a capital opportunity to show the superiority of his Leipzig University theologians—who were to judge it—over Frederick's Wittenberg theologians. He also simply disliked his cousin and resented his increasing political power. He openly sneered at Frederick's weak-kneed tolerance of the rebellious Wittenberg theologians, especially this Luther. But when Duke George discovered that his own Leipzig theologians were for several reasons unwilling to do their duty and host the debate, George the Bearded was enraged. He was a no-nonsense fellow who wouldn't countenance their fussy objections. When the local bishop opposed the debate too, Duke George roared, "What good is a soldier if he is not allowed to fight, a sheep dog if he may not bark, and a theologian if he may not debate?"[1] He fulminated against the lot of them as gluttonous and lazy and declared, "If the theologians at Leipzig cannot stomach these debates and are afraid of losing them, they should be replaced by old women who are paid to sing and spin yarn for us!"[2] In the end, the theologians complied.

All along it was Luther whom Eck really wished to debate, not Karlstadt. The duplicity of Eck's crabwise approach infuriated Luther. In a letter to Spalatin, he wrote,

> Our Eck, that little glory-hungry beast, has published a small sheet of paper regarding his planned debate with Karlstadt at Leipzig. . . . That foolish man obliquely attempts to satisfy his long-standing grudge against me, naming one person as contestant yet attacking someone else who has to handle the whole affair, he storms against me and my writings. I am fed up with that man's senseless deceit.[3]

Indeed, the Twelve Theses Eck now proposed as subjects for the debate made it loud and clear that he had Luther in his sights far more than Karlstadt. One of these theses concerned Luther's contention—which he had made in his *Resolutions*—that it was not until the reign of Pope Sylvester in the early fourth century that the Roman church had put itself forward as above all other churches. Thus the claim that the church's and the pope's authority was total—and essentially no different from the authority of Jesus himself—was erroneous. Luther was furious that Eck had underhandedly slipped this into the debate, because Luther had never meant to speak publicly about this most provocative of all subjects. But the overzealous Karlstadt's actions had allowed Eck an opportunity to shove these things out into the open, for all to see. Luther had not publicly spoken about his views of canon law and the fallibility of the church's "decretals"—those official documents that, like the one Cajetan had recently authored on indulgences, Luther did not accept as binding in the way that the Scriptures were binding. Nor did he wish to embarrass the church and further inflame the situation by speaking about this issue. But thanks to Karlstadt, there was now no going back and Luther knew it. Against his own inclinations, things had now entered a new and more public stage. Though he certainly didn't like it, he nonetheless felt that somehow God must be behind these strange developments, pushing him forward.

So now Luther felt obliged to answer Eck's theses with his own counter-theses and did not shrink from being combative. He boldly reasserted the idea that our own good works were nothing apart from God's grace. He also seriously questioned the doctrine of purgatory and again attacked the idea of indulgences. But then he saw Eck's theses and raised him one extra thesis. This one concerned the primacy of the Roman church and the limited authority of the papacy. It stated, "That the Roman church is superior to all others is proved only by the utterly worthless decrees of the last 400 years. Against these stands the testimony of the authentic history of 1,100 years, the text of Holy Scriptures, and the decree of the council of Nicaea, the holiest of all councils."[4] This was because it was at the Council of Nicaea that the Eastern Orthodox Church and the Western Roman Church had been declared equal.

As the debate drew near, things heated up more and more. For one thing, Luther still had not received official permission to participate from the cranky Duke George, who certainly disliked him for being in the camp of George's rival cousin, Frederick. So it wasn't until the time of the actual debate in June that Luther was sure he would be allowed to debate at all. For another, Eck and Luther had a number of ugly written exchanges in which Luther accused Eck of being interested not in truth but in flagrant showboating. He called him "a prankster and a sophist,"[5] and it is clear that he had been hurt by his former friend's vicious attacks. Eck fired back by saying that anyone who attacked the beloved church could be no friend, that his first responsibility was to defend the church.

Luther's friends—and Karlstadt too—all thought that his raising the white-hot topic of papal supremacy was ill-advised and did all they could to dissuade him from bringing it into this debate. Spalatin was especially forceful, thinking something so impolitic could lead only to trouble. But Luther would not be moved. "I beg you, my Spalatin," he said, "do not fear anything and do not let your heart be torn to pieces by human considerations. You know that if Christ were not leading me and my case, I would have been lost long ago."[6] The way things had transpired had galvanized Luther profoundly. In his mind, there was no doubt that the truth would win, whatever became of him. He had not asked for this fight, but neither could he hide from it. The more he saw that the facts were on his side, the more emboldened he was to present them, to uphold the truth. What especially irked him was the idea that the church—and Eck—were twisting the Scriptures to make their silly points. If only they hadn't done that, his sense of justice would not have been so provoked, but this was far beyond the pale, and he felt he must expose it.

And the further Luther looked into this specific issue of papal primacy in preparation for the debate, the more horrified he became. In March 1519, he focused especially on the subject, tracing it carefully in canon law and church history, and the more he uncovered, the more convinced he was that he must pull this pernicious lie out root and branch. Because during this time he wasn't yet sure that Duke George would allow him to debate, he published his *Resolution on the Thirteenth Thesis Concerning the Power of the Pope*. He was sure the papacy was not against God's will, but neither did he think it was ordained by God, as the church now maintained. All he read made it clearer and clearer that it was a human institution. It was not possible from Scripture to find any evidence that it had been divinely ordained. This was the issue, and by declaring otherwise, the current pope—and such as Cajetan and Eck—had put the papacy on impossibly rotten foundations. If one loved the church, one must fix this, and Luther would do so. That month seems to have been a turning point for Luther. It was on March 13 that he whispered to Spalatin, "I know not whether the pope is the Antichrist himself or whether he is his apostle, so miserably is Christ (that is, the truth) corrupted and crucified by the pope in the decretals."[7]

It is clear that the fire of this growing crisis and now the specific pressure to prepare for this debate were forcing Luther theologically forward into places he had never intended to go. But in it all, he somehow understood that the Lord's hand was pushing him along. And Luther's years of teaching the Bible gave him an unwavering confidence as he proceeded. He had started with indulgences but was now confronting the thorniest of all issues, that of papal authority itself. He came to see that the Roman church, while certainly an institution of God, could not plausibly claim utter authority as it had been doing for four hundred years. And certainly not from Scripture. For Luther, it was faith (*pace* Romans 1:7) that created the Christian and the body of Christians, called the church. Wherever faith existed in Christ, all followed, including beyond the Roman church, which is to say in the Eastern Greek church as well.

Therefore, by themselves, without faith, the sacraments and the church were empty and must no longer pretend otherwise. It was faith in Christ that was the foundation for the church, and this faith did not come from us, who were all broken sinners, but was a free gift from God. So to bend the Scriptures to claim that the human institution of the Roman church was inevitably and undeniably divine was itself heresy and an abomination. The more he stared at what was in front of him, so clear and so awful, the more he became convinced that the church had for four hundred years been in a kind of Babylonian captivity, just as Israel had been. And if he like a prophet did not point this out and call for the church to repent and return to God's truth, he would himself be guilty. He therefore had no fear in doing so.

In anticipation of the debate, which was to be a sprawling three-week affair beginning at the end of June, Karlstadt was already in January working with Lucas Cranach to create an ambitious piece of heavy-handed early print propaganda. It would also have served as an advertisement for the spectacle several months away. It was a large satirical woodcut cartoon that would come to be known as *Karlstadt's Wagon*. It depicted two processions, each composed of a team of horses pulling a wagon. Both were extremely crowded with figures and superimposed explanatory bubbles of text. The text of the first edition was in Latin, but soon a second edition appeared in German. The upper half of the divided poster depicted a procession leading to Jesus, who was labeled "*Unser Fri[e]d*" (Our Peace), and featured God the Father hunched unobtrusively in the wagon, which crushed a simian devil under its unrelenting wheels. But the procession in the lower half was marching directly into hell itself through a monstrous pair of gaping jaws filled with flames, grotesque demons, and some of the writhing damned. And who was in this wagon, smiling and accompanied by a shaggy, backward-facing demon? Who but Eck himself, and if anyone was unclear about Eck's theology, he had been helpfully labeled as "*Eigner Wil*" (My Own Will).

The Leipzig Debate Begins, *Aetatis* 35

The debate itself was slated to begin June 27, but on that very same day the imperial diet had chosen the nineteen-year-old scion of the Hapsburg dynasty, Charles I of Spain, as the new Holy Roman emperor. He replaced his deceased grandfather, Maximilian I, and would himself become

Emperor Charles V. The German estates at the diet had initially chosen none other than Saxony's own Frederick the Wise, but Frederick knew that any German prince would not have sufficient power to maintain the empire properly, so he self-sacrificially threw his vote to the young Charles of Spain, even though Pope Leo had desperately hoped he would not do this. History has often praised Frederick as the consummate statesman, more concerned with what and whom he governed than with himself, and this is a clear example of that. But because the new emperor would be too occupied with duties in Spain to bother much with Germany, Frederick's great importance to Leo did not change much afterward.

Because the debate would last three weeks and the late June weather was glorious, vast numbers of people hiked to Leipzig from great distances to enjoy the rare spectacle. Eck himself arrived with his servant on June 22, to no fanfare. But his timing was perfect, because the following day was the city's Corpus Christi festival,* an important local event, and it was shrewd of Eck to participate. He processed in his ecclesiastical chasuble and doubtless ingratiated himself with the locals. He also lodged with the mayor of the city during his stay, so there was little doubt who would have the home advantage in the upcoming contest.

Two days later, the Wittenberg contingent made their comparatively grand entrance via the city's Grimma gate. Karlstadt was in the first wagon, and he had brought with him such a mountainous library of books that the wagon groaned with their weight. The second wagon bore Melanchthon and the rector of the University of Wittenberg, along with Luther himself. Also part of this procession were Johannes Agricola and Nicholas von Amsdorf, both of whom were Wittenberg colleagues to whom Luther was close and who would figure prominently in the Reformation in the years ahead. But the most extraordinary aspect of this moving assemblage were the two hundred rowdy Wittenberg students who had come along too, carrying fearsome-looking halberds (also called pikes or battle-axes) as they walked. Many of them also carried staves (or spears).

In an unintended and unpleasant reminder of the eponymously named woodcut that he had created with Cranach, Karlstadt's wagon, doubtless due to its preposterous burden of reference literature, got stuck in the mud just outside the city gate and suddenly broke its axle. The hapless Karlstadt was thus indecorously pitched headlong into the mud and

---

* A religious festival held in many countries around the world in which the body and blood of Christ are celebrated.

understandably shaken. Was this a bad omen? The accident was of such violence that many believed it accounted for Karlstadt's less than stellar performance in the days ahead.

One of Duke George's court clerics, a certain Jerome Emser,* thought it unfortunate that the Wittenberg team had arrived with such pomp and circumstance, whereas Eck had had none, so he took it upon himself to organize an honor guard to be present for Eck's first official appearance. The horde of Wittenberg students had clearly traveled here to cheer on their professors, but they seem also to have intended to generally cause mischief. One night they staged a boisterous hullabaloo outside the mayor's home, where Eck himself was staying, which they certainly knew. For the remaining days of the debate, a guard was posted there.

As for Luther, he stayed at the house of the printer Melchior Lotter, who would make a mint from Luther's writings over the years ahead. Luther also was entertained at the homes of two prominent citizens. But for the most part, he and his colleagues were treated with derision. "The citizens of Leipzig," he later wrote, "neither greeted nor called on us but treated us as though we were their bitterest enemies." As if that weren't enough, whenever Luther entered a Dominican church, the clerics hustled the monstrance bearing the host away, as though Luther presented a grave threat to it. At some point during the three weeks, Duke George himself had a private conversation with Luther in which he felt free to bluntly criticize some of Luther's views. And as if to assure Luther he was the dunderhead some suspected, he easily solved the thorny theological question of papal authority by gruffly declaring, "Whether by divine or by human right, the pope is still the pope!"[8]

Before June 27, the two parties needed to settle the terms of the debate. Eck strongly lobbied for the "Italian" style of debate, which was more freewheeling, but Karlstadt did not agree to it. They then had to decide who would be the judges. Luther's view was that theologians were typically already set in their views, so he hoped not just the theological faculty but the entire faculty of the university could participate. Luther knew that he was more likely to find common sense and fair judgment outside the predictably hide-bound Scholastic theologians. But Eck was hostile to the idea. "Why then don't you refer the case to shoemakers and tailors?" he blurted.[9] The eminently practical Duke George agreed and

---

* Emser's coat of arms boasted a goat's head, so that when he became Luther's bitterest antagonist, Luther thenceforward invariably referred to him as "the goat Emser."

promptly shot the suggestion down. And so the theologians would be the sole judges of the debate.

When June 27 dawned, the debate proceedings began with great ceremony. At 6:00 a.m., there was a worship service at the Church of St. Thomas, where a twelve-part Mass was sung. The company then proceeded to the thirteenth-century Pleissenburg castle. Because there was no space in the university large enough for all who wished to attend, the castle courthouse would serve as the debate site. The room was duly festooned with tapestries, and seventy-six local citizens stood guard. Two lecterns faced each other. Eck's bore the image of the dragon slayer Saint George, whereas the Wittenbergers' bore the image of Saint Martin. Each morning's disputation began at 7:00 and ended at 9:00. The afternoon's session ran from 2:00 to 5:00. But on this first day, the events began with an oration of more than two hours, given by the Leipzig Humanist and Greek scholar Peter Mosselanus. In it he took great pains to warn the debaters not to wrangle indecently but long-windedly instructed them to debate God's truth in a manner befitting the subject. Duke George was stunned such things needed to be said. Did not these fool theologians already know this?

When the oration was over, it was already time to repair to midday dinner. It was said that Duke George "had an eye for the delicacies of the table."[10] So he graciously sent a deer to Eck and a tasty roebuck to Karl-stadt. Luther received nothing. When the actual debate began, the first subject was the freedom of the will and whether one was able to do anything good apart from God's grace. Luther felt that Karlstadt was debating well, always backing up what he said with quotations from his many books. But then Eck objected that he would not "debate against a library."[11] Eck insisted that Karlstadt refrain from inanely parroting what others had said. This caused a tremendous uproar, but in the end Karl-stadt was obliged to set his well-traveled helps aside.

For reasons lost to history, Luther was widely reported to have a nose-gay during much of these early debates, which some of the public found irritating. For the first four days of the debate, Karlstadt and Eck went at it, but on July 4, at last, it was Luther's turn to step to the rostrum. Mosselanus has given us this indelible portrait of the actors:

> Martin is of medium height with a gaunt body that has been so exhausted by studies and worries that one can almost count the bones under his skin; yet he is manly and vigorous, with a high, clear voice. He is full of

learning and has an excellent knowledge of the Scriptures, so that he can refer to facts as if they were at his fingers' tips. He knows enough Greek and Hebrew to enable him to pass judgments on interpretations. He is also not lacking in subject material and has a large store of words and ideas. In his life and behavior he is very courteous and friendly, and there is nothing of the stern stoic or grumpy fellow about him. He can adjust to all occasions. In a social gathering he is gay, witty, lively, ever full of joy, always has a bright and happy face, no matter how seriously his adversaries threaten him. One can see in him that God's strength is with him in his difficult undertaking. The only fault everyone criticizes in him is that he is somewhat too violent and cutting in his reprimands, in fact more than is proper for one seeking to find new trails in theology, and certainly also for a divine; this is probably a weakness of all those who have gained their learning somewhat late.[12]

Much the same can be said of Karlstadt, though in a lesser degree. He is smaller than Luther, with a complexion of smoked herring. His voice is thick and unpleasant. He is slower in memory and quicker in anger.[13]

Someone else in attendance remarked that Karlstadt possessed a "repulsive, unbearded face."

Mosselanus's description of Eck is the most detailed:

Eck, in contrast, is a great, tall fellow, solidly and robustly built. The full, genuinely German voice that resounds from his powerful chest sounds like that of a town crier or a tragic actor. But it is more harsh than distinct. The euphony of the Latin language, so highly praised by Fabius and Cicero, is never heard in his mode of speech. His mouth and eyes, or rather his whole physiognomy, are such that one would sooner think him a butcher or common soldier than a theologian. As far as his mind is concerned, he has a phenomenal memory. If he had an equally acute understanding, he would be the image of a perfect man. He lacks quickness of comprehension and acuteness of judgment, qualities without which all the other talents are vain. And this is the reason that, in debating, he throws everything together promiscuously and without selection—arguments from reason, Scripture texts, citations from the fathers—without considering how inept, meaningless and sophistical is most of what he says. He is concerned only with showing off as much knowledge as possible, so as to throw dust in the eyes of the audience, most of whom are incapable of judging, and make them believe that he is superior. In addition, he has an incredible audacity which, however, he covers up with great craftiness. As soon as he sees that he has made a rash statement, he gradually turns the discussion into another channel. Sometimes he embraces the opponent's opinion in somewhat different words, and then, with astounding guile, attributes to his antagonist, in a completely changed form, his own previously held opinions. Thereby not even Socrates appears wiser than he, except Socrates admits his ignorance and confesses that he is not certain about anything, while Eck vaunts his peripatetic confidence in his own knowledge and engages in the art of flattery.[14]

One of Luther's Wittenberg students, George Benedict, was also in attendance and inside his Bible wrote the following about Luther: "His voice could be sharp as it could be gentle, i.e., gentle in tone, sharp in the enunciation of syllables, words, and caesuras. He spoke with a quick wit and expression in such logical fashion as if each thought flowed from the previous one."[15]

As soon as Luther and Eck were facing each other, the main event for which everyone had been waiting could at last begin. And as expected, immediately the whole machinery of things lurched into full gear, with Eck cannily bringing up the hot-button issue of papal authority at the outset. He hit Luther squarely amidships, citing the famous passage from Matthew 16, in which Jesus tells Peter, "You are Peter and upon this rock I build my church."[16] This had always been interpreted as meaning that here he metaphorically gave Peter the "keys" that only he had previously held, and that Peter, as the first pope, now stood in the place of Christ, with the same authority as Christ. For many in attendance, Eck's quoting this Scripture to prove his point was as though he had shouted, "QED," and raised his hands in triumph. Eck then said that to deny this most basic of doctrines was to side with the Bohemian heretic Jan Hus, who a century earlier was condemned at the Council of Constance and burned at the stake. The acrid smoke of Hus's horrible death had not fully dissipated in this part of the world, close as it was to Bohemia, so to say such a thing was purely a rhetorical and incendiary device but a powerful one. It was name-calling in lieu of argument, but Eck was renowned for this sort of tactic. Luther, however, unflappably countered with the facts. He explained that it had been only in the last four hundred years that the church declared the pope to be supreme. For a thousand years, the Greek church had existed. Did the church believe that a millennium's list of holy saints of that church were consigned to the flames of hell? But Eck countered with the obvious question. Was Luther now maintaining here in public for all to see and hear that the church council had erred? This too was heresy. So again the logic was to be wiped away and the question of authority made paramount.

In a letter to Spalatin, Luther recounted this part of the debate:

> At length there was even a debate over the authority of a council.
> I openly confessed that [councils] have faithlessly damned some
> articles that have been taught by Paul, Augustine, and even
> Christ himself in so many words. This truly enraged the snake,
> and it exaggerated my crime. . . . Nevertheless, I proved from the
> very words of the Council [of Constance] itself that not all the
> condemned articles were heretical and in error.[17]

When Luther said that the Council of Constance had along with some heretical articles condemned some articles that were "pious and Christian," Duke George had had enough. Arms akimbo, he shook his bearded head and harrumphed, "A plague on it!"[18] Luther was indeed treading precisely where Hus had trod a century earlier, so we might ask ourselves, why should his end be different?

At some point, Eck produced some letters that were part of canon law, which were reportedly from a bishop of Rome in the first century. One read, "The Holy Roman and Apostolic Church obtained the primacy not from the apostles but from our Lord and Saviour himself, and it enjoys pre-eminence of power above all of the churches and the whole flock of Christian people." Another excerpt cited said, "The sacerdotal order commenced in the period of the New Testament directly after our Lord Christ, when to Peter was committed the pontificate previously exercised in the Church by Christ himself."[19]

But Luther had done his homework and did not believe that these documents, even though they were part of canon law, were authentic. He denounced them plainly, saying they all belonged "to the spurious Isidorian decretals,"[20] which were medieval forgeries. And that they were.

At one point, Luther switched from speaking Latin to German. Part of his genius and the ultimate success of his efforts lay in his ability to communicate with common men, most of whom did not speak Latin but all of whom smelled problems with the church as it then was. "Let me speak German!" he said. "I am being misunderstood by the people."

> I assert that a council has sometimes erred and may sometimes err. Nor has a council authority to establish new articles of faith. A council cannot make divine right out of that which by nature is not divine right. Councils have contradicted each other, for the recent Lateran Council has reversed the claim of the councils of Constance and Basel that a council is above a pope. A simple layman armed with Scripture is to be believed above a pope or a council without it. As for the pope's decretal on indulgences I say that neither the Church nor the pope can establish articles of faith. These must come from Scripture.[21]

It was true that the recent ham-fisted decretal on indulgences drafted by Cajetan—with the specific intention of silencing Luther—was a perfect illustration of such a false article of faith, what we might call a *Deus ex curia* decree. It was a tautology and a logical impossibility, a bubble that had blown itself.

The debate raged for seventeen days, but it doesn't seem to have been exciting to be there in person. Melanchthon lobbied for notaries to record everything that was said. Eck was strongly against this idea, but Melanchthon won, and so everything that was pronounced must be scribbled down. Thus the audience and debate participants had to wait idly as the writing caught up to each statement before things could again move forward. Many of the Leipzig theologians, who ate their meal just before the afternoon sessions, struggled to stay awake and often failed entirely so that they had to be awakened when it was over, at which point they would file out to enjoy another hearty meal. After a few days of these halting forensics, most of the Wittenberg students had seen and heard enough—and had spent all their money—so in groups they eventually all dribbled back to Wittenberg.

Even after seventeen days, many of the things they had wrangled over had only been touched upon. Despite all that was said, much more time was needed to do proper justice to the great and eternally important subjects. But the important Duke George could not occupy his castle with this endless wrangling until doomsday. It so happened that he soon planned to entertain Joachim, the Margrave of Brandenburg. The margrave was returning from the diet at which the new emperor had just been elected, and it wouldn't do to have the Pleissenburg cluttered up with all of these theologians and rabble. So he determined that the Leipzig debate must come to an end.

What is of greatest importance in this Leipzig disputation is that because he was in a debate, Luther said things he would likely never have said in another context. He felt compelled to respond to whatever falsehoods were being put forward and to win, and this forced him into territory he wouldn't have treaded on if he had been given a choice. But in the heat of battle, he took some new and shocking theological positions from which he could never again retreat. He came out decisively for the idea that the Bible must supersede the church, which came to be known as the idea of *Sola scriptura*. He also derided the doctrine of purgatory, asking where in the Bible it could be found. These were dangerous and provocative stands that no one had any idea he would take—not least himself—when two years earlier the subject of indulgences first prompted him to write his Ninety-five Theses. He was somehow being compelled to expose more and more of the rickety underpinnings of some church doctrines, and as a loyal son of the church he felt and indeed knew that to speak these truths, he was doing the Holy Church a great service. And he was sure that God was pushing him forward as he did so. But would the church leaders ever see it that way? Was there anyone in Rome who would have the courage to take seriously what he was saying, who would follow him along these new pathways backward to the truth, for the sake of the whole church?

After Leipzig

After the debate, Luther got a letter from some disciples of Hus. They applauded his efforts and hailed him as "the Saxon Hus," an honor and appellation he might happily have lived without. With their letter, they enclosed a gift of some excellent knives and a small book that explained Hus's views. Luther was naturally very cautious in his reply. To be caught receiving praise from and communicating with the zealous disciples of a known heretic would not do at all. Luther dictated his answer through Melanchthon with a cover letter addressed to the courier himself, so that his own letter could not be traced back to its author. But when at last Luther read the little book on Hus's views, he was bowled over. It too set forth this most basic idea that Christ alone was the head of the church, and it took the pope to task for being unable to declare this unequivocally. And Hus had said that unless his accusers could clearly show him where he had erred from Scripture, he would not recant. For these things, Jan Hus had been condemned and burned at the stake. Luther was quite flabbergasted. "We are all Hussites without knowing it!" he said.*22

The idea that the pope put himself in the place of Christ—when Luther saw that no one could stand as the true head of the church but Christ—was what caused Luther to begin calling the pope anti-Christ. To stand where only Christ should stand was to be anti-Christ. More and more now, Luther accustomed himself to seeing the papacy in this way, and he became less and less shy about saying so. But this wasn't the only way that the tone of the larger debate became coarser. After the debate, many Humanists who had been greatly impressed by Luther's performance and arguments, including Mosselanus, wrote and spoke in his favor, and often without the humility toward the church and the pope that Luther had expressed. And of course those who sided with Eck wrote their own vicious polemics. After Leipzig, the great issues of this debate had overleaped the standard theological fences and now bounded pell-mell through the countryside.

Still, it was Luther and Eck who continued to lead the respective charges in their writings. Immediately after the debate, both published their own accounts of what had happened, reiterating their points with ascending shrillness. Because of some attacks on Erasmus and because his style in the debate had been so nakedly aggressive and polemical, Eck's reputation immediately suffered, while Luther's grew. For example, because of what he had seen and heard in the Leipzig debate, one of Luther's future colleagues, Justus Jonas, came over to the Lutheran side. He was ten years Luther's junior but a brilliant scholar of Greek and Latin who had just been appointed rector of the University of Erfurt. The Leipzig debate changed everything for him, and he would become one of Luther's very closest friends and allies in the years ahead. But when Erasmus learned that Jonas had gone over to Luther's side, he was grieved and wrote the following:

---

* It is often reported that as the executioner lit the pyre to execute Jan Hus (whose surname in Bohemian means "goose"), he declared, "Now we will cook the goose." To which Hus replied, "Yes, but in a century will come a swan which you can neither roast nor boil!" This was later widely interpreted as a prophecy regarding Luther, who is frequently depicted with a swan.

You will ask me, dearest Jonas, why I spin this long complaint to you when it is already too late. For this reason: Although things have gone farther than they ought to have, we should be watchful in case it is possible to still this dreadful storm. . . . If there are things we do not like in the men who govern in human affairs, my view is that we must leave them to their Lord and Master. If their commands are just, it is reasonable to obey; if unjust, it is a good man's duty to endure them, lest worst befall. If our generation cannot endure Christ in his fullness, it is something nonetheless to preach him as far as we may.[23]

Erasmus was a different kind of reformer, quite unlike Luther, and so their lives would take dramatically different paths.

After the debate, Eck paid a visit to Frederick to let him know that he had only just begun in his efforts to end Luther's reckless career as a heretic. He said he would be traveling to Rome to give a full report against Luther. Indeed, from now until Luther's death, Eck would be his implacable and persistent foe. The debate had made Duke George a dedicated opponent of Luther's too, and he would remain so until his own death in 1539.

After the debate had ended, George became infuriated that the Erfurt faculty refused to judge it. Their reasons for this are unclear. They cited certain formal reasons, but it seems likely that they knew they would pay a price if they came out against Luther, and they saw no reason for weighing in. George confronted them in a meeting to force them toward a decision, but even so they would not render one. And the Paris theologians who also were to render an official judgment finally sent him a surprisingly hefty bill before they were willing to do so. They had appointed a commission of twenty-four, each of whom was to receive the sum of thirty golden crowns, in addition to an expensively printed copy of the lengthy debate proceedings. But by now George had had enough of these indignities, so he refused to pay the villainous bill and therefore never got an answer.

But it was not the official outcome of the debate that would have much effect; it was the hearsay in smaller circles, such as the Nuremberg Humanists. The whole Reformation juggernaut was now moving forward. Because all of Luther's and Eck's and others' writings on the debate and the issues that had been debated were being printed and disseminated far and wide, the relatively fledgling free market itself now came into play and moved steadily in Luther's direction. Eck was further discredited by a brilliant but vulgar anonymous satire thought to have been written by the Nuremberg Humanist Willibald Pirckheimer* titled *The Unecked Eck*, which made much fun with the word *Eck*, which in German means "corner." To some extent, it was as a result of this popular satire that Eck's works sold less and less. Publishers were therefore increasingly less likely to print them. Luther's writings, on the contrary, began to sell well, making printers and publishers very happy and zealous to print more of them, which they did. Luther, incidentally, never took a pfennig for anything he wrote. He was happy his thoughts were finding audiences wherever they went, and indeed they went everywhere. When Duke George forbade the Leipzig printers to publish Luther's work, their profits plummeted. The reading appetite was dramatically now for Luther, and there would be no going back. In fact, it was not only in Germany that he was now being read. And others were picking up the tune and writing their own works along "Lutheran" lines.

Part of Luther's appeal came from his escalating outspokenness. Just when he said one thing that everyone insisted no one must ever say, he said another and then another. It was as if the zeitgeist itself could barely keep up with him. The reason for this was that as Luther's sense of his own danger increased, so did his boldness. He thought, what do I have to lose? I am speaking the truth and therefore my life is in danger, so I might as well say what I can while I have breath in me. His willingness to go further and further, wherever he felt the truth led him, became breathtaking.

For example, in a sermon he published in December 1519, Luther proclaimed—in German, so all could understand—that he advocated that the church should allow the laity to take both the bread and the wine at Communion. Hus had argued the same thing, so by doing this Luther was taunting all those who had accused him of being a Hussite, especially Eck. The implications were staggering. Luther was in effect reestablishing the biblical idea that everyone who has faith in Christ is equal and that the church's position that priests are somehow different from the people in the pews is wrong. For him, the Scriptures established the idea of "a priesthood of believers," and anyone who truly believed was a Christian

---

* Pirckheimer was a Humanist who was close to both Erasmus and Albrecht Dürer. Pirckheimer eventually grew troubled by Luther's break from the church and sought to have his name removed from the 1521 bull of excommunication that mentioned him by name. Like his friend Erasmus, who initially sided with Luther, he never dreamed things could go so far.

equal to any other Christian, so why should only the priests take the wine at Communion? The Greek Orthodox and other Eastern churches had not done this for fifteen centuries, and the early Christians themselves had not done it either. Why should anyone do it? Where did the idea come from? Because Luther published the sermon in German, it was read and talked about far and wide. The laypeople's persistent sense of grievance against the clerical class had found a specific issue and in a way had found a voice. Indeed it was this very issue that became one of the main ways the Reformation spread from parish to parish, as more and more believers demanded that they too receive the wine along with the host.

But this was a trickling freshet when one considers what was to come. The snow of fifteen centuries was melting, and in the next year alone Luther would gush forth a roaring torrent of writings that a year earlier would have been undreamed by anyone, including Luther himself. Between October 1519 and October 1520, he would write three of his major works, one after the other. The first of these was titled *To the Christian Nobility of the German Nation*, the second *The Babylonian Captivity of the Church*, and the third *The Freedom of a Christian*. The events at Leipzig had unchained Martin Luther. The details of why and when are unclear, but at some point during this time he even took his own Humanist name: Eleutheros. It sounded like a Latinization of Luther, but in fact it was the Greek word for "free." So now Luther was "the free one," whom Christ had set free to speak the truth. And whom Christ had set free was free indeed.

Luther really did feel that somehow he had been liberated to say whatever he must. He felt that he was being blown forward by the Holy Spirit, and he would suffer it to blow where it listed, confident it knew better where he should go than he ever could. So with the freedom he now enjoyed—and with the temporary cease-fire with Rome, which was owing to several factors—Luther found himself rapidly and dramatically rethinking everything, and saying so in his writings. Until now, he had been rather tame and timid. He had been measured and moderate. But now he would be wild and aggressive, attacking everything that needed attacking with seemingly no patience for considering how it might come across. "The time for silence is over!" he had written. "The time to speak has come!"[24] But precisely what had happened to make him go for broke?

A number of things, really, but two in particular. The first is that in February 1520 Luther read Ulrich von Hutten's preface to a new 1517 edition of Laurentius Valla's work proving the famous *Donation of Constantine* was a forgery. Hutten was a celebrated Humanist who after traveling in Italy had come to despise the papacy, and by bringing new attention to Valla's work from a century earlier, he reignited the scandalous idea that the church had used a rank forgery to shut up its critics for the last thousand years. *The Donation of Constantine* was a document purported to have been written by Emperor Constantine early in the fourth century, giving all authority over Western Europe to the pope, and the church had used it for centuries to underscore the inviolability of the pope's authority. When Luther saw that it was now proven to be a forgery, his fury increased the more. That the church had used a lie to silence its critics for centuries was horrifying and infuriating. To a faithful son of the church it felt like a stinging betrayal, and it made him wonder: What else was a lie?

And then in June he read a second Prierias document that was now published, making anew the same hoary pseudo-argument for the unquestioned authority of the pope. It not only did *not* use Scripture and reason, but essentially swept both of them away as beside the point, as even beneath consideration. The pope's authority trumped everything, and Prierias said things in the document that were too much to be believed, going so far as to declare that the pope could not err "even if he were to give so much offense as to cause people in multitudes . . . to go to the Devil in Hell."[25] How much more strongly could it be put? This was power at its most naked. It was the bloody sword of Satan unsheathed, and it had but one message to anyone who earnestly questioned the church's teachings: *Tremble and submit.*

Luther now felt that he was dealing directly with the powers of hell. Alas, there was nothing else to think. What had happened before was one thing, but now he had shone a light down into the hole and saw the writhing nest of serpents within. The crudest, vilest means were being brought out against him and against what he knew without a doubt to be the good and holy and glorious Gospel of Jesus. There was no longer any pretense of logic from those who opposed him and certainly no fragrance of Jesus in any of it. He now believed what he had feared, that the church had in his own generation been overtaken by the forces of Antichrist. Therefore, not to speak against it boldly when he had finally seen it so clearly and unmistakably was impossible. It was not only impossible; it was unthinkable and would be an abrogation of everything good and true and beautiful. If the End of All Things was at hand, somehow he had been given the privilege to know it, and he could not be silent. He feared God more than death, and God would not allow him to be silent.

This was a unique moment in history, and he would do what God called him to do. He had no excuse for hesitating, and he would not hesitate. God would see him through as God saw fit.

And suddenly now there was at least one rumor of a death threat against him. In April, Luther wrote to Spalatin that he had been "warned and advised" of it by the provost of the Neuwerk chapter in Halle:

> Even certain of my enemies who were sorry for me sent me a warning through friends from Halberstadt that there is a certain doctor of medicine who, with the help of magic, can make himself invisible at will and then kill someone; he [supposedly] has the order to kill Luther and is to arrive here next Sunday when the relics are being shown. This is a persistent rumor. Farewell.[26]

In a world that was still breathing the vapors of the Middle Ages, it should be little wonder the prospect of an eerie assassin crawling out of thin air was thought possible. In a letter to Spalatin, Luther wrote, "I think that everyone in Rome has gone crazy; they are ravingly mad, and have become inane fools and devils." In a response to Prierias's lunatic writing, Luther proclaimed God's judgment like an Old Testament prophet: "So farewell, ill-fated, doomed, blasphemous Rome; the wrath of God has come over you."[27] Luther and his pen would be a goodly part of that wrath.

But it was with the three aforementioned manifestos that Luther would be most identified during this twelve-month caesura in Rome's mad hunt; so let us look at each of them in turn. But one other reason Luther was freer than previously to write these three groundbreaking and theologically breathtaking treatises may also have to do with something fairly mundane. During this time, Luther's monastic practice of saying the daily hours might at last have caught up with his theology. In other words, he stopped doing them altogether. Ten years later, he wrote,

> Our Lord God pulled me away by force from the canonical hours in 1520, when I was already writing a great deal, and I often saved up my hours for a whole week, and then on Saturday I would do them one after another so that I neither ate nor drank anything for the whole day, and I was so weakened that I couldn't sleep, so that I had to be given Dr. Esch's sleeping draught, the effects of which I still feel in my head.*[28]

---

* Because he was writing these words ten years later, this is obviously a joke.

Cranach's 1520 portrait of Luther.

He said that eventually he was behind by three full months and the idea of ever catching up so much overwhelmed him that he was finally forced to end this practice he had been doing for fifteen years. So it is entirely possible that the writing of these three treatises brought him to this breaking point or that he had ended this habit before writing them. In any event, it's clear that abandoning the hours enabled him to be that much more productive.

Part of what makes Luther sui generis is the mad unpredictability and speed at which he tossed these three bombs. He made up for lost time and said everything he thought must be said. While his opponents were still choking from the dust of one explosion and then blinking to fathom the damage around them, Luther threw another—of another kind and in an unexpected place—so that they were stymied and flummoxed into paralysis and confusion.

Luther's first major work during this time was his *To the Christian Nobility of the German Nation.* It was published in August 1520, and Melchior Lotter presciently printed no fewer than four thousand copies, a giddily optimistic number in the world of early sixteenth-century publishing. But Lotter's gamble was well rewarded. Within two weeks, every copy had been sold. Luther emended a second edition slightly, which was printed within the month, and eventually ten editions were printed, making their way from the printing centers of Basel, Strasbourg, Augsburg, and Leipzig out to the wider world.

Luther's tone in this treatise was sharply polemical—his friend Johannes Lang thought it "frightful and wild"[29]—and he brilliantly played to the concerns of the German nobles that the pope and the Italians in Rome with their typical cunning were stealing what was rightly German and tyrannizing the German faithful. And he called upon these nobles to "take back their country," as it were, to establish Germany as a sovereign nation—or something like it—so that the blubbery maw of Roman bureaucracy that had been feeding on their money would wither and die. With typical creativity, Luther denounced the vast money-hungry bureaucracy of papal officials as "a crawling mass of reptiles"[30] and said that they knew that the Germans had no choice but to put up with them.

Despite the treatise's title, it was clearly addressed to the German people, because it was written not in Latin but in German. So Luther was using the new technology of printing to do an end run around the cultural elites who formed the previously impenetrable wall of ecclesiastical power. Suddenly history—via Gutenberg—had provided options that had not hitherto existed, and Luther would master this new way of reaching the people and fomenting a widespread uprising against the distant, out-of-touch taskmasters. For Luther, that wall was a Maginot Line he could simply march around with his pen. In a letter to Wenceslas Linck, he defended his polemical tone:

> The womb of Rebecca also [had] to bear children who were
> contentious and kicked each other. . . . Even Paul calls his
> enemies now "dogs," now "mutilation," now "Babblers," "false
> women," "servants of Satan," and names of that kind. . . . Who
> does not see that the prophets attack [the sin of the people] with
> the greatest violence? Here we have become accustomed to these
> [examples], and therefore they no longer disturb us.[31]

Luther's theology was leading him to one new place after another. For example, his understanding of the "priesthood of all believers" meant the whole structure of the church was a pretense. The idea that there was a special caste of people who alone had the privilege to preach and to pastor and to hear confession was simply not biblical. It had been invented out of whole cloth by human beings and had no basis in scripture. Therefore for every Christian to have to submit to this, especially now that it was being used to tyrannize people—to bully them into submitting to a power and authority that was not given by God—was intolerable.

> In name the empire belongs to us, but in reality to the pope. . . . We Germans are given a clear German lesson. Just as we thought we had achieved independence, we became the slaves of the craziest of tyrants; we have the name, title, and coats of arms of the empire, but the pope has the wealth, power, the courts, and the laws. Thus the pope devours the fruit and we play with the peels.

Luther was openly declaring that the Roman church's monopoly on the spiritual must come to an end. God had never separated priests from laymen. The whole idea of Jesus's coming to earth was to forever smash these distinctions, to open the gates of heaven to all who had faith, and to call everyone to be a "royal priesthood." All who were "born again" were part of his church, so the idea that one needed to be tonsured and ordained in order to serve God was a rank fiction.

> It is pure invention that pope, bishops, priests, and monks are to be called the spiritual estate, while princes, lords, artisans, and farmers are called the temporal estate. . . . All Christians are truly of the spiritual estate, and there is among them no difference except that of office. . . . Their claim that only the pope may interpret Scripture is an outrageous fancied fable.

So based on this new understanding, Luther now did what would at any time before this have been unthinkable. He appealed to the various rulers throughout Germany, telling them they could and should throw off their shackles and be free. But then he went further: they were the rulers in the temporal realm, and they must now be the rulers in the spiritual realm too. God had called them to this, and they must do their duties to him and his people. So if the pope and his deputies will not do their jobs, you the German nobles can do it yourselves. He was appealing to the nationalistic and anti-Roman sentiment, but only up to a point. Others wished he had gone much further in this direction, but taking a page from his savior, who had refused to do what the zealots of his day wished and become a political leader who by means of force overthrew the pagan Roman yoke, Luther refused to overthrow the "Christian" Roman yoke. Luther was obviously not ignorant of the political implications of what he had discovered, but he was wisely chary of being lured toward making an idol of politics, of "immanentizing the eschaton" through a utopian nationalistic program and making the Gospel an afterthought. It must be front and center; of that he would be certain.

Some of his allies in the Humanist camp were not so afraid to think in more nationalistic directions. Ulrich von Hutten and Franz von Sickingen were two. Hutten was a colorful Humanist figure who was named poet laureate by the emperor and who despised Rome's treatment of Germany. He said that Rome treated his Germany like some "private cow" to be milked for nefarious Italian purposes and thought that if Germany could unify its various territories and free cities into something resembling a bona fide nation, as Spain and France had done, they would be more successful in dealing with the pope's grasping greediness. Hutten had hoped to enlist Emperor Maximilian in his efforts, but when Maximilian died, this possibility died too. But Hutten would not be discouraged. He colorfully blasted the papacy as "a gigantic blood sucking worm" and "insatiable corn weevil." He imagined this weevil squatting hideously in the midst of the barnyard as it

> devours piles of fruit, surrounded by many fellow gluttons, who first suck our blood and then consume our flesh, and now seek to grind our bones and devour all that is left of us. Will not the Germans take up their arms and make an onslaught on them with fire and sword?[32]

Hutten was a knight and more than willing to take up arms against the papal see of troubles. "We seek to defend the common freedom," he wrote, "we seek to free the long downtrodden fatherland."[33] For him it was an issue of liberty and justice, not unlike what would happen 250 years later across the Atlantic. It was taxation without representation. Many other knights in German territories shared Hutten's sentiments against greedy and overreaching Roman power and for German nationalism as a bulwark against Rome.

Franz von Sickingen was the leader of these knights and styled himself a kind of Teutonic Robin Hood, so Hutten introduced him to Luther's writings, after which the two of them, Hutten and Sickingen, joined forces. Later, when Luther was unsure whether Frederick would protect him, Sickingen let him know that one hundred knights stood at the ready to do so at any moment. Luther wasn't inclined to take him up on his offer, but neither was he decided against it. He was still trying to see God's hand in all of it and wrote to Spalatin, "I do not despise them, but I will not make use of them unless Christ, my protector, be willing, who has perhaps inspired the knight."[34] In any case, he knew that increasingly now he had options; so if Frederick were to buckle under the relentless papal pressure to give up Luther, Luther could find other safe havens in Germany, wherefrom—freed from his near-crippling load of teaching and preaching duties in Wittenberg—he might do considerably more damage to Rome.

One thing we see is that in 1520 Luther had accepted the idea of an irreparable breach with Rome. There was only the very slimmest of possibilities that Rome would do the right thing, but Luther was sure that he had done the right thing and would not gainsay it now in the slightest. Everything had changed since Leipzig. He more than ever felt confidence that God was with him, that the truth was unassailable, and that not to defend it would be genuine heresy, of a kind the pope and his minions could not fathom. It would be to sin against God. So Luther had become increasingly bold. "Unless I am unable to get hold of a fire," he declared, "I will publicly burn the whole canon law."[35]

The events of the past year had drawn him out into lonelier and more dangerous theological territory, but there was a newfound freedom and a faith that bloomed in this situation. He knew that God was with him in a way he couldn't have known before, so his fear of Rome, if ever any had existed, had vanished. In all he wrote and did this year, he would not just pull up the drawbridge with Rome; he would set it aflame. Unless a gaggle of papal nuncios could be persuaded to swim the alligator-filled moat with olive branches in their teeth, the back-and-forth had ended forever.

Perhaps the most dramatic example of this was in his second treatise, *The Babylonian Captivity of the Church*, in which he parsed the theological errors of the whole sacerdotal system in which a caste of priests perform seven sacraments. Luther first shot down the hoary idea of the seven sacraments as utterly subjective and without biblical basis. Whether with prophetic authority or sheer mad hubris, he excised five of the seven, saying that only two stood the true test of whether something was indeed a genuine sacrament. The only ones instituted by Christ himself, he said, were Communion and baptism. Thus the other five—confirmation, marriage, ordination, penance, and extreme unction—were man-made and must be tossed outside the camp to rot. For Erasmus, this marked the end of any hope about holding Luther within the church.

Before Luther completed the third part of his acid triptych, he again met with Miltitz, who seems somehow to have gamely swum the fetid moat with an olive branch after all. For taking the trouble to do so, Miltitz was actually able to wheedle Luther into writing another letter to Pope Leo. Luther did write it, and this time it found its way to the pope. It was attached when he sent the treatise *The Freedom of a Christian* to Rome. In the letter, Luther generously and some would say disingenuously separates the pope from those around him, casting the hapless Leo as "more sinned against than sinning." He was the victim of evil flatterers, who hovered about the papal throne like red-hatted succubi. In the letter, it is the papacy itself, with all of its attached ecclesiastical machinery, that has become anti-Christ, not Leo himself. In the letter, Luther calls him "my father" and "most excellent Leo," trying to peel the man away from the farce and sin that surround him. He was trying to give Leo an opportunity to see things as they were and to save face, to do something that might allow the church to survive and reform.

So in the letter, it was for the soiled church itself that Luther reserved the licking flames of his attack:

> The Church of Rome, formerly the most holy of all churches, has become the most lawless den of thieves, the most shameless of brothels, the very kingdom of sin, death and hell, so that not even the Anti-Christ, if he were to come, could devise any addition to its wickedness. . . .
>
> Let not those men deceive you, as they pretend that you are lord of the world who will not allow any one to be a Christian without your authority, who babble of your having power over heaven, hell, and purgatory. . . . They that call thee blessed are themselves deceiving thee. They cause thee to err, and destroy the way of thy paths.

He said that those trying to deceive the pope were "godless flatterers," which he explained was why he felt compelled to appeal to a church council. He didn't wish the pope himself to be offended. But then, just in case the pope wasn't offended, Luther added something more:

I have truly despised your see, the Roman curia. Neither you nor
anyone else can deny that it is more corrupt than any Babylon or
Sodom ever was. As far as I can see, it is marked by a completely
depraved, hopeless, and notorious godlessness.

What must the effete Leo have made of it all? Luther's certainty and
confidence and faith and courage in speaking to no less than the pope
are at least impressive, but he would speak just as openly with the emperor himself. Indeed, just a few months earlier he had written the
emperor, saying,

I beseech Your most Serene majesty, Charles, foremost of kings on earth,
to deign to take under the shadow of your wings not me but this very
cause of truth, since it is only by this truth that authority is given you
to carry the sword for the punishment of the evil and for the praise of
the good.[36]

Though always humble and respectful in talking to pope and emperor,
Luther nonetheless consistently made it clear that they too were under
the authority of the truth and God and that their rights and their own
authority stemmed not just from the truth and God but from their properly executing their authority in accordance with God and his truth. So
in a way Luther was reminding them of the true order of things as per the
Gospel, that no man was above the truth or the laws of God and that
even such as he, a lowly monk, had the right to demand of his superiors
that they behave in accordance with the truth and with God's laws. Luther's theology had dragged a startling egalitarianism out of the Gospels
and into the center of history, and history and the world would never be
the same.

The treatise itself, however, is something of a different order. It began
with a remarkable and marvelous syllogism that Luther puts forth of
"two propositions concerning the freedom and the bondage of the spirit":

A Christian is a perfectly free lord of all, subject to none.
A Christian is a perfectly dutiful servant of all, subject to all.[37]

In this final of these treatises, Luther spelled out the implications of
sola fide (faith alone), which boldly declares that it is faith in Jesus that

brings us salvation and not our own moral efforts. Jesus did all that was necessary to bring us to heaven by his death on the cross, and we need only trust in him. But to try to add to what Jesus did with any works of our own is absurd, not to say offensive to God and heretical. We cannot earn heaven by our acts, because Jesus has already done that for us. We need only accept his free gift. And if we see the magnitude of that gift, we are moved to do good things. But it is as gratitude for what God has already done in saving us, not as a way of earning our own salvation. Once we receive God's free gift of love in Jesus, we are properly moved to want to love him back and to love our fellow man.

> When God in his sheer mercy and without any merit of mine has given me such unspeakable riches, shall I not then freely, joyously, wholeheartedly, unprompted do everything that I know will please him? I will give myself as a sort of Christ to my neighbor as Christ gave himself for me.[38]

Once we embrace Christ, we are instantly made righteous because of his righteousness, and not because of anything we have done or could do. So our good works do not earn us God's favor. That favor we already possess, even though we are sinners who sin and cannot help sinning. By turning to God in faith—as sinners who understand that we are sinners—and by crying out for God's help, we do all we can by acknowledging our helplessness. At this point—in which our faith acknowledges the truth of our situation—we are instantly clothed with the righteousness of God. And it is now our gratitude to God for this free gift of his righteousness and salvation that makes us want to please him with our good works. We do them not out of grievous and legalistic duty or out of a hope to earn his favor but out of sheer gratitude for the favor we already have. Our service to him is redeemed and transmuted into a free servitude. That is the power of faith in Christ. All that is base and dead can be redeemed by faith unto glory and life.

Luther summed it up in this typically colorful image. "Is this not a joyous exchange," he asks, "the rich, noble, pious bridegroom Christ takes this poor, despised wicked little whore in marriage, redeems her of all evil, and adorns her with all his goods?" Paul and Augustine might never have put it that way, but their theology implies it not merely strongly but inevitably and irresistibly and inescapably. Thus this foundational theological idea is the infinitely fecund soil out of which the whole world grows for Luther. If we as hell-bound sinners are redeemed wholly, then every ugly and vile thing in this world can be transformed and redeemed. So all that is in this world—including our bodies and every corporeal activity, including our sexuality—far from being things that must be escaped or transcended through our pious efforts, are things to be fully accepted with our open arms, and then with God's open arms they are fully redeemed. All things, rather than be lost forever or discarded away into despised oblivion, are joyously and in every aspect redeemed unto God's eternal glory.

Eventually, this period of riotous productivity would end. The new emperor would finally turn his attention to Germany, and Rome would once again resume its furious efforts to catch the wild boar that had been cavorting so destructively in the pope's delicate vineyards.

CHAPTER NINE

The Bull Against Luther

Because you have confounded the truth
of God, today the Lord confounds you.
Into the fire with you!

—Martin Luther, upon burning the papal bull

As LUTHER WROTE and wrote in 1520, some nine hundred miles south in the shining marble palaces of Rome the golden wheels of the papal machinery once again shuddered into motion. In February, Cajetan had co-chaired a commission to examine Luther's writings, and in March he got the University of Louvain to condemn them, and then the University of Cologne did so too. On catching a whiff of this foul wind, Luther was unmoved: "We will pay no more attention to their condemnation than to the silly ravings of a drunken woman."[1]

Eck had traveled from Leipzig to Rome, not arriving until sometime in March 1520, but as soon as he arrived, he began making as forceful a case as possible against his entrenched adversary. His account of Luther's statements at the Leipzig debate of course took things far beyond the issues of indulgences. He related how Luther had at last quite plainly gone over to the Hussite side of things and had even criticized papal councils and the papacy itself as capable of errors. Of course neither Eck nor anyone else involved in Luther's case in Rome knew of the three major treatises Luther was furiously cooking up that very year, all of which would go far beyond what he had said even in Leipzig. In any case, Eck was added to the small group drawing up their bullish indictment of Luther. Cajetan felt that the document must methodically list the indictments against Luther, weighing each one, but Eck disagreed, thinking the various troubling statements should simply be enumerated. In the end, Eck prevailed, so the bull* mentioned forty-one articles that are condemned as "heretical, or scandalous, or false, or offensive to pious ears, or seductive of simple minds, or repugnant to Catholic truth, respectively,"[2] but because of this it is unclear precisely which of these forty-one actually rise to the level of heresy. Evidently, something similar was done in the case of Jan Hus a century earlier.

On May 2, Eck was chosen to take the freshly composed bull to Pope Leo, who was supposed to append his own statement in a preface. Leo was at this time luxuriating outside fetid Rome at his sumptuously outfitted hunting lodge in Magliana on the Tiber. He spent a great deal of time there, usually hunting boars, and was evidently very taken with the noble sport. He is known to have scandalized the papal master of ceremonies by daring to throw off his constricting papal habit in order that he might caper freely about in full hunting costume.[3] History records that the hares and other animals native to that area were often insufficient to fire the imagination of the papal nimrod, so he had animals bred nearby that upon his command were released for the chase. But even these sometimes failed to scale the heights of his ambitions; thus he sometimes had more exotic animals delivered to serve as his quarry too. Once an elderly and infirm leopard was captured and ferried to Magliana, there to meet its merciful end at the terrible snow-white hands of Leo himself.

Exsurge Domine, 1520, Aetatis 36

And so it was in these halcyon environs, influenced by the imagery of the hunt, that Leo in his Latin preface to the bull now likened Luther to a "wild boar" that had invaded the Lord's vineyard. Later in the short preface, Luther is magically transformed into a slithering serpent that has invaded the field of the Lord. Whether this shift in pejorative bestial imagery from porcine to serpentine was intentional, or whether everyone was simply disinclined to point it out to the profligate pontiff, can never be known. But it is the mighty first words of Leo's preface that have given the bull its name, *Exsurge Domine*, which means "Arise, O Lord." In what surely must have struck Luther as ironic, perhaps even to the point of cheekiness, Leo also wrote, "Arise, O Paul, who by thy teaching and death hast and dost

---

* For more on papal bulls, see page 23.

illumine the Church. Arise, all ye saints, and the whole universal Church, whose interpretation of Scripture has been assailed."[4]

The bull was dated June 15, and then, on June 24, it was officially published, being posted at St. Peter's in Rome. And now the bull must make its cheerless way north to be posted everywhere it might be posted and then at long last to be placed under the eyes of the very one whom it condemned, nearly nine hundred miles away. The two nuncios given the task of carrying the one hundred copies of the document into some hostile pro-Luther territories were Eck himself and Girolamo Aleandro—also known as Jerome Aleander—a brilliant theologian who had been the chancellor of the Sorbonne but who by this time had been plucked by Pope Leo to serve him under the title "librarian of the Vatican." It was Aleander who was charged with carrying the bull to the emperor, then in the Netherlands, and also to the cathedral cities in western Germany, which included Mainz and Cologne. Eck's task was considerably more difficult. He was to carry the damning document to cities in southern Germany and then into Saxony itself. Only then, once the bull had been posted in the three cathedral cities of Saxony—Meissen, Merseburg, and Brandenburg—would the clock officially begin ticking down the sixty days specified in which Luther had to appear in Rome.*

Wherever the bull was posted, the works of Luther were also to be burned. But especially as Eck proceeded farther on his journey toward those areas closest to Wittenberg, not all cities received him and his mission joyfully. Nor were all of them eager to comply with the incendiary demands of the document. The acceptance of Luther and his writings had been increasing steadily throughout Saxony, so that even in Leipzig, where Eck had been cheered the previous year, the atmosphere was surprisingly lukewarm. Duke George himself, whose violent ragings against Luther had originally been instigated by Eck's attacks in the debate, had at first welcomed Eck with a golden chalice filled with gulden, but even he eventually came out for postponing the bull's posting, so that it was actually never posted in Leipzig. Nor were Luther's works burned there. In the end, only a single member of the Leipzig faculty—his Humanist name, appropriately, was Vulcan—rather pathetically set a small handful of Luther's writings aflame.

---

* Emperor and pope both understood that traveling great distances required time and therefore stipulated the date of one's commanded appearance before them with the particular details of travel in mind.

Delivering the bull to Wittenberg itself was of course not something Eck looked forward to doing. So he crept around the problem by sending a copy of the bull to the University of Wittenberg via a courier. When it finally found its way into the hands of the university's rector, he opined that it had been delivered in a "thieving and rascally manner."[5] Frederick himself was at that time not in Wittenberg but in Cologne to attend the imperial crowning of Charles. Eck was likely very glad of this, for he had certainly not looked forward to delivering the bull to Frederick. Eck also begged off delivering the bull in person to Frederick's brother Duke John. John was then at his ducal residence in Coburg. Eck—allowing as he hadn't packed the proper clothing to be received at court—once again was pleased to farm out the dirty work to a courier.

Still, Eck had in the final days of September at least succeeded in delivering the bull to the three cathedral cities in Saxony, which was his principal task. Because the last of these was posted in Brandenburg on September 29, it was from that date exactly that Luther's sixty days were counted. By the end of November, then, Luther must appear in Rome to face the Inquisition, or he would instantly be branded a heretic and outlaw.

Luther himself heard about the bull on October 1, and ten days later a copy found its way into his hands. He was so surprised by the harsh tone of it that he sincerely questioned its authenticity, supposing that perhaps the sly Eck, in a fit of pique, had written it himself. But when Erasmus read it, he thought the same thing. Erasmus actually met with Frederick in Cologne, and because the two were long-standing friends, he frankly offered his thoughts on the Luther business, saying Luther's language had often been troublingly blunt and that he feared it would cause them all a great deal of harm. But he also complained of the intemperate language of the bull, and he is likely the one who eventually persuaded Frederick to do whatever he could to protect Luther. So when Frederick did finally meet with the new emperor, he persuaded him not to simply condemn Luther at the upcoming diet, which was to be held in the imperial city of Worms, but at least to give him a hearing there.

Meanwhile, in Wittenberg, Luther had no plans whatever of traveling to that immoral swamp called Rome, and so the sixty days passed one by one. At the end of November, he had not budged. But he had heard that wherever the bull had been posted, his works had been burned—but not always as enthusiastically as the nuncio had hoped. The first public burning had taken place on October 8, in Louvain, under the supervision of

Aleander, with the university faculty present, although many of them were not pleased about it, because they too doubted the bull's authenticity. In Cologne, the archbishop gave his consent that Luther's books be burned, but the officious city executioner, whose task it was to do the actual burning, refused to proceed unless he saw an imperial seal, and of course these copies of the bull did not have the seal that the original bull would have had. But in the end, the archbishop got his way, and Luther's works were consumed by the flames.

In Mainz, there were similarly mixed results. That city's archbishop, Albrecht, had of course been the one to whom Luther sent his famous letter on October 31, 1517, and Albrecht had sent that letter and Luther's theses on to Rome, kindling this conflagration in which they now all found themselves. But by the end of 1520, Albrecht was not at all settled on what he thought of Luther and his teachings. A large part of the reason for this was that he had himself come under the influence of Ulrich von Hutten, who was of course firmly in Luther's camp. In the end, Albrecht gave his assent to the burning of Luther's books. But when the Mainz executioner was set to light the pyre ablaze, like his officious brother in Cologne he balked. Before doing so, he had formally asked the crowd whether the books had indeed been legally condemned. The crowd was hardly on the same page as Aleander and the pope, and they answered with a deafening "No!" Upon hearing this, the executioner immediately leaped down from the pyre and refused to proceed. Aleander was of course greatly vexed, not to say embarrassed, so he immediately scurried back to the archbishop's residence to seek justice. Albrecht assured him that the following day they would try again. And on November 29, though the executioner still refused, Albrecht managed at last to unearth a humble grave digger to do the job. Evidently, the only witnesses to the act that day were a few women driving their geese to market.[6] But enough Luther supporters showed up eventually to pelt stones at Aleander, who it seems, if not for the intervention of the archbishop himself, might have been killed.

Luther Burns the Bull

Thus, on December 10—sixty days after Luther had read the bull himself— on the same wooden door where Luther had three years earlier posted his historic theses, Philip Melanchthon posted an invitation to an event, the likes of which had never taken place in Christendom. The poster described it as "a pious and religious spectacle, for perhaps now is the time when Antichrist must be revealed."[7] But to what could this advertisement be referring? It referred to a book burning, but not of Luther's works, as the papal bull against Luther had commanded. Rather it referred to the papal bull itself. In its way, it was what in the 1960s was called a "happening"—a theatrical event staged to make a public statement. And Luther's fiery statement was that he was turning the tables by himself now symbolically excommunicating the false church that had thought to excommunicate him.

One of Luther's and Melanchthon's avid students, Johannes Agricola, had been the one to organize the event, which was to take place outside the city gate, very close to the place where animals were butchered and on the very spot where the ghastly clothes and rags of those who had died of the plague were burned. Here by the repugnant carrion pit, Agricola and others had erected a pyre, and on the hour appointed—9:00 a.m.—after several hundred fellow professors and students had assembled as witnesses to this great moment, Luther cast into the flames one after the other the writings of the false church. Papal decrees were now defiantly hurled into the fire, and even a book of canon law found its way into the flames, and then the writings of Eck and Emser "the goat" too. Agricola had hectored his fellow Wittenberg students to contribute a copy of Duns Scotus's commentary on the *Sentences* and Aquinas's *Summa*. But in the end, none would part with their copies of these expensive books, else these prime examples of Scholastic teaching too would have fed the bonfire. And then, as these other works burned, Luther with a sense of drama like some magician reached into his cloak and produced the very papal bull that threatened to excommunicate him. He spoke the words from Psalms 21:10—on which he was during this time lecturing—"Because you have confounded the truth of God, today the Lord confounds you. Into the fire with you!" And then, in a final flourish, brazen and wild he flung the papal decree into the raging flames.[8]

Excommunicated, *Aetatis* 38

On January 3 of the New Year, 1521, the pope, realizing it was long past the sixty days he had set, and having seen neither hide nor hair of Martin Luther, set his papal seal to a brand-new bull, which carried out the threat of the previous bull by officially excommunicating Martin Luther. But the power of this second bull went far beyond merely condemning Luther himself. It was a legal notice to all in the empire that whoever in any way aided or abetted this outlaw would also himself be excommunicated. It also declared that all territories or cities that supported him were officially under "interdict," which is to say they were themselves as it were excommunicated from the church. They were forbidden to offer any of the seven sacraments of the church. This was the ultimate weapon Rome could use, denying the sacraments of the church—which is to say denying salvation itself—to any who did not now heed its warning. For people who knew hell was real and that the pope had this power, there could be no dithering. One would be gambling with one's eternal soul.

One of the cardinals, Pietro Accolti, who had had a hand in drawing up the bull, said the obvious: "It is hoped that as soon as the bull is published in Germany, most men will forsake Luther."[9] But quite the opposite happened, and Rome soon saw just how much authority it had lost, because once the bull had been published, many Germans even took it as an invitation to follow Luther's Wittenberg example from a month earlier. They now staged book burnings of their own, boisterously casting their copies of the bull, and many other hated writings, into the flames.

The distracted hedonist Leo and his curia had misplayed this situation from the beginning and would only blunder forward in increasingly foolish and tragic ways. Part of their miscalculation had to do with the ferocity of the sentiment into which Luther and his writings had tapped. Everywhere across Germany and in other countries too, Luther's pointed questions and answers regarding Rome were being hailed and applauded by the common folk, who had never had any kind of champion, but also by figures as august and learned as Erasmus. Because Rome had not properly attended to the fire when it first broke out, the fire had eventually been able to go underground, and now it would flare up here and there and everywhere and never again be contained.

But for Luther, it was during that first week of what would be a historic year that he saw there was no going back. And he officially bade farewell to the place he had once considered the spiritual home of every Western Christian:

Farewell, thou unhappy, lost, blaspheming Rome. . . . The wrath of God has come upon thee, as thou hast deserved. We have cared for Babylon, but she is not healed. Let us then leave her, that she may be the habitation of dragons, specters, and witches, and true to her name of Babel an everlasting confusion, a new pantheon of wickedness.[10]

The pope, for his part, knew that with his power on the wane, he must shore up his support with the emperor, because if Charles V did not enforce the ban on Luther, it would mean little. So in a letter to Charles, Leo now increased the altitude of his flattery to heavenly metaphors:

> As there are two planets in heaven, the sun and the moon, which
> surpass in brilliance all the stars, so there are two great
> dignitaries on earth, the pope and the emperor, to whom all
> other princes are subject and owe obedience.[11]

Whereas the lunar comparison must have been encouraging, the metaphor also subtly reminded Charles that whatever light it was that he was able to project to the world—and therefore whatever strength and authority he had—came from the papal Sun, the source of all light in the European solar system. Politically speaking, the emperor would have had no difficulty seeing he had to side with the pope against Luther, but he also understood that throughout Germany, Luther had become wildly popular, so he must also contrive to walk something of a political tightrope. His solution was not to compel Luther to frog-march to Rome but rather to do what had been done when Luther was last ordered to Rome. Maximilian I had asserted his authority by inviting Luther to appear within the borders of Germany—at Augsburg. This time Charles would do the same by inviting Luther to appear before the next imperial diet. It had originally been scheduled to take place in Nuremberg, but because the plague had struck there, the venue was changed. And so it was decided that the next diet would take place in the central German city of Worms.

But Leo was not quite through with his flattery. On February 25, he twittered his great "joy that His Majesty was rivaling Constantine, Charlemagne, and Otto I in his zeal for the honor of the Church." In March, however, when Charles sent his letter to the wild boar of Wittenberg, it must have sounded to the pope's ears like a gushing billet-doux. "To our noble, dear, and esteemed Martin Luther," it read, "both we and the Diet have decided to ask you to come to Worms under safe conduct to answer with regard to your books and teaching." Still, lest anyone be confused, it made its principal point quite clearly. "You have 21 days," it said, "in which to arrive."[12]

The emperor's letter arrived in Wittenberg on March 26, and because it was a summons from the highest secular authority—and because Worms was infinitely closer (and therefore safer) than Rome—Luther had no qualms about going. "I am heartily glad that His Majesty will take to himself this affair that is not mine," he wrote, "but that of all Christianity and the whole German nation."[13]

In fact, three months earlier, at the end of the previous year, Luther already knew that the next diet would be held in Worms, and suspecting he might be summoned to appear there, he wrote to Spalatin about whether he would do so:

> Of course I would by all means come, if called, in so far as it would be up to me, even if I could not come by my own power and instead would have to be driven there as a sick man. For it would not be right to doubt that I am called by the Lord if the Emperor summons. Further, if they would employ force in this matter, which is most probable (for they do not want me called there because they want me to learn something), then this matter can only be commended to the Lord. For He who saved the three men in the furnace of the Babylonian king still lives and rules. If he does not want to preserve me, then my head is of slight importance compared with Christ, who was put to death in greatest ignominy—a stumbling block to all, and the ruin of many. We must rather take care that we do not expose the gospel (which we have finally begun to promote) to the derision of the godless and thus give our enemies a reason for boasting over us because we dare not confess what we have taught and are afraid to shed our blood for it. May the merciful Christ prevent such cowardice on our part and such boasting on their part. Amen.[14]

When Luther at last received the summons from the emperor to appear at the diet, he knew it was something of historical importance. Indeed, in his mind, what would take place there was not less than a clash of the two forces that had been at odds since Eden. Luther is known not to have saved many documents, but this letter he saved, and it was passed down through his family.

CHAPTER TEN

The Diet of Worms

Here I stand. I can do no other.

God help me. Amen.

—Martin Luther

If I am shown my error, I will be the first
to throw my books into the fire.

—Martin Luther

LUTHER DEPARTED WITTENBERG for Worms* on April 3, the Wednesday after Easter. Charles had sent his summons to Luther via his imperial herald, Caspar Sturm, and now he—along with his servant—would ride at the head of the procession along the three-hundred-mile journey, guaranteeing Luther's safe-conduct. On his sleeve he wore the imperial eagle, which would have alerted any troublemakers along the way that to molest this party in any way was as if they had attacked the emperor personally. Wittenberg understood the importance of Luther's trip and appearance and wanted to play its part. The wagon in which Luther would travel was provided by the Wittenberg city council

---

* In German, the city of Worms is pronounced something like "*Voh*-arms." The German *W* is pronounced like the English *V*, and the *o* in "Worms" is pronounced less like a schwa ("uh") and more like "awe." Thus any phonetic resemblance to the vermicular is doubly reduced. Whereas the term "diet," in concert with the city's name, has for many invariably suggested the image of a plate heaped with wriggling protein, it has no connection to what one eats, but rather refers to the council or assembly of nobles gathered at the behest of the emperor (of the Holy Roman Empire), hence the more fulsome term "imperial." "Diet" harks back to the Latin word for "day," which is *dies*, and from which we today get the word "diurnal" (daily). Furthermore, the German word for meeting has a connection to the sense of a daily meeting. This is further underscored in that the German for "day" is *Tag* and the German for "meeting" is *Tagung*. With their *-tag* suffixes, the German words for a National Assembly or Congress—*Reichstag* and *Bundestag*—obviously retain that meaning as well.

Cranach's 1521 profile portrait of Luther wearing his doctor's biretta.

and the goldsmith Christian Döring. The university kicked in twenty gulden for traveling expenses, to which Duke John—Frederick's brother—added his own contributions, as did Luther's friend Johannes Lang.

Although Luther had been absolved of his obedience to the Augustinians by Staupitz, he nonetheless followed their tradition of traveling wherever he went with a fellow brother, and so an obscure member of the Wittenberg monastery—Johann Petzensteiner—was assigned to be his companion on this trip. But Luther would hardly lack for company. His friend Nicholas von Amsdorf would be along for the ride in the wagon, as would Peter Swawe, a nobleman from Pomerania, who had become sufficiently enamored of Luther in Leipzig that he had moved to Wittenberg, where he studied under him. Much of the way, Luther edified his wagon companions by teaching a Bible study on the book of Joshua and sometimes entertained them by gaily playing his lute.

Everywhere their party traveled, Luther was greeted by throngs of admirers. How his writings and teachings had spread could never have been fully known to him until now, and there is no doubt that it was a stunning and humbling revelation. If he had ever doubted it before, he had by this time become a celebrity, although there was no such thing at that time in the world. But whatever he was, everyone knew the details of his case and wanted to see the man who was defying the pope in Rome and who would now stand before the emperor himself.

When before now, in Germany or anywhere, had there been a champion of the people, someone who seemed to speak for them against the mighty, resplendent, fearsome, and oppressive powers arrayed against them? Martin Luther was, to this extent, very much a new phenomenon in history. Because of Cranach's by now widely distributed woodcut portraits of him, Luther's countenance was known everywhere his publications were sold, and where were they not sold? Except for royalty—for emperors and caesars and kings—whose face in history had ever been mass-produced so that it was recognized far and wide? The hero of the people had been born, and so, in their way, had the people themselves. They now strode onto the world's stage for the first time, led by the monk from Wittenberg, and they would never again go into the wings. In this way too the future was now being born.

So for these people waiting to see him come through their town in his wagon, this was all something out of a fairy tale, and here was their hero, the man who stood for them and for the truth, riding where they could actually see him. Many were sure he was going to his death, and told him so. When the wagon passed through Naumburg, a well-meaning cleric gave Luther a painting of Savonarola, who was burned at the stake in 1498 for doing much of what Luther was now doing. What Luther made of this well-meant but strange and macabre token is not recorded.

That Luther was in some ways the first celebrity of modern culture had everything to do with the extraordinary reach of his publications, as well as with the Cranach portraits. A month earlier in a letter to Spalatin, Luther had enclosed a handful of copies, which Cranach had suggested he autograph.[1] The technology to print a near infinity of his many writings and to add to them the fanciful woodcut illustrations by Cranach made something possible that had never been possible before, to blast a persona—an image and a lively voice that knew how to communicate to the common man—into the wide world, where it would touch the butchers, bakers, and candlestick makers, none of whom spoke Latin or had previously ever been invited into these important discussions about the world in which they lived, about the institutions that affected them and shaped their lives. How it must have flattered them that this genius of great influence was speaking to them and representing their concerns before pope and emperor. It was simply unprecedented.

The first stop on the party's journey was Erfurt, the city where Luther had studied and had become a monk and where—once he had gone to Wittenberg—bad feelings had been engendered by the Erfurt monks. But now it was a dramatically different story. As Luther's wagon approached the city, some sixty horsemen appeared to escort Luther and his entourage through the city gates and into the city's heart. They were led by the Humanist Crotus Rubianus, who had studied with Luther at Erfurt all those years ago and who was now the rector of the university. Once inside the city, Luther must have been deeply moved at what he saw. The Erfurt streets were everywhere lined with admirers. Some had even climbed walls and up onto rooftops to catch a glimpse of this famous figure who had once lived and walked among them. The poet Eobanus Hessus sang Luther's praises in verse, comparing his efforts in the church to Hercules's fifth labor—the mucking out of the Augean stables.

When Luther preached there that Sunday, the church was so impossibly filled that the large balcony in which an unprecedented number of people stood began to creak, as though about to break. A number of people proactively opted to leap out of the windows before this could take place and now began breaking the panes that they might do so. But Luther was convinced it was only Satan trying to interrupt him, and so he calmed the people, telling them merely to stand still, that the gallery would hold them, which it did. At Erfurt, Justus Jonas, who was on the Erfurt faculty, decided that he too would join this triumphal procession to Worms, and now did so.

When they came to Gotha, Luther preached there too. But at the very time that he was in the pulpit preaching, some stones strangely came detached from the church tower and fell loudly to the ground. Once again, Luther was convinced it was the devil. Those great stones had been part of that venerable tower for two hundred years. Why must they come loose just as Luther was preaching the Word of God and making this historic confrontation? Luther knew that the spiritual import of his journey was greatly disturbing to Satan, who would have done anything to prevent it but who could do nothing now but stand impotently on the banks of this river in which the Holy Spirit coursed powerfully on its way.

Their journey next took them through Thuringia to Luther's beloved Eisenach. But that evening, Luther suddenly became very ill, with a high fever. It seemed so serious that his friends were concerned for his life. A doctor was called and did what doctors often did in those days when they had no real idea of what malady they were treating: he bled Luther and then prescribed a hearty dose of schnapps. Evidently, however, these things did the trick, and eventually Luther felt at least well enough to continue the journey. But he was convinced that all of these things were the work of the enemy of mankind and truth who was raging against God's purposes, and these disturbances only confirmed to him that nothing must prevent him from getting to Worms. Myconius, who wrote a chronicle of Luther's journey in 1541, said that Luther roared defiantly that even if the fires against him should reach from Wittenberg and Rome up to heaven itself, he would still answer the summons and appear at Worms, and once there he would not fail to "kick the Behemoth in the mouth between his big teeth."[2] He was well aware that he was a man on a mission.

When they arrived at Frankfurt, Luther was feeling rather well again, and played the lute for his companions. Spalatin was by this time already in Worms, and having taken in the atmosphere there, he was gravely concerned for Luther. So he wrote to his friend advising him not to come, saying that condemnation and then death seemed the only possible outcome. But Luther was resolute. He had set his face toward Worms; replying to Spalatin from Frankfurt, he defiantly wrote,

> I am coming, my Spalatin, although Satan has done everything to hinder me with more than one disease. All the way from Eisenach to here I have been sick; I am still sick in a way which previously has been unknown to me. Of course I realize that the mandate of Charles has also been published to frighten me. But Christ lives and we shall enter Worms in spite of all the gates of hell and the powers in the air. I enclose copies of the Emperor's letters. It is not wise to write further letters until I first see in person what has to be done, so that we may not encourage Satan, whom I have made up my mind to frighten and despise. So prepare the lodging. Farewell.[3]

Spalatin later wrote, "He wants to come to Worms. Even if there be as many Devils there as tiles on the roof!"[4]

When Luther's party reached Oppenheim, they came to the banks of the river Rhine. A ferry took them and their wagon and horses over, and on April 16, around ten in the morning, their procession entered Worms at last, most likely through the Mainz gate. All who have written of it say that it was a spectacle for the ages. Trumpets from the cathedral announced Luther's arrival, and two thousand people thronged to greet him. (The entire population of the city was seven thousand, but in the course of the diet this would double.) The imperial herald was now joined by a jester wearing a fool's coxcomb and singing,

> *The one we sought so long has arrived at last;*
> *we expected you even when days were at their darkest!*[5]

Swawe wrote that it was all just like Jesus's entry into Jerusalem on Palm Sunday. It was breathtaking. Of course Luther could not help wondering whether that meant that he was days away from his Good Friday, but over and over he gave it all to God. *Thy will be done.*

The tremendous reception Luther got upon his entry into Worms deeply peeved the papal nuncio Aleander, and he blamed the emperor for allowing it. He was sure that any kind of rapprochement with this insolent monk—whom he dubbed "the Saxon dragon"—was impossible. And of course Aleander's own arrival at Worms was as far a cry from Luther's as can be imagined. No one was there to greet him, and he was bitterly put out that the only room he could find was cramped and unheated. It all must have been exceedingly unpleasant and fatiguing. In fact, the whole time he was in Worms, people hissed at him and made threatening gestures when they saw him on the street.

Aleander saw only too well that Luther was a German hero. He wrote to Rome, "Now the whole of Germany is in full revolt; nine-tenths raise the war cry 'Luther,' while the watchword of the other tenth who are indifferent to Luther is 'Death to the Roman Curia!'" This monk and his revolution had better be destroyed mercilessly, and soon. Aleander was amazed that not only did all of the people root for Luther, but they seemed well acquainted with the details of his case. "All of them," Aleander wrote, "have written on their banners a demand for a council to be held in Germany, even those who are favorable to us, or rather to themselves."[6] He was particularly nettled to see people everywhere peddling woodcut images depicting Luther with a dove, firmly answering the question whether he was inspired by the Holy Spirit, and others with him piously sporting a numinous nimbus, as though his sainthood had already been established beyond any doubt.

Later Aleander wrote a cranky account of Luther's arrival:

> I gathered from various reports as well as the hasty running of the people that the great master of heretics was making his entrance. I sent one of my people out, and he told me that about a hundred mounted soldiers . . .

had escorted him to the gate of the city; sitting in a coach with three comrades, he entered the city [at ten in the morning], surrounded by some eight horsemen and found lodgings near his Saxon prince. When he left the coach, a priest embraced him and touched his habit three times, and shouted with joy, as if he had had a relic of the greatest saint in his hands. I suspect that he will soon be said to work miracles. This Luther, as he climbed from the coach, looked around in the circle with his demonic eyes and said: "God will be with me." Then he stepped into an inn, where he was visited by many men, ten or twelve of which he ate with, and after the meal, all the world ran there to see him.[7]

After his arrival, Luther had lunch with the Hungarian delegation to the diet, but while they were eating, the door had to be guarded and blocked, because a crowd decided it would try to force its way in to see the great man up close. After lunch, because there was no room for Luther to lodge in the place where Frederick was staying, he stayed in another place, not without its charms. It was the quarters of the Knights of St. John, an order that cared for the sick. Still, Luther's quarters were far from grand. He was obliged to share a bedroom with Hans Schott and Bernhard von Hirschfeld, who were officials of electoral Saxony. But while there, Luther entertained one impressive guest after the other. A number of counts and lords came, along with several princes. Everyone who was in town wanted a few moments with the fabled monk who had come to stand before emperor and pope.

And the following day he would have his chance to do so. On the morning of April 17, Luther was informed by the imperial marshal—Ulrich von Pappenheim—that at four o'clock that afternoon he would appear before the emperor. Later that day, the marshal reappeared, along with a familiar face, Caspar Sturm, who had escorted Luther from Wittenberg. The marshal and Sturm now had the job of escorting Luther to the bishop's residence, which adjoined the cathedral. Somehow the word must have gotten out that Luther would be going there, because crowds thronged the Kämmerergasse—the same main street he had taken to enter the city on the previous day. So the marshal and the herald decided to sneak Luther via a back way that took them first through the garden of the Knights of St. John's property and then through various narrow alleys until at last they arrived at the rear entrance to the bishop's residence. Even though they took this clandestine route, many people nonetheless discovered the route and clambered over roofs to catch a glimpse of him.

Wearing his simple Augustinian cassock, Luther was escorted past the emperor's Spanish troops and on into the chamber where there was assembled such a host of dignitaries as would take anyone's breath away. Some of the most powerful people in the world were here. The seven electors themselves were here, plus innumerable archbishops and princes and dukes and other nobles, all decked out in their sumptuous and bejeweled best, replete with gaudy golden chains and befeathered hats, and all of them stood agape at the curious spectacle of this humble monk walking into their midst, who in turn goggled back at them, doubtless staggered by the sheer breadth and wealth of dignitaries here assembled.

Luther was obviously not used to this sort of environment, and just as he entered, he saw Conrad Peutinger, the Augsburg dignitary, whom he knew. Unaware that it was considered rude in the emperor's presence to behave in any way other than with extreme gravity, Luther cheerily greeted his friend. At this point, the marshal Pappenheim rebuked Luther. He was not to speak unless bidden to do so. It must also be said that this would have been the first time that Luther and Frederick had ever laid eyes on each other. They would again see each other in the chamber the following day, and then never again. They communicated only through letters, and never spoke.

One of the delegates in the room remembered the scene: "A man was let in who they said was Martin Luther, about forty years old, somewhat more or less,* robust in physique and face, with not especially good eyes and lively features which he frivolously changed."[8]

In a letter to the pope's vice-chancellor, the prickly nuncio tsked about Luther's outrageous demeanor: "The fool entered with a smile on his face and kept moving his head back and forth, up and down, in the presence of the emperor."[9]

And there, at the focal point of the grandiloquence sat the fabled young emperor himself, duly elevated upon a dais. What did the elegant grandson of Ferdinand and Isabella of Spain make of this crude, impertinent monk? Portraits of Charles from this time give the unmistakable impression of a perfect twit, a cruel victim of spoiling and aristocratic inbreeding. But Charles V was very far from that.

What must it have felt like for Luther to come into the presence of such worldly power? That he smiled seems evidence of equanimity born of his

---

* Luther was thirty-seven.

deep faith. When he came to the designated spot in the room where he was to stand, he beheld a table piled high with his own books, some forty in all. They were the Basel editions of his works, especially bound for the occasion.

The man now charged with being Luther's interlocutor—as the emperor's spokesman—was Johannes von der Ecken, who is not to be confused with Luther's Leipzig opponent, Johannes Eck. This Johannes von der Ecken was the secretary to the archbishop of Trier, who was one of the seven electors, and von der Ecken had himself been the one to oversee the burning of Luther's books in that city. Because some in the room understood Latin, while others understood German, everything must be spoken in both languages. Most to the point, Emperor Charles himself spoke German rather poorly, so it might have been mostly for his benefit that everything was also spoken in Latin.

So von der Ecken now addressed Luther—first in Latin and then in German—saying that the emperor had summoned him here to answer but two questions. The first was whether all of these books, bearing his name, had indeed been written by him. The second was whether he wished to recant anything from them. That was all and that would be all. Luther's appointed legal counsel at Worms was Hieronymus Schurff, a professor of law from Wittenberg who had already been at Worms since February, at the behest of Frederick. But Schurff now leaped up and demanded that the books' titles be read aloud. Thus von der Ecken now read from the long list to the assembly.

The sheer number of books and the titles themselves must have rung through the chamber and the minds of all who listened. They went on and on. These were the writings that had caused this revolution, that had been printed and that had been disseminated throughout most of the known world and translated into many languages—and that had been read and discussed and read and discussed. One by one, the names of these works were announced. The long list of volumes itself spoke volumes. How the world had already changed as a result of them.

When at last the titles were ended, Luther spoke, first in German, and then translating what he had said in Latin. One observer remarked, "He spoke with subdued, soft voice, as if frightened and shocked, with little calm in his visage and gestures, also with little deference in his attitude and countenance."[10] It seems that many listening that day found it quite difficult to understand him. But what he in fact said now was "The books are all mine. And I have written more." Then von der Ecken asked the second question: Did Luther defend them, or wish to recant them?[11]

Included in the long list, near the end, was Luther's recently published volume of lectures on the psalms. Aleander had ordered it from the Frankfurt book fair and added it to the list of books. This recent book, like many others on the long list, was not the source of any of the troubling statements cited in the papal bull.

Von der Ecken had made it very clear that they wanted only simple yes or no answers. They would not be drawn into a debate. So Luther said, "This touches God and his Word. This affects the salvation of souls. Of this Christ said, 'He who denies me before men, him will I deny before my father.' To say too little or too much would be dangerous. I beg you, give me time to think it over."[12] He said that he wanted to answer "satisfactorily" and in a way that did "no violence to the divine Word and danger to my own soul."

To be sure, this was not the response anyone expected. It was irregular and confusing. And indeed, what was it exactly? Was it merely Saxon cunning, a buffoonish stunt to buy time and enable the crafty Luther to do something that would throw sand in the faces of these august men here arrayed? Or was it a sign that Luther was frightened and like a rabbit must scamper back to his warren to cower, for he knew not what else to do?

But the simple answer to this conundrum, which scholars have debated for five centuries, is likely that Luther was fully expecting to be confronted with his own purportedly heretical statements and assertions, which he would be given a chance to reiterate or deny. That, and nothing more. He never expected to be confronted with an impossibly jumbled pile of his many works and to be asked from his mind to make a definitive statement upon them all. He had certainly prepared none. If people thought that fear of a painful death at the stake would have prodded Luther simply to say, "Yes they are mine, and yes I recant anything you wish me to recant," they were mistaken.

Luther's odd and unexpected request for more time must have an answer, so von der Ecken conferred with the diet and the emperor. Then he returned to speak. But before he gave the court's yea or nay, he must first express his prickly dismay and astonishment that a theological professor should be unable to quickly give the simple answer for which he had come to this diet. Such things were hardly to be endured. Then he said,

And therefore [you] do not deserve to be granted a longer time for consideration, yet, out of innate clemency, his imperial majesty grants one day for your deliberation so that you may furnish an answer openly tomorrow at this hour—on this condition: that you do not present your opinion in writing, but declare it by word of mouth.[13]

It seems the diet feared that Luther—whose ensorcelling powers of persuasion via the printed page had brought them to this difficult pass— might have asked for time so that he could repair to his room to summon from his pen yet another mesmerizing manifesto that would doubtless be printed over and over and read far and wide and cause much further damage to the Holy Church. Was that the Saxon fox's plan? And even before that, the manifesto would drag them all into an open disputation with this clever fellow, which is precisely what they had worked so hard to avoid in structuring things as they had done. If he could bamboozle them into responding to a lengthy piece of writing, their whole reason for being here would have been for naught, and Aleander's fears that this whole tawdry German affair was giving Luther yet another platform— and the best platform yet—to spread his pernicious ideas would be shown to be disturbingly well-founded.

So they sent Luther from the chamber. In his communiqué to papal headquarters, Aleander—who had criticized Luther's cheerful countenance upon his entry into the chamber—now smirked: "When [Luther] left he no longer seemed so cheerful."[14]

Back at his quarters, many nobles visited Luther to encourage him not to fear for his life, that all would be well. But Luther was not observed to waver from his stance at all. Afterward, he found time to write a letter, in which he declared, "With Christ's help, however, I shall not in all eternity recant the least particle!"[15] Later that evening, Luther met with Spalatin to talk about what he should say the next day. It is probable that Amsdorf was there that evening, as well as Justus Jonas and Schurff. What they discussed, we cannot know. And though it well might go without saying, we know that in the time he had to do so, Luther prayed with his customary ardor.

The next day Luther met with Conrad Peutinger, whom he had inappropriately greeted as he entered the previous day's session. Peutinger was a high official in Augsburg who was there at Worms representing the free imperial cities, of which Augsburg was one. He later reported that when they met, Luther was in good spirits.

There was likely a full meeting of the diet the next day, so more were in attendance and they met in a much larger chamber. To be there ahead of the appointed time—again four o'clock—Luther was led by Pappenheim and Sturm to the bishop's residence. But because this meeting with

Luther had not been planned, it was tacked onto the end of the official meeting of the diet, and it so happened that the emperor and the German estates were not finished with their business until six. So Luther waited two hours, standing in a warm crowd of people. Although the chamber was vast, it was nonetheless extraordinarily crowded. It seems fitting that not merely a part but all of the empire's representatives should be here to witness what was about to transpire. But many others had come here too, and it was so crowded that many who wanted to enter could not.

By the time Luther was at last summoned before the emperor, it was dark. All was therefore lit by torches, whose flickering lent an undeniable drama to what has since been acknowledged to be one of the seminal meetings in history.

Von der Ecken began by once more dressing down the reprobate before him, reminding Luther that he had had no right to the extra time he had been given, inasmuch as he knew very well why he had been summoned and also because he was a theologian who was expected to be able to answer in matters of faith. Aleander so approved of this masterful and somewhat sarcastic belittling of Luther that he later recommended von der Ecken be rewarded with a papal promotion. So after putting Luther in his place, von der Ecken at last asked the previous day's second question a second time: Did Luther stand by all of these many books, or was there something in them he wished to retract?

On this day, Luther was prepared, and his voice was neither quiet nor meek, as on the previous day. Though he spoke with respect and humility, he spoke with courage and boldness too. No one would complain that they couldn't understand what he was saying. Luther began, "Most serene emperor, most illustrious princes, most clement lords." He then humbly asked that everyone forgive his inexperience in knowing the correct titles for everyone and for perhaps using the wrong gestures than what was appropriate. Doubtless someone—perhaps it was Peutinger—had informed him of his faux pas from the previous day. "I beseech you," Luther said, "to kindly pardon me, as a man accustomed not to courts but to the cells of monks." What followed was a speech of between ten and fifteen minutes that he delivered smoothly and forcefully and calmly, according to all witnesses. First in German, and then in Latin.

He began by saying that to answer the question whether he would retract anything from these books, he must first point out that the books themselves fell into three categories. First, there were those works in which he dealt with the Christian faith in a very straightforward manner and which even his critics acknowledged were good and useful in instructing the faithful. Even the papal bull itself that had so roundly and harshly condemned him had admitted this. It was rather clever of Luther to begin by establishing that he was not merely some troublemaker but that everyone had agreed he had written many approved and instructive things. Then he said there was the second category of books that "inveighs against the desolation of the Christian world by the evil lives and teaching of the papists. Who can deny this when the universal complaints testify that by the laws of the popes the consciences of men are racked?"

At this, the emperor himself interrupted: "No!"

But Luther went on. Playing to the audience of German nobles, most of whom passionately agreed that Rome had abused them in all manner of ways, he said, "Property and possessions, especially in this illustrious nation of Germany, have been devoured by an unbelievable tyranny!" Even his enemy Duke George would have agreed on this score. Luther went on, "Should I recant at this point, I would open the door to more tyranny and impiety, and it will be all the worse would it appear that I had done so at the insistence of the Holy Roman Empire."

Then, Luther said, there was a third category of books. This third class, he said,

> contains attacks on private individuals. I confess I have been more caustic than comports with my profession, but I am being judged, not on my life, but for the teaching of Christ, and I cannot renounce these works either, without increasing tyranny and impiety.

It was canny of Luther to invoke tyranny, because the nationalistic mood against Rome was strong in the room. But then Luther referred to Christ's appearance before the Sanhedrin.

> When Christ stood before Annas, he said, "Produce witnesses." If our Lord, who could not err, made this demand, why may not a worm like me ask to be convicted of error from the prophets and the Gospels? If I am shown my error, I will be the first to throw my books into the fire.[16]
>
> From this, I think, it is apparent that I have sufficiently considered and weighed the arguments and dangers of scholarly disputes that have been aroused in the world as a result of my teachings, because of which I was so sharply and forcefully admonished yesterday. It is my nature to see

the positive side of things—that because of the Word of God, zeal and disputes arise. For that is the course, the manifestation, and the effect of the Word of God. As Christ says, I come not to bring peace but the sword: for I am come to set a man at variance against his father, and so on. That is why we must bear in mind that God is wonderful and terrible in his counsel, so we will not strive to smooth out differences if by doing so we condemn the Word of God. Through this a flood of insufferable evil will most likely pour over us.

If our God is so severe, let us beware lest we release a deluge of wars, lest the reign of this noble youth, Charles, be inauspicious. Take warning from the examples of Pharaoh, the king of Babylon, and the kings of Israel. God it is who confounds the wise. I must walk in the fear of the Lord. I say this not to chide but because I cannot escape my duty to my Germans. I commend myself to Your Majesty. May you not suffer my adversaries to make you ill disposed to me without cause. I have spoken.

Von der Ecken was not at all impressed by what Luther said, and replied sternly,

Martin, you have not sufficiently distinguished your works. The earlier were bad and the latter worse. Your plea to be heard from Scripture is the one always made by heretics. You do nothing but renew the errors of Wycliff and Hus. How will the Jews, how will the Turks, exult to hear Christians discussing whether they have been wrong all these years! Martin, how can you assume that you are the only one to understand the sense of Scripture? Would you put your judgement above that of so many famous men and claim that you know more than they all? You have no right to call into question the most holy orthodox faith, instituted by Christ the perfect lawgiver, proclaimed throughout the world by the apostles, sealed by the red blood of the martyrs, confirmed by the sacred councils, defined by the Church in which all our fathers believed until death and gave to us an inheritance, and which now we are forbidden by the pope and the emperor to discuss lest there be no end of debate. I ask you, Martin—answer candidly and without horns—do you or do you not repudiate your books and the errors which they contain?

In answer, Luther now spoke the words for which he has become most famous:

Since then your serene majesties and your lordships seek a simple answer, I will give it in this manner, plain and unvarnished: Unless I am convinced by the testimony of the scriptures or clear reason, for I do not trust in the Pope or in the councils alone, since it is well known that they often err and contradict themselves, I am bound to the Scriptures I have quoted and my conscience is captive to the Word of God. I cannot and will not retract anything, since it is neither safe nor right to go against conscience. I cannot do otherwise. Here I stand. God help me. Amen.[17]

In fact, we don't know whether the most famous of those words—"Here I stand. I can do no other"—were actually spoken by Luther, although there is no reason to believe they were not. Those who recorded his words in the room that day did not write them, but they were put in the first printed versions of the speech, either as a correction from the transcribed version or as an incorrect addition. These are nonetheless the lapidary words that have been recited and inscribed in many millions of places over the last five centuries, and even if Luther did not speak them, they nonetheless perfectly encapsulate his position, which is surely why they have stuck.

All of this Luther said in German. He was then as expected asked to say all he had said in Latin. But a Saxon counselor, Friedrich von Thun—one of those with whom Luther was sharing his living quarters—now called out, "If you cannot do it, Doctor, you have done enough!"[18] Everyone was hot and tired. It is said that Luther was sweating profusely. The crush of so many bodies for so many hours must have made it warm, and doubtless there was not sufficient oxygen in the room. Nonetheless, Luther insisted on continuing and now said everything once more, this time in Latin. It is recorded that Frederick the Wise was particularly charmed by the Latin rendition.

Where Luther stood as he said those words is today memorialized in the simplest of stone plaques, but where the plaque itself sits is strangely out of the way. There are no hints that at one's feet is where the history of the world is widely reckoned to have pivoted. Long gone is the great palace of the emperor of the Holy Roman Empire. Here and there are excrescences of the walls of that long-ago palace, but it all happened here, the great assemblage and the memorable exchanges, five centuries ago.

History invariably records Luther's final words of the speech, "Here I stand. I can do no other," as the culmination and therefore the end of the scene. But the reality is that it did not end so cinematically. The crowd of princes conferred with each other on what had just transpired, and there was doubtless much peripheral gabbling. Then Luther was told that his remarks had not answered the question sufficiently. Von der Ecken said that Luther must simply put aside his conscience, something that shocks the modern ear, principally because we now live in the world that came into being as a result of Luther's stand that day, a world in which one's conscience is considered sacred. Others in the room held that Luther's details were mistaken, that no councils had actually ever erred, but Luther retorted that he would be happy to give them chapter and verse. And yet because the hour was late and because they did not want to give Luther a further opportunity to do damage by answering as he surely would, the session was brought to an end.

Luther was then escorted out of the chamber by two men from the imperial entourage. Many in the great hall assumed he was being taken prisoner and said so as the escorts moved past with Luther, but the imperial escorts made it clear this was not the case. But then as Luther was led down some stairs, he was followed by a group of taunting Spaniards who had come to Worms with the emperor. They spat that Luther should be hurled into the flames for his opinions. Of course Luther had heard this many times before. When he was at last returned to the bosom of his friends, he threw up his hands as German soldiers did to proclaim a victory, and smiling, he shouted, "I've come through! I've come through!"[19]

Later that night, Frederick the Wise spoke with Spalatin. "Dr. Martin spoke wonderfully before the emperor, the princes, and the estates in Latin and in German," he said, "but he is too daring for me."[20] Frederick meant not that he disapproved of what Luther said but that he was concerned for how Luther had come across to the emperor and about the verdict that would follow.

CHAPTER ELEVEN

An Enemy of the Empire

*I am resolved that I will never again hear
him talk . . . and to act and proceed against
him as against a notorious heretic.*

—Emperor Charles V

T HERE ISN'T A historian the last five centuries who could argue
against the idea that Luther's stand that day at Worms—before the
assembled powers of the empire, and against the theological and
political and ecclesiastical order that had reigned for centuries, and therefore
against the whole of the medieval world—was one of the most significant
moments in history. It ranks with the 1066 Norman Conquest and the 1215
signing of the Magna Carta and the 1492 landing of Columbus in the New
World. And in its way, it far outweighs all of those historic moments.

If ever there was a moment where it can be said the modern world was
born, and where the future itself was born, surely it was in that room on
April 18 at Worms. There can be no question that what happened that day
unequivocally led to all manner of things in the future, among them the
events 254 years and one day later, on April 19, 1775, when the troops at Lex-
ington and Concord took a stand for liberty against tyranny. So much followed from that moment and so much has been made of it that it bears our
taking a closer look at what exactly happened at Worms, and what did not.

Luther's Appeal to Conscience

Much of what has been written about that moment homes in on the word
"conscience." Luther declared, "My conscience is captive to the Word of
God." He continued, "To go against conscience is neither safe nor right."[1]

But so many historians have conflated our modern ideas about conscience with Luther's very different ideas about it that we have accepted a deeply mistaken idea about what Luther meant, and therefore about what his stand at Worms meant. Of course Luther never said the English word "conscience"; that word is a translation from his German and Latin. The words he used, usually translated as "conscience," cannot perfectly be translated as what we today mean by that word. The German word he used, *Gewissen*, really means "knowing." And the Latin word, *conscientia*, means "with knowing." But there is nothing about these words in Luther's day that even implies what we today mean by the word "conscience." The modern concept of conscience has come to mean something almost completely subjective, as though each of us has his own barometer and that barometer were sacrosanct, as though each person's truth were comparable to truth itself. Indeed, the subjective idea of each person's truth has fairly trumped the idea of an objective truth. It implies that each of us has his own truth, and that truth is one's conscience.

Many of the toughest critics of Luther rightly aver that the line between the one and the other concepts of truth and conscience was crossed when Luther took his stand at Worms. Once the interpretation of the Scriptures and the concept of truth was taken away from the church itself, it was given away to each individual, and real and objective truth itself was effectively abolished. Once the authority of the church was broken up and the opportunity to disagree with the church was possible, anyone might disagree with any authority, and a thousand churches might spring up, each with its own version of the truth. This is indeed precisely what happened.

But it is important to see that despite what both his critics and his defenders have often said, Luther was never coming near anything of the kind. His concept of the word "conscience" was not our modern view, in which conscience takes its cue from the autonomous self. On the contrary, his concept of truth did not vary one iota from the accepted Roman Catholic view. The only difference between his view and the church's view was in the idea that one's conscience must obey God himself. The Catholic church reserved the right to say that it and it alone spoke for God, whereas Luther, in pointing out that the pope had erred and church councils had erred, was saying that the church could not reserve the right to speak for God. Therefore, if the church—via pope and councils—was able to err and to sometimes not speak for God and God's truth, Luther asserted the idea that only the Scriptures could be that inerrant standard to which everyone—including the church—must repair. Thus, if the Scriptures plainly said something different from what councils and popes said, it must be the councils and the popes who were in error and were obliged to change their views. There was no other recourse. And Luther, in saying that he could not go against conscience, was simply saying that if his own understanding, his own knowledge, as guided by plain logic and clear arguments, showed him that Scripture said one thing and anyone else—even the church—said another, he had no choice but to go with what the Scriptures said. The Word of God trumped all else. So it was not Luther's conscience that trumped anything. It was the Word of God that trumped everything. One's conscience was only one's ability to understand these things, and because he understood the Word of God clearly, he had no choice but to follow it. Luther was one of few who during that time had studied the Word of God carefully, so he had opportunity to observe that it was inerrant in a way that the church councils and popes were not. He therefore concluded that only the Scriptures spoke for God. The church must therefore bow to that greater authority.

But something else that arises out of this discussion about conscience has to do with the difference between power and truth. By demanding over and over that he be shown where he was mistaken—if he was indeed mistaken, as the church was saying—Luther appealed to the idea that anyone could understand what the Scripture said if one only dared to look at it. He knew that if he could force them all merely to look at it, to show him his error, they would see that in fact it was they who had been in error. There was no other way for him to convince them than to bother them to look for themselves. But because they were unwilling to do this, they were ignoring what the Scriptures said and were asserting the naked power of the church. Forcing people to believe did not comport with Luther's view of the God of the Scriptures. God was all powerful and omniscient, and he alone defined truth and indeed was truth. But he did not assert that power in a way that ever smacked of power in the worldly sense. He had always and ever shown himself in weakness. Jesus washed the feet of his disciples. Jesus died on the cross for those who had mocked and rejected him. God did not crush us but showed us mercy, and Luther could see that the church had not adopted this view, but had itself become wed to worldly power. It took money that was not its own and burned those who disagreed with what it taught. Luther was trying to call the church back to its true roots, to a biblical idea of a merciful God who did not demand that we obey but who first loved us and first made us righteous before he expected us to live righteously. This was the good news of the Gospel that the church had so horribly obscured. And it was what had freed Luther from the horrors of his previous life. This was truth itself, and the church's disturbing response to his attempts to get it to see these things only proved that God was not on its side in this. He would do all he could to get it to see this, including be willing to die for it, if it came to that. He feared that less than he feared God and denying God's truth.

Many historians have put Luther forward as the first to put "individual conscience" before the authority of the church and empire. But ironically, he was not at all asserting the freedom of the individual to do as he pleased. He was asserting the freedom of the individual to do as God pleased—if and when the church or the state attempted to abrogate that freedom. Luther was asserting the modern idea of freedom of religion and freedom of conscience for the first time in history. These things point not to man as a new free agent but to God himself. That it would be possible for someone to abuse these ideas to do what God did not want him to do was always the risk, so to the extent that Luther made that risk and error possible, he may be held responsible for that. But the alternative to opening things up to this risk is to accept the sheer authority of church or state, and that was far worse. So yes, to some extent, Luther's stand at Worms created new problems that we did not have before, but to a larger extent it gave us genuine liberty in a way that would lead to a new freer and deeper understanding of what God wanted. Just as Jesus had called upon the Pharisees to stop their outward obedience to God and go far deeper, to inward obedience, so Luther called upon every Christian to cease the petty obedience to church that was nothing when compared to the freedom and joy of actually obeying God.

The Morning After

On April 19, on the morning after Luther had taken his historic stand, Emperor Charles conferred with the estates—with the electors and a number of princes—to see what should be done. Aleander and the other papal nuncios were there too. But the Germans were not quite sure what to say just yet, and like Luther they said they needed more time to think about it. "Very well," said the young emperor. "Then I shall read to you my opinion." And now he read aloud a statement he had written in his own hand that morning. He had written it in French:

You know that I am descended from the most Christian emperors of the noble German nation, the Catholic kings of Spain, the archdukes of Austria, and the dukes of Burgundy, who all were, until death, faithful sons of the Holy Roman Church, and they have always defended the Catholic faith, the sacred ceremonies, decretals, ordinances, and laudable customs, for the honor of God, the propagation of the faith, and the salvation of souls. After their deaths they left, by natural law and heritage, these holy Catholic rites, for us to live and to die following their example.... What is true and a great shame and offense to us is that a single monk, going against God, [is] mistaken in his opinion, which is against what all of Christendom has held for over a thousand years to the present. I am therefore determined to use all my kingdoms and possessions, my friends, my body, my blood, my life, and my soul. For it would be a great disgrace for you and me, the noble and greatly renowned German nation, appointed by privilege and singular eminence to be the defenders and protectors of the Catholic faith ... I declare that I now regret having played so long the proceedings against him and his false doctrines. I am resolved that I will never again hear him talk ... and to act and proceed against him as against a notorious heretic.[2]

A number of those in the room were aghast. It seemed that Luther's fate was sealed. Aleander was especially tickled to hear this and now realized he had been too hasty in condemning the emperor's relatively kind invitation to Luther to come to Worms. Joachim of Brandenburg, who was probably Luther's strongest opponent among the seven electors present, reminded the room that they all had agreed that if Luther did not recant, they would proceed against him. Thus, they must go and sign the emperor's document. On the next day, however, despite initially all declaring themselves to be in full agreement with the emperor, only four of the electors consented to sign. Frederick the Wise declined to do so, as did the elector from the Palatinate region of the Rhine, Ludwig von der Pfalz. Frederick would maintain until his death that Luther had not been given the debate and disputation that he deserved so that he could explain and defend his points, and without this it was all something of a sham and certainly not sufficient to condemn a good man to death. Still, with four electors having signed, the emperor felt he had enough support to proceed with formally declaring Luther an enemy of the empire.

But then, overnight, something happened that would cause a change in plans. Some troublemakers had under cover of darkness posted a number of placards around Worms. Most of them featured the image of the *Bundschuh*, the peasant's shoe, which was the symbol of the working classes and stood in contrast with the high boots worn by the nobles. The inevitable political implications of Luther's stand had at last forced them into the wider conversation. The posting of these placards around Worms was clearly a threat. Or so many believed. The message was "Beware! If you convict Luther, we shall rise up!" There were other placards too. The one that most boldly had been posted on the door of the city hall itself read, "*Bundschuh! Bundschuh! Bundschuh!*" Another placard read, "Woe to the land whose king is a child."[3] There were even verses lampooning the papal nuncios Glapion and Chièvres, and they spoke of a force of four hundred horsemen and a thousand foot soldiers. This was hardly the work of a single troublemaker.*

It had been the case for some time—and was greatly underscored as Luther made his triumphant procession to Worms—that the common German people had found in Luther a champion and now were clearing their throats to announce themselves. They had for several years read Luther's works and had talked about his ideas, and his heroic stand against the tyranny of Rome was what they had been waiting for. He spoke for them—with the wit and fire of the common man—and they would certainly not stand aside while some Spanish emperor and Italian papal flunkies strove to crush one of their own.

They despised the unquestioned power of the church and had seen the rank abuses of that power, and the hypocrisy of much of the clergy, and the fat monks begging for money, and they had had enough. The elites had had their day, and now Luther like a German Hercules had risen up to smite them, and they would be his passionate allies. He had struck a blow for the common man in demanding that they were equal to the priests and could take both the bread and the wine, just as the priests could, and the unmistakably egalitarian implications of Luther's theology were now elbowing their way to the fore.

When Albrecht of Mainz saw these threatening posters, he turned the color of milk. Already at dawn he flew to Charles's residence to sound the warning. But the young emperor only laughed in his face. He hardly thought a few posters warranted changing the course they had settled

---

* That Ulrich von Hutten was behind these things is likely.

on. But Albrecht knew more of what these German peasants might do than this callow Spanish stripling, and he would not relent, so he returned with his brother, Joachim of Brandenburg, and the two of them convinced the other estates, all of whom now petitioned the emperor. They asked him to give them time to persuade Luther to recant. Perhaps a deal could be struck to forestall the disaster that might lie ahead. The emperor wanted nothing to do with any of it himself, but he would give them three days to do what they could.

What follows has rarely been mentioned in books about Luther, and it is a strange omission, because in these three days with the representatives of the German estates, Luther finally did get something far closer to the hearing he had always longed for. The desperation of the German nobles to avoid a bloody social uprising had brought them to this place where they hoped to reason and forge some kind of compromise with the wild monk from Wittenberg. Even if they failed, at least they would have tried, and the peasants would have seen that they took their concerns to heart and had attempted to give Luther the fair hearing he had asked for. So they praised the emperor for his stand for the faith, but now they would take the three days he had given them to see what they might accomplish. What followed in the next three days is an extraordinary last-ditch effort to avoid all that lay ahead. Because it did not provide anything as powerfully symbolic as Luther's stand before the emperor a few days earlier, it is usually overlooked. Nor did Luther or anyone else say anything as memorable as his last words at the diet. Nonetheless, it is significant because it shows how very differently things might have gone and how close this final attempt came to diverting the river of history into another channel.

The group of ten who would meet with Luther was a variegated one and included the archbishop of Trier, Richard von Greiffenklau zu Vollraths, as well as Albrecht's brother, Joachim of Brandenburg, and Duke George the Bearded, who even in this group was Luther's staunchest opponent. More on Luther's side were the Humanists Dr. Conrad Peutinger of Augsburg, whom we have already met, and Chancellor Jerome Vehus. On April 22, Luther was summoned to appear at the lodgings of the archbishop of Trier at six in the morning, two days hence.

And so early on the morning of the twenty-fourth, they met. Initially, the commission of ten wanted to deal with Luther's demeanor toward the church, rather than with the theological substance at issue. Vehus and

Peutinger were the most in favor of Luther's point of view, and Vehus was chosen to lead the discussion. They bemoaned the awful situation and appealed to Luther to consider whether anything could be done to preserve the unity of the church. Surely he should not have utterly disdained the councils as he had done. Their power and authority were still to be respected—were they not?—even if sometimes they had perhaps erred. That they would admit this as any kind of possibility was already a tremendous concession and must have been startling to some in the room. But then they backtracked a bit, saying that even though councils had expressed different things, this didn't necessarily mean they had contradicted each other. They appealed to Luther's notion of simple brotherly love and a desire not to tear apart the fabric of Christendom, if it was possible to avoid it. And they said that if he was to proceed recklessly and insist on standing by every word of his writings, it would unnecessarily destroy all of the good he had written forever, which would be tragic.

Luther was humbled that they should come to him in this way, and said so, but he could not relent one hair's breadth from his position with regard to church councils. He made it clear that in this matter he had only criticized the Council of Constance because, regarding the case of Hus, that council had clearly departed from Scripture. He made it clear that it was not his own opinion that mattered—God forbid—but only what the Scriptures clearly said. If his had been an offense against love, or if the church's offense had been against love, as he had said in his speech at the diet, that would be something else entirely. One could and should forgive such offenses. But when it came to the Scriptures, his hands were tied. Their authority and what they said were not open to his or any other's equivocation.

Then it was proposed that Luther submit all of his books to the judgment of the emperor and the imperial estates. But Luther again averred that the judgment of men was not enough. They must judge according to Scripture, and unless they promised to do so, he could not accept their judgment.

Next the archbishop of Trier stepped in. On his side of the debate were von der Ecken—who was his official—and Johannes Cochlaeus, who had been favorable toward Luther until 1520, at which point he turned against him, eventually becoming perhaps his fiercest opponent. On Luther's side were Schurff and Amsdorf. At one point, Cochlaeus put a direct question to Luther: Had the Word of God been revealed to him? Luther said that it had, at which point Cochlaeus demanded that Luther show them the nail prints in his hands. The rancor only increased from this point, with von der Ecken and Cochlaeus sometimes attacking Luther together, and with Schurff having to aggressively step in to break things up. Cochlaeus was clearly infuriated at Luther, accusing him of having attacked the pope personally. When the archbishop suggested they take a break and meet again later, no one seemed to think there was any real point to doing so.

But later Cochlaeus took matters into his own hands and snuck off to Luther's lodgings alone. He later recalled that the atmosphere there was chaotic, with people coming and going and no one watching the door, so that he was able to slip in unnoticed. He first conversed with Luther's friend Petzensteiner, who intemperately argued with Cochlaeus to the point that Luther himself had to mediate. Cochlaeus had come in good faith and somehow even managed to join them at table and found himself seated between Luther and a nobleman he took to be Frederick the Wise but who certainly was not. The animated conversation turned to transubstantiation, at which point Cochlaeus proposed to Luther that he forgo his safe-conduct from the emperor and engage in an open debate with him, Cochlaeus. It would be a no-holds-barred battle for the truth of God. Of course if Luther lost, he would likely die. Luther's friends were outraged at Cochlaeus, supposing he hoped Luther would die, and as a result one of them, Rudolf von Watzdorf, nearly came to blows with Cochlaeus. But Luther had no fear of martyrdom and was on the very verge of accepting Cochlaeus's challenge if his friends had not so forcefully intervened.

After the hubbub subsided and Luther went up to his bedchamber to retire, Cochlaeus followed him, unable to resist a final personal appeal. He showed Luther he was carrying no weapons, and Luther allowed him in so they could continue their conversation alone. By all accounts, what followed was amicable. Luther explained to Cochlaeus that even if he were himself to recant anything, some of his followers, who were now many, would lift the fallen Gospel standard out of the mire and hold it high themselves and keep marching and fighting. This was now something that went far beyond one man's opinions. Cochlaeus informed Luther that if Luther would not back down, he was obliged to take up his pen against him. "I cannot become a Hussite," Cochlaeus said, before departing.[4] For the rest of his life, he claimed that he had that night almost persuaded Luther to recant. He even said that Luther had wept during their discussion, although Luther vigorously denied this. None-theless, Cochlaeus's efforts were genuine and heartfelt, but Luther's allies were so enraged at him for nearly succeeding in getting Luther to give up his safe-conduct that they immediately penned verses that savagely mocked him and infamously punned on the similarity of his Humanist name to the German for "snail." These writings traveled quickly, sud-denly making Cochlaeus persona non grata with Ulrich von Hutten and the other Humanists with whom he had previously enjoyed favor. When most of his friends in Frankfurt joined Luther's side, he ended up having to flee to Rome. Eventually, Cochlaeus became Luther's most furious de-tractor, hastily and unrelentingly writing against him for many years.*

After the late night tête-à-tête with Cochlaeus, though, things were still not finished. The very next day, Luther met once more with a smaller contingent, this time made up of the Humanists Peutinger and Vehus on one side, with Schurff and an unnamed Saxon knight on the other. Again they tried to persuade Luther to submit his writings to the judgment of the emperor and the imperial estates, but Luther said he could not turn things over to the judgment of men unless they agreed they would use the standard of Scripture for their judgments. Peutinger and Vehus seemed to be so eager for an agreement that they insisted that this would go without saying and that for Luther to insist upon it would only insult the emperor. This conversation went round and round in much the man-ner of the previous day's, until at last it was proposed that Luther submit his writings to a church council. To this he was much warmer, but once again this was something he could assent to only if the council referred to the Scriptures in making its judgment. In their zeal to finalize a deal with him, Peutinger and Vehus reported the good news of an agreement to the archbishop but likely left out the detail that it must all be done with the guarantee of Scripture being used as final arbiter. So the arch-bishop summoned Luther to seal the agreement, but in the subsequent conversation it became clear nothing had actually been achieved. Luther's stipulation that any judgments be based on the Scripture had not changed, even with a church council.

The final conversation between Luther and the Trier archbishop was not acrimonious. This archbishop was known to be the guardian of one of the holiest relics in Christendom, which was a piece of cloth purported

---

* Cochlaeus would work his way to the head of the invective class when he asserted the spectacularly vile notion that Luther was conceived when the devil raped his mother in an outhouse.

to be the seamless garment of Christ, for which the soldiers had cast lots. So the archbishop was alluding to this when he asked Luther to please not tear the seamless garment of the church asunder. And when the archbishop asked him who might be a suitable judge, Luther joked that he would simply name any child of eight or nine.

Toward the end of their conversation, the archbishop asked Luther whether he himself might propose a solution; Luther almost offhandedly replied that the only thing he could think of was what Gamaliel had said in Acts 5, to "let the future decide" whether Luther and what he preached was of God or not. Luther was referring to that passage in which the Jewish religious leaders in Jerusalem had become furious that Peter and the apostles refused to stop preaching about Jesus and wanted to put them to death. But Gamaliel, who was one of the most respected of them, counseled that they be left alone. "Let them go!" he said. "For if their purpose or activity is of human origin, it will fail. But if it is from God, you will not be able to stop these men; you will only find yourselves fighting against God."[5] So Luther was comparing himself to the early apostles, who were also persecuted, and asking that he be allowed to continue doing what he was doing. In addition, he asked that the archbishop simply allow him to depart Worms gracefully.

After this meeting, Luther was determined to take a well-earned powder, but Spalatin informed him he was not yet free to go. Then, on the evening of the next day, the twenty-fifth, von der Ecken and two other men visited Luther to inform him what had been decided. Von der Ecken said that because of his unrepentant attitude the emperor would indeed be taking action against him. Therefore Luther must be back at Wittenberg within twenty-one days. More important, during that time, he was forbidden to preach and even to write. They especially didn't want Luther to write an account of what he had experienced at Worms, which would likely stir up further dissent. The emperor granted Luther safe-conduct during this time. That was all. Luther's response was cheerful: "As it pleases the Lord; blessed be the name of the Lord!"[6] He knew that he was free, that he had done what he needed to do, and that God would do the rest. What that was, was God's business. He agreed to obey all that had been asked of him and even shook von der Ecken's hand in parting.

But what would become of him if he returned to Wittenberg? Even if the emperor granted him safe-conduct, as he surely would have done,

Luther's return to Wittenberg would only have been until the emperor issued his edict declaring Luther an outlaw, which Luther himself surely knew, because Spalatin would have heard from Frederick what the emperor had written the morning after April 18. Frederick had determined that he wished to help Luther, but he would be wise to keep from appearing to have done so, so as not to incur the wrath of the emperor. It had been bruited about among Luther's friends in Wittenberg since 1519 that should it come to that, they could hide him away someplace. Well, it had certainly come to that. We assume Frederick initiated this idea, but he made it clear that he himself mustn't know any of the details. But where would Luther go? Somewhere. Luther's friends Amsdorf, von Feilitzsch, and von Thun told him that he shouldn't worry. All had been prepared, but no one must know the details.

On Luther's last night in Worms, he had a farewell dinner, likely provided by Frederick, who also gave him forty gulden for traveling expenses. Aleander throughout his accounts had painted a picture of Luther as a man of the flesh, wholly given over to the lusts of the body and addicted to the delicacies given him by the deluded nobles, such as Frederick. Somehow Aleander discovered the details of this last dinner and with typically pinched spite reported that the "reverend rascal" had gulped several glasses of the malmsey wine he so favored. It was a sharp parting kick. But at nine in the morning on April 26, Luther at last departed the city that would henceforth be known for what he had just done there. Where he was now going, however, he had no idea.

The Outlaw Luther

After Luther had departed, the emperor still wanted to get those at the diminishing diet to side with him against Luther. On May 6, he presented to those still at Worms his final draft of the edict Aleander had prepared. It was not written to spare anyone's feelings. Part of it read thus:

> He has sullied marriage, disparaged confession, and denied the body and blood of our Lord. He makes the sacraments depend on the faith of the recipient. He is pagan in his denial of free will. This devil in the habit of a monk has brought together ancient errors into one stinking puddle and has invented new ones. He denies the power of the keys and encourages

the laity to wash their hands in the blood of the clergy. His teaching makes for rebellion, division, war, murder, robbery, arson, and the collapse of Christendom. He lives the life of a beast. He has burned the decretals. He despises alike the ban and the sword. He does more harm to the civil than to the ecclesiastical power. We have labored with him, but he recognized only the authority of Scripture, which he interprets in his own sense. We have given him twenty-one days, dating from April the 15th. We have now gathered the estates. Luther is to be regarded as a convicted heretic [although the bull of excommunication still had not been published]. When the time is up, no one is to harbor him. His followers also are to be condemned. His books are to be eradicated from the memory of man.[7]

Aleander took the document to the emperor for his signature, but although the emperor took up his pen to sign it, he paused. One doubts this was because he was having second thoughts about the line that accused Luther of living "the life of a beast." Then, still without signing it, the emperor oddly announced to Aleander that he must bring it to the diet, for its approval. Aleander could not fathom why the emperor felt this was necessary. Besides, the diet was diminishing day by day, with more and more nobles departing to make their long journeys home. But Charles, though merely twenty-one years old, nonetheless possessed an uncommon measure of political acumen and shrewdness. He had realized that because Frederick had departed, as had Ludwig von der Pfalz, he now had a sympathetic audience left, most of whom would surely condemn Luther. In fact, although the edict had been presented for his signature on May 6, he waited until May 26, when yet more nobles who would present obstacles to his goal had departed. Whether he put the word out to those favorable to his idea to linger a bit while the others left, we do not know. But we do know that it was not until May 26—when only a bare rump favorable to the sentiment of this edict remained—that he signed it.

When he did sign it, Luther was a wanted and a marked man, an outlaw in every corner of the vast Holy Roman Empire. The edict warned that everyone within the empire was

not to take the aforementioned Martin Luther into your houses, not to receive him at court, to give him neither food nor drink, not to hide him, to afford him no help, following, support, or encouragement, either clandestinely or publicly, through words or works. Where you can get him, seize him and overpower him, you should capture him and send him to us under tightest security.[8]

It goes without saying that whenever Luther was finally captured, he would for his crimes be put to death by burning. But where was this renegade Luther on the day this edict was signed, precisely one month after he had left Worms?

On the Run

Luther left Worms at nine in the morning on April 26 in the wagon that had been provided by the Wittenberg goldsmith Döring and the city council. With him were his previous companions for the journey to Worms, including Amsdorf, Jonas, the Pomeranian Swawe, and Petzensteiner. They were now joined by Schurff too, because his destination was also Wittenberg. Aleander did not think Luther would actually go to Wittenberg, and in this he was proven correct; he believed Luther would now escape to the safe spaces of Denmark or Bohemia, presumably to live with his fellow Hussites.

Luther and his party traveled exactly along the path on which they had come. On this first day of travel, they went the sixteen miles due north toward Oppenheim, where they crossed the Rhine and then took a northeasterly route through Frankfurt and on to Wittenberg. When they departed Worms that morning, they did so without the escort of the imperial herald, who joined them later. But waiting outside the gates of Worms was a company of twenty horsemen—allegedly furnished by the bellicose knight Franz von Sickingen—who along with von Hutten were favorably disposed toward Luther and had plans to upend the existing political system that then existed under the emperor and the pope. Sickingen's territory was on the Rhine, and we assume his cavalry took Luther and his companions this far. In Oppenheim, the imperial herald caught up with them and rode with them on toward Frankfurt.

From Frankfurt am Main, two days into their journey—on April 28—Luther wrote a letter to his friend Lucas Cranach in Wittenberg. It is in this letter that Luther explained what was to take place. "I shall submit to being 'imprisoned,'" he wrote, "and hidden away, though as yet I do not know where." We remember that the night before leaving Worms, Luther was assured by Frederick, through his friends, that something like this would happen, but neither Frederick nor Luther knew the details. He would be taken to some unknown hideaway for safekeeping. Where it was and how long he would be there and any other circumstances were unknown.

Luther continued, "I would have preferred death at the hands of the tyrants, especially those of the furious Duke George of Saxony, but I must not disregard the counsel of good men; [I must await God's] appointed time."[9] He had a sense of the high danger of what he had done, and he had settled in his mind before God that he would do what he must and suffer such consequences as the Lord allowed. He still had the conviction that while he had enjoyed the laurels and adulation of his Palm Sunday entrance at Worms, a Good Friday lay ahead. But he knew that to recklessly push toward that would be wrong. He must play the role God had appointed until such time as God himself clearly opened the door to Luther's martyrdom. And so now he submitted himself to the still-hidden plans arranged by his prince, Frederick the Wise. He then wrote to Cranach, explaining his version of the strange events at Worms:

> I thought His Imperial Majesty would have assembled one or
> fifty scholars and overcome this monk in a straightforward
> manner. But nothing else was done there than this: Are these
> your books? Yes. Do you want to renounce them or not? No.
> Then go away! O we blind Germans, how childishly we act and
> allow the Romanists to mock and fool us in such a pitiful way!

Luther then made explicit his sense that he was walking the path toward his own Calvary.

> For a little while the Jews have to chant: "Crucify him!" But
> Easter Sunday will also come for us, and then we will chant
> "Alleluia." For a little while one has to be silent and suffer. For a
> little while you will not see me, and again in a little while you will
> see me—so said Christ. I hope it will now be the same way [with
> me]. But God's will, the very best possible, be done in this—as in
> heaven, so also on earth. Amen.[10]

We can only imagine the host of things in Luther's mind at this juncture. He was not so spiritually minded that he was no earthly good, so he not only thought about the possibility of his own martyrdom but recognized that we must render unto Caesar the things that are Caesar's,* just as Jesus commanded. So he was respectful of the governing authorities, and now thought it appropriate that he write to the emperor, who he knew was furious with him and had been for some time.

Later that day, from Friedberg, just north of Frankfurt, Luther wrote a long letter to the emperor. It is a humble and respectful letter, but in it Luther asserted this new and earth-shattering idea that he had recovered from the Gospels, that neither pope nor emperor possesses any authority unless it is given to him from God. It is an echo of what Jesus said to Pilate, when Pilate asked, "Don't you know that I have the power to crucify you?" and Jesus replied, "You have no authority over me, except that which has been given you from above."[11] Luther had rediscovered the lever that can move the world, and the leveler that puts all on equal footing before God. It was that which made us all free, our equality as subjects of the King of Kings.

While at Friedberg, on the next day, April 29, Luther told Caspar Sturm, the imperial herald, that he, Luther, was now safe and he therefore relieved Sturm of his duties, dismissing him. In fact, Luther wrote a statement to this effect, because this was not a simple affair, and with that statement he included a letter that the herald was to deliver to Spalatin. In the letter to Spalatin, he passed along his greetings to Pappenheim, the imperial marshal. Also—and of course this was most important of all—he enclosed the long letter to the emperor. Whether Luther and company had craftily planned all of this in advance, we don't know, but what we do know is that the principal reason Luther now dismissed Sturm was what was about to take place.

Kidnapped

We presume that Luther spent the night of the twenty-eighth in Friedberg and that Sturm was dismissed on the twenty-ninth. That day Luther

---

* The German cognate for "Caesar" is *Kaiser*, so Luther and all Germans referred to their emperors as kaisers, because they were not merely kings but the rulers of an empire. In this case, it was the Holy Roman Empire, which of course styled itself as a kind of continuation of the original Roman Empire.

proceeded with his remaining company to Grünberg, where he spent the night, and then traveled forty miles to Hersfeld. In Hersfeld, Luther was honored with a tremendous welcome by the city council and the abbot of the Hersfeld monastery. He described it in a letter to Spalatin:

> You would hardly believe in what friendly fashion the abbot of Hersfeld received us! He sent the chancellor and treasurer a good mile out to meet us; then he himself together with many riders met us at his castle and accompanied us into town. The city council welcomed us inside the gate. The abbot fed us sumptuously in his monastery and made his private chamber available for my use. [The next morning] they compelled me to preach. In vain I pled that the monastery might lose its royal privileges if the emperor's officials should interpret my sermon as a breach of the safe conduct, since they had forbidden me to preach while on my way. But I said that I had not consented for the word of God to be bound; and that is true.[12]

The next day Luther and his friends traveled on to Eisenach, where Luther preached again. Luther believed and declared that the Word of God could not be bound, so as far as he was concerned, he could not obey any man who wished to bind it, and his first obedience was due to God. In smaller matters, Luther felt differently, but as he made clear in his letter to the emperor and many other times, the Word of God was sacrosanct, and his duty to declare it wherever he went trumped any man-made constrictions.* He knew that he was endangering his life by doing this, but now and at other times Luther seems genuinely to have trusted God. But the pastor in Eisenach was not willing to go as far as his Hersfeld counterpart. He let Luther preach, but realizing this could put his own life in danger, he hedged his bet by proactively lodging a protest with the city notary.

Because Luther had relatives nearby, south of Eisenach, whom he wished to visit, he sent Justus Jonas on ahead to Wittenberg, along with Schurff and Swawe. Luther was now alone with his fellow monk Petzensteiner and with his friend Amsdorf as he traveled on to nearby Möhra, the village where his father, Hans, had been born. The three of them stayed there overnight with Luther's relatives and departed the next day.

---

* See Luther's nascent sense of religious liberty, that the rightful power of the state must never encroach upon the territory that belonged to God.

But after they had traveled about five miles—just as they were passing through a ravine near Schloss Altenstein—the three of them were violently set upon by a group of armed horsemen. Whether Petzensteiner was in on the ruse, we don't know, but we do know that seeing the armed horsemen approaching, he leaped off the wagon and fled on foot, arriving in Waltershausen that evening. The kidnappers—for such they now revealed themselves to be—pointed their fearsome crossbows at the wagon driver, demanding with rough curses to know whom he was carrying. Certainly not privy to what was going on and fearing for his life, the driver blabbed what they surely already knew. Amsdorf too was in on the ruse, but to keep up appearances with the driver, he shouted angrily at the armed men. Nonetheless, the men rather roughly grabbed Luther, but not before he had grabbed his New Testament and the Hebrew Bible. They likely forced him to run alongside their horses until they were out of sight. When the coast was clear, they could reveal themselves as friendly, which Luther had certainly suspected. They now stripped him of his monk's habit and dressed him in a knight's cloak, so that anyone seeing him would have no idea that he was a monk, and at this point probably let Luther mount one of their horses. Because they didn't want anyone to be able to follow them or trace their path, they took a wildly circuitous, serpentine route toward their mysterious destination, deep in the Thuringian forest.

And who were these kidnappers? Both were friends of Frederick's, as one might have expected. One was the castellan* of the fabled Wartburg castle, Hans von Berlepsch; the other was the lord of the nearby Schloss Altenstein. Both had played their roles convincingly, and after riding many hours through the blackness of the forest, just before midnight they clattered across the wooden footbridge to deliver their exhausted abductee to safety. The plan that Frederick had instigated—while preserving his own "plausible deniability"—had thus been executed. Luther was at the Wartburg castle, and almost no one in the empire knew about it, although, just as was hoped, many soon heard about the kidnapping and wondered whether Luther had been killed.

The idea that the emperor had issued this edict against Luther helps us see how the medieval world, where church and state essentially formed a theocracy of sorts, was very much like a Muslim caliphate. We see that where the church and the state are essentially one, there can be no

---

* A castellan—or chatelain—is the governor or keeper of a castle.

genuine—or "free"—church, and although Luther did not have what we think of as the separation of church and state on his mind, nor religious liberty, what he was doing nonetheless amounted to the same thing. To free the Gospel—to free freedom—meant tearing it out of the world and letting it stand alone.

In any case, with the Edict of Worms, something like a fatwa had been put on the head of Luther for his "heretical" beliefs, and he would now be captured and likely executed. Perhaps a single assassin or group of assassins would catch up with him someplace and end his life out of sight, without announcing who had sent them, though people would naturally assume it was the emperor or the pope who was behind it. That's exactly what many people thought had happened in this kidnapping. Over the months of Luther's semi-self-imposed exile, many wondered whether he was still alive. And if Luther had died, would the great movement he had ignited fizzle out?

Far away in the Netherlands, Albrecht Dürer wrote,

> I know not whether [Luther] lives or is murdered, but in any case he has suffered for the Christian truth. If we lose this man, who has written more clearly than any other in centuries, may God grant his spirit to another. His books should be held in great honor, and not burned as the emperor commands, but rather the books of his enemies. O God, if Luther is dead, who will henceforth explain to us the gospel? What might he not have written for us in the next ten or twenty years?[13]

CHAPTER TWELVE

The Wartburg

How I wish that Karlstadt had tried to refute
celibacy with more fitting Scripture passages!

—Martin Luther

PERCHED ATOP AN impossibly high ridge that itself sits like a
lone island amid a sea of greenery stretching to the horizon lies
what is called the Wartburg.* Begun in 1067 by a Thuringian
count known as Ludwig der Springer,† the Wartburg was already by Luther's time a fabled site. For Luther, the Wartburg would be something
like an ark floating above the surface of the world. The time Luther spent
there would soon become legendary, and the Wartburg itself a byword
for Luther's exile.‡ But most people today when gazing up at the Wartburg remember that it was the place where Luther did the one thing that
would more than anything symbolize all else that he did when he translated the New Testament into German, forever releasing from its Latin
prison the simple song of freedom itself, which would fly around the
world and never again be hidden away.

But when Luther first arrived, he had no plans to do any such thing.
Here at the Wartburg, he was alone and unknown. Apart from the castellan Berlepsch himself, no one in the castle knew who their fellow oc-
cupant was. Berlepsch settled him in a very small apartment—containing
a humble and sparsely furnished living room and a tiny bedroom—that

---

* To get to the Wartburg today, one must park far below and then either take a shuttle bus up the impossibly winding switchbacks or ride a donkey, as was done in olden times. In any case, the journey will
soon impress upon the pilgrim the great remoteness of this redoubt.
† This is typically translated as Louis the Jumper or Louis the Leaper. The nickname came as the result
of a dramatic leap he took from a high tower in which he was imprisoned into the river Saale.
‡ When Dietrich Bonhoeffer saw the Wartburg from his train window as he passed in 1941, he was
horrified to see that the Nazis had replaced the prominent cross atop its highest tower with a grotesque, floodlit swastika.

*Cranach's 1522 woodcut portrait of
Luther in his "Junker George" phase.*

was sometimes used as a temporary prison for errant knights. It was next
to Berlepsch's own quarters in the outer castle, far from anyone else,
where Luther would escape notice by the others in the castle. A small set
of stairs led from Berlepsch's quarters to Luther's, and each night these
were pulled up via a chain and secured with a lock. For the first period of
his time at the Wartburg, Luther was cut off from all human contact save
Berlepsch and the two noble lads serving as pages who brought him his
meals. What they were told about this mysterious man, we don't know.
But we do know that as far as anyone was concerned, save the handful in
on this historic stunt, the celebrated and vilified monk known as Martin
Luther no longer existed. From the moment he stepped over the threshold of the castle, he was to be known exclusively as Junker* George. He

* Pronounced "Yoong-kerr," the word "Junker" is derived from *jung* (young) and *Herr* (lord).

must henceforth look and act like the other knights residing in the castle and therefore now began to grow out his tonsure with all alacrity. He also grew a beard and cast aside his rough-hewn cassock for the stylish accoutrements of a noble knight. He would sport a fashionable doublet and hose, as well as a linen shirt, all of which was punctuated by a handsome codpiece. Whenever he was ready to leave the confines of his room, no one must know his real identity.

Arriving here in this quiet place after the historic hubbub of what had just taken place at Worms must have been a dramatic shock, nor did Luther have the slightest idea how long he would need to remain here. He was not used to being utterly alone, nor to having a moment's time on his hands. But now he seemed to have nothing else. What to do? The only one with whom he could converse at first was Berlepsch, so the days yawned before him and all he had by way of books was his Greek New Testament—it was the 1516 edition that Erasmus had translated—and his Hebrew Bible, both of which he had snatched from the wagon. For a man who lived and breathed books, this must have been a draconian limitation. Still, these were books of books, and he would make great use of them, as we shall see.

He now had breathtaking vistas of the Thuringian forest in early May. On the clearest days, he could look northeast and see Mount Meissner rising thirty miles away in Hesse. In his letters to his friends Spalatin, Amsdorf, and Melanchthon—the only ones who knew of his location, besides the two men who had carried him here—he referred to himself during this time as being "in the realm of the birds" and "in the domain of the air." He was as far removed from the world of students and preaching and controversy as ever before, impossibly high up in his glorious aerie in the sky. He once wrote that he could hear the birds "make melody from their perches, praising God day and night for all they were worth."[1] But he also referred to the Wartburg as his "Patmos," the island where late in life the apostle John had been exiled by the Roman emperor for "the word of God and for the testimony of Jesus Christ."[2] John there produced what we today know as the book of Revelation, and Luther too would eventually produce a tremendous literary outpouring, the final part of which was his German translation of John's book itself. For beginning that December, Luther took on the mighty task of translating the entirety of the New Testament into German.

But that was still months away. In his first days at the Wartburg, before his pen would find its torrential voice, he simply wrote a few letters.

The first—probably written four days into his residence—was to his dear friend Philip Melanchthon:*

> I have had much ado to get this letter off, so great is the fear that my whereabouts may somehow be revealed. Therefore you people, too, be careful. . . . With the exception of you and Amsdorf, it is not necessary that other people know anything else than that I am still alive.[3]

In his first days there, Luther was desperate to receive letters from his friends and to hear news of what was happening in the wider world. He knew that much concerning him and his cause was going on, and it maddened him to be unable to know everything, much less to do anything about it. So in this first letter, he turned to the subject of something he had heard, perhaps from Berlepsch. It concerned some rioting that had happened in Erfurt just two days before Luther was taken to the Wartburg. The rioting was a result of an incident from a month earlier, after Luther had been grandly received by a number of monks as he passed through Erfurt on his way to the diet. The day after Luther had left, the dean of St. Severin decided to punish those clergy who had taken part in that fulsome reception welcoming this excommunicated heretic. When one of the clergy—a certain Johannes Drach, who was a canon—had refused to comply with the dean's punishment, the dean humiliated him by physically grabbing him while he was in the chancel, dragging him out of the church, and peremptorily excommunicating him. The Erfurt students and other young people—who had also taken Luther's side in the wider controversy—protested loudly and rioted against this action. That Erfurt artisans and others took part in this violent protest marks the first time that the Reformation movement had moved beyond its previous academic and ecclesiastical boundaries. This was a trend that would continue from this point on. But the pent-up frustration of the Erfurt citizenry exploded again on May 1 and 2, perhaps because they had word that Luther was then passing nearby on the road home from Worms. Nonetheless, the Erfurters now insisted that Drach be reinstated. Eventually, the dean complied with this demand and nullified

---

* It is unclear whether this letter was actually mailed, because only a fragment survives and Luther later mentions writing things but tearing them up and not sending them, for fear of being discovered.

the excommunication. Luther was amazed to hear all of this and was desperate for further details, which were slow in coming. Following his reinstatement, Drach nonetheless resigned his post in Erfurt and went to Wittenberg. This sort of thing would happen more and more in the years ahead as what had become the Reformation spread far beyond Luther's control and unrest spread all across Germany and far beyond too. Wittenberg became the safe place for all who held Luther's views, and like Drach many of them came there to stay. Luther wondered what effect his disappearance from the world and his present silence—when he had previously been anything but silent—would have on the wider and developing situation:

> Who knows what God plans to work with these mighty men* by this counsel of silence? The priests and monks who raged against me while I was free now dread me as a captive, so that they start to soften their campaign against me. They cannot bear the weight of the common people's threats, but also they do not know how to escape them. Behold, the hand of the Mighty One of Jacob, what it accomplishes while we are silent, suffer, and pray. Is not the word of Moses true: "You will be silent and the Lord will fight for you"?[4]

But that same day or another day soon thereafter, Luther wrote another letter to Melanchthon in which he expressed his great dismay at these outbreaks of violence by people who are ostensibly on his side:

> I hear that there has been violence in Erfurt against the houses of priests. I am amazed that this is tolerated and bypassed by the city council and that our Lang is also silent on this. Although it is good that those lazy, ungodly priests are harassed, yet this method creates disgrace and just repulsion for our gospel. I would have written to Lang [about this], but I still can't. This kind of service toward us on the part of these people shocks me tremendously.[5]

This would be a continuing problem for Luther in the months and years ahead. What he had started had taken on a life of its own, and he would increasingly spend his time trying to deal with the adverse effects

---

* This is a possible allusion to those in the book of Isaiah who go against God and are vanquished.

of people motivated by his ideas who advocated for those ideas in ways
that he thought deeply mistaken, that in his mind brought shame to the
sacred cause of Christ's Gospel.

But there was no going back. Luther had said and done things with
real consequences, some good, some bad, and some indifferent. Close to
home, some followers were doing things Luther would stand against, but
many others were reading his works and joining and spreading the ferment of these new ideas just as he had hoped. The German common folk
had been aroused, and as with all movements some had been aroused for
the right reasons and some for the wrong. The wheat and the tares must
grow up together and God would decide in the end.

> If the Pope will take steps against all who think as I do, then Germany
> will not be without uproar. The faster he undertakes this, the faster he
> and his followers will perish and I shall return. God is arousing the spirits
> of many, especially the hearts of the common people. It does not seem to
> me likely that this affair can be checked with force; if [the pope] begins to
> put it down, it will become ten times bigger. Germany has very many
> *Karsthansen.*[6]

His followers were increasing in number every day, so that soon
enough people far from Germany were forced to take sides in this now
open war of ideas. For example, eight days after Luther arrived at the
Wartburg, there was in faraway London a public burning of Luther's
books. The bonfire was lit in the churchyard of St. Paul's Cathedral and
had been organized by Cardinal Wolsey and the dean of St. Paul's, Richard Pace. Henry VIII had already taken a stand against the impolitic
Wittenberg firebrand by personally penning an attack on Luther's *Babylonian Captivity*. It was suddenly felt that Luther's audacious writings
called for Catholic orthodoxy to be more strongly defended, so the open
atmosphere of Humanist "free thought" that had allowed Erasmus to
write his critiques of the church, and had allowed England's Thomas
More to write his *Utopia* in 1516, was more or less quenched. This larger
desire to stand with the church against "heresy" was keenly felt all across
Europe. In Paris, Francis I oversaw the public burning of Luther's works,

---

* The German word *Karst* means "hoe," so *Karsthansen* became the term for manual laborers and peasants in general, especially those who were opposed to the nobles.

and in distant Poland, King Sigismund himself that July issued a stern edict against Luther's ideas.

Being holed up at the Wartburg was in many ways very frustrating for the young man used to skipping off to preach sermons and give lectures and do the myriad things he must do in his various capacities as Augustinian district vicar, doctor of theology at the university, and so much else. "Lazy and full," he wrote to Spalatin, "I sit here all day long."[7] This was not the life he was used to. Not being in the midst of things back at home was difficult. And there were other problems. For one thing, he would again suffer from the *Anfechtungen* that hadn't plagued him in a while and that likely had been kept at bay by his busyness.

But he also sometimes wondered whether he should have allowed himself to be hidden away like this. Had he made an error in not insisting on pushing things to their logical conclusion, even if it meant that he might well have been put to death? In any case, he had confidence that his Wittenberg colleagues—Andreas von Karlstadt, Gabriel Zwilling, Nicholas von Amsdorf, and Philip Melanchthon—could ably handle all that needed doing there. The diffident twenty-four-year-old Melanchthon had been charged with leadership while Luther was away, but Melanchthon would never be the kind of leader Luther was. Luther had far more confidence in him than Melanchthon had in himself. Melanchthon was of course first and foremost a scholar and often felt ill-equipped to do what was necessary in his temporary new role. Luther had always been concerned for him, and because he thought it would be good for Melanchthon, he had practically arranged his marriage to Katharina Krapp, the daughter of the Wittenberg mayor.

On the twelfth, Luther wrote to Melanchthon,

> What are you doing these days, my Philip? Are you not praying for me that this retreat to which I unwillingly consented may result in something great for God's glory? I am quite eager to know your reaction [to my disappearance]. I was afraid it would look as if I had deserted the battle array; and yet there was no way to resist those who wanted and advised this. [Yet] I desire nothing more than to meet the fury of my enemies head on.[8]

This thought would not let him go during his months in the Wartburg, that he ought not to have left Worms and ought not to have allowed himself to be hidden away. But now he was here, and he would make the best of it.

In the letter, he encouraged Melanchthon to "be steadfast" in his absence and "fortify the walls and towers of Jerusalem." Luther said that thus far he alone stood in the battle, but soon enough they would come after Melanchthon too. He then passed on what he had heard in a letter from Spalatin, that his archenemy Duke George—whom he typically called the "Hog of Dresden," but whom he now refered to as the "Rehoboam of Dresden"*—was excited to comply with a new edict demanding that everywhere throughout the empire Luther's books be sought out and burned. He also said that the emperor was even reaching out to the king of Denmark—which had been a potential haven for Luther's followers—demanding that he no longer harbor them. And then Luther broached an infinitely more personal matter, one that would bedevil him for some time at the Wartburg and throughout his life.

"A Relic of the Cross"

Luther's life during what would become ten months at the Wartburg was different from the life he had led before. He was sedentary, spending most of his time, especially in the early weeks, alone in his room. The stultifying lack of exercise and the rich foods served to him by his overzealous host seem to have exacerbated an affliction that already troubled him at Worms. Luther broached the painful subject in a letter to Melanchthon:

> The Lord has afflicted me with painful constipation. The elimination is so hard that I am forced to press with all my strength, even to the point of perspiration, and the longer I delay the worse it gets. Yesterday on the fourth day I could go once, but I did not sleep all night and still have no peace. Please pray for me. This affliction will be intolerable if it continues as it has begun.[9]

That same day he told Amsdorf in a letter, "My constipation has become bad. The Lord afflicts me."[10] But it was his closest confidant, Spalatin, on

---

* Rehoboam is the arrogant king of Israel after his father, Solomon.

whom Luther would bestow the most detailed descriptions of his gastrointestinal sorrows. And in these epistles we see—in keeping with his incarnation theology—how comfortable Luther was mixing the highest and lowest of subjects. A month after the letter to Amsdorf, he wrote,

> The trouble from which I was suffering at Worms has not left me but rather has increased. I am more constipated than ever in my life, and despair of remedy. The Lord thus afflicts me, that I may not be without a relic of the cross. May he be blessed. Amen.[11]

The condition became so severe that Luther desperately hoped he could get permission from Frederick to travel to Erfurt, where he might see a doctor. But because of the danger involved all around—that he might actually be kidnapped and brought before the emperor as an outlaw—Spalatin said this was not possible. Spalatin was, however, able to procure special medicine from the doctors at Frederick's court, which he quickly sent to Luther. After Luther received and used this medicine, on July 15, he wrote to Spalatin:

> I tried the pills according to the prescription. Soon I had some relief and elimination without blood or force, but the wound of the previous rupture isn't healed yet, and I even had to suffer a good deal because some flesh extruded, either due to the power of the pill, or I don't know what.[12]

Two weeks later, he wrote with an update:

> Concerning my health, I have easier elimination now, due to the strong and powerful medications, but the way my digestion functions has not changed at all. The soreness continues, and I am afraid it may develop into a worse evil with which the Lord afflicts me, according to his wisdom.[13]

Most have seen Luther's constipation for precisely what it was, which is to say constipation. But we should return once more to Erik Erikson's excruciatingly Freudian view of Luther's gastrointestinal gestalt, because for decades many Luther scholars seemed to feel the need to take Erikson's views seriously. Here is a vintage passage on this vital topic:

One could say that Luther was compulsively retentive, or even that he was mentally and spiritually "constipated"—as he was apt to be physically all his life. But this retentive tendency (soon to alternate with an explosive one) was part of his equipment; and just as we assume that psychosexual energies can be sublimated, we must grant that a man can (and must) learn to derive out of the modes of his psychobiological and psychosexual make-up the prime modality of his creative adaptation.[14]

And all God's people said: *Amen*.

Writing

Luther's room at the Wartburg contained a tiled oven for warmth, a simple desk and chair, of which he made ample use, and one especially curious object, likely a gift from Frederick, via Spalatin, though any letter in which it is referenced has been lost. It was the gargantuan vertebra of a whale, doubtless from the remains of a cetacean that had beached or washed up someplace very far away, probably on the coast of the North Sea. Whale bones were at that time prized for their healing powers, and one assumes that because Luther complained so regularly of the various maladies affecting him, Spalatin had found it and sent it along as a happy surprise and encouragement. And how could Luther help to have been cheered by something as outrageous and singular as this colossal white bone from a leviathan that once swam endless miles beneath the waves of a distant sea? Luther had never seen the ocean, and never would in his life, so the exotic quality of the object must have been all the greater. One assumes Luther put his feet upon it as he sat at his desk during the endless hours he spent there writing and writing.*

The amount of writing Luther did during what would stretch to ten months in the lofty castle beggars the imagination. To be fair, there was little else he could do while he was there. He was unable to regale his friends in person and unable to lecture and preach several times per week as he used to do. Before his tonsure and beard had grown out, he was even unable to walk anyplace beyond the courtyard of the castle, nor

---

* This extraordinary object is the only piece of "furniture" or decoration from Luther's time at the Wartburg that has survived. It is there still, where any visitor can see it.

could he even do this much for fear of appearing aimless and drawing attention to himself with the other knights there. Whatever he did, he mustn't appear outside his room with a book. That would be a dead give-away that he wasn't a knight at all, for books were such newfangled objects at that time that they weren't so easily come by, and few noble knights would spend their time with one. Eventually, Luther would be able now and again to take horse rides through the forests that stretched in every direction, but always with a servant or two alongside who must scour the woods for trouble. He was even allowed to walk on the forested paths around the Wartburg to pick strawberries—something he had done as a youth not far from there while in Eisenach with his relatives—but always accompanied by the two noble pages entrusted to him by Berlepsch. But because Luther really had little at all that he must do, he leaped headlong into the opportunity to scratch ink onto paper and wrote furiously, accomplishing more in his ten months of seclusion than many writers do in a lifetime.

Incidentally, there is a tremendously popular legend that Luther literally threw ink at the devil while at the Wartburg, though this seems only to be one more cock-and-bull story, this time owing to an erroneous literalization of a metaphor. What Luther clearly meant was that he was fighting the devil by writing against him, not by actually trying to bean Old Scratch with an inkpot. The ink stains on the walls of his cell that are there today were certainly put there after Luther, by other "authors."

But Luther could not write anything in his first days at the Wartburg. He must first have the proper materials. So as soon as he could, he badgered his friends in his letters to send him various books and to send him his own uncompleted manuscripts. Before any of this arrived, however, he busily spent hours upon hours reading Erasmus's Greek New Testament and also his Hebrew Bible. This would prepare him for the monumental work he was going to do come December, of translating the entire New Testament into German.* But as soon as other books and manuscripts arrived, he went to work on smaller projects, of which there were many. In a letter to Spalatin on June 10, he wrote, "I am both very idle and very busy here; I am studying Hebrew and Greek and writing without interruption."[15]

Luther's time away from the hurly-burly of life in Wittenberg did not

---

* There had been earlier translations of the New Testament into German, but none that had been done directly from the Greek, and none that were written in the language of the common German people.

entirely keep him safe from the back-and-forth that he had been engaged
in with his opponents. He was in some ways above the fray he had begun, but in many ways he was still very much in the thick of it. Cajetan
had in early 1520 succeeded in getting the universities of Louvain and
Cologne to weigh in on Luther's writings and to condemn them. As soon
as Luther read what they had written, he had in turn condemned their
condemnation, saying that it lacked even minimal scriptural foundation,
which it did. But now, in May 1521, another piece of writing with what
was meant to pass as scriptural foundation appeared. It was by the Louvain academic James Latomus and was titled *Reasons from the Holy Scriptures and Ancient Writers for the Condemnation of Brother Martin Luther's
Articles of Doctrine by the Louvain Theologians*. With his boundless hours
of time at the Wartburg, Luther penned a reply. He also wrote a bitterly
sarcastic reply to something written by the "goat" Emser, who was chaplain to George the Bearded. He wrote a number of these kinds of things
at the Wartburg, but far fewer than he had been writing in the years
preceding this time. While at the Wartburg, he was able to shift to writing things that had a more permanent quality than the fiery pamphlets
he had tossed off so easily and frequently.

Another work to which he now turned his attention was a work on
the Catholic sacrament of confession. In his book *Babylonian Captivity*,
he had explained that he no longer recognized it as a sacrament. Now
he wrote a small book titled *On Confession: Whether the Pope Has the
Power to Require It*. Luther was not against confession, but as someone
who had suffered enormously in his first years as a monk because of
what had been the standard approach, in which every sin must be rig-
orously remembered and confessed, he saw that it ended up being more
of a woeful burden to Christians than the relief it was intended to be.
In his work, Luther quoted James 5:16 ("Therefore confess your sins
one to another") to prove that the biblical idea of confession was something Christians can do with one another, so it wasn't necessary or even
advisable to abide by the onerous ecclesiastical strictures insisted upon
by the church. Luther also felt that confession must not be mandatory,
but rather should be something Christians could do when they felt the
need. Many Christians simply felt guilty if they hadn't gone to confession, so it had become only one more burden in a life of religious burdens, rather than the glorious freedom from burdens it was meant to
be in the first place.

Before leaving for Worms, Luther had been working on a commentary on the Magnificat—Mary's song of praise in the Gospel of Luke's nativity narrative. The text comes directly from the first chapter of Luke's Gospel and Luther's exegesis got to the heart of his theology, that Mary can receive God precisely because she is lowly and has humbled herself. Far from recommending her as a great saint to be looked up to for her great moral exploits, he praised her for abasing herself unto nothingness. It is in her emptiness that she can receive God—in her case literally—and it is in our emptiness, offering him nothing, that we can receive him too. Luther dedicated this small book to Duke John Frederick, the seventeen-year-old prince who was Frederick's nephew and who would one day replace him as elector. But toward the end of the commentary, he spoke with typical prophetic boldness to this rich, young ruler:

> All these things were foreordained by God in order to verify those in authority, to keep them in fear, and to admonish them of their peril. For great possessions, glory, power, and favor, as well as the flatterers no lord may be without, surround and lay siege to the heart of a prince, moving it to pride, to forgetfulness of God, and neglect of the people and the common weal, to sensuality, blasphemy, arrogance, and idleness, in short to every sort of vice and evil. Indeed there is no castle or city that is so heavily besieged and assaulted. Unless therefore, one fortifies himself by means of such examples, and takes the fear of God for his defense and rampart, how can he endure?[16]

Luther's prophetic boldness in speaking to pope and emperor—and to Frederick and Albrecht of Mainz and to so many others in power—is one more example of what might well be considered the shining center of his larger rediscovery and rescue of the true Gospel from under its crushing welter of ecclesiastical and political medieval structures. He had seen that he was not under these leaders as much as *they were all under God together.* All authority came from God, and as in Christ all were one and all were judged equally, it was Luther's right and indeed his duty as a Christian to speak the truth to these powers, to point out to them where they were wrong and where they might go wrong, for the sake of their souls and for the sake of all those whom they ruled over. Luther's fear of God trumped his fear of these rulers, so he was free to speak with perfect candor, knowing that his authority to speak came not from selfish desires but from a desire to bring God and his Gospel to bear on the situation. So it was not just his right to speak to them as he did but his solemn duty. This is what started him along this course, when he posted his theses in 1517, but we see as time passed that whatever timidity and fear he once had of offending those in power had diminished, to the point that it ceased to exist altogether. He began to reckon being careful to speak as mere worldly wisdom and "fear of man" than as born out of genuine faith in the God he served.

Luther's demeanor toward his opponents changed over the course of his time at the Wartburg. Before Worms, when he was meeting with Cajetan, Luther had generally been gracious and even loving much of the time. But at some point while in hiding, he felt that he had made a mistake at Worms in not letting them all have it in the manner of an Old Testament prophet. He knew that would likely have led to his death, but, as we have said, he didn't fear losing his life. He only feared not doing what God had called him to do, and he had the idea that at Worms perhaps he had failed. We see this in his September 9 letter to Spalatin, in which he criticized Erasmus for being congenial to the point of cowardice. He said he had seen that he might someday part ways with Erasmus and Fabricius Capito:*

> For I saw that Erasmus was far from the knowledge of grace, since in all his writings he is not concerned for the cross but for peace. He thinks that everything should be discussed and handled in a civil manner and with a certain benevolent kindness. But Behemoth† pays no attention and nothing improves by this. . . . [Erasmus's and Capito's] writings accomplish nothing because they refrain from chiding, biting, and giving offense. For when the popes [and bishops] are admonished in a civil manner they think it is flattering and keep on as if they passed the right to remain uncorrected and incorrigible, content that they are feared and that no one dares to reproach them.

So this line of thinking made him wonder whether he had himself erred in being too gentle:

> I, too, am very afraid, and my conscience troubles me because I yielded in Worms to your advice and that of [our] friends, held

---

* A colleague of Erasmus's.
† As Saint Jerome did, Luther equated the Behemoth of Job with the devil.

my spirit in check, and did not show myself as an Elijah to those idols. They would hear other things, if I would come before them again. But enough of this.[17]

He said something similar in a letter on November 1, regarding his willingness to go to the Wartburg and stay out of the emperor's grasp:

I have withdrawn from the public and thus obeyed the advice of friends. I have done this against my will, and I am uncertain whether with this action I have done something which is pleasing to God. I certainly thought I should expose my neck to the public fury; but [my friends] were of another opinion.[18]

Luther had also been working on two devotional works called postils, which he completed at the Wartburg. The word "postil" derived from the Latin phrase *post illa verba texta* (after these words) and generally was a commentary on a biblical text. So Luther's postils were his commentaries on the biblical texts upon which a pastor would preach each Sunday. In a way, they were outlines for sermons themselves. Luther wrote many postils over the years, and they tended to sell well and were another way he spread his theological thinking to the German people.

Meanwhile, Back in Wittenberg

Now that Luther was far away in "the land of the birds"[19] atop the fabled Wartburg, life would go on in the valleys below. Luther's writings had over the course of the last months unlatched a number of theological barn doors, and they had done so with such persuasiveness that others had been emboldened to pull or push these doors open. A number of horses seem to have gotten out. Many things about which Luther had written in *Babylonian Captivity* were now beginning to be put into practice by those he had left in charge back in Wittenberg, but Luther was not there to oversee any of it.

For example, Justus Jonas, who had so disappointed Erasmus by leaving Erfurt to join Luther's party, had in June 1521 decided he would no longer lecture on church law, although this was precisely what he had been hired to do by the All Saints' chapter of Wittenberg. But Justus

Jonas had seen the new light, and it shone wholly from the sacred Word of God, and not at all from the musty books of canon law or the fusty *Sentences* of Peter Lombard or Aristotle's god-awful *Ethics*.

But there were more central issues than this. What Luther had written about priestly vows and about celibacy and about the Mass and so many other things would now suddenly be put into actual practice in Wittenberg. But in almost all cases these practical leaps forward were made by people who were generally not as thoughtful and careful as Luther himself would have been.

Celibacy or Marriage?

Some priests had decided it was time to take Luther's views on marriage seriously, and without consulting Luther or anyone else on the details, they promptly found wives and got married. When Luther got word of this, he was surprised, though he was not at all against it. He knew it was decidedly courageous, because things were far from where one could do such things without serious consequences. Indeed, Archbishop Albrecht of Mainz hauled one of the men before a court, while Duke George had another arrested and sent to the bishop at Meissen.

But not only was it two priests who were married, but then a monk too, and this made matters even more complicated. In his *To the Christian Nobility of the German Nation*, Luther had taken pains to differentiate between the vows of priests and those of monks. He made it clear that the necessity of celibacy for priests was not biblical, but he had never made this case with regard to monks, who had freely and quite specifically taken such a vow. But before Luther could weigh in further on this tricky issue from the Wartburg, Karlstadt once more galloped ahead of things and wrote something in which he declared that all the vows of priests and monks were invalid, essentially rendering those vows null and void in Wittenberg by doing so. Melanchthon thought he was correct in what he said, but Luther was not so convinced. He had to think it through and clarify some things. But Karlstadt had written what he had written, and now it was Luther who was playing catch-up.

One could almost get the idea that in springing ahead as he did, Karlstadt was somehow trying to lead the Reformation in Luther's absence. Things weren't yet at a point where this caused problems, but when

Luther read the theses that Karlstadt had written on the subject of the
vows of monks and priests, he quickly discovered a fly in the ointment.
Luther said in an August 3 letter to Melanchthon that he was bothered
by some sloppy biblical exegesis that Karlstadt had used to make his argument against monkish vows:

> I highly approve of his effort and diligence, of course, although I
> rather wish that he had not twisted that passage about the "seed"
> which was sacrificed to Molech into a reference to the emission of
> semen. [Our] enemies will ridicule the distortion of this passage
> since it is clearer than light that it refers to the sons and daughters
> who were being sacrificed as a burnt offering to the idol.[20]

In Scripture, "seed" often refers to one's offspring—as in Genesis 3,
where, talking to the serpent, God says he will "put enmity between you
and the woman, and between your seed and her seed."[21] What Karlstadt
had done was confuse the onanistic idea of spilled seed with the word
"seed" in a passage about Moloch, an idol to which pagan tribes sacrificed
their children. Luther saw this childish mistake immediately and felt
that it compromised Karlstadt's entire argument, and therefore brought
down the whole of their cause. And there were other errors too.

Three days later, Luther was complaining about Karlstadt's work to
Spalatin:

> How I wish that Karlstadt had tried to refute celibacy with more
> fitting Scripture passages! I am afraid he stirs up quite a lot of
> talk for himself and for us. What kind of exegesis is this: the
> giving of seed to Moloch is the same as becoming unclean by a
> natural emission of semen? Everyone knows that in this passage
> "seed" means the same as "children" or "offspring." . . . The cause
> he has undertaken is important, and an excellent endeavor, but I
> wish it were also done in an outstanding, skillful, and successful
> way. For you see what great clarity and strength our enemies
> demand of us, since they misrepresent even the most evident and
> fitting [of our] statements.

Then he worried about those who would be influenced to marry based
on Karlstadt's work:

For what is more dangerous than to incite such a big crowd of
unmarried people to matrimony on the basis of such unreliable
and uncertain Scripture passages, only to have them harassed
afterward with continual anguish of conscience, worse than the
cross they now have to carry. I too wish to see celibacy made a
matter of choice, as the gospel requires. I do not see clearly yet
how to accomplish this. But my warning is in vain. Maybe
[Karlstadt] does not want to be held back in his course.
Therefore one has to let him continue.[22]

It's instructive to see how scrupulous Luther is. He wanted the case
for everything he put forward to be rock solid in every way; anything less
wouldn't do. The differences between him and Karlstadt would widen,
but for now Luther was willing to let things stand. After all, he was at the
Wartburg and could hardly micromanage everything in faraway Wittenberg, though he would certainly do what he could. It is somewhat
curious that although Luther wrote innumerable letters to Spalatin and
many to Melanchthon during this period, he wrote none to Karlstadt.
Nor had he asked him to come along to Worms in the spring.

Later in the long letter, Luther told Spalatin that he went on a two-
day hunting party with some of the knights. "We caught two hares and a
few poor partridges," which was of course an extremely pathetic bounty
for several men hunting for two days. He explained that he would have
preferred to hunt "bears, wolves, boars, foxes, [etc.]" and judges it "a worthy occupation indeed for men with nothing to do." Then he related how
he had himself saved a baby rabbit, slipping it into the sleeve of his cloak.
Nonetheless, the hounds by smell discovered it and succeeded in "biting
through the cloak, broke its right hind leg and killed it by choking it." In
this incident, as in so many others, Luther saw an allegory: "Thus pope
and Satan rage to destroy even the souls that have been saved, and care
nothing about my efforts."[23]

In a letter to Spalatin that September, Luther circled back to the grim
details of his most fundamental struggles:

Today, on the sixth day, I had elimination with such difficulty
that I almost passed out. Now I sit aching as if in labor
confinement, wounded and sore, and shall have no—or little—
rest this night. Thanks be to Christ who has not left me without
any relic of the holy cross. I would have been healed from all

soreness if the elimination had moved more easily. But whatever heals in four days is wounded again by elimination.[24]

But then, in early October, good news. Not only had his stubborn constipation problem been alleviated, but the subsequent recurring painful anal rupture had at last healed too. "At last my behind and my bowels have reconciled themselves to me," he gushed. He exulted that he wouldn't be needing any more medication. He then told Spalatin to watch out for Melanchthon, because he was always concerned for him and feared that if the plague broke out in Wittenberg, his more frail friend must be spirited away to someplace safe. "That head," he says, "must be preserved so that the Word, which the Lord has entrusted to him for the salvation of souls, may not perish." And finally he reported on a priest at the Wartburg "who daily celebrates mass with great idolatry."[25] We can only imagine how that priest would have shuddered had he known that the taciturn bearded fellow observing him was none other than Martin Luther of Wittenberg.

The Mass

Just as Luther's views on marriage were suddenly being put into action in Wittenberg, what he had written about the Mass was being acted upon too. Luther had argued that the Catholic Mass, by being a reenactment of the sacrificial death of Christ, put forth an idea that was unscriptural, so the Mass as it had been practiced was theologically wrong. This was, of course, a monumental idea: to dismiss the single thing most central to medieval ecclesiology. Luther, of course, had also made it clear that separating priests into a special caste apart from laypeople was unbiblical, and therefore the idea that only they and not the laypeople should take the bread and the wine both during Communion was wrong. But suddenly in Wittenberg, Gabriel Zwilling—who was one of Luther's Augustinian brethren—Melanchthon, and Karlstadt were putting these things into practice. They were celebrating the Lord's Supper and giving both the bread and the wine to all who came. Laypeople had never drunk the Communion wine before—or at least not for many centuries. And the Wittenbergers were even going a step further by allowing the laypeople to handle the Communion chalice.

Luther was not entirely against these things, but he always wanted to be measured and responsible in moving forward. But once again Karlstadt skipped cavalierly ahead of things by declaring in writing that anyone who did not take both bread and wine together during Communion was committing a sin. When Luther learned of this, he was furious. It was one thing to say that laypeople should be permitted to take the bread and the wine together, as the priests did—and he certainly agreed with that—but it was a step too far to say that not doing so was actually itself a sin. The Gospel gave us the freedom to do these things if we chose, but it did not in any way compel us.

Then Gabriel Zwilling preached very critically about monasticism and encouraged the monks in the Augustinian cloister to abandon their cowls. On November 12, no fewer than thirteen of them took him up on this. By the end of the month, another fifteen would leave. It was a startling development, and the prior of the monastery, Conrad Helt, was so upset that he wrote to Frederick, asking for his help. Luther wrote to Spalatin, saying that his concerns over this exodus en masse were similar to the concerns he had over Karlstadt's mutton-headed exegesis regarding celibacy and marriage. Luther wanted to be sure that the monks who had left would not later regret what they had done. In both cases, one may see evidence of Luther's pastor's heart. He was concerned more about the people than about the correctness of the theology. So Luther decided to write on the subject, again trying to undo the damage that those to whom he had entrusted everything in his absence had done. The treatise he wrote was *The Judgment of Martin Luther on Monastic Vows*. In this treatise, Luther wrote a lengthy preface in the form of a letter to his own father, essentially apologizing for his own ill-considered monastic vow of sixteen years earlier. The preface and treatise are in Latin, so one doubts whether Luther's father, who did not read Latin, ever knew of it. Nonetheless, it gives us a beautiful picture of Luther's love for his father and of his own thinking on what he had so impetuously done so many years before.

But then Zwilling also took on the issue of private masses, declaring on October 6 that he would say them no more and also telling the Wittenberg townspeople that they ought not to attend any masses if the bread and the wine were not offered together to all. Luther had written that private masses were not biblical, not least because the Greek word for the Eucharist in the New Testament was *synaxis*, which meant an assembly. Nor had anything like them been done until about the seventh century. Still, it is remarkable that the man who had put forth all of these radical ideas was not there to oversee them first being put into practice. The Wittenbergers also incorporated the German language into the Mass by using German for the words that Jesus spoke when he instituted Communion at the Last Supper. Thus *Hoc est corpus meum* became *Das ist mein Körper* (This is my body). The radicalness of hearing one's own language spoken by the priest at the holy culmination of the Mass must have been jarring and even shocking for some in the pews, but the Wittenberger leaders were kicking out the traces and roaring ahead, and Melanchthon evidently didn't feel he had the authority to slow them down.

Part of the problem in Wittenberg at this time was that there was no clear consensus and no clear leader, even though Luther had deputized Melanchthon as his personal choice to lead in his absence. But Melanchthon was simply not up to the responsibility. So there was often confusion and disagreement, mainly because things were moving too fast and some of the faithful were indeed not at all ready to accept these radical changes. In the absence of a leader, therefore, Frederick now stepped in. He sternly ordered the lot of them to resolve their differences and come together on how to proceed, and he appointed a committee—consisting of Melanchthon, Jonas, Karlstadt, Schurff, and one of his own advisers—to investigate the influence of Zwilling.

Luther still believed he had left Melanchthon in charge, and in a famous letter that August he urged him to lead and not to be afraid of making mistakes, not to be afraid even of sinning. Luther wrote,

> Be a sinner and sin boldly, but believe and rejoice in Christ even
> more boldly, for he is victorious over sin, death, and the world.
> As long as we are here [in this world] we have to sin. This life is
> not the dwelling place of righteousness, but, as Peter says, we
> look for new heavens and a new earth in which righteousness
> dwells. It is enough that by the riches of God's glory we have
> come to know the Lamb that takes away the sin of the world. No
> sin will separate us from the Lamb, even though we commit
> fornication and murder a thousand times a day. Do you think
> that the purchase price that was paid for the redemption of our
> sins by so great a Lamb is too small?[26]

Luther was hardly saying that Melanchthon should try to sin, as many have misinterpreted this quotation, but that he should forget about trying not to sin, because in the end this was not possible. He must understand that in all that we do, we will doubtless sin—because we are sinners—but if our faith is in Christ, who has already defeated sin and paid for our sins on the cross, we are redeemed. Luther hoped that Melanchthon could put away his fussy academic concerns and simply lead, even if he would not do so perfectly, but his hopes along these lines were certainly in vain. Melanchthon during these months was also heavily under the sway of Zwilling's preaching—which by all accounts was extremely powerful and compelling, to the point that he was called a "second Luther"—so it seemed that the only thing that could help the situation was for Luther himself to come back and see for himself what was going on.

Luther had tried to have Melanchthon installed as the main Wittenberg preacher back in September. He knew that if Melanchthon were not preaching, things might go wobbly at this crucial time, and of course he was quite right. Melanchthon's skills as a preacher were superb, and any idea that someone must not preach simply because he was not ordained no longer made sense. It was theologically erroneous, and now, if ever, was the time for the non-ordained Melanchthon to take the pulpit and steady the tippy canoe through his preaching and leading. In a letter to Spalatin, Luther made the case:

> For if we have broken all laws of men and cast off their yokes, what difference would it make to us that Philip is not anointed or tonsured but married? Nevertheless he is truly a priest and actually does the work of a priest, unless it is not the office of a priest to teach the Word of God. In that case Christ himself would not be a priest, for he taught now in synagogues, then in ships, now at the shoreline, then in the mountains. . . . Since, therefore, Philip is called by God and performs the ministry of the Word, as no one can deny, what difference does it make that he is not called by those tyrants. . . . May Christ compensate for my absence and silence with Melanchthon's preaching and voice, to the confusion of Satan and his apostles.[27]

Luther still hoped that with Cranach and Christian Döring appealing to the city council, Melanchthon could be appointed the preacher. Because he was not ordained, this would also powerfully underscore the idea of "the priesthood of all believers." But the council was simply not up to this dramatic departure and rejected the appeal. So Zwilling and later Karlstadt filled that vital role in Luther's absence, and the very events that Luther hoped would not happen did happen. So until he was able to come back for good and right the wrongs and clarify what was confused, things would rumble forward in bumpy fits and starts.

These included episodes of violence in Wittenberg too. On October 8, a number of monks from St. Anthony's cloister in Lichtenberg had come to Wittenberg on one of their standard begging tours. But now when they came, they unwittingly stumbled into an atmosphere decidedly hostile to them and their mendicant behavior. It was even reported that students pelted them with stones and clods of earth.

Luther was gratified that things were moving forward, but how they were moving was often dismaying. Usually they moved a bit too quickly. But in one instance, they were not moving forward at all. Luther now learned that Albrecht of Mainz, who had inadvertently kicked off everything in 1517 with his abuse of indulgences, was again short of cash and hoping that his refurbished relic collection—with the subsequent boon of indulgences that came with viewing them—would be the best way out of his troubles. When Luther discovered this, he boiled with fury.

Albrecht had spared no expense in advertising the collection. Dürer himself was commissioned to do an engraved portrait of the archbishop for the sumptuously printed catalog of relics. And the garish mélange of novelties outdid even those of which we have already read. It purported to include two "jugs" of wine from the wedding at Cana; two vials of milk from the breasts of the Virgin Mary; actual manna* from Moses's sojourn in the wilderness; a finger of Saint Thomas the apostle;† the Johannine digit with which Jesus's cousin had pointed to the Savior as he came to be baptized in the river Jordan; another thumb from Saint Anne;‡ yet more branches from the burning bush; numerous pieces from the bodies of the twelve apostles, forty-three of which were from Peter alone; nine thorns from the crown of Christ;§ an actual piece of the body of Christ,

---

* Because the manna was known only to last one day before it rotted and bred worms, its existence thirty-five centuries after Moses was the more impressive.
† It was purported not to be merely one of the eight Didymean possibilities, but that very one with which Thomas had demonstrated his infamous doubt by placing it in the side wound of the resurrected Jesus.
‡ Logic dictates that it formed a matched pair with its cousin in Wittenberg.
§ One of these was said to have distinguished itself by miraculously separating from its eight immovable brethren, and in the sight of many witnesses.

somehow said to be transubstantiated; and a single pinch of the very soil from which Adam was created.*

Luther's anger at the news of Albrecht's elaborate relapse was unparalleled. Like some bearded Thuringian Zeus on his Olympus, Luther rose on December 1 to hurl an epistolary lightning bolt from the ramparts of the Wartburg. The letter was to the wayward Albrecht himself, informing him that Luther not only was alive but would prove it by coming after such scurrilous abominations as this with more zeal than ever before.

> You may think me out of the fray, but I will do what Christian love demands, without regard to the gates of hell, let alone unlearned popes, cardinals, and bishops. I beg you, show yourself not a wolf but a bishop. It has been made plain enough that indulgences are rubbish and lies. See what a conflagration has come from a despised spark, so that now the pope himself is singed. The same God is still alive, and he can resist the Cardinal of Mainz, though he be upheld by four emperors. This is the God who breaks the cedars of Lebanon and humbles the hardened Pharaohs.
>
> You need not think Luther is dead. I will show the difference between a bishop and a wolf. I demand an immediate answer. If you do not reply within two weeks I will publish a tract against you.[28]

Luther might as well have said, "Don't make me come down there. . . ." In fact, as a result of this and the other things that were happening, Luther felt he should slip away from the Wartburg if possible, if only to see with his own eyes what was taking place and to let his friends know that he was well.

---

* How it was soil from which he had been created but was not a part of his body must remain a mystery.

CHAPTER THIRTEEN

The Revolution Is Near

Should one continue only to debate about the
Word of God and forever refrain from action?
But why do I talk to the deaf?

—Luther in a letter to Spalatin

S O IN DECEMBER the knight known as Junker George decided he
would descend from the Wartburg heights and travel again among
the faithful in the valleys below, carefully revealing to no one that
he was in fact the notorious heretic monk Martin Luther. The distance
back to Wittenberg was nearly 150 miles, but because he was playing the
role of knight, instead of sitting idly in a clumsy wagon, Luther rode a
horse and was accompanied by a servant. Thus accoutred in his gray
knight's cloak and with a red beret under his hat did the bearded zeitgeist
ride, unrecognized through hill and dale. We know that he stopped in
the inn of Johannes Wagner in Leipzig and that sometime on the next
day he rode through the gates of Wittenberg, from which he had been
absent since departing for Worms, eight months before, on April 3.

But early in the morning on the day before Luther's arrival, the Wittenbergers' frustration with the clerical resistance to their proposals had
boiled over. Townspeople and students had forcibly prevented worship-
pers from entering the town church to attend daily Mass. After some
priests did manage to get into the church and began chanting the Magnificat, they were accosted and pelted with stones and the missals
wrenched from their hands. The following day mocking posters appeared
on the town's Franciscan cloister, and later more troublemakers arrived
to verbally abuse the friars and then forced their way into the chapel and
even destroyed a wooden altarpiece.

Luther arrived in Wittenberg, hoping for a short, sub rosa visit. He stayed not at the Augustinian cloister but at the home of his friend Nicholas von Amsdorf.* Very few people knew he was in town. Melanchthon spent considerable time with him. Someone must have had the idea that Cranach should paint a portrait of Luther during this short-lived doublet-and-beard phase. But when Cranach was summoned, he at first had no idea whom he spoke with. Cranach did paint Luther's portrait and made a woodcut too, giving us a precise picture of Luther during this period. It was also during this time that Melanchthon reportedly urged Luther to spend his remaining time at the Wartburg translating the New Testament into German.

What Luther observed in Wittenberg did not bother him very much at all. He had observed on his journey from the Wartburg that the townspeople wherever he went were stirred up over the issues of the coming changes, so he was not so surprised by the small outbreaks of violence that were reported. In fact, while he was in Wittenberg, forty rowdy students and townspeople had marched through the town carrying small swords, even threatening to storm the Franciscan cloister. Nonetheless, Luther thought everything would be all right. Perhaps he was surprised and thrilled to see with his own eyes that the dream that all of these things could actually happen was in fact coming true, despite some rattling hiccoughs. In any case, he promised his friends that upon his return to the Wartburg he would immediately write a strong rebuke against the violence. Coming from him, it should have an effect. But Luther felt that generally things were proceeding well enough. So he would return to the Wartburg and stay until Easter and in that time planned to pour himself into translating the New Testament into German.

The only thing that bothered Luther very much while he was in Wittenberg was discovering that some of the writings he had sent to Spalatin for publication had in fact never been published. So on December 5, the day after his arrival, he wrote Spalatin, upbraiding him in as strong a manner as ever he had done or would do. "Amid all the delight of being with my friends again," he said, "I found this drop of bitterness, namely, that none of them has ever heard of or seen my little books and letters. Judge for yourself whether I should not consider [my] disappointment justified." Earlier in the letter he explains,

---

* He might also have lodged with Melanchthon during this time.

I have sent you, along with letters, the [manuscripts of the] little books on vows, on the masses, and against the tyrant of Mainz [Albrecht]. I had hoped that they all were given to the proper people. Now, since I find everything different, I have to draw my own conclusions. . . . There is nothing that would disturb me more at this moment than to know that [these manuscripts] had reached you and that you were holding them back, since I have dealt in these little books with themes that require the greatest possible haste. Therefore if you have them, for goodness' sake curb that moderation and prudence of which I suspect you, for you accomplish nothing by rowing against the stream. What I have written I want published, if not in Wittenberg then certainly somewhere else. If the manuscripts have been lost or if you have kept them, I will be so embittered that I will write more vehemently than ever on these points. Whoever destroys lifeless paper will not also quench the spirit.[1]

Once again we see that Luther would not brook dissent of a certain kind, namely that kind which seemed to him to be full of "the fear of man" and insufficiently full of the fear of God. He seemed to know that things ought to move forward at a certain pace and was determined to confront those who would stop that from happening. Presumably, Spalatin responded favorably to allowing the two "little books" to be printed, but he was successful in persuading Luther to let the harsh letter to Archbishop Albrecht wait a bit before he sent it. Still, Luther insisted that Spalatin forward the letter to Melanchthon so that he could edit anything that was too harsh. In persuading Luther to hold off with this letter, Spalatin had maintained that the archbishop was somehow already mending his ways, and as evidence for this he told Luther that the archbishop had released those priests he had earlier imprisoned for getting married. But Luther was clearly enraged by what he perceived as Spalatin's lack of faith in this situation. Quite bitterly, he said, "For the Lord lives, whom you people—as is becoming to courtiers—do not trust unless he arranges his works according to your way of thinking, so that faith would no longer be necessary."[2] He had never before spoken to Spalatin as he did now, but a new seriousness and fire had come into Luther over these months. He had long ago crossed the Rubicon, and anything like Spalatin's caution now struck him not only as offensive but almost as though it were in league with the devil against him and God's purposes.

> Should one continue only to debate about the Word of God and forever refrain from action? But why do I talk to the deaf? Your mind does not believe; it is too much occupied with the affairs at court, that is, it is both too sophisticated and too timid. . . . I finally see that in this case the counsel of men must be overcome. Up to now I was hindered by them in many ways; but they vainly fear that heaven will go to pieces.[3]

Once back at the Wartburg, Luther in two days wrote his promised tract, *A Sincere Admonition to All Christians to Guard Against Insurrection and Rebellion.* He counseled in it that God could not be stopped from doing what he was already doing, so to take up arms or resort to any violence to push it along was a lack of faith and would only do the devil's work by bringing the Gospel into ill repute. "I will always be on the side of those against whom insurrection is directed," he wrote.[4] God must do the work, and God cannot be stopped.

> Just see what has been accomplished in a single year, during which we have been preaching and writing this truth. See how the papists' camouflage clothing has shrunk in length and breadth. . . . What will be the result if the mouth of Christ continues to thresh* by his Spirit for another two years?[5]

This is the same piece of writing in which Luther decries the name "Lutheran," which was being taken by many who sided with him. He asked that such people simply call themselves Christians. "What is Luther?" he asked. "After all, the teaching is not mine. Neither was I crucified for you. . . . How then should I—poor stinking maggot-fodder that I am—come to have men call the children of Christ by my wretched name?"[6] Of course his plea was in vain.†

---

* Because we no longer live in an agrarian society, the violent image of a wooden threshing flail beating the daylights out of something—whether grains of wheat or something else—has generally been lost to us, but Luther used it rather often. Our contemporary images of martial arts nunchakus may suffice as an idea, or perhaps those wildly flailing plastic figures used by car dealerships to draw the attention of passing motorists.

† It is likely that had his name been more difficult—as were the names of his friends Melanchthon and Oecolampadius—this sincere request might have been more readily complied with.

On December 22, Karlstadt, ever forcing things forward, announced that on New Year's Day a simple evangelical Lord's Supper would be held in the Castle Church, in which every one of the new reforms would be included. Both wine and bread would be served to all. Those communing must hold the chalice themselves, and the words of the Communion ceremony would be spoken in simple German. The host would certainly not be elevated, as is done in the Catholic Mass. Of course there would be a sermon. But as soon as Frederick's counselors caught wind of this service, they made clear they would shut it down. It was one thing to take such steps in more private quarters, as they had been doing, but to do this in the Castle Church itself was too much and much too soon. But Karlstadt cleverly moved the date up one week, to Christmas Eve, before anyone had time to organize against it. And not only did he conduct things as promised; he even dispensed with the usual clerical vestments, simply wearing his academic gown. Many hundreds came. Some said a thousand were there. It was said that many of those who took Communion did not fast beforehand, as was typical, or go to confession, both of which were somewhat scandalous. Twice during this landmark service, the sacred Communion wafer was dropped on the floor, with the offending layperson too horrified by what he had done to bend down and pick it up, so Karlstadt took it upon himself to do so. But word of this contributed to the controversy with which this service was regarded.

Afterward, Karlstadt—clearly emboldened by this service—decided that on New Year's Day he would hold a similar one in the Wittenberg City Church. The pastor there was not against it, but all of these reforms happening so quickly contributed to the revolutionary atmosphere in Wittenberg, and rather than calm the mobs, it seemed to further inflame them. At the Christmas Eve service, lamps in the church were broken, and popular songs were caterwauled in the streets, doubtless drunkenly. Then, on the day after Christmas, as though he must do everything radical in one fell swoop, Karlstadt became engaged to a fifteen-year-old. He was himself thirty-five, and it was the fashion among those of nobler birth to marry much younger women, and she was indeed from a noble family. But things were now shooting forward at a pace that was not long sustainable. The clash of traditionalists with Karlstadt and Zwilling and the others had contributed to an atmosphere at times tense and violent, at other times giddy and reckless.

The Zwickau Prophets

On December 27, in the midst of the developing maelstrom, three men arrived from the town of Zwickau, a textile center ninety miles south of Wittenberg. They claimed to have direct communication from God and immediately betook themselves to the home of Melanchthon to tell him all about it. The first two, Nicholas Storch and Thomas Drechsel, were a pair of wild-eyed weavers, while the third, Thomas Stübner, was a former student of Melanchthon's, but because his father was a bathhouse attendant, he had taken the pointedly egalitarian name Stübner, which was the German word for that profession.*

Zwickau had already been solidly receptive to Luther's teachings for a couple of years, so reformation had taken root there rather quickly. But there were far more radical roilings there too, most of them instigated by an especially colorful radical named Thomas Müntzer, who claimed Luther as his spiritual father. But Müntzer had dark depths of which Luther knew nothing just yet. This was why Luther had felt quite comfortable in recommending him for a post in Zwickau at St. Mary's Church and did so. But it was in Zwickau that Müntzer fell in with the weaver Nicholas Storch. Described as "lean and goggle-eyed,"[7] Storch had an uncanny ability to draw listeners into his eccentric, ethereal orbit. He spoke of mystical visions and revelations, and before anyone knew it, he and Müntzer were attracting many glassy-eyed adherents and diverging not only from the Catholicism of Rome but from the Reformation of Luther and the Bible too. Müntzer publicly praised Storch from the pulpit and deputized him to conduct secret meetings so that he could teach others this more direct pathway to God. In fact, he was convinced there were several clear spiritual stages by which one mystically achieved the "righteousness of God." First, he said, there was "amazement" and then "disengagement," and then "contemplation," and then "endurance," and then one finally achieved "the righteousness of God" itself. Not only was this not in any way biblical, but it seemed the precise inverse of everything Luther had taken such pains to teach. One must run from the idea of climbing up a ladder of "religious works" to God. That was the clear lesson of his failed monastic efforts. One only realized one could not

* To be a bathhouse attendant was considered an especially lowly position, but given the egalitarian atmosphere of those in Stübner's theological circle, he had likely taken the name as a badge of honor.

climb to God and then via the miraculous door opened by faith, God came to you. But there was no one in Zwickau to point this out, so these men continued swimming in these rarefied and confused theological waters. Rumors flew that they were about to appoint twelve apostles to preach their new gospel—and seventy-two further disciples—just as Jesus had done.

But things in Zwickau turned sour when in one of his sermons Müntzer passionately denounced someone, after which that someone was beaten to a frothy pulp by the bloodthirsty mob he had "inspired." At this point, the city council had to step in, but even after this ugliness Müntzer was unwilling to slow down. More violence soon followed, until the authorities decided Müntzer must simply be expelled from the town altogether, causing widespread furor among his disciples. In the ensuing melee, fifty-six weavers' apprentices were arrested and jailed. After this, Müntzer happily fled to Bohemia. But even after he had gone, some of his adherents continued to stir the pot, most notably Storch. Even Duke George had seen that something must be done, and he prodded his cousin Duke John to take action, which he did, calling for an investigation. But preferring not to squirm under questioning, Storch made his own escape southward. With him he took his friends Drechsel and Stübner. And where would these myrmidons of the Future expect to find spiritual succor? Where indeed, if not in Wittenberg?

Thus did this trio find themselves at Melanchthon's home, where they quickly overwhelmed the shy genius with their confident biblical interpretations and stories of heavenly ecstasies. Amsdorf too was taken in. It is easy to see how in that extraordinary environment Melanchthon and others seriously wondered whether they were in some kind of new apostolic era, especially when Storch and his followers had no doubt about it—and there was no Luther nearby to show these miscreants the door. Melanchthon and Amsdorf could not help but be intrigued at the idea that these three Zwickauers had revived the early church's spiritual gifts. Of course Paul and Peter and other disciples had seen visions. No one doubted this, nor that the apostles had experienced the miracles of speaking in tongues. Who knew but that this was something the Lord wished to bring back now, through these three men? Who knew whether all that had transpired meant that they were living in the last days, just before the Lord's promised return? For some strange reason, none of the outlandish things these men said seemed theologically iffy—until they shared with Melanchthon their views on infant baptism, which they were implacably against. Of all things, it was this that got his attention. But they said other things that ought to have alerted him, such as the idea that direct revelation from God himself could now supersede the Bible. After all, they said, if the Bible were so necessary, God might have sent it to them directly from heaven. Now they had the Holy Spirit. Melanchthon was in a dither. He didn't feel confident enough to understand whether these fast-talking holy men were onto something or not, and he felt sure that Luther needed to return again to judge the situation properly. And this was what the prophets themselves wanted too. Where was Luther? They must meet with him and were aggressively pushing on this front. So Melanchthon now wrote to Frederick, asking whether Luther might again be recalled to Wittenberg:

> I can scarcely tell you how deeply I am moved. But who shall
> judge them, other than Martin, I do not know. Since the gospel
> is at stake, arrangements should be made for them to meet with
> him. They wish it. I would not have written to you if the matter
> were not so important. We must beware lest we resist the Spirit
> of God, and also lest we be possessed of the Devil.[8]

That the prophets had considerably rattled the subdued Melanchthon seems clear. But the stolid Frederick was hardly one to be taken in by flaky Zwickau weavers. As far as he was concerned, these three troublemakers should be clearly instructed from the Scriptures. Besides, it was out of the question that Luther should be recalled from the Wartburg; the political situation was far too dangerous. Frederick stoutly insisted that Melanchthon and the others have nothing more to do with these batty agitators, and let that be an end of it. So Melanchthon rather meekly agreed.

Of course Melanchthon would write to Luther about the Zwickau visitors, and Luther also had little patience for what he heard. First, he scolded Melanchthon for the umpteenth time about his everlasting timidity, saying that Melanchthon knew the Scriptures far better than he himself did and should be able to puzzle this out without Luther's personally traveling to Wittenberg to hold his hand. He then said that the Scripture commands us to "test the spirits" (1 John 4:1) and not to feel rushed into making any decisions about them. First prove they are of God. He also said that there was nothing he had heard that could not easily have been a satanic counterfeit, and he went to some pains to say that the mark of someone who has encountered God or who is truly called by God is suffering. So had these self-proclaimed prophets of Zwickau experienced *Anfechtungen*? Had they only had pleasant experiences in God's presence, or had they sometimes been terrified, as so many had been in their encounters with God or his angels? If their experiences only partook of a peachy keenness, one had better beware.

Meanwhile, Karlstadt continued to blithely leapfrog ahead of things. Without Luther in the way, he must have felt that he himself was the actual leader of this burgeoning movement. Things were happening with increasing rapidity, and it must have been a heady experience. His wedding—of which Luther approved, trilling, "I know the girl"[9]—took place January 19, and besides spending lavishly to do the occasion justice, he invited a veritable throng of distinguished guests. Karlstadt even dared to invite Frederick, though he did not attend. A month later Justus Jonas too would take the happy plunge.

But there were all along the way signs that did not bode well for Karlstadt's future. The townspeople were sometimes driven to violence by their enthusiasm, with one group of rowdy goons venting their passions by storming a local pastor's house. And then, on January 6, the Reformed congregation of Augustinians had convened right there in Wittenberg, at the Augustinian cloister. The affair was presided over by Luther's friend Wenceslas Linck, who had come from Nuremberg. Johannes Lang was there too, from Erfurt. But the Augustinians had come to a strange pass. The Wittenberg cloister alone had already lost a third of its monks and at this convention, the leaders decided to adopt some drastic reforms, which would have widespread ripples throughout monasteries everywhere. They now officially allowed any monks who wished to leave to do so, making their lifelong vows officially voluntary and therefore essentially meaningless. Actually, Luther had hoped they would do this. But without him in Wittenberg, some of the usual suspects got carried away.

For example, a few days after this convention, Zwilling decided it was time for some public theater. So he instigated and oversaw the destruction of some of the cloister's previously sacred objects. Figures of the saints had their arms and heads chopped off. Images of them were burned. Karlstadt had in his sermons agitated against images in church, saying that the commandment "Thou shalt not make for thyself any graven images"[10] must be obeyed, so all images were now considered nothing but worldly temptations to sin. He even said crucifixes should no longer be displayed. Luther might have agreed with some of what Karlstadt said, but he would never have taken things so far so fast and would certainly not have allowed the destruction of these statues, images, and other things. A number of the wooden altars were smashed and destroyed too, as were banners. The unbridled perpetrators even burned the consecrated oil that was used in administering last rites.

Karlstadt's views on images were far more radical than Luther's and partook of a kind of Gnostic dualism in which everything that tempted the senses was suspect and outlawed. "Our eyes make love to [images] and court them," he wrote. "The truth is that all who honor images, seek their help, and worship them, are whores and adulterers."[11] We know that Luther would diverge from Karlstadt's severely iconoclastic view on art in churches, but Karlstadt went further yet, asserting that church music too was beyond the pale. "Relegate organs, trumpets, and flutes to the theater," he wrote. "The lascivious notes of the organ awaken thoughts of the world." King David might have had something to say about these prohibitions on worship music, but Karlstadt was rarely in a temperate mood. "If there is to be singing," he declaimed stingily, "let it be no more than a solo."[12] Luther not only would have disagreed but would soon enough bring about a glorious revival of music and congregational singing in the life of the church, one that would peal and resound around the globe for centuries. But the winds in Wittenberg were then synonymous with the legalistic howlings of Karlstadt, and who could stand against it?

But the doughty Duke George would suddenly volunteer. On hearing of all these barbaric outrages, the superlatively irritated duke—then attending the diet at Nuremberg—bloomed into a fulminating bouquet of rage. He was not about to let this madness continue. He demanded immediate action. So he persuaded the diet to send the following excoriation to his delinquent cousin Frederick and to the bishop of Meissen too:

> We have heard that priests celebrate mass in lay habit, omitting essential portions. They consecrate the holy sacraments in German. The recipients are not required to have made prior confession. They take the elements into their own hands and in both kinds. The blood of our Lord is not served in a chalice but in a mug. The sacrament is given to children. Priests are dragged from the altars by force. Priests and monks marry, and the common people are incited to frivolity and offense.[13]

Frederick must have felt grieved at what was happening himself. So it is no wonder that he heeded the diet's warning and agreed that putting the brakes on these shenanigans was a wise idea. What would the emperor and the pope do when they heard of these shocking excesses? And they surely would hear of them. Frederick knew that if things continued along these lines, he could himself suffer great consequences and perhaps even lose his territory to his perpetually livid cousin. So on February 13, Frederick wrote letters to the university and to the Castle Church. "We have gone too fast," he said. He declared that the images must not be disturbed anymore—Luther would have agreed with this—and that any "essential portion" of the Mass must remain.[14] Finally, he said that Karlstadt must no longer preach. Frederick hardly wished to stop the Reformation, but it was only prudent to slow things to where cooler consideration could be brought to some of the most divisive issues. Nonetheless, this was a considerable blow to Karlstadt, who doubtless felt he was being scapegoated in the messy situation.

But the Wittenberg city council took umbrage at the elector's instructions and decided it would not comply. The one thing that the Gospel had done and would always do was embolden people to think for themselves and demand relative freedom from those in authority. At the very least, they would call those leaders to account. And so now in Wittenberg the people dared to push back against their own prince. They felt strongly about these reforms, and of course they were heartily egged on in their views by Karlstadt and Zwilling. Despite these leaders' excesses and sometimes poor judgment, the people felt theologically justified in managing their own affairs if their leaders were being negligent. So in brazen defiance of Frederick, the Wittenberg council decreed that the church services were indeed to go forward precisely as Karlstadt had been conducting them. Moreover, public immorality must immediately be sent packing. Thus prostitution was outlawed, all brothels were to be closed immediately, and all begging was outlawed too. And the idea that the people of God had an obligation to the poor leapt into the picture too, and a community chest was set up to help them. But the local ordinance went so far as to insist that all images in the churches be removed. There were other drastic measures too. What Karlstadt had in mind seemed to be a kind of utopian society, based on Christian doctrines, and Wittenberg would be the first in a series of Christian towns freed from the encumbrances of leadership outside the community.

Melanchthon was not on board. He knew that Karlstadt and Zwilling had not managed things well, that events had taken an unnecessarily unpleasant and strident turn. But he never felt himself the person to restore order. He even now thought of leaving Wittenberg altogether. "The dam has broken," he wrote, despondent, "and I cannot stem the waters."[15] Many students at the university, caught up in the emotional and rather millennialist tumult of these days, came to the conclusion that their studies were a waste of time. An outbreak of the plague in Wittenberg during this period must have exacerbated this end-time atmosphere. If all that mattered was "preaching the gospel" and saving souls before the Final Reckoning, which was soon to arrive, what was the blessed point of all their Humanistic studies? Why read the obscure thoughts of poets from antiquity when eternity yawned just up ahead? The sloppy anti-intellectualism that has plagued those most zealous about evangelism had here for the first time reared its ignorant head. Another reason some students left was that many of them survived financially by begging. It was something one saw in all university towns in Germany, so if begging was now prohibited by Wittenberg law, how were they any longer to survive? So, many of the students simply took the opportunity to go home. Wittenberg had now come to a genuine crisis, and the city council knew there was only one thing to do: Luther must be summoned home to help. No one had emerged with anything near his leadership abilities, and the time had come for him to put his Wartburg period in the rearview mirror.

Luther Translates the New Testament

Luther was no longer restless at the Wartburg, as he had been in his first days there. His constipation had passed, and upon returning from his quick trip to Wittenberg in December, he had dived headlong into translating the New Testament into German. He reckoned that with a few months' hard work, he really could finish it. The plan was to do so and then return to Wittenberg around Easter, this time for good. He had first mentioned the idea of translating all twenty-seven books of the New Testament in December, to his friend Johannes Lang, who was himself then translating the book of Matthew. That Luther managed to pull off the entirety of this project in eleven weeks has boggled the mind of scholars for half a millennium. This is because such an undertaking requires an extremely rare set of skills, and history has judged that Luther performed it exceedingly well, so well that his is still today the principal German translation that is used or upon which subsequent translations have been based. Perhaps most important in translating an ancient language into a modern language is maintaining the innate poetry of the language, even and perhaps especially when that "poetry" takes the form of prose. The language should be supple and vivid and powerful, but the theological ideas behind the words must not suffer along the way. On the contrary, Luther wanted to clarify the theological meaning of many previously poorly translated and therefore misunderstood passages. These bad translations and ideas had contributed not only to the misunderstanding of individual verses and theological ideas but also to the wider problem of general unfamiliarity with the Bible. Who wished to read something that was swollen and opaque? And if people did not read it for themselves, they would be reliant on a priestly caste to interpret it for them, which had of course been the case for many centuries, with results that Luther hardly considered positive.

Luther relied mostly on Erasmus's second edition of his Greek New Testament, which came out in 1519. Although there were a number of rather turgid German New Testament translations in circulation, they had all relied on the Latin Vulgate—with its innumerable errors—rather than on the original Greek, which had not existed until Erasmus's 1516 edition. So Luther mostly ignored these previous German translations. But he brought not only accuracy to this new work but the supreme genius of an ear so attuned to the dramatically variegated German language of his day that what he accomplished in translating the entire Bible—for after finishing the New Testament, he would turn to the Old—not only succeeded in revolutionizing the Christian faith in Germany but also had the effect almost of creating a new German language. In his magisterial biography, Heinrich Bornkamm sums it up thus: "It was from Luther's Bible that the German people learned to speak the language they were to have in common."[16] The numerous dialects throughout Germany had only recently begun to compete with what is now called High German, which was a unified German language being used in more and more places. "I speak the language of the Saxon chancery," Luther said, "which all the German princes are now using."[17] It is a startling fact of linguistic happenstance that a number of these dialects, which were merging to become a universal or "High" German around that time, were doing so in precisely the area of Luther's Saxony. By using this new language with what can only be reckoned virtuoso skill, and putting it into a book that was the only book many families would own, he helped Germans find a national voice in a way that he never particularly intended but that can never be sufficiently appreciated. In doing so he helped create a German national identity, pulling a common scarlet-and-gold thread of Scripture through each of the more than three hundred patches on the rich linguistic quilt.

What Luther put in his German Bible would affect the German tongue forever. A number of Saxon words—such as *Krippe* (crib) for "manger"—have become the words now universally used by all Germans. Luther also came upon terms which had no German equivalent, such as "scapegoat," and was forced to invent a word, which he did: *Sündenbock*.

Luther had intended to stay at the Wartburg and finish this monumental work, along with a number of sermons—or postils—that he had been working on. In fact, even when he planned to return at Easter, he was not expecting to resume his pastoral duties, but rather hoped to hide away in or near Wittenberg so that he could finish polishing the German New Testament with the help of his linguistic superior Melanchthon—and after that to leap into taking on the Old Testament, with the help of Melanchthon and numerous others. But the news from home stirred his pastor's heart and made him think that an earlier return must be considered. He saw that the church in Wittenberg sorely needed him in this official capacity. The city council included his dear friend Lucas Cranach and the goldsmith Christian Döring, and when they summoned him, he saw it as nothing less than a call from God himself. For Luther, of course, that was everything. He would not fear what man could do, neither Duke George nor the emperor nor the pope. If God called, God would protect him, and if God did not protect him, that would be God's business. His business was to obey.

On February 24, he wrote to Frederick. In his inimitably jolly way, Luther joked that with all of these new troubles the elector—who was so extremely enamored of relics—was to be congratulated on now getting the biggest relic of them all, and at no cost whatsoever. It was "the whole cross, together with nails, spears, and scourges."[18] Ha-ha. It was Luther's firm belief that those who supported the Gospel would suffer and be attacked and would in their way be crucified. It is not clear whether the elector appreciated the joke. And he certainly did not think it safe or wise for Luther to return. On February 28, a bailiff was dispatched to the

Wartburg, to apprise Luther of Frederick's sincere request that he not return to Wittenberg. Frederick did not think Luther deserved to be turned over to the imperial or papal authorities, despite the Edict of Worms, because Frederick felt that Luther had not yet gotten the fair hearing and disputation that his honest concerns merited. But if Luther returned, Frederick would feel pressure to hand him over. Frederick hoped to avoid these political problems for some time yet. And no matter what, Luther's life would be endangered if he left his redoubt "among the birds." But by now Luther had made up his mind that God wished him to return, and he could not be dissuaded.

CHAPTER FOURTEEN

Luther Returns

Men can go wrong with wine and women.
Shall we then prohibit wine and abolish women?
The sun, the moon, and stars have been worshiped.
Shall we then pluck them out of the sky?

—Martin Luther

LUTHER DESCENDED FROM his island in the sky on March 1, 1522. About two days into the trip, he came to the town of Jena, where he stayed at the Black Bear Inn. Johannes Kessler, a nineteen-year-old student from St. Gall, Switzerland, was also staying there. Kessler was headed to Wittenberg too, traveling with a fellow student, Wolfgang Spengler. Kessler wrote a firsthand account of his time at the inn, saying that he and Spengler observed a knight at a table, dressed in a scarlet-red doublet with woolen breeches and wearing a red hat. One hand touched the pommel of his sword, the other held a book, which they observed to be a Hebrew Psalter. How curious for a knight to be reading such a book! But the mysterious knight bade them join him and asked whether they knew anything about the nascent Reformation. They certainly did. As it happened, they were themselves headed to Wittenberg. At some point in their conversation, they inquired after the famous Martin Luther, asking whether he was then at Wittenberg. The knight volunteered that he could with certainty say that Luther was not at Wittenberg but would soon be. And he told them that when they reached that fair city, they must send greetings to Schurff from "the one who is to come."[1] At some point, the innkeeper took the young men aside and told them the man with whom they were eating was none other than Luther himself, but they mustn't let on that they knew, because he was traveling incognito, no thanks to this blabbering innkeeper. But the students didn't believe this preposterous claim, assuming the ill-informed innkeeper had mistaken the name of Ulrich von Hutten—who they knew was a real knight and a friend of the Reformation—for Luther's and that this knight, conversant in the things of the budding Reformation, therefore must be he. But when they arrived at Wittenberg on March 8, they gave their letters of introduction to Hieronymus Schurff and soon afterward were introduced to Melanchthon, Nicholas von Amsdorf, and Justus Jonas. And then they met Luther too. Here he was in his natural habitat—sans beard and doublet. They were taken aback to understand that this smooth-shaven monk was indeed the same figure with whom they had spoken at the Black Bear Inn. Eventually, Kessler would return home to become a noted reformer in his native Switzerland.

Before his arrival in Wittenberg, on March 5, Luther came to the town of Borna, near Leipzig. There he stayed at the nobleman von der Strassen's home, where he wrote the following letter to Frederick. It has become one of his most famous. "I wrote for your sake," he began, "not for mine."

> I was disturbed that the gospel was brought into disrepute at Wittenberg. If I were not sure that the gospel is on our side, I would have given up. All the sorrow I have had is nothing compared to this. I would gladly have paid for this with my life, for we can answer neither to God nor to the world for what has happened. The Devil is at work in this. As for myself, my gospel is not from men. Concessions bring only contempt. I cannot yield an inch to the Devil. I have done enough for Your Grace by staying in hiding for a year. I did not do it through cowardice. The Devil knows I would have gone into Worms though there were as many devils as tiles on the roof, and I would ride into Leipzig now, though it rained Duke Georges for nine days.

The image of a steady rain of scowling Duke Georges is entertaining enough, but Luther's faith and fearlessness are on dramatic display here. It is clear that when he knows he is in God's will, he not only has no fear but has a tremendous boldness. In fact, he is now so clear that he is walking with God for God's purposes—and therefore cannot go wrong, come what may—he speaks to Frederick in a way that sounds at least somewhat arrogant:

I would have you know that I come to Wittenberg with a higher protection than that of Your Grace. I do not ask you to protect me. I will protect you more than you will protect me. If I thought you would protect me, I would not come. This is not a case for the sword but for God, and since you are weak in the faith you cannot protect me. . . . [Y]ou should do nothing but leave it to God. You are excused if I am captured or killed. As a prince you should obey the emperor and offer no resistance. No one should use force except the one who is ordained to use it. Otherwise there is rebellion against God. But I hope you will not act as my accuser. If you leave the door open, that is enough. If they try to make you do more than that, I will then tell you what to do. If Your Grace had eyes, you would see the glory of God.[2]

These are powerful words. He has no doubt that the Lord of hosts is real and will protect him, so much so that he dares to tell the man who has long protected him that Luther's faith—which is to say God—will now protect Frederick. And then he speaks not simply of God's protection but of his glory.

When Luther arrived back in Wittenberg, he knew he owed the elector the kindness of writing a letter to the Imperial Council of Regency, explaining why he had returned, thus relieving Frederick of bearing the whole responsibility in it, which was certainly politically costly. In the letter, he clearly and humbly confessed his obedience to the imperial government. He explained that he had returned for the sake of his "children in Christ," meaning his congregation at Wittenberg. But the larger issue of precisely how one comports oneself as a Christian now came into play here. To Luther, what Karlstadt and Zwilling had done smacked more of angry political protest than of humble Christian faith. Luther felt that their behavior had brought shame to the Gospel. They had as much as turned receiving the body and blood of Christ into a political protest. Luther was also troubled at the mobs that had jumped into the fray, obviously with no regard for the Gospel but with a carnal desire to swat at the authorities. Luther was never simply antiauthoritarian—far from it, as we shall see in the events of the Peasants' War. So he now made clear in this context what he had previously made clear in other contexts: one must allow God the freedom to do what he wished to do. But to force things by dragging one's own dead flesh into what ought to be done only by the living Spirit of God was to play into Satan's hands and to do Satan's work. Luther was quite clear that the excesses of Karlstadt and Zwilling—and for sure those of the Zwickau prophets too—were guilty of this. As with any such thing, they were theologically sloppy, falling into the errors of legalism with regard to certain things, such as the prohibition of all images in church, and falling into the opposite errors of libertinism. It was all a muddle, but Luther was back, and he must now put things right again.

"No One Can Die for Another"

Luther was back in Wittenberg on March 6 and spent the next two days talking with his kitchen cabinet of Jonas, Amsdorf, and Melanchthon. Then, on Sunday the ninth, Luther climbed up into the pulpit of the City Church for the first time in nearly a year to preach the first of what would be eight sermons in eight days, to commemorate the beginning of Lent. According to the Luther scholar Michael Mullett, Luther was well aware of the theater of this moment, of how the Lenten severity now cast all that had gone before in the lurid light of carnival and excess. But Mullett goes much further, suggesting it was all perfectly preconceived, that Luther,

> showing his calculated mastery of visual symbolism and costume, matched his own appearance to the time and season. He now very deliberately abandoned the louche splendors of his knight's costume, in favor of his dramatic black monastic habit, cutting off his jaunty cavalier's beard, and having his skull shaved to restore his monk's tonsure, emphasizing once more the power of his austere cephalic structure.[3]

One doubts whether Luther was indeed conscious of the "power of his austere cephalic structure" or that he was even conscious of the austerity of his "cephalic structure." Are not most severely shorn heads inherently "austere"? Nor does Cranach's earlier rendering of Luther's facial hair support the adjective "jaunty." In any case, the moment was pregnant with drama, and it seems likely the clean-shaven speaker knew it. There can be no doubt that the atmosphere in the church was electric. What would the man say who had been taken from their midst this longest of seasons? He was like one returned from the realm of the dead, but here he was again, our Luther, come back to us. Even if the congregation had been as indifferent to him as they were attentive, his first words would have fixed their attention as a pin fixes a beetle in a specimen display case.

"The summons of death comes to us all," he said, "and no one can die for another." Who could fail to be drawn in by that, whatever the speaker's "cephalic structure"? How these first startling words from the man thought dead himself must have echoed in the ears of the congregation. "Everyone," he went on, "must fight his own battle with death by himself alone. We can shout into another's ears, but everyone must himself be prepared for the time of death, for I will not be with you then, nor you with me."[4]

In some ways, these words may well stand as a summation of the entire Reformation to come: that we may not rely upon nor blame others for our relationship with God—and all things related—and must take our new-found freedom in this not as license, but as the gravest and most sacred of responsibilities. And so, with this most provocative of opening salvos, Luther began the first of his octave of now famous "Invocavit Sermons." In preaching them, he was clearly taking authority over the broken situation, and in a way that only Luther seemed able to do, he definitively and clearly explained the issues that were dividing people and corrected the excesses that had crept in under Karlstadt and Zwilling. Luther never rebuked Karlstadt in these sermons. Still, it must have been embarrassing and even at times stinging for Karlstadt to listen to Luther theologically dismember his previous bold and public assertions. No one doubted whom Luther was criticizing in these sermons.

But the old hands of Wittenberg were thrilled. Hieronymus Schurff happily wrote to the elector that

> great joy and exultation from the learned and the uneducated has
> sprung from Dr. Martin's return and from his sermons. By his
> mediating divine help he is putting us angry and misled people
> back on the way of truth by daily showing us where we went
> wrong and by using irrefutable arguments to get us out of the
> mess into which the interloping preachers led us.[5]

And the young students too were gushing. One of them, Albert Burer, wrote, "Luther has come to restore order and to straighten out what Karlstadt and Gabriel [Zwilling] had messed up with their violent sermons."[6] Burer goes on to say that Karlstadt and Zwilling had not shown any consideration for those who disagreed with them and for whom the changes were too fast and dramatic. They had charged forward with the wild-eyed and typically insensitive zeal of new converts. Burer felt that Luther was sensitive to those not yet ready for everything at once and was like a Paul in his judiciousness. And Luther was theologically clear and helped his listeners to grasp what he said. "Whoever has heard him once," Burer wrote, "unless he is a stone, would gladly hear him again and again. For he drives home his points, like nails, into the minds of his hearers."[7]

Luther's genius and what made him the unquestioned leader of this movement comprised two things. First, he had the all-important pastor's heart, such that he was deeply concerned not merely with being right but with how what one said affected the simple faithful. Luther knew that some had felt pushed too quickly and too hard by the changes that Karlstadt and Zwilling had championed, and this was a fatal error, for it was unavoidably part of administering the Gospel to care about those people whom Paul called "the weaker brethren." Luther saw catering to these more timid members of the body not as any kind of abrogation of the truth but as central to the larger and most important issues of love and grace. In their hopped-up ardor to be right, Karlstadt and Zwilling had been somewhat too willing to step on toes. Luther memorably declared that such zealots, after drinking their own fill of milk, would "cut off the teat," forgetting that others would still need to drink milk.[8] One must be concerned for those who are not yet fully on board and must bring them along patiently. So to be right required being right not just in what one did and said but *in the way one did and said things*. If one was not concerned with how one implemented some of these new practices, one would set everything back, as Luther was certain that Karlstadt and Zwilling had done.

But the second way in which Luther here distinguished himself had to do with his theological insights. He was the one who had put many years of careful study into the Scriptures and who possessed the theological insights that had carried them all to this place, so he could see some of the theological problems that lay behind the more superficial issues. In other words, it was one thing to debate whether images in churches were appropriate, but it was another to understand the theology behind debating theology, to know that not all questions and issues were equal, and to know that this itself was a theologically important point, one that had been missed in the months he had been away.

The way Luther framed this was by saying that the underlying laws of freedom and love must obtain over all. So where things were nonnegotiable, yes, one must be firm and clear and uncompromising, but where things were optional, one must be clear that they were indeed optional. And one had to know which were which. So while Karlstadt had said that not to take both elements at Communion was a sin, Luther said no, people were free to do either. Where Karlstadt and Zwilling had insisted that images were clearly forbidden in Scripture, Luther said no. There were cherubim on the ark, and there was a bronze serpent in the wilderness. This was not so simple. Furthermore, just because images or statues might be the occasion of causing people to sin because some people were tempted to pray to the saints did not automatically mean that the images and statues must be abolished. Someone might take overweening pride in a church building. Did that mean we should not build churches? And whatever they did or didn't do, they must do it slowly. "Give men time," Luther said.

> I took three years of constant study, reflection, and discussion to arrive where I now am, and can the common man, untutored in such matters, be expected to move the same distance in three months? Do not suppose that abuses are eliminated by destroying the object which is abused. Men can go wrong with wine and women. Shall we then prohibit wine and abolish women? The sun, the moon, and stars have been worshiped. Shall we then pluck them out of the sky? Such haste and violence betray a lack of confidence in God. See how much he has been able to accomplish through me, though I did no more than pray and preach. The Word did it all. Had I wished I might have started a conflagration at Worms. But while I sat still and drank beer with Philip [Melanchthon] and Amsdorf, God dealt the papacy a mighty blow.[9]

Luther was saying that freedom and love must be at the center of Christian faith. A faith "without love is not enough; indeed, it is no faith at all," he said.[10] Luther also took pains to point out the similarities between the bondage of works in which the papal system had held people and the bondage of other kinds of works in which this recent movement in Wittenberg had held people. There were people who had grown up revering the host and the chalice of wine in such a way that it was impossible for them quickly to behave as though these were nothing special, as though they, who were common laypeople, should be able to touch the host with their hands and handle the cup of wine without terror. Luther well remembered his own paralysis at his first Mass. So to force people to handle the cup with their own hands was no different from forbidding them to partake of the cup. In these and other things, freedom must be the only guide. Let people be free to take the cup, but let them not be coerced to do it. As an example of this freedom, Luther chose to wear his monk's cowl when he preached. He might easily have done as Karlstadt had done and worn his academic gown, but Luther wanted to be clear that if he is not coerced to wear his cowl, then perhaps he will wear it after all. It was in the freedom to wear it or to refrain from wearing it that he rejoiced. Karlstadt and Zwilling had, as it were, forced nonconformity in the same way that the pope had forced conformity. It was as though in rebelling against a forced uniform of suit and tie, a group would cast a suspicious eye on anyone not wearing the new anti-uniform of denim and tattoos. Both attitudes represent a kind of bondage, and both are against the greatest laws of all, the Gospel laws of love and freedom. "Formerly the devil made us too papistic," Luther said, "and now he wants to make us too evangelical."[11]

In a pamphlet about the Lord's Supper, titled *Receiving Both Kinds in the Sacrament,* he wrote the following, which reprises the heart of his earlier book *The Freedom of a Christian:*

> I have taught in such a way that my teaching would lead first and foremost to a knowledge of Christ, that is, to pure and proper faith and genuine love, and thereby to freedom in all matters of external conduct, such as eating, drinking, clothes, praying, fasting, monasteries, sacrament, and whatever it may be. Such freedom is to be used in a salutary way only by those who have faith and love, that is, those who are real Christians. On such people we can and should impose no human law—nor permit anyone else to do so—which would bind their conscience.[12]

In what he now said and did in Wittenberg, Luther even won over some old foes. Fabricius Capito, who was a representative of Archbishop Albrecht of Mainz, had been one of the severest critics of Luther, so much so that Luther had called him a "virulent beast." But when Capito heard that Luther was back in Wittenberg, he paid a visit to hear him preach and was moved by all he saw and heard. "Already," Capito said, "the people are flowing together as if into a procession and then continuing on into the liberty of Christ."[13] He would within a year's time leave his post with the archbishop and become a leader of the new evangelical movement in Strasbourg.

Luther's relationship with Karlstadt, however, was badly damaged. He was three years Luther's senior and did not easily swallow Luther's public rebukes of what he had been doing in Wittenberg. Zwilling, who was younger, rather quickly took Luther's criticisms to heart and indeed mended his ways, but Karlstadt was more inclined to want to prove that Luther was wrong. He clearly smarted from being told by the elector he could no longer preach and from having been at the center of a burgeoning movement one moment and suddenly being put in the dunce's corner and watching Luther lead the class. Karlstadt understandably became embittered at the turn of events, in which Luther was suddenly telling people that what Karlstadt said they must do they must in fact not do. "The honey-lined net," Karlstadt wrote bitterly, "was more effective than the unyielding fetter."[14]

At one point, he wrote a series of theses that he hoped he would be able to debate with Luther publicly, but the university forbade him even to have them printed. It is hard not to think that Karlstadt was at least in some ways a convenient scapegoat for all that had happened and that had been allowed to happen and even fomented by Melanchthon, Amsdorf, and the city council. Karlstadt began spending less time in Wittenberg and eventually became the pastor of a tumbledown parish in rural Orlamünde, from which he began writing pamphlets critical of Luther and where he would be free to put into action those things he had been forbidden to do in Wittenberg. He would conduct all services in German and without vestments; he would give Communion in both kinds; and he would utterly forbid images and infant baptism.

Luther's idea that God's Word—that the good news of the Gospel—would have its way and needn't be forced or rushed is at the heart of most of his theology. In one of his Invocavit Sermons, he preached,

> Do you know what the Devil thinks when he sees men use violence to propagate the gospel? He sits with folded arms behind the fire of hell, and says with malignant looks and frightful grin: "Ah, how wise these madmen are to play my game! Let them go on; I shall reap the benefit. I delight in it." But when he sees the Word running and contending alone on the battle-field, then he shudders and shakes for fear.[15]

Luther more than did his part in preaching the Gospel in these years. In 1522, he preached 117 Sunday sermons in Wittenberg. The next year he preached 137 sermons there. And he preached many sermons on the road too.

The Prophets Return

Luther and company had not heard the last of the gung ho Zwickau prophets, whom Luther eventually lumped in with other radicals under the derisive term *Schwärmer* (fanatics). Sometime in early January, Storch and Drechsel had fled Wittenberg as hastily as they had come and were now traveling throughout Germany to spread their loopy doctrines wherever they might. Storch's ability to work his hypnotic voodoo on crowds was unparalleled, especially as he wove increasingly spine-tingling tales of what he had seen in the heavenlies. He spoke often of seeing the archangel Gabriel, and even went so far as to claim that Gabriel had told him that he himself would one day sit on Gabriel's throne, although he failed to explain where Gabriel would then sit.

The youngest of the trio, Thomas Stübner—who had been Melanchthon's student—remained behind with Melanchthon, who kindly put him up in his own home and defended him against a growing number of deeply suspicious Wittenbergers. Stübner stayed with Melanchthon and his wife for some time and did not cease to harry them with increasingly apocalyptic prophecies. At some point, he claimed the Muslim Turks would soon arrive to kill every priest, including the ones who had presumably done the right thing in marrying. He also claimed that in five—or seven—years a violent revolution would come, although those who had remained devout would survive, and there would be no more divisions in Christendom. We can only imagine how the cerebral and sweet Melanchthon dealt with all of this. Things came to a bizarre pass when one day they were all sitting at the table and Stübner—perhaps exhausted from weeks of nonstop prophesying—nodded off. He then awoke quite suddenly, declaring that he was in fact John Chrysostom, the fourth-century archbishop of Constantinople.

Early in April, Luther himself had a conversation with Stübner and another of his band, named Magister Cellarius, who was visiting Wittenberg. Stübner now explained his doctrine of spiritual stages to Luther. He explained that he had himself achieved the second mystical stage of "steadfastness" and he then had the great temerity to inform Luther that although he only stood in the first stage—which he called "mobility"—Stübner was confident he too might achieve the second stage. Luther was flabbergasted at these absurdities and said so. There wasn't as much as a shadow of any of this in the Bible. Either Stübner and his friends had manufactured them out of whole cloth, or they had been told these things via "revelation," but because the Bible did not confirm it or even hint at confirming it, Luther flatly rejected it. There were revelations from God and revelations from other sources. These were obviously not from God.

Stübner then attempted to convince Luther that the Bible did not speak of original sin. Of course the Bible didn't mention original sin—nor the Trinity, nor the printing press—but to leap from that to refuting the doctrine would be a stretch, especially with the man for whom the Bible had been as air and water for so many years. Then Cellarius got into a rather boisterous exchange with Luther, so that Luther quoted Zechariah to him. "The Lord rebuke you, Satan!" he said, at which point things continued speedily downhill. Cellarius had previously been flattering to Luther, but now he whirled about and unleashed such an unrelenting torrent of vulgarity that Luther could not find a space to reply. Unsurprisingly, Stübner and Cellarius soon departed Wittenberg. Later, Luther summed up his meeting by saying, "I have spoken with the devil incarnate."[16] He was not speaking hyperbolically, but sincerely believed that the god who was behind their mystical gifts was not God but the devil himself.

Although this was the last Wittenberg saw of Stübner, some time later Drechsel made another entrance. He told Luther of two extraordinarily vivid visions he had had that he interpreted as clear warnings of God's imminent wrath. Luther was not impressed, and after Drechsel had breathlessly delivered himself of his dire Delphic pronouncements, Luther sarcastically asked whether that was all he had to say. Drechsel now mystically perceived that his visions were not being appreciated and made his exit. But the leader of the original Zwickau trio, Storch, circled back to Wittenberg that September. For some reason, the "prince of the prophets" was now garbed in the attire of a foot soldier, and with him was a new convert, Dr. Gerhard Westerburg, of Cologne, who, like many of the others initially attracted to the Zwickau prophets, would later become a part of the violent Anabaptist movement. Storch engaged Luther directly on the subject of infant baptism, mocking the preposterous idea that a sprinkle of water could have eternal consequences. The conversation didn't proceed much past that.

On his return to Wittenberg, Luther had entered a new season, one in which challenges from such as Duke George—on the more hidebound traditionalist right—were matched by such as Karlstadt and Müntzer on the free radical *Schwärmer* left. He must now focus not merely on parrying the attacks on both flanks but also on defining what the new way forward would look like, although having people pushing on both sides helped bring definition to what lay between them. Still, the last thing Luther had ever expected to do was be saddled with the unfathomable challenge of creating what amounted to a new church—or at least a new denomination. But the events of the past years had brought him to this curious historical pass, and now he faced the task of figuring out what things should be, not only for his own congregation in Wittenberg, but for all those others in surrounding towns—and some very far away too, who looked to him for leadership. He would have to puzzle out exactly what a worship service would be like, and in the course of doing this, would find himself writing music and hymns, for one of his signal achievements in history would be bringing congregational singing into the church.

In this first year back, Luther wrote a great deal in which he was trying to clarify what real faith meant and how a Christian ought to live. He wrote the *Personal Prayer Book*, in which he attempted to help counteract much that had passed for prayer and devotional life under the medieval church, in which rote prayers were said multiple times, as though God were doddering or distracted or simply disinclined to hear what we had to say. Luther understood that the God of the Bible was a loving father eager to hear the prayers of his children. What Luther wrote in a letter to an Austrian nobleman two years later helps us see the heart of this idea. This nobleman's wife had died, so he had written to Luther about praying for her soul, saying that he had paid many priests to say private masses for her. Luther minced no words, saying that paying priests to pray for his deceased wife was "faithless."

> It is sufficient for your grace earnestly to pray once or twice for her. For God has promised that whatever you ask for, believe that you will receive it and you will certainly have it (Luke 11:9–10). In contrast, when we pray over and over again for the same thing, it is a sign that we do not believe God and with our faithless prayer only make him angrier. True, we should regularly pray, but always in faith and certain that we are being heard. Otherwise, the prayer is in vain.[17]

It is vintage Luther that he says that praying over and over is in fact not only utterly useless but actually counterproductive because it demonstrates our lack of faith. By praying in that way, we are only proving that we don't know to whom we are speaking and are insulting him. It is as though we were to bribe a kindhearted policeman who is already trying to help us, or as though we were to bribe our own dear parents. It would not help the situation but in fact bring them grief and horror to see that we do not know them at all and actually deeply distrust them. It would create distance between us where there had been none, except in our own minds.

Much of Luther's time during this first year back was spent in traveling to nearby towns to preach. He was invited to preach in Zwickau, in Torgau, in Borna, and in Altenburg. He also preached in Erfurt and at the court of Duke John in Weimar. His message of evangelical faith had caught on, but now he must help it spread in a way that was orderly. Over and over in these sermons, he stressed the basics:

> Christ came down from heaven to make himself known to us. He stepped down into our mire and became a man. But we do not know him, nor do we accept him, who came to help us out of every need and fear. But he who accepts Christ, acknowledges and loves him, he fulfills all things and all his works are good; he does good to his neighbor; he suffers all things for God's sake.[18]

Letter to Staupitz

On June 27, Luther wrote to his dear old friend and mentor, Johannes von Staupitz. It had been a long time since they had corresponded, and the impact of the Reformation on the Augustinian order and in general had made things rather difficult for Staupitz. Although he agreed with Luther in many ways, theologically speaking, he could never follow his brightest student along the difficult path that directly challenged the pope and had now led away from the church itself. In fact, having seen the handwriting on the wall in the Augustinian order already in 1520, he resigned his post as vicar-general, being replaced by Luther's friend Wenceslas Linck. A year later Staupitz left the Augustinians entirely and joined the Benedictines. Luther had heard a rumor that Staupitz was being considered for the abbacy of the Benedictine cloister in Salzburg, which upset him. He also knew that Staupitz had been hearing things about him that were simply untrue.

One thing I beg of you: for Christ's mercies, do not indiscriminately believe the accusations that are made against either Wenceslas [Linck] or me. You say that my teachings are praised by those who patronize brothels, and that my recent writings have given great offense. I am not surprised or afraid of this. Certainly we have done nothing here other than publicize the pure Word among the people without [creating] a disturbance, and this we are [still] doing. Both the good and the bad are making use of the Word; [and] as you know, it is not in our power to control [how they use it].... We will do what Christ predicted when he said that his angels would gather out of his kingdom all causes of offense. My Father, I must destroy that kingdom of abomination and perdition which belongs to the pope, together with all his hangers-on. He [Christ] is doing this without us, of course, without the help of a human hand, solely through the Word. The Lord knows the end of it. The matter is beyond our power of comprehension and understanding.

Therefore there is no reason why I should delay until someone is able to understand it. Because of the greatness of God, it is most fitting that there should arise proportionately great disturbance of minds, great causes of offense, and great monstrosities. Do not let all these things disturb you, my Father. I am very hopeful. You can see in these things God's counsel and his mighty hand. Remember how from the beginning my case has always seemed to the world to be terrible and intolerable, yet it has grown stronger day by day. It will also prevail over that which you so greatly fear; just wait a little while. Satan is feeling his wound; this is why he is raging this way, and throwing everything into confusion. But Christ, who has begun this work, will tread him under foot, and all the gates of hell will strive against Christ in vain.

... I am daily challenging Satan and his armor all the more, however, so that the Day of Christ may be hastened in which he will destroy the Antichrist.

Farewell, my Father, and pray for me. Dr. [Hieronymus Schurff], Rector Amsdorf, and Philip send their greetings....

Yours,
Martin Luther[19]

The German Bible

Without question, the largest of the projects Luther now faced was translating the entirety of the Bible into German. The manuscript of the New Testament translation that he brought back from the Wartburg in early March was breathtakingly impressive, although not quite finished. Luther knew that it still required the close and rigorous attention of Melanchthon. This linguistic savant knew the Greek better than anyone alive and now spent many weeks carefully combing through the text for nits, which he and Luther picked out. Luther also required extraordinary help with the very end of the book. In fact, it was with the penultimate chapter of the ultimate book, Revelation, that he needed assistance. In that chapter the New Jerusalem is described as having foundations covered with every kind of jewel. But how in the world to figure out the German word equivalents of such rare gems as chrysoprase, chrysolite, jasper, beryl, and carnelian? For this conundrum, he turned to his friend Lucas Cranach, who was creating twenty-one original illustrations—which were heavily influenced by Dürer—for the book of Revelation, which would be published with the New Testament itself. Cranach in turn appealed to his friend Frederick, asking whether he and Luther could borrow some of the gems from his treasury, which they did, enabling them to identify each one by color. Cranach's illustrations were a powerful selling point for the book, which was printed in September and came to be known as the September Testament. Unbound copies of this tremendous literary sensation sold for half a gulden, while bound copies sold for a gulden, which Cranach's biographer Steven Ozment tells us was roughly the price of a slaughtered hog.[20]

Showing his own theological leanings in his illustrations, Cranach slyly placed on the head of the whore of Babylon the distinctive and recognizable three-tiered papal tiara. When Duke George saw this, he once more blew his everlasting stack, condemning the tiara in no uncertain terms and demanding that his wayward cousin see to it that this triple crown be duly plucked from the whore's head by the next printing. Luther sent early copies of the Bible to Spalatin and Frederick, as well as to Frederick's brother Duke John and to John's son Duke John Frederick, both of whom were at this time living in Weimar.* Three thousand copies were

---

* Duke John would succeed his brother as elector in 1525, and Duke John Frederick would succeed his father in 1532.

The whore of Babylon wears the three-tiered papal tiara.

initially printed, all of which sold quickly. The second printing of an additional two thousand copies occurred in December, at which point the tiara had indeed been left at home. But the popularity of this epochal and groundbreaking book was so extreme that three months after the second printing, all copies had sold, at which point the price going forward was tripled.

The book is a masterpiece of the bookmaker's art, in large part because of Luther's extensive clarifying commentary and margin notes. It can hardly be seen by us as it was first seen, because thanks to Luther so many are today familiar with the Bible and what is in it. But if we imagine a population that had never seen the Bible in a language they could read and had no idea of what was in the book, we may understand it as a revelation to almost all who first saw it, as not less than historic and indeed as revolutionary. Luther's commentary prefaces in front of each book were for many Germans the very first explanations they had of what was in this book that had been for centuries hidden from them. There are innumerable examples of simple clarifying explanations that would have forever changed how people viewed things. In the beginning of the New Testament, for example, Luther explains the meaning of the word "gospel" as "good news," and he explains that although the four Gospels—Matthew, Mark, Luke, and John—are all the stories of Jesus's life, crucifixion, resurrection, and ascension, nonetheless the actual and true Gospel is to be found all through the New Testament. The whole of the story is the Gospel.

Luther's view of this was so central to his reading of the New Testament that he gave that precedence over all else, meaning that whereas he considered the Word of God sacred, he nonetheless felt comfortable ranking things in accordance with how closely they hewed to this central message of the Gospel. So Luther did not consider all of the books of the Bible equal, as one might expect. In fact, he even had his doubts whether the books of James and Revelation ought to be considered canonical and apostolic. At the end of the New Testament, he wrote,

John's Gospel and St. Paul's epistles, especially that to the Romans, and St. Peter's first epistle are the true kernel and marrow of all the books. They ought properly to be the foremost books, and it would be advisable for every Christian to read them first and most, and by daily reading to make them as much his own as his daily bread. For in them you do not find many works and miracles of Christ described, but you do find depicted in masterly fashion how faith in Christ overcomes sin, death, and hell, and gives life, righteousness, and salvation.[21]

For Luther, it was this central message of the good news of the free gift of Jesus's love and righteousness that was the Gospel. Everything else was there to support that. So Luther most infamously called the book of James an "epistle of straw," for a number of reasons, not least that it seemed to emphasize good works, although, to be fair, this dramatic comment was only included in the first edition of 1522. Still, it can be very difficult to see how Luther pushed the books of Hebrews, James, Jude, and Revelation to the side, as though they ought to be somehow on probation. But one ought not to go too far, either. Common sense has always tacitly understood that not all things in the Bible are equal. For example, who would say that the famous verse from John 3:16, "For God so loved the world that he gave us his only begotten Son, that whosoever believes in him should not perish, but have life everlasting," is equal to this verse from 2 Timothy 4:13, "When you come, bring the cloak that I left with Carpus at Troas, and my scrolls, especially the parchments"? Or even to the following verse, which cannot help but strike the reader as peevish: "Alexander the metalworker has done me great harm. The Lord will repay him according to his deeds."[22]

There are today many Scripture verses that are quoted endlessly, while some are hardly known, and the reason for this is precisely what Luther is getting at. The difference between Luther and many other Christians in this is that he is not afraid to make explicit what is clearly implicitly understood. The idea that all Bible verses are technically equal by dint of being part of the "Word of God" should not prohibit us from saying that some verses are more important than others. Some would say that we can somehow find the Gospel in every jot and tittle of Scripture, because it is alive and should not be read the way we read other books, but even if this is the case, we will look much harder in some verses than in others, where it is on the very surface for everyone to see. This is all that Luther meant, but we shouldn't be so theologically prickly as to shoo away this plain reading of things.

Translating the Old Testament

Despite all else he was doing, Luther's greater and far more ambitious project of translating the entire Bible into German would not lie fallow, even in 1522. Not long after handing his New Testament manuscript to Melanchthon, Luther sprang into this years-long project. His plan was to attack it from the beginning books first and publish it in stages. The Pentateuch (Genesis, Exodus, Leviticus, Numbers, and Deuteronomy) would naturally be the first part. Luther and his team, consisting of Melanchthon, Amsdorf, and others, got through these five long books with such speed they were able to nearly finish the first volume of the Old Testament in late December of that year and actually publish it in February 1523. But translating from the Hebrew presented fresh and sometimes extraordinary difficulties. For one thing, the Latin Vulgate was riddled with errors, which Luther was thrilled to discover and correct, although knowing they had been promulgated by the church for centuries must have caused him pain too.

In a letter to Spalatin, Luther rather desperately asked for help in solving the riddle of many obscure animal names found in Leviticus and Deuteronomy. By the time of his letter, the manuscript was essentially finished, but before it could go to the printer, there remained a handful of sticky taxonomic wickets to be negotiated. One can only imagine what Spalatin thought in reading this letter and in being urgently tasked with these overwhelming details:

> Please make your help available to us, and describe for us the following animals, classifying them by their species:
>
> Birds of prey: kite, culture, hawk, sparrow hawk, the male sparrow hawk.
>
> Game animals: gazelle, chamois, ibex, wild goat, or forest goat.
>
> Reptiles: Is *stellio* correctly translated as "salamander," and *lacerta limacio* as "orange-speckled toad"?
>
> ... Among the Hebrews, Latins, and Greeks, [the names of] these animals are terribly confused, so that we have to guess at what they are on the basis of the genus and species of the animals. If possible, therefore, I want to know the names, species, and nature of all birds of prey, game animals, and venomous reptiles in German. ...
>
> There are so many names of night birds: owl, night heron, great horned owl, wood owl, screech owl.
>
> These birds I know: vulture, kite, hawk, sparrow hawk— although I cannot identify them too well.
>
> These game animals I know: stag, roe deer, chamois (which [the Vulgate] renders as *bubalus*).
>
> I do not know what [the Vulgate] is thinking when [it] mentions among the kosher animals the goat, stag, antelope, and giraffe.*

*Any animals with cloven hooves such as these were obviously not kosher.

I wish that you would undertake this part of the work. Take a Hebrew Bible and try to find out all about these animals through careful research, so that we can be sure about these things. I do not have so much time.

Farewell, and pray for me.[23]

Luther's New Testament proved to be a sensation for many good reasons. For one thing, its language was powerful. Many phrases were so good that they entered the German language forever. Luther did not write a book to be read so much as a book to be read aloud. It was deftly attuned to the ears of the average German, and this would give it wings and legs both.

But more than the translation's excellence were the prefaces, which helped explain and frame everything. Of course this idea was itself central to Scripture, that the Scriptures could not be understood unless someone explained them to us. The episode in the book of Acts in which the Ethiopian eunuch speaks to Philip illustrates this:

So Philip ran up and heard the man reading Isaiah the prophet. "Do you understand what you are reading?" Philip asked. "How can I," he said, "unless someone guides me?" And he invited Philip to come up and sit with him.[24]

It is often overstated that Luther opened the Bible for everyone to read, because this implies that all interpretations of it are equal, which Luther clearly did not believe. He set himself up as a guide and teacher and knew that there was no substitute for this any more than there was a substitute for people reading the Bible on their own. He had no difficulty in seeing that either one taken to an extreme would create grave problems. Anyone reading the Bible without an understanding of what he read was certain to fall into error, just as anyone who refused to read the Bible and only allowed others to interpret it made it possible that he would be listening to interpreters who were theologically wrong. Just as no one can die for us, no one can have a relationship with God for us, and therefore no one can take full responsibility for how we read the Scriptures. At some point we have the personal responsibility to be involved.

So all of Luther's commentaries were meant to be helpful, but none of them were meant to be exhaustive or definitive. Of all of Luther's prefaces, the one he wrote to the book of Romans is almost universally regarded as the masterpiece:

> Faith is a divine work in us which changes us and makes us to be born anew of God. . . . Faith is a living, daring confidence in God's grace, so sure and certain that the believer would stake his life on it a thousand times. This knowledge of and confidence in God's grace makes men glad and bold and happy in dealing with God and all creatures. And this is the work which the Holy Spirit performed in faith. Because of it, without compulsion, a person is ready and glad to do good to everyone, to serve everyone, to suffer everything out of love and praise to God who has shown him this grace. Thus it is impossible to separate works from faith, quite as impossible as to separate heat and light from fire.[25]

Luther's words in this preface so purely communicated what it meant to be "born anew" that more than two centuries hence, in May 1738, John Wesley heard them read aloud and instantly had a profound conversion experience.[*26]

This led to Wesley's preaching this same Gospel message on a grand scale, which had tremendous historical ramifications, including the Methodist revival of the eighteenth century, which in turn led to the conversion of William Wilberforce, who led the battle to end the slave trade in the British Empire. It also led to the ministry and preaching of George Whitefield in the American colonies, which over several decades led to the unification of the colonies under the same egalitarian ideas as those that Germans were encountering in the early sixteenth century through the preaching of Luther and other Reformation preachers. Ideas have consequences, and Luther's had more than most.

---

* In his journal, Wesley wrote, "About a quarter before nine, while the leader was describing the change which God works in the heart through faith in Christ, I felt my heart strangely warmed. I felt I did trust in Christ alone for salvation; and an assurance was given me that He had taken away my sins, even mine, and saved me from the law of sin and death."

CHAPTER FIFTEEN

Monsters, Nuns, and Martyrs

No natural exhalation in the sky,
No scope of nature, no distemper'd day,
No common wind, no customed event,
But they will pluck away his natural cause
And call them meteors, prodigies and signs,
Abortives, presages and tongues of heaven.

—Shakespeare, *King John*, 3.4

NOW AND AGAIN the world of Luther seems positively modern. Other times it seems anything but that, and the story of the Papal Ass and the Monk's Calf is one of those times.

In this same December 1522 in which Luther and Melanchthon were putting the finishing touches on Luther's German New Testament, many miles to the east of Wittenberg, in the village of Waltersdorf, a certain cow gave birth to a severely deformed calf. Because the world of that time was keenly attuned to comets, anomalous births, and other potential portents in the skies and on the earth, this grotesque creature, which was said to look like a monk, drew much attention, and news of the bovine freak quickly spread. When the court astronomer in Prague learned of the creature, he immediately perceived that this monk's calf was a clear omen referring to Martin Luther, so he wrote a poem on the subject that became popular in certain precincts. Luther, unsurprisingly, had another interpretation of the oddnik veal.

Only a few months earlier, a large whale had become stranded on a beach in Haarlem in the Netherlands, and news of this captured Luther's attention. Before this, Melanchthon had been investigating the story of an alleged monster that was found washed up on the shore of the Tiber River, near Rome in 1496. It was said to possess the body of a woman, the head of an ass, and the skin of a fish and to have two different kinds of feet. Because it was discovered near Rome, it quite naturally was interpreted as a divine commentary on the papacy and quickly came to be known as *der Papstesel* (the Papal Ass). One wonders how much interest in this bloodcurdling curio arose from having an occasion to pronounce the transgressive phrase "Papal Ass."

In any event, Luther and Melanchthon dutifully set to work on a gaily titled pamphlet, *Interpretation of Two Horrible Figures, the Papal Ass in Rome and the Freiburg Monk's Calf Found in Meissen*. It was graphically illustrated with Cranach woodcuts and had to be the most far-fetched thing to which Luther ever set his pen, itself something of a distinction. The monk's calf was said to have a coat resembling a cowl, and perhaps also some slight suggestion of a tonsure. Thus Luther confidently took it to be a symbol of all monks and monkery in general. The calf, of course, could be nothing but a symbol of idol worship, because every fool had heard of the golden calf in Exodus, and the fact that all calves eat grass indicated that monasticism focused on "earthly" things. The purported holes in the misshapen animal's hide were obviously a pointed divine gloss on the unfortunate doctrinal lacunae among the various monastic orders. At the end of this surpassingly ludicrous work, Luther passionately appealed to all those in holy orders to abandon them and become "true Christians." But the fact that—even without reading this screwball tract—innumerable monks and nuns were leaving their monasteries and nunneries would soon become a serious problem for Luther, although not without at least one significant upside in the shape of a dozen nuns from Nimbschen.

Escape of the Nimbschen Twelve

On April 8, 1523, only a few months after Luther and Melanchthon had created their inimitably outré pamphlet, Luther wrote to his friend Wenceslas Linck, "Yesterday I received nine nuns from the Nimbschen convent."[1] Before this letter, we have only heard about runaway monks, of which there had been many—so many, in fact, that Luther was overrun with problems of what to do with them. It was one thing for people to escape the bondage of life in a dull monastery and another thing to figure out what they ought to do with themselves once they were out. Of course many of them made their way to Wittenberg, somehow expecting Luther to solve their problems. But it was that much more difficult for nuns to escape than for monks, so in the case of the Nimbschen convent, it was Luther himself who served as proud midwife. It was a genuinely brazen flouting of Duke George's laws, because the town Nimbschen was within his territories. It's easy for us to forget how serious such a thing was at this time.

As the story goes, Luther had finagled things so that on Holy Saturday, April 4, a certain Leonhard Koppe, who was a burgher from the town of Torgau, drove his covered wagon to a nunnery in Grimma, where he typically made deliveries. As the story has been told for five centuries, his wagon at this time contained empty but nonetheless foul-smelling herring barrels. At a certain juncture, twelve nuns suddenly appeared and sprang aboard the wagon, at which point Koppe blasted off, hell-for-leather toward freedom. The decidedly fishy but colorful tale that the sisters were actually crouched inside the filthy barrels is in nearly every biography of Luther, but it is, alas, simply untrue.

As we have said, the Nimbschen nunnery was within the borders of ducal Saxony, over which the irascible martinet Duke George held sway. He had expressly outlawed monks and nuns leaving their orders, so to be sure this was a daring escape. Three of the twelve castaways were immediately hustled to relatives, while the other nine were four days later delivered to Luther in Wittenberg. Because there was almost no way for a woman to support herself in the 1520s, situations had to be found for each of the nine, and the simplest path forward was to find them husbands, which is its own story and weaves itself into Luther's tale rather dramatically.

First Blood of the Reformation

During the seventeen years that Johannes von Staupitz was vicar-general of the Augustinian order, many Augustinian monks were drawn to Wittenberg to study, because this was Staupitz's university. Of course, if not for Staupitz, Luther himself would never have been there. The time of Staupitz's vicariate (1503–20) coincided with all of Luther's tenure there, and as a result many of the Augustinians who came to Wittenberg became acquainted with Luther and his theology. One of the monasteries with which Staupitz had had a special connection was the one in

Antwerp in the Netherlands. The monks there had embraced Luther's teachings very early and as a result came under intense persecution when they returned to their homeland. This was because at that time the Netherlands was under the regency of Queen Margaret of Austria, who was an aunt to Emperor Charles. After her nephew in 1521 had issued the Edict of Worms, she—with the help of Jerome Aleander—brutally attempted to stamp out the spread of Luther's rogue doctrines. Thus it happened that the first three men martyred for their Reformation faith were burned at the stake in her territories.

Already in 1519, the Antwerp Augustinians were preaching against indulgences, and as a result of this and other good things they began to attract the attention of some enemies, as well as some friends, including Dürer and Erasmus. Erasmus wrote Luther a friendly letter, saying, "In Antwerp there is a prior in the [Augustinian] cloister, a genuine Christian with nothing false about him, who glows with love for you; a former student of yours, as he boasts. He is virtually the only one who preaches Christ. Nearly all the others simply prattle and think of profit."[2] Erasmus was referring to Jacob Propst, who had studied in Wittenberg in 1505–9 and returned there in 1520 to get his theological degree. Albrecht Dürer lived in Antwerp during this time and was so taken with Propst that he painted his portrait, and when Propst left Antwerp for Wittenberg, Dürer gave it to him as a gift. But no sooner had Propst returned from his studies in Wittenberg than he was arrested and imprisoned at Brussels. Under cruel imprisonment and severe interrogation, he eventually recanted publicly, after which he was sent to the Augustinian monastery in Ypres. But once there, Propst publicly repudiated his recantation and continued preaching in the Lutheran manner, after which he was arrested a second time. Astonishingly, he managed to escape and made his way to freedom, arriving again in Wittenberg.

Propst's successor as prior in Antwerp was Henry von Zütphen, who also had studied at Wittenberg for two years, living with Luther in the Augustinian cloister. He picked up where Propst had left off, bravely continuing to teach Luther's theology among the Antwerp Augustinians. But on September 29, 1522—Michaelmas—Zütphen was lured away from the cloister on a false pretext and arrested in what ended up being a major crackdown on the Antwerp cloister. Luther wrote about it in a letter to Wenceslas Linck:

The friars were expelled from the monastery; some were held
captive at other places; some were dismissed from custody after
they had denied Christ; others stand firmly until now.... All
utensils of the monastery have been sold. The church and the
monastery are closed and sealed, and are even to be demolished.
The Host was transferred with great pomp, as if from a heretical
place, to the Church of the Blessed Virgin, where it was received
with all reverence by Lady Margaret [of Austria]. Some men and
women of the city were harassed and punished.[3]

Zütphen was to be transported to Brussels, but the very night of his
capture he was freed from his imprisonment by a crowd who were incensed at his arrest. He fled to Bremen, intending to continue to Wittenberg, but when he was persuaded to preach in Bremen, he so captivated
his hearers that they enjoined him to stay and preach regularly at
St. Ansgar's chapel, which he agreed to do, garnering a growing following. But the hue and cry against him from those who thought him a heretic did not stop, although Henry's behavior in it all was remarkable for
its grace and courage, and he continued preaching regularly.

After Zütphen's arrest and escape, the entire contingent of monks in
the Antwerp cloister were arrested and taken fifty miles south to be imprisoned at Vilvoorde, near Brussels. It is presumed they were all interrogated and held under harsh conditions. When it was clear that if they
did not recant they would be burned at the stake, most of them eventually recanted and were released. But three continued to refuse. These
were Johannes Esch, Henry Vos, and Lampertus Thorn. They were all
interrogated again by the Inquisition but again refused to recant. Finally,
they were turned over to the secular authorities, who pronounced their
sentences of death by burning, to be carried out July 1. One final time
they were pushed to recant. Esch and Vos refused outright, but Thorn
asked to have an additional four days to consult the Scriptures. He was
not executed, but died in prison five years later. Esch and Vos, however,
were taken to the Brussels marketplace on the appointed day and burned
to death.

When Luther received the horrific news, he was with Johannes Kessler, one of the students he had spoken with that night in the Black Bear
Inn. Kessler said that Luther "began to cry silently" and then said, "I
thought I would be the first to be martyred for the sake of this holy

gospel; but I was not worthy of it." But then, in what many said was his typical way, he quickly began giving thanks to Christ, who was at last beginning to "create fruit for our—no, his—Word and to make new martyrs."[4] Luther almost instantly was able to see the bigger picture, to see God's larger perspective on the situation, and he knew that despite the sadness of what had happened on a human level, it was nonetheless something for which to praise and thank God.

In fact, the painful news of what these young courageous men endured for their faith caused Luther to want to do something he had never done before, something he would do much more of in the years ahead, and something that would be one of his principal contributions to Christian worship over the next half millennium. Luther wrote a hymn.

It is ten or twelve stanzas and narrates the story of their martyrdom. The first stanza reads,

> *A new song to the Lord we'll raise,*
> *Of what His truth hath done;*
> *For His great glory and His praise*
> *A triumph He hath won.*
> *At Brussels in the Netherlands,*
> *His might has been made known;*
> *Two boys who loved the Lord's commands,*
> *The power of truth have shown:*
> *Great was the faith the Lord of heaven*
> *To these two Christian boys had given.*[5]

Luther was sensitive to the historic and spiritual import of what had happened in Brussels. The new work that God had graciously chosen him to bring into the world had just been crowned with the greatest honor. God had confirmed the truth of what they all were engaged in by allowing two innocents to be murdered just as Christ himself had been murdered, so that what man and the devil had done for evil, God would now turn to good. The news of their bravery would be sung about and spread abroad, encouraging others in their faith. It was a moment in the newly kindled life of God's people that deserved to be honored, and in Luther's telling of their story in the hymn it was and would continue so to be honored. For Luther, their martyrdom represented a new stage in the movement God had begun. The last words of the hymn make that clear:

> *The summer now is at the door,*
> *The winter's gloom is gone;*
> *The vernal gales are flitting o'er,*
> *Bright days are coming on:*
> *God hath Himself His work begun,*
> *His work He never leaves undone.*[6]

The deaths of these two young men and the brutal treatment of all the other monks from the Augustinian cloister in Antwerp bring home to us that Luther himself knew he might be asked to make the ultimate sacrifice for his beliefs, something he was always ready to do.

Luther and others had at first heard that Lampertus Thorn was martyred around the time of Esch and Vos but then learned that he was still imprisoned. In January 1524, Luther wrote to him,

> Grace and peace in the Lord. Christ has given me abundant testimony of you, dear brother Lambert, that you do not need my words, for He Himself suffers in you and is glorified in you. He is taken captive in you and reigns in you, He is oppressed in you and triumphs in you, for He has given you that holy knowledge of Himself which is hidden from the world. Not only this, but He strengthens you inwardly with His Spirit in these outward tribulations and consoles you with the double example of Henry and John. Thus both they and you are to me a great consolation and strength, to the whole world a sweet-smelling savor, and to the Gospel of Christ a special glory. There is little need, then, to burden you with my consolations. Who knows why the Lord was not willing to have you die with the other two? He will preserve you for another miracle.
>
> . . . And so, my brother, do you pray for me as I for you, mindful that you are not suffering alone, but that He is with you Who says, "I am with him in tribulation; because he has hoped in Me, I will deliver him; I will protect him, because he hath known My name." But we, too, are with you, as the Lord is, and neither He nor we will desert you. Be a man, let your heart be strong, wait for the Lord.[7]

To know that others were being cruelly treated, were being imprisoned under horrendous conditions under the threat of death, and to know that some would make this ultimate sacrifice, was surely more difficult for

Luther than had he himself endured such things. But there can be no question that they drove him closer to God and made him the more passionate to spread the truth God had entrusted to him. This is one of the practical ways that we can see Tertullian's famous phrase "The blood of the martyrs is the seed of the church" being borne out.

The persecution of the Antwerp brethren continued in the story of Luther's friend Henry von Zütphen, who settled for a time in Bremen, where he preached regularly, despite opposition. Luther was grateful to know that God's Word was being preached far beyond Wittenberg, and in the fall of 1524 he wrote to Zütphen, simply wanting to maintain their connection. That God's Word was courageously being preached in Bremen was greatly encouraging to Luther. But shortly after Zütphen received Luther's letter, he was called to come and preach in the village of Meldorf, in distant Dithmarschen. The brethren in Bremen opposed his leaving, feeling that his work with them was not yet finished, but Henry believed that if he was called to preach—especially in a place where such preaching had never been done—he must go, because it was a call from God. The poor souls in Meldorf deserved to hear God's Word. He promised the Bremeners that after the Word had been established in Meldorf, he would return to Bremen. So Zütphen traveled the hundred miles north to distant Meldorf and preached there on December 4 and twice again two days later. But the local Dominicans were so outraged to hear him and to know that the Reformation had invaded their distant country that they contrived to have him captured and killed without a trial.

The subsequent story of what happened to Luther's friend is a horrific one, and we only know the details of his brutal treatment and murder because Luther himself wrote them in his heartbreaking essay "The Burning of Brother Henry." Luther described the cruelty of the drunken, murderous mob that had been incited by the twin authorities of church and state to kidnap, brutalize, and then murder Henry von Zütphen for the same reason that he wrote the hymn telling the story of the burning of Esch and Vos. He knew that publicizing such things would strengthen and encourage the faithful to continue their efforts, and he also knew that the public shaming of those who had done these monstrous things was a measure of justice and truth that would have its own ramifications. He wrote that once again "in our day the pattern of true Christian life has reappeared, terrible in the world's eyes, since it means suffering and persecution, but precious and priceless in God's sight."[8]

The Nuns from Nimbschen

The story of Luther's marriage begins with his having planned and arranged the daring escape of the twelve nuns from the Nimbschen convent. He not only was waiting to give them succor in Wittenberg but had himself instigated and arranged their flight. For him, it was a moral duty, but inasmuch as it was punishable by death, it was inarguably audacious. At that point and for a long time afterward, Luther was not interested in marriage. He was reasonably convinced that he would die a martyr's death, so the joys of matrimony were far from his mind, although he was aggressively involved in pairing up others for the married estate. But to understand the details of the Nimbschen breakout, we have to go backward and ask how it was that the supremely sheltered nuns in that convent were aware of the revolutionary goings-on outside. The answer underscores how, despite the great efforts to squelch the spread of Luther's teachings and writings, they nonetheless flew like birds across the countryside.

One place in which these birds had made a happy nest was at the Augustinian monastery in Grimma. The prior of that monastery was Wolfgang von Zeschau, a Saxon nobleman, who had early warmed to the ideas originating in Wittenberg. In fact, in 1522, he resigned his priorship and left the order, taking a number of similarly inclined monks with him. He did not leave Grimma, but now took up a new role as hospital chaplain there, at the Johannite Hospital of the Holy Cross. But the vow-killing Lutheran ideas almost certainly clambered over the walls of the Nimbschen nunnery with his assistance, because two of the nuns there were his relatives—likely his nieces—named Veronica and Margarete von Zeschau, who were biological sisters and were two of the twelve to have escaped in the darkness of the night preceding Easter morning. He is likely to have had some access to the convent as their relative and as a prior of the nearby monastery.

So after the provocative notions had been planted and had germinated and bloomed, a number of the nuns sought to leave, doing what anyone would have done under the circumstances by writing to their relatives. But in every case, they were rebuffed. Their relatives would have felt about breaking nuns out of a convent as someone today might feel about springing someone from a federal prison: it was wrong, and it was illegal, in this case to the point of being punishable by death. So the nuns turned to Luther, somehow reaching him via letters, although how these letters found him and who served as courier are unknown. When Luther learned of the plight of these sisters, he felt a powerful moral obligation to free them. But how?

Luther had in 1519 and again in 1522 made a number of visits to Torgau, and while there he must have become acquainted with the established leaders of that city, among them one Leonhard Koppe. A widely respected man in his late fifties from an established Torgau family, Koppe had been educated at Leipzig and Erfurt and had served on the Torgau town council and then more recently as a tax collector for the elector. So when the canny Reformer wanted to contrive a means of escape for the Nimbschen twelve, it occurred to him that if he hoped to find someone to help who would be above reproach in every way, he could not do better than Herr Koppe, now fifty-nine years old. It would not do to allow any appearance of impropriety, and this gentleman's willingness to serve in this capacity would cover a multitude of sins. Koppe would enlist his young nephew in the raid, as well as another established Torgau burgher named Wolf Dommitzsch.

The details of the raid are unknown. For example, how it was communicated to the nuns that they ought to be prepared to leave late on Holy Saturday, when all was quiet and Christ was still in the tomb, and where they were to meet up with Koppe and his men is not known. There are innumerable versions, all with invented details. Some stories have said that the nuns had to dig through a wall to escape.

All we can say for sure is that the endlessly retold story of the nuns hiding in odious herring barrels is apocryphal. This colorful fiction originated when someone—still alive around 1600—recollected that Koppe had pulled it all off "with particular cunning and agility, as though he had been bringing out herring barrels."[9] But of herring barrels on this particular trip, there were surely none, though this is a story that more than any of these stubborn legends has affixed itself to Luther like a lamprey. Let it here be forever detached. We only know that a single large covered wagon was used. It doesn't seem at all likely that the wagon actually entered the convent. Probably it waited for the nuns in the nearby forest, and the nuns snuck there to meet it.

The wagon would have proceeded to Torgau—a long thirty miles if cramped in a covered wagon rattling along primitive roads. The nuns spent part of Easter Day and all of Easter Monday in Torgau, doubtless

recuperating from their escape. It is quite possible they worshipped in
the church there on one or both of those days. The distance to Wittenberg from Torgau is roughly the same as that from Nimbschen to Torgau. We are not sure whether it was covered in one day or whether they
stayed someplace between Torgau and Wittenberg, but we do know for
sure that on Wednesday, April 8, the wagon at last was pulled through
the gates of Wittenberg.

The whole enterprise to free them had been a wild and daring one, but
now it had been successful too. Luther so sincerely felt he was doing
God's work that he chose to blast the good news of the escape to the
world immediately. With typical speed, he wrote up his account the very
next day—framing it as an open letter to Koppe, the brave man who had
sacrificed his name and more to do this valiant deed. It was titled *Why
Nuns May, in All Godliness, Leave the Convents: Ground and Reply*. He
wanted the whole world to know that everything had been arranged so
that the young women's reputations would be protected from the vile
gossipmongers and slanderers who were sure to smell blood in such a
story. Luther also wanted it to be an example to encourage others—and
this it surely was. Luther's central role in all of this is often forgotten. He
was not merely the recipient of nine escaped nuns—one until death do
them part—but he was the one who had managed the details of their
genuinely dangerous escape, knowing that if it was successful, it would
be a dramatic victory over the forces of darkness and a bold defiance of
the devil and his various henchmen such as Duke George, who must
have been steaming indeed when he realized what had just taken place.

Luther took the plight of those trapped in holy orders very seriously,
and that of nuns especially so. He knew many of them had been put in
convents as girls and had never had the slightest say in whether they
wished to stay. Many were unhappy and had never voluntarily taken any
vows, so the idea that it should be illegal for them to leave struck Luther
as immoral. Luther also was far ahead of his time in taking the sexuality
of women seriously and in believing and saying that they were entitled to
husbands and to sexual activity. That they might be kept in forced celibacy was a sin against the manifest order of God's creation of men and
women with desires for each other, which in turn created families. To
deny them this was itself a sin.

Largely as a result of the Nimbschen escape and the attendant publicity
that came as a result of Luther's writing about it, many nuns were inspired

to leave their convents in the next years. One of them, Ursula von Münsterberg, was the cousin of Duke George himself. In fact, it was she who led an effort to attract a chaplain to her convent who was open to Luther's ideas, and she was even able to smuggle Lutheran writings into the convent, which was in Freiburg. In 1528, when she was forced to flee her convent, she stayed with the Luthers in the Augustinian cloister in Wittenberg.

In 1524, a year after the Nimbschen breakout, a woman named Florentina von Oberweimar escaped the confines of a nunnery in Eisleben and came to Wittenberg. She wrote an account of her story, telling how at age six she had been forced to go into holy orders and attempted to leave but was violently forbidden to do so. In desperation, she had written to Luther, asking his help, and was severely punished as a result by her abbess, who even had her flogged. As it happened, the abbess was her own aunt. When she escaped, Luther wrote letters to the five counts of Mansfeld, explaining that no one could or should be forced to serve God against one's will. Florentina's story was published as *A Story of How God Rescued an Honorable Nun, Accompanied by a Letter of Martin Luther to the Counts of Mansfeld*, and Luther wrote a preface.

But now that the nine Nimbschen nuns were safely in Wittenberg, each of them must find a living situation. The eldest of them was the sister of Luther's mentor, Johannes von Staupitz. We mustn't overlook the poverty of these nuns and of Luther too. No one had cash to spare to buy clothes for these girls, who were still wearing their habits days after they arrived. For everything, Luther and others must beg the nobility. Luther wrote to Spalatin that very Friday, asking for help. The next day Amsdorf wrote to Spalatin too. "I pity the girls," he wrote, saying that they had "neither shoes nor clothing." He asked Spalatin to inquire among his noble friends who would donate food and clothing to the cause. He also teased his friend in the letter:

> They're beautiful, dignified, and all from the aristocracy. I do not find
> a fifty-year-old among them. The oldest among them, the sister of my
> benevolent lord and uncle, Dr. Staupitz, I have appointed for you, my
> dear brother, to be her husband. . . . If you want a young one,
> however, then you are to have the choice among the most beautiful.[10]

But each of these now former nuns would find her way in the world. Johannes von Staupitz's sister would for a while live with their brother,

Günther, and a few years later opened a school for girls back in Grimma, eventually marrying one of the citizens of that city. Another of the nine, Lonatha von Gohlis, was taken in by her sister and eventually married. Two sisters, Ave and Margarethe von Schönfeld, lived with the Cranachs in their palatial home until they were married off. It seems that Luther singled out Ave as the one of the group he would have married, were he interested in marrying, but Ave was shortly snapped up by one of Cranach's employees, Basilius Axt, the young medical doctor who oversaw Cranach's apothecary business. Ave's sister Margarethe later married a nobleman from Braunschweig.

Katharine von Bora—known as Kathie—was also of noble birth, but Luther dismissed her as a match for himself, saying that he was not interested in marrying and that she was somehow "too proud." She initially lived with the family of Philip Reichenbach, a distinguished lawyer who the next year became Wittenberg's city clerk. But Kathie also spent much time at the Cranachs', which was her prime residence in Wittenberg at that time, and eventually went to live there. The Cranachs' home was so distinguished that for a time during this period they hosted the exiled king of Sweden, Christian II, who was the emperor's brother-in-law. The king honored Kathie with a golden ring, which kings in those days handed out like lapel pins.

Kathie von Bora also spent time in the Melanchthon household, and it is likely that she there came to meet the young nobleman Jerome Baumgärtner, who had studied in Wittenberg under Melanchthon and who returned to visit a short time after Kathie's arrival. The two of them rather quickly fell in love, and Kathie was well regarded in his circle of Wittenberg friends, so much so that they dubbed her Katherine of Siena, one assumes for her piety. Baumgärtner remained in Wittenberg for two months, at the end of which time it was assumed he would propose to Kathie. But first he must depart for a time, which he did. However, that time stretched past what everyone expected, causing not a little wonderment at the state of Baumgärtner's mind. Had some unknown event or obstacle been raised against his desire to marry Kathie? The summer gave way to fall, and still there was no word from him. Winter came and spring too and then a second summer. Luther esteemed Baumgärtner greatly and wrote to him in October 1524, "If you want to hold on to your Kathie von Bora, then hurry before she is given to someone else, which is already imminent. She has not yet gotten over her love for you. I would surely be delighted at your union. Live well!" Luther in this letter is alluding to another man—Dr. Kaspar Glatz—an older gentleman who was now pressing his suit with Kathie. It is also possible that Luther was pressing the man's suit for him, because he was always eagerly playing matchmaker with the nuns whose liberty he had encouraged. Glatz was a doctor of theology who also went by the Latin Humanist name Glacius. He had become rector of the University of Wittenberg in 1524, and we gather had expressed interest in the lively and intelligent Kathie, even though she expected the now long-lost Baumgärtner to return and marry her at any moment.

In September 1524, Luther sent Glatz to Orlamünde, where Luther's old rival Karlstadt had been causing some trouble. But Kathie was never interested in spending her life with Glatz, who some of his own colleagues characterized as "an old skinflint." In fact, she was enough averse to Glatz that she eventually approached Amsdorf to tell him so. But she explained to him that she did not wish anyone to think she was averse to marriage itself, and she then rather forthrightly and forwardly said she was quite open to marrying either him—Amsdorf—or perhaps Dr. Martinus. Thus was the door opened, neither by might nor by power, but by a maiden, proud, strong willed, and available.

But Amsdorf was even less inclined to marry than the little-inclined Luther and would remain a dedicated bachelor his whole life. So the question became whether the esteemed Dr. Luther himself could be persuaded to leap off that high crag from which he had been pushing so many others. There were so many other things pulling at him that it was nearly impossible for him to focus on personal matters. For one thing, there was Thomas Müntzer and the brewing rebellion of the German peasants. This would unleash upon the landscape a nightmare of blood and horror that would for a season seem to blot out the sun itself, making love and marriage the distant ideas of a forgotten world.

CHAPTER SIXTEEN

Fanaticism and Violence

YOU BREATHE OUT NOTHING BUT
SLAUGHTER AND BLOOD.

—Agricola in a letter to Thomas Müntzer

What courage has he, Dr. Pussyfoot,
the new pope of Wittenberg,
Dr. Easychair, the basking sycophant?

—Müntzer, writing about Luther

THE TROUBLES THAT Luther once had with those still hewing to the pope's line on things were soon replaced by the troubles he would have with Karlstadt and then with Thomas Müntzer, and those with Müntzer would breed still greater troubles. But for Luther the question was always: What was God's course between these extremes?

> We however take the middle course and say: There is to be neither commanding nor forbidding, neither to the right nor the left. We are neither papistic nor Karlstadtian, but free and Christian, in that we elevate or do not elevate the sacrament, how, where, when, and as long as it pleases us, as God has given us the liberty to do so. Just as we are free to remain outside of marriage or to enter into marriage, to eat meat or not, to wear the chasuble or not, to have the cowl and tonsure or not. In this respect we are lords and will put up with no commandment, teaching, or prohibition.[1]

Nonetheless, as far as Karlstadt would push things in the wrong direction, it would all show itself to be almost as nothing when compared to the excesses of Thomas Müntzer. For example, that July Müntzer preached a sermon in front of Duke John. It was essentially a threat disguised as a sermon. Either the princes would join in with the All-stedt reforms, or God would smite them. Müntzer was not one to mince words:

> What a pretty spectacle we have before us now—all the eels and snakes coupling together immorally in one great heap. The priests and all the evil clerics are the snakes . . . and the secular lords and rulers are the eels. . . . My revered rulers of Saxony . . . seek without delay the righteousness of God and take up the cause of the gospel boldly.[2]

In other words, slaughter with your swords those who disagree with me, or you yourselves will be slaughtered. Müntzer is one of those cases in history when a madman rises to power and draws others into his madness, resulting in an unrelenting bloodbath. Müntzer, like all utopianists, was divorced from reality and wished to be so divorced, thinking the reality of this world as something to be fled as soon as possible. All political and religious reform movements are tempted in the direction of cultishness and violence, and at the time of Luther, Müntzer was the one who led this charge over the cliff.

Throughout history and in the last decades particularly, many have rejected religion precisely because of this sort of pharisaical judgmentalism, harsh legalism, and in the end cruelty and violence that have been manifested in various groups. But just as in Luther's time, these things have manifested on both ends of the theological spectrum. In Luther's day, there was on one side the ultra-traditionalist medieval papacy that would ultimately use violence to protect its power and on the other side the radical "left" of such as Thomas Müntzer and his disciples whose intolerance would bring about violence in another way. Luther rightly saw that freedom and truth and love cannot be separated. They partake of each other, and whenever they are divided from each other, the devil gains a foothold and violence enters.

On the one hand, he understood that the pope and the church had combined with the emperor to squelch true freedom, to repress honest inquiry, and to do so with deadly force. They were so invested in preserving the status quo that any who persisted in disagreeing with them would be cruelly persecuted and perhaps burned alive. Luther had been crusading against this since the day he posted his theses on the doors of the Castle Church, and this side of things had so merged church and state that these twin powers were essentially a single dreadful authority, one that would not brook dissent.

But on the other hand, there had now arisen a new version of the same problem, as extreme in the other direction as ever the papal errors had been. It was far on the other side of freedom, where sweet freedom became license and then bondage. The papal church had become so powerful that it had cozied up to the power of the state to the extent that no one could tell them apart; they seemed to have become one iron oppressive state, albeit with one part having more religious gilt besprinkled over its unyielding surface. It was a case of the church keeping no distance whatever from the state. But in Müntzer, there was a utopianist urge to utterly nullify all state authority, and therefore to usurp all that was political by assuming it into the church community. In either case, authoritarianism and bloodshed must be the result.

To tell the larger story concerning how things spun far out of control with Müntzer, we first have to backtrack to Karlstadt in Orlamünde. It's hard to avoid the impression that at least to some extent Karlstadt had repaired thither in order to lick his wounds and have some measure of the freedom denied him in Wittenberg by Luther and Frederick. It is not unreasonable that he should have felt resentment toward Luther, who was allowed to play the role of the bearded Moses descending from the Sinai of his Wartburg to mete out judgments and exile Karlstadt for doing what Karlstadt doubtless thought of as God's good work. To some extent, Karlstadt was the victim of guilt by association. He had allowed the mad Zwickau prophets into Luther's henhouse, and before coming to Wittenberg, they had been influenced by the increasingly febrile Thomas Müntzer, so the shadow of their collective unhinged utopianism unavoidably fell on Karlstadt. He had also allowed an atmosphere that ended in the burning of images and the destruction of altars. Even though Karlstadt never came close to the excesses of the Zwickau prophets or Müntzer, he had nonetheless preached against images and other things with such vigor that he could rightly be accused of legalism. But even in Orlamünde, he aroused Luther's suspicions. He was said to have eschewed the world and weeds of academia for those of the peasantry. He no longer allowed people to call him Dr. Karlstadt, but preferred the somewhat pretentious egalitarian sobriquets of "Dear Neighbor" and "Brother Andreas." He was also sartorially transformed, now presenting himself as a clodhopping son of the German soil. He had swapped his previous finery for shapeless rural duds: a gray peasant's uniform and a bumpkin's felt hat.

Before he had left Wittenberg for Orlamünde, Karlstadt had only confirmed Luther's opinion of him as someone who had gone too far, who had to some extent thrown his lot in with Müntzer and the Zwickau prophets, all of whom pushed a kind of forced egalitarianism that smacked more of pure social ferment and anger at the nobles than of the Gospel of Christ. Karlstadt—who, although no longer allowed to preach, was still lecturing at the university—had overseen a doctoral ceremony and in the midst of it declared that such ceremonies were inherently godless because Jesus had forbidden his disciples to call anyone "master." We don't know whether Luther rolled his eyes, or whether anyone did so in those days, but we do know that he was sorely tempted to walk out. Karlstadt and his forced and legalistic interpretations of the Scriptures smelled to Luther like fanaticism, so it is no great wonder he put Karlstadt in the *Schwärmer* category with the Zwickauers and Müntzer.

At Orlamünde, Karlstadt also had free rein to push his dualistic theories about the wickedness of images. He believed that the material world and the world of "creation" must be transcended, and that meant images and statues too. And he twisted the Scriptures themselves, claiming Jesus had said that we as his bride were to present our "naked souls" to the bridegroom. So anything having to do with what he called the "clothing" of the "creation" was strictly verboten. All of this had a vague idea of getting back to the soil and nature, as though "nakedness" were more natural than clothing. But Luther would have seen this as a leap back to Eden without the cross, as though we could go back through our own efforts and forget that blood had ever been shed for our sins. And so it was heresy and foolishness both.

Luther also sniffed Old Testament legalism in some of what Karlstadt was brewing and quipped that they would soon be introducing circumcision. But it was all a harebrained hodgepodge, because added to these things was a reliance on "hearing from God" via inner voices and revelation that was unmoored from the Scriptures and therefore wide open to excess and theological confusion. Luther had never put much truck in "hearing God" in the way of the mystics, but it was less this—which could in some circumstances be respectable and biblically grounded—than the idea that Karlstadt and the other *Schwärmer* were using this mainly as an excuse to slip free from the strictures of Scripture or, as they might have seen it, to be "free" and "natural."

Thomas Müntzer

All of this brings us back to the terrible story of Thomas Müntzer. Müntzer had studied in Wittenberg in 1517, when Luther was still dabbling in German mysticism, so it seems that what first attracted him to Luther, Luther soon thereafter abandoned, while Müntzer developed it further, and much further, as we shall see. It was during his time in Wittenberg that Müntzer met Karlstadt. After leaving Wittenberg, Müntzer was a pro-Luther Christian, so much so that in 1520 Luther recommended him to the pastorate in Zwickau. But there Müntzer fell in with the Zwickau prophets, Storch, Drechsel, and Stübner, and also grew close to the so-called *Tuchknappen,* the radical journeymen weavers of the town. It was from being in their circle that he presumably developed his ideas of a revolution of the working classes against the nobility.

Müntzer's mystical ideas were the very antithesis of Luther's theology. Müntzer believed that in order to hear the Word of God, one must first be cleansed "of the clay of cares and lusts."[3] In other words, one must do what Luther tried and failed to do as a young monk—confess one's way into heaven. In our own time, the Scientologists talk about becoming "clear." In all of these cases, it is a rigorous religious program, and the results are meant to be achievable. But it never has anything to do with God's grace and has everything to do with one's own strenuous efforts. One must simply white knuckle up the rungs of the various spiritual stages until one has strained and striven into the very throne room of heaven. This was what the Zwickau prophets had spoken of to Luther, and it seems that they got their ideas along these lines from Müntzer. But by the time of his last days in Zwickau, Müntzer's ideas had gotten daffier still.

When Müntzer was first in Zwickau, his screw had become sufficiently loose that his sermons were often downright disturbing. During this time, Johannes Agricola wrote a strong letter to Müntzer, begging him to see that what he was saying was going too far. For example, Müntzer would from the pulpit sometimes attack people by name.

Agricola made it very clear in his letter that he must stop that immediately, and his frustration with Müntzer boiled over at one point when he urgently burst into all caps, writing, "YOU BREATHE OUT NOTHING BUT SLAUGHTER AND BLOOD."[4] As he certainly did. But Müntzer was too far gone in this direction to be called back. The world was on the brink of conflagration. And God had chosen him to lead the elect into the New Jerusalem.

It was hardly surprising when the burghers of Zwickau decided to show their mad prophet the door. So Müntzer fled to Prague with Stübner and wrote to a friend, "I am traveling the entire world for the sake of the Word."[5] He was sure that in Prague he could find a perch from which to fly to heaven, but the people of Prague weren't buying either. But this didn't stop him from penning his crackpot "Prague Manifesto," a critique of the clergy combined with his mystical ravings that he scrawled on a huge yard-square sheet of paper, hoping to post it as Luther had posted his now famous theses and thereby ignite the true revolution, the one that would make people's heads spin and usher in the millennium.

But first Müntzer had to find another job. He bounced from temporary post to temporary post. In March 1522, he wrote to Melanchthon, criticizing Luther's doctrines as too soft and wrong on several counts. He did not like Luther's "concern for the weak."* There was no room for compromise with those who couldn't keep up with the pace of change. And Luther's respect and deference to Frederick and the other princes disgusted him. Luther was too much in bed with the governing authorities. God had given his people all the authority on heaven and earth, and they must take it, by force if necessary. For his part, Luther thought Müntzer insane.

All through 1522, Müntzer was beating the bushes for a permanent job as a preacher. Then, in April 1523, he pratfell nicely into a heaven-sent sinecure at Allstedt, a rural village north of Erfurt. Here he was able to bamboozle a fresh group of disciples and begin work on the metaphorical spaceship that would blast them all into another world. Allstedt was in Thuringia, in the territory of Duke John, Frederick's brother, so from the moment Müntzer arrived, Spalatin kept a close eye on him, though they were not inclined to give him the boot quite yet. Müntzer quickly married a former nun, Ottilie von Gersen, and then went about his program

---

* Saint Paul in Romans 15:1 enjoins Christians to show grace to those who are weaker in the faith: "We then that are strong ought to bear the infirmities of the weak, and not to please ourselves."

of convincing his parishioners that they were the ones God had chosen as his elect. Now they must prepare to take up arms and smite those who were outside their circle. It was only logical, and there was no time to be lost. Müntzer's confident crackers preaching drew more and more listeners, until one Sunday there were two thousand in attendance to hear his latest "sermon."

Luther knew that Müntzer presented a diabolical challenge. For one thing, he was spreading his bizarre doctrines in the friendly territory of electoral Saxony. If he had tried such things in Duke George's territory, he would not have gotten farther than the nearest dungeon. Frederick, however, was inclined to let things ride without worrying too much, but here was a case where a little more worrying might have been advisable. Luther knew that what Müntzer was preaching would likely lead to violence, and when a chapel dedicated to Mary was burned down at Mallerbach, it became clear Müntzer's vitriolic sermons had incited it. He had already by then organized thirty members into his "secret league." Their goal was "to stand up for the gospel, to pay no more assessments to monks and nuns, and to help expel and destroy them."[6]

Müntzer eventually succeeded in persuading most of the town to follow him. He got five hundred to join his "league" before it was all over and had them swear a formal oath. Many of those who did so were not Allstedters but miners from Mansfeld or peasants from the surrounding towns. Müntzer even carved them up into military units, who prepared to repulse the princes, should they dare to step in. Luther knew that Müntzer's time in Wittenberg had set him on this course, just as it had set Karlstadt on his, and it bothered him deeply that what was born of his own good efforts could lead to such madness. But it bothered him the more that he could not rein in what so many on the Catholic side would surely end up attributing to him. Any violence that was a result of his ideas—even if those ideas were twisted into unrecognizable pretzels that would have their own ramifications—would be traced to him, and the blame for them laid at his feet. Luther could not do much to suppress these things, but he would do what he could to clarify the difference between his position and theirs, hoping to prevent further harm.

So that July, Luther published his *Letter to the Princes of Saxony Concerning the Rebellious Spirit*, which he dedicated to Frederick and Duke John. He knew that at some point the governing authorities would need to face the inevitable violence and he hoped to rouse them to the gathering threat. Still, Luther did not advocate the use of force against Müntzer because of his ideas. Although he would deviate from this principle in the years ahead, Luther believed in the relative freedom of religion and ideas, and he felt that the good ideas—meaning the true Word of God—would win out over the counterfeits. But he knew Müntzer was soon to step from the world of ideas into the world of action and would then have crossed the line into that territory in which the governmental authorities had the right—and much more than that, the solemn duty before God—to act.

Somehow, that same month, Müntzer agreed to preach to Frederick's brother Duke John and his son Duke John Frederick. They were passing through Allstedt and on July 13 summoned Müntzer to the castle there. His goal was to pull them into helping fulfill his supremely wiggy plans. Indeed, what Müntzer preached that day would have set anyone's hair on fire. He invited the princes to whom he spoke to "step up boldly onto the cornerstone (Christ)"[7] and use the swords they had been given to do God's work. But what, precisely, was this work? Only wait, and Müntzer will tell you. It was to help him lead a revolution of the "elect," and these elect must of course wipe out those who were not elect. And who would determine who was the elect? Müntzer thought he might take a crack at doing so. He would reveal his thinking by taking the book of Daniel as his preaching text. He declared to the seated nobles that Daniel was the prophet who interpreted the dreams of the king, and then he put himself forward as the Daniel of their own day, as the one chosen by God to do all the interpreting that needed doing. So if they only knew what was good for them and the universe, the Saxon princes should install him as their "Daniel." Then he could boldly lead them into the conflagration at the End of All Time. Who could fail to be interested? And to seal the deal, he punctuated his message by howling that "the godless have no right to live except as the elect are willing to grant it to them."[8]

But where did he come by this interpretation of the divine will? He twisted the Scriptures, which by definition can only be twisted away from God. In referring to the parable of the ten minas, which Jesus tells in Luke 19, Müntzer misread the context of the final line—"But as for these enemies of mine, who did not want me to reign over them, bring them here and slaughter them before me."[9] In Müntzer's self-aggrandizing version, these words are spoken not by the character in the story invented by Jesus but by Jesus himself. Thus Müntzer believed he had a biblical mandate to call for the slaughtering of all those who were not the elect. And then he threatened the Saxon princes, saying that if they would not step up and seize this moment, God would take their swords from them.

Müntzer also made it clear that Luther must be one of those slaughtered. He called him "Brother Fattened-Hog"—and Melanchthon "Brother Soft-Life"[10]—and derided Luther for his love of pleasure and for living only "to devour juicy morsels at court."[11] Then Müntzer demanded an "international" hearing for his ideas. To those in power—which was to say, to those listening to him—Müntzer threatened unleashing the peasant hordes. Either the nobles before him would use their swords for God's purposes—as he saw them—or God's "people" would take things into their own hands. All must either accept his gospel or confess themselves heathen and die.

There is nothing quite like religious madness, and that it is a foretaste of hell can hardly be debated. Müntzer's vision was a fever dream from the mind of Satan, that same fever dream as bubbles from the minds of numerous like figures through history unto our own day, for whom the devil is God and life is death, for whom grace is weakness and cruelty is justice. This is the hellish apotheosis of self, in which all "others" are either enslaved or killed.

And so Müntzer—having delivered himself of this cheery homily to the territorial lords—awaited their decision. Won't you help me smash the sky and ascend with me into the empyrean? Or will you consign yourselves to be slaughtered and go to hell? How Dukes John and John Frederick had squirmed during this message we can only guess, nor will we ever know whether when it was over they shook Müntzer's hand on the way out and told him they had enjoyed his sermon. We do know that Müntzer soon after had this "sermon"—along with an added bonus section on dreams—printed.

Then, on July 17, Müntzer contacted Karlstadt in Orlamünde, inviting him to join his "league of the elect" and inviting him to prevail upon fifteen villages to join them. To his eternal credit, Karlstadt immediately saw that Müntzer was about to do what everyone had feared, to lead an armed "people's" revolt against the nobles, and so he promptly tore up the letter. But then he rode his horse to a friend's home and reconstituted the letter to show his friend what Müntzer was proposing, so he would have proof. Karlstadt had never promoted violence, and two days later he wrote to Müntzer, firmly refusing to participate and counseling him to cease and desist from his martial plans. To be sure, they had some important things in common, but leading hordes of peasants to slaughter nonbelievers—and forcibly drag the End of All Things from the distant future into the present—was not one of them.

After Dukes John and John Frederick pondered Müntzer's immodest proposal, they knew action must be taken against him. So he was summoned to be interrogated at the Weimar court, as were a number of his Allstedt followers. But some of these followers, who were interrogated separately, easily volunteered Müntzer's plans to lead an armed revolt. It was not as if this hadn't been clear enough in the sermon, but in this different context it must have come across to Müntzer that his plans were not met with approval. In any event, Müntzer now somehow intuited that the jig was up for him. Witnesses said that after he left the chamber, he was ashen. But late on the night of August 7, he did what he always seemed to do in such awkward spots: he opted to skedaddle, literally climbing over the Allstedt city wall. But this time, he left a wife and child behind. All those who had joined his "secret league" and whom he had whipped up into an ungovernable frenzy were humiliated at his ignominious departure. Everyone else, however, was tremendously tickled to see him take his leave. But Luther rightly believed they hadn't heard the last of him. Indeed, Müntzer next settled in Mühlhausen and once again began attracting followers. There he met up with a fitting partner in one Heinrich Pfeiffer, who was himself an accomplished agitator of the first water. It was in Mühlhausen that Müntzer now wrote his most rousing and bitter philippic against Luther, titled *Highly Necessary Defense and Answer Against the Soft-Living Flesh of Wittenberg, Which in Miserable and Perverted Fashion Has Soiled Poor Christendom Through the Theft of Holy Scripture.*

Müntzer's burning hatred of Luther was now further irritated because of his earnest belief that Luther was a wart-ridden toady to the princes, that he sided with them against the suffering peasants:

> The princes bleed the people with usury and count as their own the fish in the stream, the bird of the air, and the grass of the field, and Dr. Liar says, "Amen!" What courage has he, Dr. Pussyfoot, the new pope of Wittenberg, Dr. Easychair, the basking sycophant? He says there should be no rebellion because the sword has been committed by God to the ruler, but the power of the sword belongs to the whole community. In the good

old days the people stood by when judgment was rendered lest the ruler pervert justice, and the rulers have perverted justice. They shall be cast down from their seats. The fowls of the heavens are gathering to devour their carcasses.[12]

But if whom the gathering fowls would devour were to be judged as dispositive, Müntzer must be reckoned a false prophet. Still, to those who, in the end, would be devoured, his keening self-righteous voice was a temporary and soothing balm, one with which "Dr. Pussyfoot" could not at this point compete.

Back to the Black Bear Inn, *Aetatis* 40

Later that August of 1524, Luther was dispatched to the town of Jena to preach a sermon. He had been sent on a preaching tour by the Saxon princes, to determine where Karlstadt's and Müntzer's "enthusiasm" had spread, with the idea of scotching it by pointing out its theological faults. Of course Karlstadt did not take kindly to being lumped in with the murderous Müntzer, so when Luther preached at St. Michael's Church in Jena, which was close to his village of Orlamünde, Karlstadt traveled thither, slipped into the church, and—wearing the unconvincing "disguise" of his felt bumpkin's hat—slumped in a pew to listen. Luther thundered against all of the things that separated him from the likes of Karlstadt and Müntzer. He took on the issues of "images," infant baptism, and the Lord's Supper. Luther had now moved from his position of being ambivalent about images to saying that churches should in fact display them. He saw that the *Schwärmer*, as he called them, tended toward legalism—which Luther saw as directly opposed to the message of grace in the Gospel—and he linked legalism with the Law of the Old Testament, and therefore with Pharisees and with Jews. That there was a prohibition against images in synagogues therefore made sense to him, and thus he was now against both legalism and any prohibition of images. He also implied that the fruits of all these things must logically lead to the murderous evil of Müntzer's insurrection. When he was through, he returned to his lodgings at the Black Bear Inn, the same place where two years earlier he had snookered the students on his return journey from the Wartburg. But Karlstadt had had enough and wanted to have it out with his old friend. So he wrote him a letter at the inn and asked for a meeting.

Luther agreed to the meeting and some hours later greeted Karlstadt in the inn's parlor. Luther was traveling with a number of Saxon court officials, and Karlstadt had with him his brother-in-law and two colleagues. Karlstadt opened aggressively by objecting to being attached in Luther's sermon to those "riotous murdering spirits" in Müntzer's camp. "He who wants to . . . put me in the same pot with such murdering spirits," he said, "ascribes that to me without truth and not as an honest man."[13] This was a very strong statement to make in a public setting in those days, but Karlstadt was hardly through. He then poured forth the pain of having been prohibited from preaching in Wittenberg and even of having his books kept from being printed, both of which he not entirely incorrectly saw as Luther's doing.

The conversation went back and forth, and it was clear the two of them had different views of how things had proceeded over the previous two years. To his credit, Luther wholeheartedly accepted Karlstadt's position as being implacably against violence, but he struggled to determine whether Karlstadt's and Müntzer's positions nevertheless somehow partook of the same "spirit." Both of them believed in the mystical idea of hearing God's voice. Both of them believed infant baptism a wicked idea. Both of them believed images must never be used. Both of them seemed to be antiauthority in their disdain for nobles and their special affinity with the peasants. Luther was not adamant in making his larger point, but he was sincerely trying to puzzle it through. Was there a "spirit of Allstedt" common to both men? Of course no one questioned Luther's own doctrine of "spirits," which was itself at least unclear and not at all scripturally based. Did he mean to say that there was a specific demonic power leading Müntzer onward and that one was either wholly against that "spirit" or for that "spirit"? Could there not be a host of such demonic spirits? Luther's insistence at times that one be clearly on board with him in all matters, or else anathema, ironically betrayed the same inflexibility that he had experienced with the papists and the *Schwärmer* both.

At some point in their long conversation, Karlstadt accused Luther of having changed his position on something. At this point, Luther cheerfully said, "My dear doctor, if you really know that to be the case, then write it out freely and boldly so that it comes to light."[14] This was an important moment. Soon Luther repeated the challenge, pulling a gulden from his pocket as a token of his seriousness and tossing it to Karlstadt. "The more boldly you attack me, the dearer you will be to me."[15] Karlstadt then bent the soft gold coin—presumably with his teeth—to take it out of circulation and thus made it a permanent token of Luther's promise that he was free to write against him. So it seemed that things ended on a reasonably friendly note, but what happened two days later casts doubt on that interpretation.

Luther two days after this meeting arrived in Orlamünde to preach, but when he did, he was not greeted by the townspeople, all of whom claimed to have been in the fields, harvesting. Luther seemed in a sour mood already and likely took offense at what he perceived as a lack of courtesy toward him. So when some of the town council appeared, he pointedly did not deign to doff his hat, as was customary and polite, and promptly took them to task over a letter they had sent him complaining of his treatment of Karlstadt, which he had found exceedingly rude and harsh in its tone. He even accused Karlstadt of having written it himself, which the Orlamünders flatly denied.

When Karlstadt himself appeared, Luther imperiously bade him take his leave, saying they were now enemies, which was evidently his interpretation of their recent agreement to air their differences in print. Luther even said that unless Karlstadt left, he would not continue the conversation. After Karlstadt left, the village fathers invited Luther to preach to them, as he had been doing in so many towns and villages on this tour, but he sharply declined and then engaged in an *in situ* argument with them about the issue of "images." He then endured their foggy interpretation of the already painfully cloudy theology Karlstadt had been peddling about transcending the physical world. It all sounded spookily enough like the folderol he had heard from the bug-eyed Zwickau prophets and Müntzer, not to mention like the soul-crushing devilment of his earliest years as a monk. Luther could take no more, and so, amid a cannonade of choicest insults from his ungracious hosts—including being told to go to the devil and having actual stones thrown at him—he departed. After he left, Karlstadt mounted the pulpit and fulminated against his former friend as a "perverter of the Scriptures."[16]

The horror for Luther was that now he was fighting those who had previously been in his own camp. It was deeply disheartening. Again, he felt betrayed by his old friend, who doubtless in turn felt betrayed by him. Things grew even less amicable when Duke John on September 18 expelled Karlstadt from the entire electoral territory. Karlstadt had never been given the pastorate in Orlamünde, despite the community's desire that he be their preacher, and now the "old skinflint" Dr. Kaspar Glatz—whom Luther was trying to fob off on one of the Nimbschen nuns—would have the Orlamünde pulpit. But with a congregation in full revolt against Luther and the Saxon princes, it proved to be something of a hardship post. Glatz did not last very long.

But now, freed by Luther at the Black Bear Inn from his previous muzzling, Karlstadt poured out ink upon ink in five pamphlets that took Luther to task over their principal differences. In November, he wrote *A Dialogue or Conversation Concerning the Abominable and Idolatrous Misuse of the Most Honorable Sacrament of Jesus Christ.*

As would often happen in the years ahead, Luther's personality led him to harsh and sometimes mulish views on certain issues. Just as he seemed to say that to agree with Müntzer in any way meant that one partook of "the spirit of Allstedt"—as if this were something one could determine clearly—he was not able to appreciate nuance or difference on the issue of the Lord's Supper. For his own reasons, he saw the denial of the "Real Presence" of Christ in the Lord's Supper as a denial of everything that mattered, as beyond the seamless and impenetrable pale he had erected. To deny the "Real Presence" was to side with all of his enemies on that side of things, and that was that.[17]

In December 1524, Luther responded to Karlstadt's writings, publishing the first part of what would be a two-part polemic against him and all the others who differed with him on images, infant baptism, and Communion. It was titled *Against the Heavenly Prophets in the Matter of Images and Sacraments.* Going hammer and tongs at the positions laid out by his onetime friend and collaborator—whom he now certainly considered his new chief enemy—Luther cited what he saw as popish legalism and a concomitant obsession with unimportant externals, over and against the true Gospel. For him, this was Old Testament legalism. It was an overzealous anti-popery that had run so far away from Rome that it had stupidly circled the globe to end up back at Rome without ever knowing it. "The pope commands what is to be done," he wrote, "Dr. Karlstadt what is not to be done."[18] Luther saw both as the opposite of the freedom promised in the Gospel. It bound the conscience and kept people in a stance of perpetual guilt for not having done enough. "For in no place," he wrote, "do they teach how we are to become free from our sin, obtain a good conscience, and win a peaceful and joyful heart. That is what really counts."[19]

Melanchthon was upset at what he perceived as the harshness of Luther's tone toward Karlstadt, but, alas, very much of what Luther would write in the years hence would read like a modern-day late-night tweet storm. The cranky Luther we associate with his later years was now only clearing his dyspeptic throat. In his critique, he repeated his previous unfortunate and polemical conflation of Karlstadt and Müntzer. But one reason that Luther did see a vital similarity between them had to do with the issue of authority and with what he saw as a common spirit of rebellion. Both Müntzer and Karlstadt were disinclined to play by the rules, and in this Luther saw something important. Karlstadt had not gotten his pastorate in Orlamünde in the proper way and flouted convention in pretentiously forgoing his former title of "doctor." Both were also cavalier in their slippery and clearly erroneous use and interpretation of certain scriptural passages. Luther was of course perceived by many as antiauthoritarian and as a renegade and rebel in how he saw the pope's authority, but Luther would have made clear that he was never against authority per se, far from it. It was because of his respect of true authority that he spoke out against false authority. But Luther believed Karlstadt and certainly Müntzer had gone too far on this score. In any case, what readers in Orlamünde made of Luther's new two-part work was not especially difficult to divine. They discovered for it what was a literally disgusting fundamental application: they used it as toilet paper.

The Peasants' War and the Limits of Liberty

It only made sense that once Luther had freed liberty from its cave, the thing would fly about and cause trouble. Liberty itself did not know its own limits. It knew it did not believe it should be crushed into nonexistence in a cave, but once it was out of that cave, it did not know how far it was permitted to fly before it would kill itself. Luther was himself puzzling over this. In *To the Christian Nobility*, he had made clear that Christians were free, but he also made it clear that their freedom made them duty-bound to behave well toward others. Christian truth was eleven parts paradox out of ten. This was its essentially mysterious and glorious nature.

So the question was, at what point did the government's authority over people cease? Whenever the true Gospel of Christ comes into history, slaves are freed and injustices are made right. The abolitionist and civil rights movements in the United States attest to that. When people know that they are free, they begin to demand that the government treat them as such. But how far can those demands go, and in what way can people make those demands without falling back on selfishness and violent force? This is the question that in the last century captured the minds of such figures as Gandhi, Dietrich Bonhoeffer, and Martin Luther King Jr.

So for some years the peasants had been making demands and expressing their grievances, but the advent of Luther's teaching—the advent of the Gospel—gave a further and deeper and more explicit justification to their views. In 1431, at the Council of Basel, the document known as "Emperor Sigismund's Reformation" declared, "Therefore everyone knows that he who claims his fellow Christian as property is no Christian. He is against Christ and nullifies all God's commandments. God has freed all Christians and released them from all bonds."[20]

So this coalescing revolt in February 1525 produced a document called "The Twelve Articles," which in obviously Christian terms laid out the case of the peasant class. It grounded their requests in divine law, and the authors clearly felt free to ask their rulers to behave justly under this law, which governed them all.

PEACE TO THE CHRISTIAN READER
AND THE GRACE OF GOD THROUGH CHRIST:

There are many evil writings put forth of late which take occasion, on account of the assembling of the peasants, to cast scorn upon the gospel, saying, "Is this the fruit of the new teaching, that no one should obey but that all should everywhere rise in revolt, and rush together to reform, or perhaps destroy altogether, the authorities, both ecclesiastic and lay?" The articles below shall answer these godless and criminal fault-finders, and serve, in the first place, to remove the reproach from the word of God and, in the second place, to give a Christian excuse for the disobedience or even the revolt of the entire peasantry.

In the first place, the gospel is not the cause of revolt and disorder, since it is the message of Christ, the promised Messiah; the word of life, teaching only love, peace, patience, and concord. Thus all who believe in Christ should learn to be loving, peaceful, long-suffering, and harmonious. This is the foundation of all the articles of the peasants (as will be seen), who accept the gospel and live according to it. How then can the evil reports declare the gospel to be a cause of revolt and disobedience? That the authors of the evil reports and the enemies of the gospel oppose themselves to these demands is due, not to the gospel, but to the devil, the worst enemy of the gospel, who causes this opposition by raising doubts in the minds of his followers, and thus the word of God, which teaches love, peace, and concord, is overcome.

In the second place, it is clear that the peasants demand that this gospel be taught them as a guide in life, and they ought not to be called disobedient or disorderly. Whether God grants the peasants (earnestly wishing to live according to his word) their requests or no, who shall find fault with the will of the Most High? Who shall meddle in his judgments or oppose his majesty? Did he not hear the children of Israel when they called upon him and save them out of the hands of Pharaoh? Can he not save his own today? Yea, he will save them and that speedily.

Therefore, Christian reader, read the following articles with care and then judge.

The first of the twelve reads:

First, it is our humble petition and desire, as also our will and desire, that in the future we should have power and authority so that each community should choose and appoint a pastor, and that we should have the right to depose him should he conduct himself improperly. The pastor thus chosen should teach us the gospel pure and simple, without any addition, doctrine, or ordinance of man.[21]

Of course the ideas in "The Twelve Articles" were profoundly buttressed by Luther's writings and Reformation thinking, so it was clear to Luther that he must have a response to this document. But even if it hadn't been clear that this article looked to him as its father, the document was sent to him with an accompanying pamphlet in which he, Melanchthon, and Johannes Bugenhagen were asked to be the arbitrators between them—the peasants who had written it—and their noble rulers. But the escalating seriousness of the peasants in seeing their demands through would put Luther in a difficult position. Already in 1522 from the Wartburg, he had written his pamphlet *Sincere Admonition to All Christians to Guard Against Insurrection and Rebellion*. He wrote it in response to the rabble-rousing and worse that had been going on in Wittenberg at that time, and in it he put forth his conviction that the Gospel must never proceed through force or violence. The Word of God would accomplish its own ends peacefully, if only people would preach it patiently and humbly. This thinking lay behind much of what he said when he returned from the Wartburg and kicked his friend Karlstadt to the curb, holding that even if what Karlstadt was saying were true, he must not forcibly insist on it being implemented but out of concern for "the weaker brethren" should take things slowly and should put up with things he found bothersome rather than demand that they be made right. They would be made right in God's time. This, it seems, was precisely Luther's position now when he read "The Twelve Articles." It wasn't that what they said was wrong but that using force or even the mere threat of force was not the way to make things right and was therefore itself wrong. And that was the underlying message of the peasants' document. Everything it said was noble and true, but the threat of force behind it all damaged it fatally.

So in mid-April, Luther wrote his *Admonition to Peace: Reply to the Twelve Articles of the Peasants in Swabia*. In it he said that if the rebellion were to "get the upper hand," the results would be tragic. He wrote, "Germany would be laid waste, and if this bloodshed once starts, it will not stop until everything is destroyed. It is easy to start a fight, but we cannot stop the fighting whenever we want to."[22] As in his *Sincere Admonition*, he cited the suffering of the innocent as a main reason not to proceed with the rebellion. But in this essay, he severely admonished both sides. He took the nobles to task for their unchristian behavior in oppressing the peasants, and he took the peasants to task for wanting to proceed impatiently with violence. Luther always had respect for authority, even when it was in the wrong, and he believed that going to war with the powers that be would be far more destructive than constructive.

> Can you not think it through, dear friends? If your enterprise were right, then any man might become judge over another. Then authority, government, law and order would disappear from the world; there would be

nothing but murder and bloodshed. As soon as anyone saw that someone was wronging him, he would begin to judge and punish him. Now if that is unjust and intolerable when done by an individual, we cannot allow a mob or crowd to do it. . . . What would you yourselves do if disorder broke out in your rank and one man set himself against another and took vengeance on him? Would you put up with that? Would you not say that he must let others, whom you appointed, do the judging?[23]

But Luther was most bothered by the *Schwärmer* who had incited this rebellion with their careless words. All of them ought to have known better. Like his namesake Martin Luther King Jr., Luther was not advocating doing nothing, but he was strongly advocating against violence as a Christian means of solving social injustices. Luther's advice was to trust God and to trust him radically. His message was scriptural: if we do not take these things into our own hands, but cry out to the Savior, we will see how he fights on our behalf. But it is clear from history that people rarely have the kind of faith that believes this sufficiently to resist taking action. To make his point, Luther quoted Romans 12:19: "Beloved, never avenge yourselves, but leave it to the wrath of God." Then he wrote,

Indeed, our leader, Jesus Christ, says in Matthew 7 [5:44] that we should bless those who insult us, pray for our persecutors, love our enemies, and do good to those who do evil to us. These, dear friends, are our Christian laws.

But then Luther lustily laid into those who had led these peasants astray: "The devil has sent false prophets among you; beware of them!" He mentioned no one by name, but everyone understood that he meant Müntzer and Karlstadt and the Zwickauers. They had foolishly whipped up thousands of peasants into a state of righteous anger that had nothing to do with the humble Gospel of Christ, and that humble Gospel is always infinitely more powerful than any righteous anger that resorts to the sword and the fist. He then reminded them of Jesus's admonition to Peter in the garden of Gethsemane, "He who takes the sword will perish by the sword." Then he gave them a contemporary illustration from his own experience:

Pope and emperor have opposed me and raged against me. Now what have I done that the more pope and emperor raged, the more my gospel

spread? I have never drawn a sword or desired revenge. I began neither conspiracy nor rebellion, but so far as I was able, I have helped
the worldly rulers—even those who persecuted the gospel and me—to
preserve their power and honor. I stopped with committing the matter
to God and relying confidently at all times upon his hand. This is why
God has not only preserved my life in spite of the pope and all the
tyrants—and this many consider a really great miracle, as I myself must
also confess—but he has made my gospel grow and spread. Now you in-
terfere with what I am doing. You want to help the gospel and yet you
do not see that what you are doing hinders and suppresses it most
effectively.[24]

As it happened—and as Luther rightly observed—those towns and
regions where the Gospel had not penetrated were the most inclined to
join this angry rebellion. It made sense that those places where the freedom of the Gospel had not been allowed were the more incensed at their
oppressive leaders and perceived their condition as worse than those who
lived in places where the Reformation ideas had been allowed to exist.
Luther thought that if only those who believed in the Gospel and lived in
territories where the Gospel was allowed had not joined these other reb-
els, there would have been hope. Their leaven would eventually spread to
these Catholic territories, and in time there would be dramatic progress.
But such restraint was not in evidence at present.

Peasant rebellions had been occurring here and there throughout
Germany since the previous fall of 1524. But by mid-April, when Luther
was in Eisleben—where he had traveled to help establish a Christian
Latin school and where he wrote his *Admonition to Peace*—their rebellion had spread and was in full swing all around Germany. The emperor's
armies were fighting in France, so it had fallen to the local princes to
defend themselves, and they had not proven equal to the sheer numbers
of pike-wielding peasants. What the emperor was doing far beyond
Germany—whether in dealing with difficulties to the west in France or
to the east with the Turks—made all the difference in that it prevented
him from doing much inside Germany that would have stanched the
flow of these revolutionary ideas, sometimes for good and sometimes for
ill. In this case, it seemed mostly for ill. What the peasants did in many
cases was very disturbing. Their actions were as far from what Luther
hoped would result from his ideas as imaginable. That Easter Sunday,

for example, peasants captured the Count of Helfenstein and his soldiers near Weinsberg. Although the count endeavored to bargain with the peasants, drunk with their power they slaughtered him on the spot and then sadistically forced two dozen noblemen and their servants to run a gauntlet in which they were all stabbed to death with lances. Their bodies were left to rot.

But Luther knew very little about what had been going on all around Germany—much less about such atrocities as happened near Weinsberg—and by the time he was finished advocating for peace, there was precious little peace left to be had. In fact, things were now boiling forward toward a final bloodbath. It was only after he had written this tract urging peace that he began to get a sense that things had moved far beyond what he had known. Everywhere Luther now traveled after Eisleben, he saw groups of peasants on the march, and he sensed the demonic spirit of murder that was in the air. He preached passionately against their violence and did all he could to exhort them to a peaceful conclusion, but those who had seen him as a friend and ally now only jeered at him. He traveled and preached through northern and middle Thuringia, but all in vain. The peasants had wandered far beyond the borders of reason, and Luther knew that the "spirit of Allstedt" had indeed taken hold of them.

At times during this period, he feared for his life. His theologically correct message of moderation and restraint could not compete with the wild tauntings of Müntzer, who appealed to their deep sense of outrage at many decades of injustice. When Luther preached, many of them not only heckled and jeered but also rang bells as a symbol of their protest. Luther finally saw that they were not to be spoken to. They had become rabid and bloodthirsty, so now there was but one thing to be done: he must rally the nobles to crush them. Already on May 4, Luther wrote to his friend Johannes Rühel, urging him not to advise Count Albrecht to "be soft." Whatever you do, Luther counseled, do not give in to the peasants' demands. Rühel later said that Luther's letter had indeed buoyed him up at a crucial time.

As Luther traveled toward home, the ugliness of warfare was everywhere around him. It was a vast landscape of death, and now "the archdevil" Müntzer appeared, inflaming it at every opportunity. After his time in Mühlhausen, Müntzer had again fled, this time to Nuremberg, and then he fled Nuremberg to return to Mühlhausen. But his lifetime of serial fleeing would soon be at an end, for here and now his great hour of action had come, and Müntzer could at last mount the world stage to play the part of his waking dreams. In Mühlhausen, he amassed and led an armed militia that he humbly dubbed the "Eternal League of God." It rallied under a rainbow banner daubed with the painfully ironic maxim "The Word of God Endures Forever."

Everywhere now, and in Thuringia and Saxony especially, thousands of peasants were looting and destroying cloisters. In Thuringia alone, more than seventy cloisters were sacked, and the monks treated despicably. The fanatic peasant mobs swarmed in every direction, burning castles and barns as they went. There was no justice being sought, nor even the pretense of such. It was nothing but vengeful murder and mayhem on a terrible scale. But Luther knew that Müntzer had been called by Satan to stir up these blind butchers, all of whom ardently believed they were doing God's work as they reveled in slaying and burning and gloried in blood and ashes.

By the time he got back to Wittenberg, Luther had seen enough, and he poured out the bile of it in his infamous *Against the Murdering and Thieving Hordes of Peasants*. Luther saw that whatever peace he had hoped for and cried out for over and over was not to be had. So he now whirled about and exhorted the nobles throughout Germany—the very men whom God had given the sword—to use that sword with all their terrible might and main. They must not hold back but do everything in their power to obliterate and smash into dust this bloodthirsty rebellion that was not of God but of the very devil himself. "Let whoever can stab, strike, strangle," Luther wrote. "If you die doing it, good for you! A more blessed death can never be yours if you die while obeying the divine Word and commandment in Romans 13[:1–2], and in loving service of your neighbor whom you are rescuing from the bonds of hell and the devil."[25]

Luther's fiery exhortations would return to haunt him, though, because they would be published far later than he had intended. So when they were finally read by most people, the peasants had already been massacred, and Luther's ferocious call to violence at that point seemed nothing but cruel. Luther had not been wholly insensitive to how his words might sound when he wrote them, but even after their context changed, he did not apologize for them. Several months later, he wrote a follow-up titled "An Open Letter on the Harsh Booklet Against the Peasants" in which he essentially defended himself against the many accusations that had been made against him and reminded his readers why he had written what he had:

> You have to answer people like that until the [blood] drips from their noses. The peasants would not listen; they would not let anyone tell them anything, so their ears must now be unbuttoned with musket balls till their heads jump off their shoulders.[26]

Luther knew that if the nobles did not stay the rebellion, it would fatally crack the skull of German society and overwhelm all civility and order for a long time to come. Everyone would suffer horribly, so the idiotic and bloodthirsty peasants were doing nothing but sawing off the very limb upon which they sat. If the raging peasant fire was not extinguished by the nobles, the result would be more burning and bloodshed and suffering than ever before. "If anyone thinks this too harsh," he wrote toward the end of the work, "let him remember that rebellion is intolerable and that the destruction of the world can be expected any hour."[27] That is, of course, always difficult to argue with.

But Müntzer had not gotten either of Luther's memos. In Mühlhausen, he was ever urging his followers onward, forward in their mindless course toward death and destruction. Müntzer fancied himself born for this hour, and how he poured himself into it! If given the chance, he would croak himself hoarse, exhorting all of Europe into an early grave.

> Now then, go to it, go to it, go to it. Now is the time. The scoundrels are as despondent as dogs.... They'll fawningly request, whimper, beg like children. Have no pity. As God gave orders through Moses, Deuteronomy 7, he has revealed the same to us.... Go to it, go to it, while the fire is hot. Don't let your sword get cold or go lame. Hammer out your cling-clang on the anvil of Nimrod. Topple their tower to the ground. So long as they are around it is impossible for you to be rid of human fear. And so long as they rule over you, no one can tell you anything about God. Go, go, while you have daylight. God leads on before you. Follow, follow![28]

Of course it was not God who was leading them but that eternal corpse who before time and forever aspired to be God. He it was who now led these lost souls into outer darkness, to that place where there would be wailing and gnashing of teeth. But now, as terrible and fearsome as the possessed hordes of peasants had been all across Germany, when they encountered their first genuine opposition, they would not prevail. Landgrave* Philip of Hesse took the lead in opposing them, bravely marshaling a force of mounted yeomen and knights in armor. First in Fulda and then in Hersfeld, he succeeded in fatally dividing the gibbering hosts. In each case, experienced leadership and much superior weapons won the day. The next move in his campaign was in Bad Frankenhausen on the Kyffhäuser, where most of the peasants had massed their forces. For this battle, Philip invited the help of his father-in-law, Duke George, whose own forces joined the fray.

Müntzer had little idea what he was now facing, and his holier-than-thou trash-talking would now ascend to its dizziest oxygen-deprived apex. He had sent a blizzard of letters during this time to buck up allies

A portrait of Thomas Müntzer (1489–1525).

---

* The German *Graf* means "count," so a landgrave is a count with territorial sovereignty.

and terrify foes, but on May 12 he wrote to both Mansfeld counts, Albrecht and Ernest. To Ernest, a Catholic, Müntzer wrote,

> Brother Ernst, just tell us, you miserable, wretched sack of
> worms, who made you a prince over the people whom God
> redeemed with his dear blood? . . . By God's mighty power you
> have been handed over to destruction. . . . I tell you: The eternal
> and living God has decreed that you be removed from your chair
> by power given us . . . for God has said about you and your
> kind . . . Your [eagle's] nest will be torn down and destroyed.[29]

To Count Albrecht, who was theologically aligned with Luther, something Müntzer clearly also thought beyond the pale, he wrote,

> In your Lutheran gruel and Wittenbergian soup, have you not
> been able to find what Ezek[iel] 37 prophesies? Besides, have
> you not been able to taste in your Martinian peasant shit how
> the same prophet goes on to say in chapter 39 that God makes
> all the birds under heaven devour the flesh of princes and all
> the dumb animals guzzle the blood of the big shots, as
> described in the secret revelation in [chapters] 18 and 19?
> Haven't you caught on that God values his people more than
> you tyrants?[30]

Was it indeed God who had said these things? Each letter bore the same cracked signature: "Thomas Müntzer with the sword of Gideon."* But two days later, the fight was over. It was a rout, as utter as can be conceived outside fairy tales, a carnival of carnage in which four thousand peasants were slaughtered, while something like four of the nobles' soldiers were killed. On the following day, the surviving peasants who were crouched above the city were challenged to turn over their "false prophets" and surrender. If they complied, they would be treated with mercy. But Müntzer was still awake inside his own mad dream and would spend his last free hours gamely firing up the weary souls around him. He crowed that whatever bullets came their way, he would catch in

---

* In the biblical book of Judges (chapters 6–8), Gideon is a prophet and military commander who with a force of three hundred Israelites defeats the far superior armies of the Midianites. The Angel of the Lord declared to Gideon, "The Lord is with you, mighty man of valor!" so Müntzer's reference is to his idea that like Gideon, God is with him and he cannot be defeated.

his magical sleeve! Of course when the nobles' demands were not met, they began the attack. When the first cannon blast fell short, Müntzer howled in triumph. But when subsequent attempts were less inaccurate and Müntzer's sleeves proved to be mortal, the mock-heroic prating died down, and the peasants did what anyone would do who is not ready to die: they lifted their skirts and speedily scattered. Most of them actually ran toward their enemies, thinking they could find safety someplace inside the city. But they did not, and when the troops caught up with them, the butchery continued.

As for Müntzer, he and his sleeves escaped to an attic and scrambled under the covers of a bed. When he was at last discovered there, he tried to pawn himself off as a pathetic invalid, but a nearby satchel of incriminating papers made everything clear, at which point he was indecorously hauled out of his garret sickbed and down into the famously bearded presence of Duke George himself. Amazingly, the duke sat with Müntzer on a bench and asked him about what had taken place at nearby Artern, where three emissaries had been sent to Müntzer by Count Ernest. Duke George said that he understood that Müntzer had in fact ordered that these peace-seeking emissaries be beheaded, which they were. Müntzer's reply was "Dear Brother, I tell you I didn't do it; divine justice did it." After this, Landgrave Philip entered the heated conversation, trading Scripture quotations with Müntzer.

The next day Müntzer underwent a trial in which he was tortured and confessed a number of things. He even recanted his sermons against the rulers. And after his extreme advocacy for taking Communion "in both kinds," he now even humbly received Communion according to the Roman rite, which is to say bread alone. Knowing he would be executed, he wrote a letter of farewell to his Mühlhausen congregation in which he confessed nothing by way of his own guilt but actually blamed the selfishness of the peasants for the defeat, saying, "Without a doubt things happened that way because everyone there was seeking his own good more than the justification of Christendom." This more than anything else outraged Luther when he learned of it later. "Anyone who saw Müntzer," Luther said, "would say that he had seen the devil in the flesh at his most ferocious."[31] In his letter, Müntzer even had the strange temerity to admonish those whom he had whipped toward deadly violence to "flee from the shedding of blood." This was the man who had said he was appointed to end the lives of all those who were not the elect, who had wailed, "I am sharpening my sickle." At the trial of Heinrich Pfeiffer, who had been Müntzer's ally since Mühlhausen, Pfeiffer guilelessly stated what Müntzer's plans had always been. "After annihilating all rulers," Pfeiffer said, "he intended to carry out a Christian reformation." But instead, eighty thousand peasants had died, and the Reformation of Luther had been so mixed up with this sprawling blood-soaked tragedy that in the eyes of any inclined against that Reformation, it was further discredited. On May 27, Müntzer and fifty-three others—Pfeiffer among them—were beheaded. Their heads and bodies were impaled upon pike staffs, where they remained to grimly decorate the outside of Mühlhausen's city walls for years.

CHAPTER SEVENTEEN

Love and Marriage

The life of married people, if they are in the faith,
deserves to be rated higher than those who are
famous for miracles.[1]

—Martin Luther

LUTHER'S WORLD AFTER the terrible Peasants' War was quite different. Although he had done whatever he could to prevent the violence that had broken out and before that had warned against the doctrines of Karlstadt and Müntzer, many nonetheless blamed him for what had happened, and the Reformation fell into greater disrepute in certain precincts. And just weeks before the final bloodbath outside Mühlhausen, the man who from the beginning had been Luther's quiet but implacable protector and champion had died.

The Death of Frederick

Frederick had been fifty miles south of Wittenberg in his hunting lodge at Lochau. This truly noble statesman who had protected Luther and who had unquestionably saved Luther's life and therefore allowed the Reformation to continue and take root died on May 5. Luther got word the next day as he traveled back to Wittenberg. Astonishingly, Luther had never spoken with him or met him, and had seen him only once, at the Diet of Worms among so many other nobles. Toward the end, Frederick had been as moderate and kind as ever, even trying hard to understand the peasants' bitterness toward the nobles. To his brother John, who now succeeded him as elector, he had written,

Perhaps the peasants have been given just occasion for their uprising through the impeding of the Word of God. In many ways the poor folk have been wronged by the rulers, and now God is visiting his wrath upon us. If it be his will, the common man will come to rule; and if it be not his will, the end will soon be otherwise. Let us then pray to God to forgive our sins, and commit the case to him. He will work it out according to his good pleasure and glory.[2]

His death had come at the very crest of fighting in the Peasants' War. The castle lodge at Lochau was deserted when he died, because all of the men were in the field with Duke John, fighting the uprising. Spalatin had made haste to his lord's bedside and when he arrived saw Frederick wearing his glasses and reading the comforting letter Spalatin had sent ahead. Spalatin usually read aloud to the elector, including nearly every letter he ever received. So now Frederick asked his faithful friend to continue reading what would be this last letter aloud, which Spalatin himself had written. Spalatin took it and read aloud what he had wanted to say to the man to whom he had been so very close. At some point, Frederick's discomfort was such that he said, "I can't anymore." Spalatin stopped. "My most gracious Lord," he asked, "have you any trouble?" Frederick's words now were the last he spoke in this life. "Nothing but the pains," he said, and fell into a sleep.[3] Spalatin nonetheless continued to read aloud to him from the book of Hebrews, and as he was doing this, Frederick slipped into eternity.

The next day the elector's body was laid upon a bier to be taken home to Wittenberg. The wagon was drawn in a cortege for fifty miles through the Saxon towns and villages where he had ruled. Bells were rung and people gathered to see and pay their respects to the man who had irenically ruled over them since his own father's death, forty years before. On the tenth, Frederick's body arrived in Wittenberg, where he would be buried in the Castle Church. Eight pallbearers from the nobility carried the bier, while other notable figures and citizens walked alongside. Thus was he borne into the town he had built. Lucas Cranach and Christian Döring stood at the doors of the church handing coins to the poor, as was customary at such times.

Twenty men carrying torches and coats of arms accompanied the elector's bier as it was carried into the Castle Church and placed in the center of the great nave. Melanchthon and Luther both spoke. Spalatin had inquired of them what would be appropriate for his funeral on the following morning, because no Saxon prince had ever had a funeral except in the Catholic church. What should the new protocol be? They determined that no masses should be held, nor black vestments worn, nor black altar cloths laid. In the letter on this subject to Spalatin, Luther wrote, "Death is oh so bitter—not so much to the dying as to the living whom the dead leave behind."[4]

That night the elector's body, now six days dead, lay in the silence of the church, guarded by sentinels. Some time before dawn, a grave was dug near the altar, and at 7:00 a.m., after Matins were sung, the church bells rang to summon the people. Luther now preached a second sermon, and the body was lowered into the ground as the choir sang the Nicene Creed.

"I Will Not Marry"

The previous fall, before the peasants' rebellion had spread into full fan across Germany, Luther was puzzling over the issue of marriage and parrying not a few attempts to corral him into that noble institution. In November, however, he remained adamantly against the idea. Argula von Grumbach, a dedicated supporter of Luther's and one of only a handful of notable women of the Reformation, had written to Spalatin, eagerly inquiring after Luther's marital status. She felt strongly that he must move forward. On hearing of her letter, Luther wrote to Spalatin,

> I am grateful for what Argula writes about my wedding plans; I am not surprised about such gossip, since so many other bits of gossip are around concerning me. Nevertheless give her my thanks and tell her I am in God's hand as a creature whose heart God may change and rechange, kill and revive again, at any moment. Nevertheless, the way I feel now, and have felt thus far, I will not marry. It is not that I do not feel my flesh or sex, since I am neither wood nor stone, but my mind is far removed from marriage, since I daily expect death and the punishment due to a heretic. Therefore I shall not limit God's work in me, nor shall I rely on my own heart. Yet I hope God does not let me live long.[5]

It seems that the detachment from this world that looked like sheer morbidity under the pear tree with Staupitz in 1505 had not changed much and that Luther was still fully expecting to meet his Maker via unnatural means, and even welcomed it. It is obvious he was not in 1524 looking forward to any future involving a wife and children, nor did this attitude seem to change throughout that winter. On April 16, 1525, however, just before he left Wittenberg for Eisleben, where he wrote his famous *Admonition to Peace*, and before he saw with his own eyes the extent of what was happening, he wrote to Spalatin, still protesting strongly against marriage. At the same time, however, he seemed to hint that this protestation was not the whole story:

> Incidentally, regarding what you are writing about my marrying [let me say the following]: I do not want you to wonder that a famous lover like me does not marry. It is rather strange that I, who so often write about matrimony and get mixed up with women, have not yet turned into a woman, to say nothing of not having married one. . . . But you are a sluggish lover who does not dare to become the husband of even one woman. Watch out that I, who have no thought of marriage at all, do not some day overtake you too eager suitors—just as God usually does those things which are least expected. I am saying this seriously to urge you to do what you are intending.[6]

Less than three weeks later, while Luther was in the midst of the horrors of the Peasants' War, making his way home, he wrote his letter to Johannes Rühel, in which he advised him not to dissuade Count Albrecht from wiping out the rebellion. But in that letter, written on May 4, he slipped in a single bright line that fairly leaps from the surrounding bleak landscape of the letter: "If I can manage it, before I die I will still marry my Kathie to spite the devil, should I hear that the peasants continue."[7] Obviously, for him to write it so offhandedly in the midst of an otherwise grim and serious letter indicates that Rühel and Luther and others were well acquainted with this person and with the possibility of Luther's marriage to her. That he should call her "my Kathie" is the most startling, because clearly things have been going on of which no other surviving letters give us any idea. But almost certainly, the one thing that would have focused his mind on marriage—such that he blurts this out in a letter about the "murdering hordes"—was his recent visit to his parents. Visiting them had been part of his recent trip, and if mentioning "my Kathie" in his letter to Rühel is any indication, he certainly mentioned her to his parents. For all we know, he visited them specifically to mention her to them. There is no doubt that they heartily approved the idea of their son's at long last marrying and having children. Luther was now nearly forty-two.

There were two other reasons that might have made marriage seem less difficult to Luther now. One we already know, and that is the death of Frederick. His views on priests and monks marrying were more traditional than not, and surely Luther was conscious that if he were to marry, it would trouble the man he so respected and who had done so much to protect him. But Staupitz had died recently too, and his death might have been even more important in clearing the way for Luther to marry. He knew full well that it would have greatly bothered Staupitz to know that his former protégé and spiritual son had married, and that he had married a nun would have seemed dramatically worse.

Oddly enough, we know that Luther took an especial delight in the scandalous outrage that marrying a nun was bound to occasion. He spoke of wanting to spite the devil—and the pope too—by doing such a thing. And yet he did not do it only out of spite. To someone for whom spiritual warfare was quite real, the act of marrying a nun was as though he had delivered a whirling roundhouse kick to the devil's own snout. He knew that this act would have meaning and very real power in the spiritual realm. It was an act of worship to God as much as anything anyone could ever do, and its spiritual significance was tremendous. Luther was in his person and with his own body countering the falsely pious antipathy to the physical, and specifically to the erotic. God had created the physical and the sexual as good, and he had redeemed them from their broken fallenness via marriage. Thus not only was there nothing dirty about this, but the opposite was true. Luther thought unnatural celibacy to be of the devil and natural and healthy marital sex to be something that glorified God.

> Whoever is ashamed of marriage is also ashamed of being and being called human, tries to improve on what God has made. Adam's children are and remain human; that is why they should and must beget more men. Dear God, we see daily the effort it costs to live in a marriage, and to keep the marital vows. And we try to promise chastity as if we were not human, had neither flesh nor blood.

But it is the God of the world, the Devil, who so slanders the marital state and has made it shameful—and yet allows adulterers, whores, and dissolute knaves to survive in high esteem all the same—that it would be fair to marry in order to spite him and his world and to accept his ignominy and bear it for God's sake.[8]

In 1522, in *Against the So-Called Spiritual Estate*, he wrote,

A young woman, if the high and rare grace of virginity has not been bestowed upon her, can do without a man as little as without food, drink, sleep, and other natural needs. And on the other hand: a man, too, cannot be without a woman. The reason is the following: begetting children is as deeply rooted in nature as eating and drinking. That is why God provided the body with limbs, arteries, ejaculation, and everything that goes along with them. Now if someone wants to stop this and not permit what nature wants and must do, what is he doing but preventing nature from being nature, fire from burning, water from being wet, and man from either drinking, eating, or sleeping?[9]

Just three days before his wedding, Luther received a letter from his friend Spalatin, who was considering marriage himself. In the letter, Spalatin asked Luther what he thought of long engagements, and Luther's typically witty response was "when you're driving the piglet, you should hold the sack ready." He also said,

Don't put off till tomorrow. By delay, Hannibal lost Rome. By delay, Esau forfeited his birthright. Christ said "You shall seek me and you shall not find." Thus Scripture, experience, and all creation testify that the gifts of God must be taken on the wing.[10]

Luther Is Married, *Aetatis* 41

Sixteenth-century marriages in Germany were typically two-stage affairs. There was first a small ceremony with a handful of witnesses and then a larger event with a church procession and guests from out of town. But the initial event was capped with the consummation of the marriage, so the marriage—actually called the *Kopulation*, which is etymologically related to the more anodyne word "couple"—was in fact consummated *before the wedding*. If the marriage was not consummated, the wedding would not happen. And if the marriage was consummated, the couple were as good as married before the wedding. This was the typical case, and Luther and Kathie were no exception. So on the evening of June 13— a Tuesday—his friend Johannes Bugenhagen, who was the Wittenberg parish pastor, conducted the ceremony in the Black Cloister. It was attended by Luther's closest friend at that time, Justus Jonas, and by Lucas Cranach and his wife, Barbara, with whom Kathie had been living for some time. Another local friend, the jurist John Apel, was there too. He had also married a former nun and was chosen by the university as the official witness to the marriage.

Odder far than the idea that these marriages were consummated before the weddings was the idea that they must be consummated in full view of a witness. So after the small ceremony, the couple were escorted to their bedroom in the cloister, where Jonas did the curious honors, watching the two become one flesh literally and figuratively. He wept to see it, knowing the huge significance of it all on every level. There was often an observation deck above the bed, though this detail seems not to have been observed in this case. It seems more likely that Jonas simply stood someplace in the room, silently beseeching the Lord of hosts not to abandon him to a coughing fit or sneeze. From our vantage point, this scenario cubes whatever ideas we have concerning awkwardness, but for those in Luther's day who were not prudes about the facts of life, and who considered the marriage bed not less than holy, and who saw in the physical union of man and woman a living picture of the union between the Bridegroom, Jesus Christ, and his Bride, the church, it was a real place and real time where heaven bowed down to kiss the earth, where alpha embraced omega, and where the dewy newness of Eden was rediscovered. And out of this came that which was impossible, the bounteous miracle of life itself. "Yesterday," Jonas wrote to a friend, "I was present and saw the bridegroom on the bridal bed—I could not suppress my tears at the sight."[11]

In the morning, Kathie—already leaping into her role as lady of the house—provided breakfast for the handful of guests. Presumably at Cranach's suggestion, the city council presented the young couple with no small amount of wine for this meal. There was a gallon of Rhine wine, a gallon of sweet Madeira, and one and a half gallons of Franconia wine.

No one knows why Melanchthon was not invited to the June 13 ceremony, but we do know he disapproved of the marriage, so perhaps Luther intuited this and wished to spare himself and his friend the emotions of their disagreement. Nonetheless, Melanchthon was upset not to have been invited or notified. Our only record of his pique is in a letter three days later to his friend Camerarius, which was cryptically written in Greek:

> Since dissimilar reports concerning the marriage of Luther will reach you, I have thought it well to give you my opinion of him. On June 13, Luther unexpectedly and without informing in advance any of his friends of what he was doing, married Bora, but in the evening, after having invited to a supper none but [Bugenhagen] and Lucan the painter, and Apel, observed the customary marriage rites. You might be amazed that at this unfortunate time when good and excellent men everywhere are in distress, he not only does not sympathize with them, but, as it seems, rather waxes wanton and diminishes his reputation, just when Germany has special need of his judgment and authority. . . .
>
> The rumor, however, that he had previously dishonored her is manifestly a lie. Now that the deed is done, we must not take it too hard, nor reproach him; for I think, indeed, that he was compelled by nature to marry. The mode of life, too, while, indeed, humble, is, nevertheless holy and more pleasing to God than celibacy.
>
> . . . I have hopes that this state of life may sober him down, so that he will discard the low buffoonery which we have often censured.[12]

We also know that Melanchthon's wife, Katharina, was not at all fond of Luther's new bride, and Melanchthon's reference to her merely as "Bora" is startling in its brusqueness, because nowhere else is she ever referred to in this way. Melanchthon's wife had doubtless seen a good deal of Bora during those first two months when Dr. Baumgärtner was courting her, often in the Melanchthon home, because he was a friend of theirs, and perhaps during this time Melanchthon's Katharina had observed some traits in Bora of which she disapproved. Perhaps it was even they who helped Baumgärtner make his decision not to return to wed her. If this is true, how much the worse it must have been to discover that she had parlayed this setback into the grand prize of Luther himself.

But Melanchthon was not the only one displeased by the news of Luther's marriage. The canon law aficionado Hieronymus Schurff was torn with deep concerns. "If this monk marries," he wrote, "the whole world and the devil will laugh, and he himself will destroy everything he has done."[13] Luther saw it quite the opposite way, but he knew that people would have an opportunity to snicker or cluck at it if they liked. Even the eely Erasmus had spread the false rumor that Luther had taken advantage of the young nun and was only marrying to cover his beastly tracks.

Martin and Kathie's wedding feast itself was to be on June 27, presumably to give out-of-town guests time to travel to Wittenberg. This was of course precisely two weeks after the marriage ceremony, and therefore also a Tuesday. Tuesdays were at that time for some reason thought to be lucky days for getting married, perhaps because there is a Jewish tradition that considers Tuesdays especially fortunate because in the first chapter of Genesis God says, "It was good," twice on the second day of the week.

On June 21, Luther invited his friend Nicholas von Amsdorf to the wedding feast:

> Indeed the rumor is true that I was suddenly married to
> Catherine; [I did this] to silence the evil mouths which are so used
> to complaining about me. For I still hope to live for a little while.
> In addition, I also did not want to reject this unique [opportunity
> to obey] my father's wish for progeny, which he so often expressed.
> At the same time, I also wanted to confirm what I have taught by
> practicing it; for I find so many timid people in spite of such great
> light from the gospel. God has willed and brought about this step.
> For I feel neither passionate love nor burning for my spouse, but I
> cherish her. To give a [public] testimony of my wedding I shall give
> a banquet this coming Tuesday, where my parents will be present.
> I definitely wish that you, too, will be there. Therefore, since I
> wanted to invite you, I am inviting you now and ask you to be
> there if you can possibly do so.[14]

Luther of course must invite Leonhard Koppe, who had driven the getaway wagon when the Nimbschen twelve busted out of the convent. Luther asked Koppe and his dear wife to please bring a barrel of Torgau beer and teased him that if it didn't taste good, Koppe would be forced to drink it all himself. Of course Luther invited his parents, as well as some other friends and family from Mansfeld. And when he invited Spalatin, he asked him to procure some venison from the Saxon court. It seems that anyone wishing to celebrate with game must become a mendicant. The city of Wittenberg gave Luther and his new bride a gift of twenty silver gulden and a barrel of Einbeck beer. Because the barrel cost nearly six gulden, it must have been magnificently large. Einbeck and Torgau were both famous for their beer during this period. Wenceslas Linck had himself been married for two years, and he came too, all the way from Altenburg, as did Melanchthon, who after all only lived down the block.

Innocent Ribbing

Another of the changes that 1525 would hold had to do with Spalatin, who had served the elector Frederick and been the main glue in Luther's relationship with his prince. But now that there was a new elector, Spalatin would move to Altenburg, where he became the pastor of a large church. And that November, he too would marry. Of course he invited Luther to attend, but because Altenburg was seventy miles due south of Wittenberg, traveling there would have entailed going through Leipzig, which was the territory of Duke George, whose ire toward the heretic Luther had not cooled. So Luther begged off the two-day journey to Altenburg but blamed it on his young, overprotective wife. "The tears of my Kathie keep me from coming to you," he wrote. "She thinks you actually want me to be put in danger." But two weeks after this, he wrote Spalatin a second letter, one that has understandably been oft quoted. This is because it proposes Luther's presence in Spalatin's marriage in a way that is far less typical than attending a wedding. But Luther is Luther, and he never set any store by being typical:

> When you have your Catherine in bed most sweetly embracing and kiss-ing her, reflect within yourself: "My Christ, to whom be praise and glory, has given me this being, the best little creature of my God." And then when I have guessed the day you will receive this letter, on that very night I will also love my wife with the same act in memory of you.[15]

These extraordinary sentences reveal or underscore a number of things about Luther. First, his relationship with Spalatin may well be the closest relationship he had in the world. Only Justus Jonas can approach it, and of course he was physically present at Luther's first performance of the "marital act." But Luther and Spalatin knew each other so intimately and had worked together so closely in forging a way forward for the Gospel in the midst of political and other dangers that Luther felt more than a little comfortable sharing his most intimate thoughts with Spalatin. Second, we know that Luther truly found the physical act of sexual union within the context of marriage to be something beautiful and holy. It really was a return to Eden, where God approved and sanctified all we did and where the idea of something being sinful or dirty was not even possible. So in this intimate and private letter, we have evidence that in his own life Luther lived what he preached and taught. This world, as well as every physical thing in it, was to be redeemed through Christ. We were not to wall it off from the spiritual but to redeem it, to drag it into the sanctified world of the spiritual, to imbue it with the real presence of Christ so that whatever it was, bread or wine or the sexual act, it was all suffused with the presence of God and made new and beautiful again.

Luther's view of the material world and especially of the sexual sphere stands in stark opposition to the dualistic, Gnostic, antimaterialist view of those who would over-spiritualize everything—as the *Schwärmer* had done—by eschewing sex and marriage and anything "non-spiritual." The otherworldly glassy-eyed look of cult members bespeaks this perspective, as though they were not really here, except in their bodies, which they have already mostly transcended. Agricola had circulated the story that Müntzer himself was so consumed with the things of God that when, on Easter Day in 1524, he was informed of the birth of his son, he didn't blink or express the slightest joy. When one stood solely in the otherwordly realm, all of these terrestrial things seemed distant and meaningless.

Paradoxically, the modern materialistic view of the world does the same thing, albeit in the opposite direction. Instead of saying the spiritual is superior to the material—and therefore we must transcend the material or depart from it as much as possible, if not entirely—it says the spiritual is a fiction and the only thing that is "real" is the material. This failed project, rather than slap away the material as something to be completely avoided, slaps away the spiritual as something invented and actually nonexistent. It holds that the reason sexual relations are not "dirty" is that there is no such thing as "dirty." Thus our ideas of shame are mere social constructs. Indeed our ideas of sin and even our ideas of what is good and true and beautiful are merely social constructs and inventions. So we have a purely materialist view of sex and the human person which holds that we are not spiritual beings—capable of falling away from God or being redeemed back into his presence—but purely physical beings for whom God is either a convenient fiction or an inconvenient fiction. According to this view, we must embrace the physical in such a way that we avoid any spiritual implications, so the sexual act is no longer shameful, but not because we have reentered Eden via the shed blood of Christ, rather because we have declared shame and sin and God to be religious fictions. We will therefore move forward purely as corporeal beings and will drown any flickers of shame or uncomfortableness as vestiges of our more primitive selves.

What Luther had done was something else entirely. Far from saying there is only this material world, he said God originally created this material world as good and had suffused it with his presence, but in Eden we fell away from that union with God. Thus the split between the "material" and the "spiritual" is the wound at the heart of the universe, and only Jesus can heal it. Therefore let us now allow him to do so by inviting him into this world. He came to Bethlehem and died on Calvary, but we must invite him into our hearts and must accept him so that he can do in our lives what he came to do. When we do this, everything is restored. So whatever we do in our humble, daily lives—whether having sex with our spouses, or raising our children, or working at our jobs—we may now do unto God's glory and may therefore redeem in him.

Luther was saying that for people who live like this, there is no longer a world in which officially religious and spiritual people only do religious and spiritual things. There is now a new world in which everyone can partake of God's goodness, in which every person is a "priest," in which every person can live fully loved and approved of by God, in which everyone can take the bread and the wine both at Communion.

So the idea that Luther had suggested his friend Spalatin invite the mental image of his dearest friend, Martin, and Martin's bride, Kathie, into his own marriage bed during the marital act is a reclamation of the childlike innocence of Eden before the Fall. It is not something strange and dirty from which our minds must recoil, because it does not believe that inviting the ultimate spiritual being who is God into our physicality and sexuality is to bring the spiritual where it has no business. On the contrary, it belongs there. It is also not something beautiful because there is no such thing as sin and broken sexuality. It is not an orgy or a group grope that says all sex with anyone is beautiful and a healthy option. It is that distant third thing of which the world knows so little. It is an invitation into the supreme health of a life fully redeemed in Jesus Christ, one that says yes, we can be born again; we can reenter God's good graces and again be as little children; we can take what the world and the devil would call dirty and make it as clean as soap.

The last line of Luther's letter to Spalatin brings their wives into things again, and with its typically Lutheran innocent ribbing wink bears the unmistakable hallmark of mankind's first joy, and even makes the connection to Eden explicit: "My rib greets you and your rib."[16]

Karlstadt Returns

Once Andreas Karlstadt had been kicked out of Orlamünde and banished by Frederick from Saxony, the hapless man could not find a home, wandering with his wife and daughter from town to town. He eventually ended up hiding in distant Rothenburg ob der Tauber, nearly 250 miles south of Wittenberg. But when the Peasants' War broke out, he found himself threatened by both sides. The man who had styled himself a humble tiller of the soil was at every turn rejected by the peasants; a peasant gang had even threatened his life. And the man who had married a noblewoman—and who had made it clear that he wanted nothing to do with violence—was accused by the nobles of being one of the peasant leaders, which might well have been punished with death. So when at last the violence came to an end, and he could come out of his hiding, where could he turn? He now turned to Luther.

On June 12, he wrote an extraordinarily humble letter to his former friend and recent enemy, begging forgiveness for "all I have sinned against you, moved by the old Adam."[17] He asked if he and his wife and young child could stay with Luther. On the twenty-seventh, the very day of Luther's wedding ceremony, Karlstadt's wife and child arrived in Wittenberg, where they were hidden under Luther's roof in the Black Cloister. Karlstadt himself arrived some time later.

Karlstadt even asked if Luther would appeal to the new elector, Duke John, so that he might be able to return to Saxony. It must have been humiliating for Karlstadt, but he even went to the length of revoking the last books he had written against Luther and promised not to write, preach, or teach again. Luther did intercede with the elector, asking that Karlstadt be given a hearing to let him prove he was not a "rebellious spirit" in the mold of Müntzer. Given the climate of those days, this might well have saved Karlstadt's life.

During the eight weeks that Karlstadt was quietly hiding under Luther's aegis, he wrote a full apology—titled *Apology*—in which he explained himself and told of his wanderings among the violent peasants. Luther himself wrote a foreword to it, making clear his sharp doctrinal differences with Karlstadt but nonetheless using his influence to make sure Karlstadt was given a fair hearing. Karlstadt even published a pamphlet in which he explained that his views on the Sacrament—which had differed from Luther's "Real Presence" views—never had been meant as a doctrinal statement but had been only his personal views, previously set forth in the manner of theses to be disputed.

Even for Luther, it was not easy to convince the elector John that Karlstadt should be allowed to return to Saxony. The fear that he would again cause trouble was something he took very seriously. Karlstadt had asked whether he might live in Kemberg, but because this lay on the main road to Leipzig, the elector feared it would be too easy for people to visit him there and subsequently spread his radical ideas. But that September, he was officially given permission to live in Seegrehna, a small hamlet five miles southeast of Wittenberg, where his wife's family lived. Spalatin had likely been the chief strategist in this, knowing that Karlstadt was best kept close to Wittenberg, where they could keep an eye on him.

But early in 1526, Karlstadt's son was to be baptized, and Karlstadt invited Justus Jonas, Johannes Bugenhagen, and Kathie Luther to be the godparents. Luther and a number of others from Wittenberg made the short journey to Seegrehna for the celebration. Karlstadt's son—who was named Andreas, after his father—was two, which was very old for an "infant" baptism, but he had been born around the same time that Karlstadt was banished from Saxony, and it is also possible that at that time Karlstadt was still opposed to infant baptism. But now was a time for reconciliation, such as was possible, and Luther himself was stunned at the development. In a letter to Amsdorf, he wrote, "Who would have thought a year ago that those who called baptism a 'dog's bath' would ask for baptism from their enemies?"*18

Married Life

Now forty-two, Luther was set in his ways. He would continue living in the same place he had been living since coming to Wittenberg fifteen years earlier. The only difference was that then there had been forty monks living in the Black Cloister and now there was only one former monk—and one former nun. But the success of Luther's marriage is a testimony both to Luther and to his Kathie. He was cheerful toward her in all the years of their marriage, and when one considers how exceedingly cranky and angry he could be to everyone with whom he dealt, that is the more extraordinary. But as extraordinary as his marital cheer is, Luther had chosen what by all accounts was an extraordinary woman. She was significantly younger than he, by fourteen years, but somehow the two of them fit together as well as any couple could. Years later, he recalled his first year as a married man:

> Man has strange thoughts the first year of marriage. When sitting at table he thinks, "Before I was alone; now there are two." Or in bed, when he wakes up, he sees a pair of pigtails lying beside him which he hadn't seen there before. On the other hand, wives bring to their husbands, no matter how busy they may be, a multitude of trivial matters. So my Katy used to sit next to me at first while I was studying hard and would spin and ask, "Doctor, is the grandmaster the margrave's brother?"19

Kathie respectfully called Luther *Doktor*, but from the full picture we get of her, we imagine she said this with a twinkle. And he always returned the favor by calling her *Doktorin*, which is the feminine version. One never gets the sense that she was out of her depth with him or that

---

* The bonds between Luther and Karlstadt didn't end with this ceremony. Only a few days afterward, Luther found himself interceding again with the elector on behalf of the miller in Seegrehna, who was Karlstadt's wife's uncle. And not long after that, when the plague struck Wittenberg, another relative of Karlstadt's wife who was stricken by the disease came to live with Luther and Kathie at the Black Cloister.

he found it difficult to relate to her because of her relative youth and lack of education.

If the change to married life was jarring for anyone, it must have been jarring for Kathie. She moved from Cranach's palatial and extremely well-appointed home to the near stable that was the Black Cloister. Since the monastery had been deserted, only Luther and another monk named Brisger lived there, plus Luther's servant Sieberger, who was famously unacquainted with cleanliness and order. Brisger was soon married and moved out, and Sieberger built a small adjoining house for himself, so that the vast, tumbledown monument to men without women became Martin and Kathie's to care for. To say that it benefited from this one woman's touch would be a historical understatement. That Luther had previously lived as the quintessential bachelor is borne out by the following disgusting admission: "Before I was married the bed was not made for a whole year and became befouled with sweat."[20] The gag-inducing image of a straw mattress soaked with the perspiration of Martin Luther to the extent that it should become "foul"—even in his eyes—is enough to make almost anyone cheer at his having taken the plunge into marriage. And indeed, the fetid horrors of the Black Cloister would soon be exorcised by the dramatically capable Kathie.

There is no question that she ran the household, doing more things than can be enumerated. Her work ranged from overseeing the much-needed paint and plaster repairs, to eventually raising hogs, cattle, and even fish. Kathie actually oversaw a fishpond that gave them trout, perch, pike, and carp, gathered via net. And then there was a nearby orchard that provided apples, pears, nuts, and peaches. Kathie also oversaw the barnyard. In addition to the pigs she raised, there were cows, ducks, and hens. It is a matter of record that the noble former nun did the slaughtering herself. Luther was in charge of the garden, where he grew melons, cucumbers, peas, lettuce, cabbage, and other things. He did much of the work himself there and was endlessly bothering his friends about sending seeds.

Kathie also managed their money, which Luther had always done very poorly, mainly because he needed little to live on and because whatever he got he tended to give away. He was notoriously generous, so much so that his friends sometimes had to step in to correct him. "I do not believe," he said, "I can be accused of niggardliness."[21] Even when they received a wedding gift that seemed to him too luxurious, Luther intended to give it back, but the savvy Kathie hid it, preventing him. Luther received no income from his torrential publications because even though the publishers made a mint from them, Luther refused to take a penny, nor did he take money for all of his preaching. He simply wanted to spread the Word and trust God would provide. But he was not averse to actual menial work. Besides what he did in his garden, he at one point decided a capital way to bring in some extra income would be by woodworking. So in the first year of his marriage, he ambitiously ordered a lathe and other woodworking implements; however, he was not adept enough to turn a profit, whether with a lathe or otherwise, so in the end this project fell by the wayside. Still, he was cheerfully game to do what he could, so whenever they tore, to save the money of a tailor, Luther always mended his own pants.

One steady source of income for them was the many boarders they took in at the Black Cloister, where they provided room and board for many University of Wittenberg students. Of course this kept Kathie extremely busy. In latter years, she bought a farm in nearby Zühlsdorf and spent time there too. Luther's letters to her greeted her comically: "To the rich lady of Zulsdorf [sic], Mrs. Dr. Katherine Luther, who lives in the flesh at Wittenberg but in the spirit at Zulsdorf." Or "To my beloved wife, Katherine, Mrs. Dr. Luther, mistress of the pig market, lady of Zulsdorf, and whatsoever other titles may befit thy Grace." She and Luther seem to have teased each other endlessly but always good-naturedly. Who would have thought that Martin Luther and marriage would have gotten along so well together? At the end of his first year with Kathie, he wrote, "My Kathie is in all things so obliging and pleasing to me that I would not exchange my poverty for the riches of Croesus."[22]

Kathie was an energetic, bright, and eminently resourceful person. Their marriage was duly and officially consummated on the night of June 13, and already in October Kathie was showing early signs of pregnancy. They would have six children. But the idea that a monk and a nun were to have a child together struck many as tempting fate. Surely God would show his displeasure for their unholy union, but how? Just what ungodly freak would spring from this dark coupling? Would their child be a monster like the Papal Ass or the Monk's Calf—or like the headless child supposed to be born in Wittenberg in the previous year? In fact, the most prevalent rumor that circulated in Saxony at that time was that the product of any such union must be a two-headed horror.

On June 7, 1526, Luther's first son was born, happily lacking a second head. Luther could not contain his joy at his first child's birth, and the very next day he wrote to his friend Johannes Rühel in Eisleben, where Johannes Agricola also lived at that time:

> Please tell Master Eisleben [Johannes Agricola] on my behalf, that yesterday, on the day which is called Dat* at two o'clock, my dear Kathie, by God's grace, gave to me a Hansen Luther. Tell him not to be surprised that I approach him with such news, for he should bear in mind what it is to have sun† at this time of year.
>
> Please greet your dear sun-bearer, and Eisleben's Else. I commend you herewith to God. Amen. Just as I am writing this, my weak Kathie is asking for me.
>
> Martin Luther[23]

They named him Hans, after his godfather Johannes Bugenhagen and also after Luther's own father, Johannes, who was also called Hans. In the child's first years, however, he would be called Hänschen, the diminutive version of the name. The child was baptized a mere two hours after he emerged from his mother's womb.

---

* The American edition of *Luther's Works* explains this as follows: "'He [she, it] gives,' written in Latin. This is the name given to June 7 by an old [medieval] calendar [called *Cisiojanus*] in which the names of dates were taken from rhymes composed from the initial syllables of the names of the important saints of each month."

† Luther is punning on sun/son (*Sonne/Sohn*).

CHAPTER EIGHTEEN

Erasmus, Controversy, Music

Erasmus is an eel.

—Martin Luther

T HE CATACLYSMIC FALLING-OUT between Luther and Erasmus must rank as one of the intellectual battles of the ages. Like the relationship between Freud and Jung or between Charles Darwin and Alfred Russel Wallace, it sheds much light on the issues of the day. But long before Luther and Erasmus came to trade blows and jabs with each other, they were largely viewed as allies. In fact, once Luther's doctrines began to catch on with the wider public, many in the Vatican laid the blame for it squarely in the Dutch lap of the "Prince of the Humanists" himself. Erasmus and his ever-loving Humanism—and his own witty and popular critiques of the church—were seen as the fecund soil in which the German weed called Luther could thrive. It's easy to see how they might have gotten these ideas. The fact is that for a time—and especially in the two years following the posting of his Ninety-five Theses—Luther's affinity with Erasmus was remarkable. At that time, though neither would have said so, they were very much intellectual comrades in arms. Both of them saw and declared publicly that the Roman church had strayed so far that reform was necessary. They weren't the only ones to see it, but their voices and pens were the principal ones making noise about it, and their works struck a chord and found vast audiences. How each of them would work toward bringing the much-needed reform would differ, but much of what they were saying was astoundingly similar, not least because it was obviously true.

Both Luther and Erasmus spoke out against the church's legalistic approach in so many things, its emphasis on silly rules and behavioral issues at the expense of deeper principles. Erasmus said that the principal teaching of the church at this time was less "loving one's neighbor" than "abstaining from butter and cheese during Lent."[1] And Luther and Erasmus both saw the pope and the papacy as one of the principal problems and said so. The Luther historian Roland Bainton says that many of the things Erasmus wrote during this time were very much meant to be read as his approval of what Luther was saying, though he wouldn't say so explicitly. For example, in his 1519 updated edition of his *Annotations on the New Testament,* Erasmus added the following passage:

> By how many human regulations has the sacrament of penitence and confession been impeded? The bolt of excommunication is ever in readiness. The sacred authority of the Roman pontiff is so abused by absolutions, dispensations, and the like that the godly cannot see it without a sigh. Aristotle is so in vogue that there is scarcely time in the churches to interpret the gospel.

And in 1519, in his *Ratio theologiae,* he added the following passage, which sums up what Luther is saying in many other ways:

> Some assert that the universal body of the Church has been contracted into a single Roman pontiff, who cannot err on faith and morals, thus ascribing to the pope more than he claims for himself, though they do not hesitate to dispute his judgment if he interferes with their purses or their prospects. Is not this to open the door to tyranny in case such power were wielded by an impious and pestilent man? The same may be said of vows, tithes, restitutions, remissions, and confessions by which the simple and superstitious are beguiled.[2]

The similarities here with Luther are certainly astounding. But Erasmus was clever in how he went about this business and was therefore canny in how his support of Luther came across. Luther thought him positively slippery, quipping, "Erasmus is an eel. Only Christ can grab him." For example, Erasmus always argued that Luther should get an open hearing, but he was careful never to endorse the man himself. There were differences between them, after all, and Erasmus was not about to let himself and his views get swallowed up like Korah into the widening rift of the Lutheran Reformation.* For example, Luther's incipient

---

* For his rebellion against Moses, Korah fell into an abyss that opened in the earth.

nationalism—or at least the Reformation's flirting with nationalism—posed a danger to Erasmus's hopes for a unified Europe. In fact, Erasmus had pointedly dedicated his commentary on the four Gospels to the four sovereigns of the new national states: Henry VIII of England, Ferdinand of Austria, Francis of France, and Charles of Spain. A pan-Europeanism under the unifying aegis of the Roman church was not a small cause for him.

But another, more fundamental difference lay in the way the two men expressed themselves. Luther was as German as Germany itself, which is to say that there was a bluntness and a love of truth that sometimes came at the expense of comity. He cared about theological doctrine in a way that was sometimes ferocious and unyielding, and he obviously thought that it must be so, and that God would sort it all out in the end. But Erasmus was opposed to confrontation. He was more a wit than a theologian—in fact, he was not a theologian at all—and he was more an advocate of finesse and satire than blunt pronouncements or cutting japery. Erasmus's indifference to theology per se is an important difference between them and would be the thing that led to their dramatic and public clash. His patron saint, for example, was the Thief on the Cross, who was saved without ever having heard about the Trinity or the *Filioque* clause—or even having heard that Jesus was fully man and fully divine. Erasmus would rather elide the details of many of these theological issues. They were simply not his focus. He endeavored to convey the basics of the faith to as wide an audience as possible. In fact, he was so intent on this that some of his writings were even translated into the Aztec language, as that society had been breached by the Europeans a few years earlier, in 1519.

This is not to say that Luther did not wish to appeal to the common man, nor that he didn't see this as a priority. On the contrary, what probably enabled him to succeed as he did was his almost uncanny ability to do this. His already remarkable talent at communicating directly with the average German in the pew was honed further yet in the years in which he preached often in Wittenberg. It is probably Luther's astonishing intellectual wingspan—to be able to go from Greek and Latin translation and deep exegesis and scholarship to preaching candidly and clearly to the open-minded peasant—that marks him as a genius for the ages. He not only did not disdain the common man but positively hated those who did. He saw the obscurantism of Scholasticism and Aristotle as enemies of

Christ and of those Christ loved and cared for. A comment on this subject is recorded from his *Table Talk* later in life. "Cursed are all the preachers that in the church aim at high and hard things," he said, "and, neglecting the saving health of the poor unlearned people, seek their own honor and praise, and therewith to please one or two ambitious persons."

In a dedicatory preface to *A Treatise on Good Works*, Luther wrote,

> Although I know full well and hear every day that many people think little of me and say that I only write little pamphlets and sermons in German for the uneducated laity, I do not let that stop me. Would to God that in my lifetime I had, to my fullest ability, helped one layman to be better!
>
> ... I will most gladly leave to anybody else the glory of greater things. I will not be ashamed in the slightest to preach to the uneducated layman and write for him in German. Although I may have little skill at it myself, it seems to me that if we had hitherto busied ourselves in this very task and were of a mind to do more of it in the future, Christendom would have reaped no small advantage and would have been more benefitted by this than by those heavy tomes and those *questiones* which are only handled in the schools among learned schoolsmen.[3]

So as far as this went, Luther could play at being the simple "son of a miner" and joke earthily with the common laborer in a way that far outstripped the scholarly and witty Erasmus. But unlike Erasmus, Luther had a German fussiness over theological order and correctness, and it was this that occasioned the great explosion between them. We might see this as where Luther departed from Humanism, or where Humanism departed from Luther. This was the divide, in the end: How far could Humanism and its adherents—principal among them the "Prince of the Humanists," Erasmus—ride along with Luther? Did Erasmus at some point realize he was riding along on the back of a tiger and simply want off?

We should recall that without the intellectual movement known as Humanism, it is unlikely that the phenomenon known as Martin Luther could have happened. Without Erasmus's restored Greek New Testament, it would hardly have been thinkable for Luther to translate that book into a German so fresh and accessible that it dramatically changed German-speaking people forever, making them a people of the Book in a way they had never been before. And we must remind ourselves that it was that great Humanist Reuchlin who helped Melanchthon become who he was, and who in turn cast all of Wittenberg in a Humanist mold.

But in the mid-1520s, the universes of Luther and Erasmus had approached the limits of how far they could coexist on friendly terms. Luther's criticisms of the church had become shrill and aggressive in a way that was unthinkable a few years earlier. Erasmus had many times commented on how deeply troubled he was by Luther's tone, which he thought was hurting the larger cause of bringing reforms to the church. Although Erasmus himself often got into trouble with the church, he never took those fatal transgressive steps beyond the church's pale that Luther had, and it was clearly important to him that he never stray beyond that palisade of what passed for orthodoxy—and the church's good graces. He had an uncanny ability to finesse things and to tiptoe back into the church's embrace whenever necessary.

So the baseline to which Luther hewed in his criticism of the church was very different from that to which Erasmus hewed, and at some point the difference between those baselines became painfully obvious to Erasmus. Doing what Luther had done after Worms, such as identifying the papacy with the Antichrist and burning the papal bull, was well beyond Erasmus's limits. In order to make this clear to the church and to show his final fealty to it, Erasmus was asked by King Henry VIII of England to write something against Luther. So the dance Erasmus had been able to dance in which he contrived to have his cake and eat it too had come to an end. The church wished him to make clear that these were two different cakes.

No matter what Erasmus did or didn't do now, many would think him guilty of having created the Humanist and critical atmosphere that made Luther possible. Still this point marks when Humanism and Luther's Reformation must clarify their limits. Many were eager to hear Erasmus on these issues. Just as there were many Humanists like Hutten who despised the church and were more for Reformation even than Luther, there were Humanists who were looking for clarification. Precisely how far could they stray? Erasmus must tell them. But Erasmus was not eager for the confrontation with Luther any more than he was eager for confrontation with the church. It was never his way.

Luther was in a similar bind on his other flank. After the Peasants' War, the Catholic church blasted Luther for his role in starting the snowball down the hill. In July 1525, his old enemy Jerome "the Goat" Emser, who had been chaplain to Duke George, wrote *How Luther Has Promoted*

Rebellion in His Books. And then his newer and future archenemy Johannes Cochlaeus—who would replace Emser as George's chaplain—wrote against him too. If this weren't enough, in October, Luther's friend Capito and the Swiss Reformer Huldrych Zwingli got in their licks. It was a dog-pile-on-the-rabbit low point for Luther.

Luther's story is a testament to how things beyond him shaped his course and the course of the Reformation in general. If the emperor hadn't been distracted by his wars with France, Italy, and the Muslim Turks, the Edict of Worms would have been enforced with far greater vigor, and Luther would never have had these four years to continue spreading his ideas. If Pope Leo hadn't been as myopic—and not merely literally—Luther and his vials of doctrinal nitroglycerin would have been handled with kid gloves rather than hammers. Also, the death of Pope Leo in December 1521 had an effect. Leo was succeeded by Adrian VI, who, like Erasmus, was a Dutchman and very much wanted to drain the papal swamp. It would be a new day, and everyone was excited that the sixth of the six popes from hell had at last taken his leave, presumably having shipped off to whatever eternal fate he had himself officially decreed. But after only twenty months in office, Adrian VI died, and as we know reformation from the inside had not gotten very far. Nonetheless, upon his election in January 1522, Erasmus wrote Adrian a congratulatory letter letting him know that he could count on his fellow Dutchman to do whatever would be helpful to him. And this is when Adrian joined Henry VIII in saying that Erasmus could be most helpful if he took up his famous pen to do battle with Luther.

Erasmus had never before openly spoken out against Luther, but the time had come. The pope had made Erasmus an offer he couldn't refuse. So this is most likely what finally pushed him to write on the subject of free will, which he believed was the principal and underlying issue between Martin Luther and himself.

But there are more specifics to how Erasmus's pen was put to paper. Luther's letter against Henry VIII, following Henry's harsh criticisms of Luther, seemed to Erasmus grotesquely indecorous in its harsh tone, and he felt obliged to let it be known that he felt this way. Then the pro-Reformation Humanist Ulrich von Hutten wrote very harshly against Erasmus in his *Expostulatio,* accusing this greatest of scholars of being cowardly, vain, and greedy for his own glory. He also categorized Erasmus's relationship to the Reformation as opportunist and worse. So

Erasmus was deeply offended and felt obliged to write a reply, which he did, titled *Spongia adversus aspergines Hutteni* (*The Sponge* Against the Aspersions of Hutten*). In it he said that his role in dealing with the Reformation had mostly to do with trying to parry Luther's "obstinate assertiveness"⁴ and complained that he was abused for his stance by both sides of the controversy. He clarified that he desperately wanted to help preserve the unity of the church, so things such as what Hutten had written were unhelpful, to say the least.

When Erasmus said these things about Hutten, Luther felt obliged to weigh in. He had no use for mere wit or for glad-handing or even for "unity" where the truth and the Gospel were concerned. So at this point, he clearly thought Erasmus cowardly and felt he was now playing both sides when it was time to choose. So Luther wrote a letter to Conrad Pellicanus in Basel, essentially saying so. He felt Erasmus had made himself irrelevant and said in the letter—which he fully expected Erasmus to see—that he should "become another man"⁵ and seize things by the horns rather than beat around the bush pathetically. Why did he not see that the Christian cause itself was at stake? Why did he not bravely enter the fray and help?

But this was not Erasmus's way, and for the genial scholar Luther's letter, with its accusations, would be the end of his silence. And so in response to this attack upon his manhood, Erasmus now finally moved forward with a book he had already written on the subject of free will at the urging of Henry VIII but had not yet published. The book was indeed "against Luther" in no vague terms. Luther didn't know this yet, but he suspected there might indeed be some response from Erasmus. As it happened, Melanchthon's friend Camerarius—to whom he had written the Greek letter crabbing about Luther's marriage—was headed to Basel, and Luther used this opportunity to convey a message to Erasmus directly. He understood that everyone revered Erasmus, but Luther was no respecter of people and wished to make it clear that if Erasmus did not come after him, he would leave him alone, but if Erasmus did write against him directly and against the Reformation openly, he would spare nothing in returning fire. He very high-handedly cast Erasmus in the role of an infirm observer who lacked the abilities necessary to the great battle for truth that Luther was fighting. In effect, he was telling

---

* In the late medieval era, teachers and students sometimes wrote on slates, to which were attached sea sponges, which served as erasers.

Erasmus to stay out of the way and he wouldn't get hurt. In his tremendously direct and undiplomatic German fashion, he might as well have called Erasmus an incontinent old man. In any event, Erasmus took it as though he had.

And so, feeling compelled to clarify his position, on September 1, 1525, Erasmus published his treatise on free will—helpfully titled *On Free Will*. The full title was *De libero arbitrio diatribe sive collatio*, which was macaronic, with the single word "diatribe" in all Greek capitals and the rest in Latin. As soon as the book appeared, everyone in the Humanist universe went mad with expectations over what was clearly shaping up as an open conflict between the "Prince of the Humanists" and the leader of the Reformation. It would be a battle for the ages, the two intellectual heavyweights of the age squaring off.

With typical élan and nuance, Erasmus eloquently laid out every aspect of the arguments. In even more classically Erasmian fashion, he took a firm stand against taking a firm stand, asserting that the question of whether free will existed could never truly be settled. He said that the idea that Luther had demonstrated free will did not exist was simply wrong. Besides, there was enough in the Old Testament to make the case for free will, and the church fathers—whose points of view were further recommended by their lives of great holiness (he said pointedly)—had also believed free will existed. So there. Also, there was no way of saying exactly whether free will might not play at least some role in our salvation, however small—although Erasmus rightly qualified this by saying that no matter what we did that could be construed as good, we would nonetheless be obliged to give the glory to God and to ascribe whatever good we did to God's grace. But did this actually mean there was no such thing as free will? He doubted it. This was the mystery of it all, but Erasmus was not uncomfortable with that mystery. If there was a mystery, there was a mystery. Why force an inscrutable text to say something because we were uncomfortable with its inscrutability? On this and some other issues, the only honest way out was to let them stand as mysteries about which we could only say so much. Luther's thesis was therefore one with many things to recommend it, but the simple and forced finality of it bore the stamp of wishful exaggeration.*[6]

---

* It is fascinating to note that already in 1522 Melanchthon had seen the principal difference between Erasmus and Luther: "In theological matters we especially seek two different things: one, how we shall be consoled in regard to death and the judgment of God, the other, how we shall live chastely. One is

Erasmus also felt that some truths were better quietly kept away from the public at large, and Luther's explosive idea that free will doesn't exist—and that what one does therefore doesn't matter toward salvation one way or another—could lead to tremendous misunderstanding, which could lead to social decay. From his point of view, this social decay was already happening because of Luther's teachings and Luther ought to be far more concerned about that. It was one thing to be against pharisaical and strained piety and another to let wildness and immorality reign and caper about. No one wished people to be puffed up with religious pride, but neither should one invite Dionysus with his thyrsus into St. Peter's to lead maenads in bacchanalian revelry. The woeful news coming out of Germany indicated that this was happening already. So to say free will did not exist was not an open-and-shut case, and the suggestion that it was was not merely a theological error but an error that could harm the faithful, who did not understand such arcane theological points and whose lives—and, infinitely more important, whose eternal future—would suffer as a result.

Finally, Erasmus did not like writing on doctrinal matters, and said so, but he had felt compelled to write on this one and privately hoped that although Adrian was dead and replaced by Leo's nephew, his own time in the papal doghouse might be ended, that he had done his penance, as it were, and could be restored. Of course, once he had written this work, the Catholic rulers naturally and perhaps somewhat greedily expected him to continue in this openly anti-Luther vein. Duke George wanted him to keep his quill moving! He hadn't had a moment's patience for nuance in his life and thought Erasmus should immediately refute Luther's execrable stand against monasticism; after all, when one had a big gun like Erasmus, it was a great pity not to blast it off once in a while, if only to remind the opposition that one had it!

Luther was so busy when *De libero arbitrio* was published that he did not read any of it until November. Usually, Luther only read bits of works that attacked him, lest their untruths and confused arguments affect him too much. He would read enough to be able to write a

the subject of true, evangelical, Christian preaching, to the world and to human reason unknown; that is what Luther teaches, and that is what engenders righteousness of the heart, in which good works then originate. The other is what Erasmus teaches us—good morals, the chaste life. It is also what the heathen philosophers knew about. What, however, has philosophy in common with Christ, blind reason with the revelation of God? Whoever follows this knows only affection; he does not know faith. However, if love does not proceed out of faith, then it is not genuine, only an external Pharisaic hypocrisy. Nevertheless, I do not hesitate to explain that Erasmus is superior to the ancients."

rebuttal, and then because of the shortage of paper at that time, and as a way of incarnationally expressing his sentiments, he did what the Orlamünders had done with his own *Against the Heavenly Prophets,* using the remainder as a *spongi culus.* In this case, Luther did Erasmus the honor of reading the entire work, but it so disgusted him that he knew it would take a great effort to respond to it. As far as he was concerned, it was a putrid goulash he greatly preferred to leave untouched. Perhaps the servants would like his portion.

But avoiding answering this would not be easy. Luther was being pressured by those on his side for a reply. Still, his busyness with other things made that difficult. That fall Joachim Camerarius was fairly drooling with anticipation for something from Luther, as were many of the other Humanists on the Reformation side. But Camerarius was more vocal about it than most. After the winter had passed, however, there was still nothing, not even something like a cloud the size of a man's hand on the horizon to give him hope. So Melanchthon wrote to him on April 4. He assured his former pupil that yes, Luther had at long last begun his reply to Erasmus and must soon be finished. For Luther, he said, it was all in the beginning, and now that he had begun, it surely couldn't be long! But Philip Melanchthon was whistling in the wind. Luther had been busy dealing with many things, but none of these things were a reply to Erasmus. In early 1525, Luther had been dealing with Karlstadt, and then in April he had visited Eisleben and had written his two works during the black crescendo of the Peasants' War. And of course in June he was suddenly married, which had prompted Melanchthon to send Camerarius his letter of Greek pique on that bitter subject. On July 19, Melanchthon wrote to Camerarius once more to tell him that his cheery April promise was in error. In fact, there was nothing in the works at all. Luther was busy lecturing again too. In midsummer, he began his lectures on Nahum and by the end of the year would have also spoken on Habakkuk, Zephaniah, Haggai, and Zechariah. When could he find time to answer Erasmus's work? It was sometimes as if he didn't even have the ability to choose to do it, as if free will didn't even exist on non-salvific issues either!

Camerarius visited Wittenberg in August. At this point, he was so desperately champing at the bit for Luther's response that he was even so forward as to importune the great man's new wife on the subject. Perhaps the twenty-six-year-old Kathie could be persuaded to force her husband to sit down and write what every Reformation Humanist was now contorted with agony to see. In the end, Kathie actually did persuade her husband of eight weeks to settle down to attack the unpleasant project. The result of his work was titled *De servo arbitrio* (contrasted with Erasmus's *De libero arbitrio*), or *On the Bondage of the Will.** Luther worked very hard on it all through the fall, and it did not appear until New Year's Eve. Its tone was hardly continent, and it so stung the venerable Erasmus that he wrote to Luther directly:

> The whole world knows your nature; truly you have so guided
> your pen that you have written against no one more rabidly and,
> what is more detestable, more maliciously than against me....
> How do your scurrilous charges that I am an atheist, an
> Epicurean, and a skeptic help the argument? ... It terribly pains
> me, as it must all good men, that your arrogant, insolent,
> rebellious nature has set the world in arms.... I would wish you
> a better disposition were you not so marvelously satisfied with
> the one you have. Wish me any curse you will except your
> temper, unless the Lord change it for you.[7]

Putting Luther's inveterate inability to play nice to the side, what had he said in his much-anticipated work? For one thing, Luther had not composed it *de novo* but decided to rebut Erasmus point by point and to follow the general form of Erasmus's own essay, so it was not a stand-alone explication of Luther's views but more a refutation of Erasmus's. Still, it is widely regarded as Luther's magnum opus, and Luther too came to see it that way. For one thing, Luther regarded this issue as the central theological issue in all that he did. This was the heart of the heart of the good news—of the best news conceivable—that we cannot choose our way out of hell, nor do anything of our own accord to be freed from sin and eternal damnation, but, *mirabile dictu*, Christ had come to set us free. All we need do is believe in him, and we are freed from sin and death forever and irreversibly. We are under no obligation to do anything at all to save ourselves; indeed we cannot do anything, and it is vitally important that we perfectly understand that we can do nothing. Nothing. So this misun-

---

* *On the Bondage of the Will* is widely reckoned Luther's greatest work, and in their introduction to the Baker edition of it, no less than J. I. Packer and O. R. Johnston judge it "the greatest piece of writing that came from Luther's pen." Is it any wonder Camerarius was so impatient?

derstanding that we might perhaps add something, even the smallest something—which idea Erasmus was in his soft way promoting—was nothing less than the most evil and harmful misunderstanding in the history of the world.

It should be said that Luther in the acerbic work nonetheless earnestly commended Erasmus for dealing with the single vital issue:

> You alone . . . have attacked the real thing, that is, the essential issue. You have not worried me with those extraneous issues about the Papacy, purgatory, indulgences and such like—trifles, rather than issues—in respect of which almost all to date have sought my blood . . . ; you, and you alone, have seen the hinge on which all turns, and aimed for the vital spot. For that I heartily thank you; for it is more gratifying to me to deal with this issue.

But then he bitingly says that if this work is the best that this greatest of intellectuals can muster, it only underscores the more his conviction that free will is a fiction. Luther is surely aware that in riding the wild bronco of his argument, his pen has leaked some acid:

> As to my having argued somewhat vigorously, I acknowledge my fault, if it is a fault—but no; I have wondrous joy that this witness is borne in the world of my conduct in the cause of God. May God Himself confirm this witness in the last day![8]

For Luther, this question is the very focus of human existence itself, the bald and unavoidable choice between life and death, heaven and hell, glories everlasting and joys unspeakable or equally enduring and unimaginable horrors and nightmare agonies. So to wittily equivocate or to elegantly skate around the hole in the ice while people are that moment drowning in that very hole is to serve evil, and there is nothing else to be said about it. That must be seen clearly and understood firmly and believed passionately, else one is in league with the devil of hell himself, whether one knows it or doesn't. Luther hoped to convert Erasmus, not simply to win an argument. This issue was only the most important thing in the world.

Luther had of course early in his life lived the hell of trying to do what he could to get to heaven. In those efforts, he had only gone backward, all the way to the antechambers of hell itself. This was where one's efforts would lead and could not help but lead, and Luther would by no means coat this everlastingly fatal poison with honey:

> As for me, I firmly confess that if it were possible, I would not wish to be given free will or to have anything left in my power by which I could endeavor to be saved, not only because, in the midst of so many adversities and dangers and also so many assaults by devils, I would not be able to stand firm and keep hold of it (since one devil is stronger than all men put together and no person would be saved), but also because even if there were no dangers, no adversities, no devil, I would still be forced to struggle continually towards an uncertainty and beat the air with my fists; for no matter how long I should live, and do works, my conscience would never be certain and sure how much it had to do to satisfy God. For no matter how many works I did, there would always remain a scruple about whether it pleased God or whether he required something more, as is proved by the experience of all self-justifiers and as I learned over so many years, much to my own grief.[9]

Luther also almost violently takes issue with Erasmus's contention that one's stance on free will is not important. For Luther, there is no doctrine more important, because for him this was the doctrine that determined how one read all the rest of the Bible. And if this one thing is properly understood, then we can sweep away all of the contrary suggestions in the Old Testament Scriptures that Erasmus cited. To say the question of free will is open to various interpretations is no different to Luther from saying the question of the bodily resurrection and the Incarnation are open to differing interpretations. Not only are they not open to different interpretations, but how we stand on these supremely vital issues determines all else. Thus Luther had worked hard to establish the clarity of this single doctrine beyond all doubt. For him, it is a treasure for emperor and peasant alike, for *Kaiser* and *Karsthans*. It is not a theological side issue; on the contrary, it is the one thing everyone can and must understand: without Jesus to save us utterly, we are utterly lost. With Jesus, we are saved. For Luther, all the flailing and the winnowing of his exegeses had produced these vital kernels that were meant to nourish mankind unto eternal life, and whatever contrary arguments Erasmus had put forth must be blown away like chaff.

The contrasting stances of Luther and Erasmus are fascinating. That their simmering feud finally boiled over in Luther's greatest work ended their communication, but not their private feuding. And for all his efforts to distance himself from Luther, the one final grunting shove that was *De libero arbitrio* still did not sufficiently distance him in the eyes of his most Roman critics, who forever saw him as suspiciously pro-Lutheran. For them, Erasmus's important work was nonetheless too little, too late. And in 1559, when Pope Paul IV published the Vatican's first *Index of Prohibited Books*, one certainly expected to find Martin Luther's books there, and did, but if one looked closely, one would have seen Desiderius Erasmus's were there too.

The Sacramentarian Controversy

Whereas the blowup with Erasmus concerned the issue of free will, the next controversy in Luther's widely controversial life concerned the nature of the Lord's Supper, and this time the challengers came not from those who sided with the pope but from within the ranks of the Reformation. It concerned the nature of the elements—the bread and the wine—at the Eucharist. In the Gospels, Jesus at the Last Supper said, "This is my body" and "This is my blood."[10] In both cases, he was holding things that appeared to be other than his body and his blood. He was holding first bread and then wine. So the question at issue was, when he said "This is my body" and "This is my blood," what exactly did he mean? This whole controversy— over which much genuine blood was eventually spilled and many bodies broken—all depended on what the meaning of the word "is" is.

The Catholic church had always taught that the priest was able via his singular spiritual authority to transform the bread and wine into Christ's body and blood—literally. When he prayed over the elements during Mass, they somehow became the actual body and blood of Jesus.* This is known as the doctrine of transubstantiation. Luther disagreed with this doctrine, holding that the plain meaning of Scripture must be grasped, and no more or less. Jesus said that the bread *was* his body and the wine *was* his blood ("This *is* my body," and "This *is* my blood"). He did not say, "This bread *will become* my body" or "This wine *will soon be* my blood."

---

* The Latin words spoken by the priest performing this ritual were *Hoc est corpus meum* (This is my body). The faux-Latin term "hocus pocus," spoken when an act of mysterious magic is performed, is a bastardization of this phrase.

Rather he simply said, "This *is* my body" and "This *is* my blood." Luther said that when a Christian in faith says these words, the body and blood of Christ are present, because he has spoken these words of Jesus in faith. Whatever the Scripture says is true and needn't be finessed into being merely a symbol or a metaphor. Luther called this doctrine the Real Presence. Jesus really was genuinely present in the elements. He did not become present when a priest prayed, but he *was* present when we believed in the words he spoke. The Word of God was true, and believing that—faith in the Word—was all that mattered. So it was the faith of the believer in the Word of God—and not the transforming words of any priest—that effected the change.

But others in the Reformation disagreed. The first of these was Karlstadt, but more significant to this issue was Huldrych Zwingli of Switzerland, who said that the word "is" actually meant "signifies." Zwingli claimed this had been revealed to him in a dream and that what Karlstadt believed on this issue had not influenced him. But these differences mattered profoundly to the men who argued about them.

Why was this so important to Luther? There were two principal reasons. First, Luther said that we must believe precisely what the Scriptures said and that when Jesus said "is" there was no way to read it other than "is." To do so was heresy. We were bound to believe the Word. Yes, it challenged us, but we could not put reason above the Word of God. It was difficult to understand how the bread and the wine could continue looking like bread and wine while being the body and blood of Jesus Christ, but it was also difficult to understand the Trinity and the Incarnation and the Resurrection and many other things, but we were obliged to believe them if that is what the Scriptures said. How it happened that the bread and wine became Christ's body and blood was as beside the point as how the Holy Spirit fertilized Mary's egg or how Jesus's corpse became alive or how he walked through walls and ascended into heaven. It was unlikely we could know how, but we were nonetheless obliged to believe.

The second reason this was important to Luther had to do with the very important idea that God did not wish us to have disdain for the physical or the corporeal. According to Luther, the Catholic church of his time and the Gnostics had taught that to be more like God meant to become less physical and more spiritual, to be somehow at war with this world. Luther said that Christ had come into the world to redeem it and he had become a human to redeem humanity. So every material thing in this world, once it was touched by Christ, was redeemed and returned to the "goodness" it originally had before the Fall. So to say that Christ himself could not be present in bread and wine but that the bread and wine must *via transubstantiation* physically be transformed into the literal body and blood of Jesus (although still looking like bread and wine) was to denigrate the bread and the wine, and the whole material and physical world. According to him, Christ could really be actually present in the bread and the wine without their becoming other than what they were.

The third reason this was important to Luther had to do with Aristotle, whom he despised. And he blamed the church for importing Aristotle's unchristian philosophy into places where it had no business existing. The church had tried to explain via Aristotelian "reason" how the bread and the wine actually became the body and blood of Christ while still looking like bread and wine. It said that the thing in "essence" became the body and blood of Christ while retaining the "accidents" of bread-ness and wine-ness. For Luther, this was pure sophistry and far worse than nonsense, because it implied that Christ could not come into our world and redeem it but must really replace it with something "spiritual"—in this case, himself in full transubstantiated actuality. The church had been maintaining and teaching that Christ replaced the bread and the wine with himself, so that the bread and the wine looked like bread and wine but were actually not bread and wine, but were the actual body and blood of Christ. But Luther maintained and taught that Christ was present in the bread and the wine but did not replace them. Both were still there. For Luther, the Catholic church taught that the physical was being not redeemed but shoved away and simply replaced with something fully "spiritual." For him, Christ was actually present in the bread and the wine, without the bread and the wine being somehow "transformed" in the way that Aristotle or rather Aquinas explained via his unconscionably smuggled-in Aristotelian thinking.

Oecolampadius rather simplemindedly and over-literally could not understand how Christ could have been bodily resurrected and then could have bodily ascended to sit at the right hand of the Father and yet simultaneously be physically also present in the elements of Communion. Luther impatiently swatted this away as "mere physics," writing,

The Word says first of all that Christ has a body, and this I believe. Secondly, that this same body rose to heaven and sits at the right hand of

God; this too I believe. It says further that this same body is in the Lord's Supper and is given to us to eat. Likewise I believe this, for my Lord Jesus Christ can easily do what he wishes, and that he wishes to do this is attested by his own words.[11]

At times, this controversy grew ugly, with Zwingli's camp mocking Luther's view of things, saying that he and those of his party were "cannibals" who worshipped "a baked God."

In 1528, Luther wrote,

Why then should we not much more say in the Supper, "This is my body," even though bread and body are two distinct substances, and the word "this" indicates the bread? Here, too, out of two kinds of objects a union has taken place, which I shall call a "sacramental union," because Christ's body and the bread are given to us as a sacrament. This is not a natural or personal union, as is the case with God and Christ. It is also perhaps a different union from that which the dove has with the Holy Spirit, and the flame with the angel, but it is also assuredly a sacramental union.[12]

Being theologically consistent, Luther felt similarly about infant baptism. It was by simple faith that the water of baptism transformed the infant baptized. The water was not "magical water" and did not become other than water, but by faith all things were transformed. So the faith of those doing the baptism that God was as good as his Word was all that was necessary. In a way, Luther believed in what we may think of as the "magic" of faith to very genuinely change things. It was not merely a spiritual transformation but the spiritual sacramentally united with the physical, forever and genuinely changing it, redeeming it from merely physical into something more, but not forgoing the physical.

Luther was of course bothered by Zwingli but did not write against him on this issue, although he had three of his sermons on the subject printed and sold. Luther saw that Zwingli and all the others on this subject had precisely the same views as Müntzer and Karlstadt. In a way that was opposite but similar to the papists, they eschewed the physical things of this world as bad, and Karlstadt and Müntzer of course had said that artistic images and church music* were bad. It was all of a piece. Paul had

---

* Zwingli, ironically, was proficient on six instruments.

written, "The letter killeth, but the spirit giveth life."[13] And John had written, "The flesh profiteth nothing."[14] But Luther knew that to divide the material world from the spiritual was not at all biblical. The Greek word *SARX* that John had used meant not *actual* flesh but that part of us that is "fleshly" and not attuned to God. Luther smelled both monastic dualism and Gnostic dualism again. This was more heresy, and as with Müntzer and Karlstadt it came from within his own camp. When Luther heard from Nikolaus Gerbel in Strasbourg that Martin Bucer too had gone over to this view, he was especially upset.

The Sacramentarians, as Luther called them, had begun where he had begun, by being anticlerical and disdaining the idea that priests could magically transform bread and wine into the body and blood of God himself, but they had kept going and had gone too far, so that they ended up agreeing with the ones they had fled from. It happened all the time, and Luther was left holding the line in the center of it all, trying to drag both sides back to the scriptural meaning:

> Here Christ is driven away by both parties. One pushes him out the front door, the other drives him out the back; one errs on the left, the other on the right, and neither remains on the path of true freedom.[15]

Luther saw that to allegorize or turn into metaphors or symbols what was plainly stated was no different than saying that Jesus rose "in the hearts of his disciples." It would be like saying the check is in the mail—"metaphorically." In a letter to those in Strasbourg, he wrote, "The text is too powerfully present and will not allow itself to be torn from its meaning by mere verbiage."[16]

> Whoever has a bad conscience from his sins should go to the
> sacrament and obtain comfort, not because of the bread and
> wine, not because of the body and blood of Christ, but because of
> the Word which in the sacrament offers, presents, and gives the
> body and blood of Christ, given and shed for me.[17]

In other words, the spiritual reality produced by faith in God makes everything even more real than physical reality, but it does not push physical reality into nonexistence or unimportance. Believing what God has said is all that is necessary for God to come all the way from heaven to earth and to transform not just the bread and the wine but us too, and eternally. This was at the heart of it all. This was the redemption that Christ brought to us and to all creation via faith in his Word.

Letting the Sunshine In

So the theological points that were at issue in free will and in the Sacramentarian controversy applied to everything. A vital aspect of Luther's theology is that God and the good news of God in Christ must be freed to overflow those sacerdotal channels to which the medieval church had restricted them. They must water the floodplains of ordinary life at all times and in all circumstances and in all things. The Bible must be made available to everyone in his own simple language; forgiveness and confession must not be restricted to interactions with priests; and Communion must be available in both kinds to everyone who believed in Christ. As far as Luther saw it, the church had over the centuries created such a rigid ecclesiastical structure that it had effectively walled God off from the faithful. It certainly hadn't done this intentionally, but it had nonetheless slowly but surely hidden God away in a place to which only those in the clerical class had the keys—or "the keys." This essentially, not to say absurdly and blasphemously, cast the church and the pope in the role of God's keeper, as though he were in a cage or a prison, as though they were not subject to him, but he to them. This was the problem. If they determined when he could come out and how, they were not mediators between him and his people but rather God's captors. How had things come to such a pass? For Luther, Jesus had come to earth—had died and risen from the grave— precisely to tear down the divisions between God and man. Jesus was the bridge between the two who had been separated since Eden, and faith in him was the way we could cross the bridge.

It therefore followed that if one truly believed, then all of life must be a life of freedom in Christ. One was truly free to go anywhere, and by faith one brought God wherever one went. For Luther, this was a large part of what the Reformation was all about, to take holiness out of the church and into the wider world. To take it from the priest and give it to every father and mother. To take it from the praying monks and nuns and give it to every laborer and every housewife. It was never meant to be hidden in religious vocations. The wall between them must be broken down forever. Just as the curtain in the temple had been torn to allow us into the holy of holies, and to allow God out of the holy of holies, so now all that was once confined to the religious and ecclesiastical spheres must fly out and into the wide world. Thus was everything that God had made redeemed by faith in Christ. On the one hand, this had happened fifteen centuries earlier, but it was as if the money had been put in the bank then and no one knew it was there, or soon forgot it was there. So no one had made a withdrawal and spent it, which was the point of the money. Luther was declaring that it was there and that it was available to all and now we must take it out and use it in our own lives for God's purposes. In this way, the Gospel would and should touch everything. Thus it was with sex and with every physical thing in this world, and so it must be with music too.

Music was not to be banished from our lives as Karlstadt and Müntzer felt it must be, nor was it to be separated into "church music" that could only be sung by priests and monks and "secular music" that was sung by the people outside the churches. All that was good was of God, and to create walls where God has built none was far worse than a mere tragic mistake. So Luther, in creating the worship services for the new Reformation church, sought to bring every kind of good music into God's service and sought to bring the "priesthood of all believers" into God's choir in church. Because it is so ubiquitous today, including even in Catholic churches, it is hard to believe that before Luther introduced it, there was no congregational singing in churches. He knew the power of music and wanted to use it for God's purposes:

> Music is a fair and lovely gift of God which has often wakened and moved me to the joy of preaching. St. Augustine was troubled in conscience whenever he caught himself delighting in music, which he took to be sinful. He was a choice spirit, and were he living today would agree with us. I have no use for cranks who despise music, because it is a gift of God. Music drives away the Devil and makes people gay; they forget thereby all wrath, unchastity, arrogance, and the like. Next after theology I give to music the highest place and the greatest honor. I would not exchange what little I know of music for something great. Experience proves that next to the Word of God only music deserves to be extolled as the mistress and governess of the feelings of the human heart. We know that to the devils music is distasteful and insufferable. My heart bubbles up and overflows in response to music, which has so often refreshed me and delivered me from dire plagues.[18]

Luther clearly wished to bring the good news of Christ into every aspect of the world so that the leaven of the Gospel could touch everything, as it was meant to do. As the nineteenth-century Dutch statesman and theologian Abraham Kuyper had said, "There is not one square inch in all of creation over which Jesus Christ does not say 'mine!'"[19] So everything would be redeemed, including the desire of the common man and woman to sing. But Luther had a very practical consideration in this too. He knew that the best way to inculcate the truths of Scripture into the minds of every man, woman, and child was to put good doctrine into musical forms. If they heard things preached from the pulpit and had them reinforced by their own readings of Scripture and their readings of Luther's catechisms, that was all well and good. But how wonderful it would be if all of that was further reinforced in congregational hymns. However, there had been no new hymns for many centuries, so Luther was in a hurry to create some. He wrote many of them himself. But he also cast his net far and wide for assistance in this grand project. At the end of 1523, Luther wrote to Spalatin, asking for help in translating some psalms into hymns:

[Our] plan is to follow the example of the prophets and the ancient fathers of the church and to compose psalms for the people [in the] vernacular, that is spiritual songs, so that the Word of God may be among the people also in the form of music. Therefore we are searching everywhere for poets. Since you are endowed with a wealth [of knowledge] and elegance [in handling] the German language, and since you have polished [your German] through much use, I ask you to work with us in this project; try to adapt any one of the psalms for use as a hymn, as you may see [I have done] in this example. But I would like you to avoid any new words or the language used at court. In order to be understood by the people, only the simplest and the most common words should be used for singing; at the same time, however, they should be pure and apt; and further, the sense should be clear and as close as possible to the psalm. You need a free hand here; maintain the sense, but don't cling to the words; [rather] translate them with other appropriate words.[20]

By inviting everyone to partake of the Christian experience in a way that had previously been impossible, Luther was really only opening the shades and the windows and letting the fresh air and the sunshine in. Both were meant to be free and to be freely enjoyed. More than that, they were essential for life. There were always risks in doing this. Sometimes insects would come into the house, and sometimes people would get sunburned, but living in a world without sunshine and fresh air was too high a price to pay to avoid these problems, so he was willing to take the risk.

CHAPTER NINETEEN

The Plague and *Anfechtungen* Return

For more than a whole week I have been tossed to
and fro in death and in hell, so that I am still drained
of all strength in my body and am trembling in all
my limbs.

—Luther in a letter to Melanchthon

Dear God, what misery I beheld! The ordinary
person, especially in the villages, knows absolutely
nothing about the Christian faith, and unfortunately
many pastors are completely unskilled and
incompetent teachers.

—Luther, *Small Catechism*

THE YEAR 1527 began with Luther calling King Henry VIII of England a Satan worshipper. On New Year's Day, he wrote a letter to his friend Wenceslas Linck:

Persuaded by the king of Denmark, I wrote a humble and
suppliant letter to the king of England [Henry VIII]; I had high
hopes and wrote with a guileless and candid heart. He has
answered me with such hostility that he sounds . . . as if he rejoiced
in the opportunity for revenge. These tyrants have weak, unmanly,
and thoroughly sordid characters that make them unworthy of
serving any but the rabble. . . . I disdain them and their god Satan.[1]

Henry's well-known decapitation of two of his wives makes Luther's statement plausible enough, but the story of Luther's back-and-forth with the ginger multi-wived tyrant began almost a decade earlier, after Luther had written on indulgences. Henry began to write against Luther on that subject but had set the manuscript aside for a time. When Luther wrote his *Babylonian Captivity* in 1520, Henry once more picked up his quill and completed the document, which became mostly a criticism of this more recent work. Henry had at that time put himself forth as a serious Catholic believer, and—presumably with some help from Cardinal Wolsey—he wrote his stinging response to Luther, titled *Defense of the Seven Sacraments*, for which trouble he earned the honorific title "Defender of the Faith" from an exceedingly grateful pope Leo X. The pope was so ecstatic over the work that he even awarded an indulgence to anyone who read it. In the book, Henry called Luther "a poisonous serpent" and "infernal wolf." Luther, never to be outdone in invective, fired back in a work titled *Against Henry, the King of England* in which he said Henry's work was overflowing with lies and Henry was the "king of liars." Luther also declared that Henry's ranting and raving made him come across like "a livid whore on the street."[2] It was this work that prompted Erasmus to publicly take issue with Luther's tone.

At some point following these traded gibes, King Christian II of Denmark intervened. He was somehow under the impression that an apology from Luther for his intemperate remarks could swing Henry over to the Protestant side. As it happened, Luther and the others who had broken with Rome needed help in dealing with Duke George, who had organized a Catholic alliance and was furiously intent on smiting once and for all the Lutheran pestilence. No one knew whether warfare would break out, and at that time Elector John even had more ramparts built to further fortify Wittenberg against such an attack. So Luther believed Christian's tale and wrote nearly as humble a letter as he had ever written. But alas, Christian had his facts wrong, and Henry cynically took the opportunity of this present of a creampuff pitch to blast it out of the park, and then to thumb his nose at the pitcher as he strutted around the bases. He was as vicious in his response as imaginable, accusing Luther of deflowering a nun and of leading scores of thousands to their deaths in the Peasants' War. This savage, mocking response to Luther's honest apology provoked Luther to pour out his feelings in his letter to Linck on New Year's Day of 1527. As we know, three years later, when Henry's cardinal Wolsey would be unsuccessful in persuading the pope to give

Henry an annulment for his marriage to Catherine of Aragon (who was the aunt of Emperor Charles), Henry would angrily cashier the cardinal and break with Rome anyway, and so become a Protestant after all, at which point the new pope would embarrassingly revoke Henry's absurd honorific title, "Defender of the Faith." But this was three years away. For now, Henry was Rome's fiercest champion.

The year 1527 was difficult in other ways. For one thing, the plague returned. It arrived in Wittenberg that summer, causing many to leave the town, though Luther stayed behind, feeling that it was his duty as a pastor and leader to do so. But even before the plague arrived, Luther had begun having health problems of his own. He had experienced a great tightness in his chest, which he evidently cured with Benedictine root. But there were also further troubles with hemorrhoids and other afflictions. Already two years before, Luther reported an abscess on his leg, which never fully healed. Then, in June 1526, he had a terribly painful attack of kidney stones. Kathie asked him what she could bring him to eat, and he asked for a fried herring and cold peas with mustard. His doctors were aghast that he would eat this, but Luther seems to have known what would do the trick, and sure enough the pains and the stones passed. But Luther would suffer with more stones in the years ahead.

But 1527 brought other difficulties. In early April, Luther's friend Georg Winkler, a pastor in the nearby city of Halle, was murdered. Halle was under the authority of Archbishop Albrecht of Mainz, and therefore still officially Catholic, but Winkler nonetheless had been bravely preaching there along evangelical lines. He also began serving Communion in both kinds to his parishioners, and it was these departures from Catholic practice that made him a marked man. He was summoned to Mainz to give an account of himself, and it was believed that on his way home he was murdered at the archbishop's behest. When Luther learned of this, he wrote a letter of consolation to Winkler's parishioners. In it, he imagines what Winkler would be saying to them from his heavenly perspective. It's obvious that Luther's own gloomy views of the spiritually dark world they all inhabited colored the words he put in Winkler's mouth, but he meant them as encouragement, saying that we are here together in this vale of tears and we should earnestly wish to join our martyred brother in the place where there are no tears and where sorrows and dying have passed away:

If you loved me, then you would indeed rejoice that in this way I
have passed from death to life. For what is certain in this life?
Today someone stands erect, tomorrow he lies there; today
someone has the right kind of faith, tomorrow he falls into error;
today someone hopes, tomorrow he despairs. How many splendid
people are now falling daily in the errors of the fanatics; how many
are yet to fall because of these same and other [sects] still to come?[3]

To know that Luther's friends were being murdered for their beliefs
helps us understand Luther's apocalyptic views. For him, the world was
approaching its last spasms of violence and historical drama, in which
the Antichrist was revealing himself, raging and raging the more at the
advance of the true light of the Gospel. "It is a sure sign," Luther wrote,
"that a great disaster is at hand, which will engulf the world, from which
God will snatch his own beforehand, so that they be not seized and perhaps fall and be lost among the godless." Who can doubt that living
through this would have been extraordinarily stressful, especially for the
man who had helped bring it all about and therefore felt a deep responsibility for all of it?

Shortly after this latest grievous episode, Luther's health failed dramatically. It had been faltering on and off in the previous years, but this
episode marked the dramatic beginning of never-ending medical difficulties for Luther. It happened on April 22, when he was in the pulpit. He
suffered an attack of such acute dizziness that he could not continue the
sermon. What caused it and how it ended that day, we don't know. But
in July it happened again, and this time it came in concert with the return
of his old nemesis, *Anfechtungen*, which he had thought forever banished.
The causes are difficult to determine, nor can anyone be sure just what
his *Anfechtungen* was, except that we must record Luther's subjective experiences of it. We know that he was deeply weary of his unending battles over the Eucharist and much else. And Luther was also very troubled
that everywhere around him there was such a poor response to the
heaven-sent message of freedom he was offering. The onset of this bout
of *Anfechtungen* occurred early on the morning of July 6. He was overwhelmed with sadness and tortured by negative thoughts of his own unworthiness before God, so much so that he summoned his friend
Bugenhagen—who was now the Wittenberg City Church pastor—to
hear his confession. At ten that morning, he had been invited to dine

with some nobles at a local inn. He decided to go but ate little and afterward went to see Justus Jonas. In Jonas's garden, he sat with his dear friend and poured out his grieving heart.

Afterward, he went home, but not before inviting Jonas and his wife to come back to the Black Cloister for supper. No sooner had they walked in the door than Luther experienced an infernal buzzing in his ear and said that he must lie down. But even before he could do so, he desperately asked Jonas to bring him some water—"or I shall die." Jonas was so flustered that he ended up spilling the water over Luther's face and back. After Luther lay down, he suddenly grew cold and became quite convinced that he was passing from this world. He prayed out loud, first the Lord's Prayer and then two penitential psalms. He was not only physically ill but also clearly tormented in his spirit, feeling guilty of past sins and generally unworthy as he had early that morning. He asked everyone around him to pray for him, quite sure he was now dying, and he lamented not having been counted worthy to shed his blood for the sake of the Gospel, as others had done. The doctor Augustine Schurff was summoned and treated Luther with hot compresses. But Luther was inconsolable, slipping away. He felt badly about the way he had spoken and written sometimes but said he only spoke that way to comfort himself in his pain, never to hurt anyone. Because he was sure he was dying, he gave his wife, Kathie, a strong word of encouragement to hold fast to the faith. He remembered his little Hänschen. He was upset that he would now be unable to counter the *Schwärmer*, who would continue to spread their confused poison, perverting the goodness of God's Gospel, leading people out of the ditch of popery, only to lead them into another ditch across the road. Luther wanted everyone who was there to witness to the fact that in his dying he had not recanted anything he had written against the pope with regard to repentance and justification.

But Luther did not die that day. Sometime the next day, he felt well enough to arise from his bed and have supper. But it had all been a deeply harrowing experience. Nor did the effects disappear quickly. For more than two weeks, he was unable to read or write.

In fact, all that month and through August and into September the effects lingered, and he was not himself. During yet another fierce spell of *Anfechtungen*, he became convinced that he had lost Christ utterly, that he was slipping away into the devil's grasp, into blasphemy and sin, but he believed the fervent prayers of his friends had held him fast and therefore he had not been lost. Luther was sure these were buffetings of the Evil One, and he later said that what he experienced during this time was more severe than anything before.

On August 2, he wrote to Melanchthon, who was away on a church visitation:

> For more than a whole week I have been tossed to and fro in death and in hell, so that I am still drained of all strength in my body and am trembling in all my limbs. I have lost Christ completely and have been shaken by the floods and storms of despair and blasphemy. However, as moved by the prayers of the saints, God has begun to have mercy on me and to snatch my soul from deepest hell.[4]

It is very difficult for the modern mind to make sense of Luther's sufferings and to understand how he himself made sense of them. We are tempted to think he must only have been suffering from depression brought on by chemical imbalances and purely physical causes, and therefore to think he was imagining the rest of it. But Luther was himself convinced that this was spiritual warfare, that the enemy of our souls was attacking him, and we have to acknowledge that on this score he is well within the boundaries of standard Christian belief. The stories ranging from the New Testament accounts of Jesus's dealing with demons all the way to present-day accounts of exorcisms attest to the persistence of such stories, all of which bear enough resemblance in their details to at least warrant being taken seriously.

What is also perplexing to us is Luther's clear suggestion that without the prayers of his friends he might have lost his faith and slipped into perdition. But here he is being perfectly consistent with his theological pronouncements elsewhere, that we are not the ones who pull ourselves into heaven but that God pulls us into heaven. All that is required of us is faith, and the barest modicum of faith is all that's necessary. But here is the more dramatic point: that even when we don't have faith, the faith of our friends and family can be enough. So he is saying that his friends' prayers sustained him when he could not sustain himself. This is consonant with his doctrine that our prayers for an infant are enough to recommend him to God, that our faith for that speechless babe will suffice to open the child to the great channel of God's mercy.

On August 21, he wrote to Johannes Agricola in Eisleben,

My hope is that my own battle is of service to many, although there is no evil that my sins have not deserved. Yet my life consists in this, that I know and boast that I have taught the Word of Christ purely and to the salvation of many. This burns up Satan, so that he would kill and destroy me along with the Word. That's why I have not suffered at the hands of the tyrants of this world, while others have been killed and burned for Christ and have perished; I am buffeted all the more in the spirit by the prince of this world.[5]

Luther was convinced that these were satanic attacks, and he was maintaining that because he had not been martyred for his faith, he was suffering in this way instead. It is always impossible to say exactly how spiritual warfare happens, because we are talking of an invisible realm, but the multitude of experiences related over the centuries has given us enough of a baseline from which to fathom these things, and Luther's interpretation of what he experienced was guided by the accounts with which he was familiar.

The Plague Returns, *Aetatis* 43

During that summer, the plague again struck Wittenberg. Many left the town, as was the custom, to avoid contagion. On August 15, the entire university temporarily moved to Jena. Melanchthon and Justus Jonas took their families away too, but Luther felt obliged to stay and care for the sick. Kathie and their son, Hans, also remained in Wittenberg. There is no question that Luther's faith is on display here, because he knew that remaining behind put him in physical danger, but he felt a responsibility to risk his life—and even the lives of his family—by remaining where he was and caring for the sick. God had called him, and he would answer God's call. The only thing he feared was not doing this. But during this period, little Hänschen did get quite sick.

Pastor Bugenhagen stayed in Wittenberg too, even moving with his family into the cloister a few months later. As was expected when the plague struck, people began to die. Karlstadt's own sister-in-law, Margarethe von Mochau, was ill with the plague and came to live at the cloister, as did the doctor Augustine Schurff's wife, who was also stricken. The Black Cloister during this time functioned very much as a hospital. When

the wife of the Wittenberg *Bürgermeister* contracted the plague, she too
came to the Black Cloister; but she did not survive, dying just moments
after Luther had held her in his arms. Bugenhagen's pregnant sister
Hanna—who was married to Luther's secretary, Deacon George
Rörer—had also contracted the plague. She had come to the Black Cloister and had a terribly difficult birth in which the child was stillborn. Not
long after the birth, she died too. This whole tragic scene affected Luther
particularly powerfully, not least because his own Kathie was herself
again pregnant and due in December:

> I am concerned about the delivery of my wife, so greatly has the example
> of the Deacon's wife terrified me. . . .
>
> My little Hans cannot now send his greetings to you because of his
> illness, but he desires your prayers for him. Today is the twelfth day that
> he has eaten nothing; somehow he is sustained only by liquids. Now he is
> beginning to eat a little bit. It is wonderful to see how this infant wants to
> be happy and strong as usual, but he cannot, because he is too weak.
>
> Yesterday the abscess of Margaret von Mochau was operated on.
> Since the pus has drained away she is beginning to feel better. I have con-
> fined her in our usual winter room, while we are living in the big front
> hall. Hänschen is staying in my bedroom, while the wife of Augustine
> [Schurff] is staying in his. We hope for the end of the plague.[6]

During this summer of *Anfechtungen* and plague, another evangelical
believer would be martyred for his faith. This was another friend who
had been at Wittenberg not long before. His name was Leo Kaiser, and
he was in Wittenberg for eighteen months before racing home to Bavaria
to see his ailing father, who died soon thereafter. But Bavaria was not
safe Lutheran territory, so the price of seeing his father on his deathbed
was a steep one. Shortly after his father died, Kaiser was arrested and
put in prison, where Luther wrote to him. Somehow Luther sensed Kaiser would be killed for his faith, and it bothered him deeply in the months
leading up to his July 6 experience of *Anfechtungen* and then afterward
too. Luther's old friend and enemy Johannes Eck had been one of Kaiser's persecutors, which made it even more painful for Luther. In the end,
Kaiser refused to recant and was publicly humiliated, stripped of his
clothing as Eck looked on, and then led around in chains before being
imprisoned again. Then, one month later, he was taken to his hometown,

where he was burned at the stake. "Jesus, I am thine! Save me!"[7] he had cried three times as they lit the wood around him. Luther was greatly disturbed to hear the gory, horrible details of his death, how the executioner had prodded the charred torso into the flames, so that it too would burn. He wrote all of it in a pamphlet at the end of the year and included a prayer in which he asked God to make him worthy to suffer a similar fate. In the pamphlet, he also asked whether he was living in a way that was worthy of the Gospel cause as Leo had been worthy. It is believed that the twin agonies of Kaiser's martyrdom and the death at the Black Cloister of Bugenhagen's sister Hanna, along with her child, were what led Luther to compose the hymn for which he is most famous, "*Ein feste Burg ist unser Gott*" ("A Mighty Fortress Is Our God"). Luther composed not only the words but the melody too.

The depression was with him on and off during this period. Bugenhagen and his family moved into the Black Cloister too, and Luther poured out his doubts to his friend and asked for prayers. The spiritual darkness sometimes felt so strong that he said he was sure they were dealing not with mere demons but with the prince of demons himself. At one point, he told Bugenhagen that he didn't have enough faith and needed Bugenhagen to speak some of the promises from God's Word to him, to declare them over him in faith, because his own faith was weakened. At one point, Bugenhagen said, "This is what God thinks: What am I going to do with this man? I gave him so many outstanding gifts, and he doubts my grace."[8]

Finally, from November 20 onward, the plague began to ebb away. Luther and Kathie were well, and their little Hänschen recovered. No one else had died in the cloister since Bugenhagen's sister and niece. But still now Luther's *Anfechtungen* tortured him until sometime in December. He was sure that after he had been married, this old and horrible malady would have left him forever, but it had not. But he said if this be the Lord's will, he would accept it, "for the glory of God, my sweetest Savior."[9]

But at least this *annus horribilis* ended on a bright note. On December 10, Kathie successfully gave birth to their first daughter, Elisabeth. After witnessing the agony of Bugenhagen's sister's death a few months earlier, Luther had been especially apprehensive. But all was well with wife and daughter, and the plague was gone. And then, on the very last day of 1527, Bugenhagen's wife too gave birth. It was a son, whom they named Johannes, after his father.

Visitations

In 1528, as a way of seeing to it that the spiritual health of Saxony was improving, Elector John deputized Luther and Melanchthon and others to make visitations to the various parishes in his territory. Part of the idea was that they would stamp out the heretical teachings of the fanatic *Schwärmer*, which continued to persist long after Müntzer's death and had broken out afresh among what would eventually be called the sect of the Anabaptists.* What Luther found in his travels was not terribly encouraging. There was profound ignorance of the Christian faith, and even where the Reformation had succeeded in abolishing the old traditions of the Catholic church, it seemed to have freed the people only from behaving with some semblance of morality and toward the barest modicum of religious activity. The true joy and liberty of the Gospel were not much in evidence. Luther wrote of his findings,

> Dear God, what misery I beheld! The ordinary person, especially in the villages, knows absolutely nothing about the Christian faith, and unfortunately many pastors are completely unskilled and incompetent teachers. Yet supposedly they all bear the name Christian, are baptized, and receive the holy sacrament, even though they do not know the Lord's Prayer, the Creed, or the Ten Commandments! As a result they live like simple cattle or irrational pigs and, despite the fact that the gospel has returned, have mastered the fine art of misusing all their freedom.[10]

It is hardly a surprise that after decades and even centuries of being taught nothing and living in their syncretistic world of medieval superstition and the barest bones of Catholic faith, many of the villagers knew nothing of the true Christian faith. A few years under a nominally evangelical preacher couldn't have cured that. The worship of Mary and other saints was still deeply ingrained, as was the religious "works" mentality that is the sine qua non of almost every religion around the world. Everyone knew he was guilty of something, that there was a gulf between him and some impossible standard, and the medieval system of guilt here and

---

* The word "Anabaptist" comes from the Greek prefix *ana*, which means "again." The Anabaptists did not believe in infant baptism and so were "rebaptizing" adults who had previously been baptized as infants.

there assuaged by some rituals had sufficed—in its insufficient way—since time immemorial. What could be done? It would be a long road, but Luther would help things along by writing a catechism.

Luther knew that for centuries no one had known the Bible nor what was in it. They had been a captive audience every week, and their own priests themselves usually knew nothing of the Bible or what was in it either. So the faith simply was not passed on in any measure. When Luther visited these villages and towns and saw the tremendous ignorance born of these dark ages, he was grieved, but his grief led him to write what is one of his greatest works, called *The Large Catechism*. It was Luther's way of promulgating the faith widely and it was published in 1529. It dealt with the basics of the faith: the Ten Commandments, the Apostles' Creed, the Lord's Prayer, holy baptism, and the Eucharist. It was written in a question-and-answer format so that it could be easily taught, and Luther knew that it would aid many pastors who themselves were not acquainted with the basics of the faith and who therefore didn't know how to teach it to their flocks. Luther also published *The Small Catechism*, intended for simple folk and for children too.

These works were not merely meant to be memorized, although they were certainly intended for memorization; Luther wanted the actual ideas to make their way into the hearts and minds of those who read them. For example, he began his exposition of the First Commandment, "Thou shalt have no other gods before me," with the following extraordinary formulation:

> What is it to have a god? What is God? Answer: A god is that to which we look for all good and in which we find refuge in every time of need. To have a god is nothing else than to trust and believe him with our whole heart. As I have often said, the trust and faith of the heart alone make both God and an idol. If your faith and trust are right, then your God is the true God. On the other hand, if your trust is false and wrong, then you have not the true God. For these two belong together, faith and God. That to which your heart clings and entrusts itself is, I say, really your God.[11]

Great sadnesses continued among Luther and his Wittenberg friends. Three months into 1528, Bugenhagen and his wife lost their little Johannes. And that August, Luther and Kathie lost their daughter, Elisabeth, just eight months old. Luther's love for this tiny girl made his grief over her loss quite overwhelming: "It is amazing what a grieving, almost womanly heart she has bequeathed me, so much has grief for her overcome me. Never would I have believed that a father's heart could feel so tenderly for his child."[12] It was therefore the more a blessing that in the following year, Kathie gave birth to a second daughter named Magdalena, who was born on May 4.

It must have been around the happy time of Magdalena's birth that Luther's parents paid another visit to Wittenberg, because in 1529 Lucas Cranach painted his portraits of both of them. His portrait of Luther's father, Hans, suggests a man fatigued and perhaps somewhat vexed by life, or perhaps he was simply impatient with his portraitist. Hans's wife Margarethe's portrait suggests a somewhat dour woman, perhaps also fatigued by life and its difficulties, and perhaps resigned to the fact that she must sit still while the painter goes through his everlasting motions. What joy could it have been to be immortalized at this stage of life? But the fact that Cranach painted them at all says much. Why he painted them as he did is another mystery.

CHAPTER TWENTY

The Reformation Comes of Age

Better be ten times dead than that our consciences
should be burdened with the insufferable weight of
such disaster and that our gospel should be the cause
of bloodshed.

—Martin Luther

As the 1520s rolled to their conclusion, the only reason Luther was still alive and the Reformation had been able to spread as it had was that the emperor had been too busy to enforce the paper tiger known as the Edict of Worms. In fact, since the Diet of Worms in 1521, Charles had not been in Germany at all. He had been busy fighting the French. In 1526, the emperor had been unable to attend the Diet of Speyer, instead asking his younger brother, Archduke Ferdinand of Austria, to preside. But in the five years since Worms, the mostly unmolested Lutherans had increased their strength dramatically. And the emperor's strength was further compromised by having to battle the Turks on the eastern border of his empire and having to battle Francis I of France on his western. Charles was getting no help in fighting the Turks from Germany, and then, when he finally defeated France in 1525 at the Battle of Pavia, Pope Clement VII—who had succeeded Adrian VI—used his authority to release the French from the harsh peace conditions that Charles had imposed on them. The emperor couldn't win.

As a result of these papal shenanigans, Charles fell out with Clement, which in turn caused Clement to ally himself with Milan, Venice, Florence, and France, an alliance called the Franco-Italian League, or the League of Burgundy. England was to have been a part of this alliance too, but when Henry VIII failed in his petulant attempts to have everyone cross the channel to sign the treaty on his turf, he stormed out of the league in a sable-colored huff.

Therefore imperial power was at a particular ebb at the diet of 1526. The emperor desperately needed help to fight the Muslim Turks in Hungary and Austria, and so he now needed to cut a bargain with the rebellious Reformation Germans. The Turks had already conquered all of Greece and much more. Suleiman the Magnificent was now pushing to extend his caliphate—and what we now call sharia law—all the way to the Rhine and would very soon be attacking Vienna. If Charles wanted the help of all the Reformation-minded leaders against the Mohammedans, all he need do was to allow them to carry on as they were doing. In a way, it was an issue of religious freedom. If he did not give them their religious freedom, he could fight the Islamists all alone. Interestingly, Luther was not convinced that his side should use its political leverage in this way. He thought it far too cynical and manipulative. After all, they must do the right thing as God showed them the right thing, and abandoning one's duties to Caesar was never an option. Surely the only right thing in this situation was to help the emperor in fighting against the marauding Turks. Nonetheless, the emperor's brother, Ferdinand, agreed to temporarily lift the Edict of Worms. Or at least not to insist on enforcing it. Instead, the issue of the edict would be decided at a church council as soon as possible. And in the meantime, the Edict of Worms would be temporarily suspended, although it would have been nearly impossible to enforce anyway, given how thinly the emperor's forces were stretched across Europe. And thus as happens in politics, the proverbial can was kicked down the road—naively and cynically both—to be dealt with at a more opportune time. Thus the Reformation could continue, and now it would do so with the official imprimatur of the emperor and the diet. So the suspension of the edict bought more time, during which the Reformation would continue to take root and grow.

But by 1529, the emperor's fortunes had turned once more. Although he had not been in Germany since the Diet of Worms in 1521, he would at last return, after eight long years away. In 1529, Luther and his compatriots would have to face the political and imperial music. But how was it that Charles's fortunes had improved? For one thing, his imperial forces had repelled the Turks at the gates of Vienna in October 1529. Heavy rains had fallen, hampering the siege efforts, followed by early snows. In the end, Suleiman and his armies retreated. The Turks would not make another attempt on Vienna for 154 years.

And then, fresh from this triumph, Charles was finally to proceed to Italy so that at last in February 1530 he would be crowned Holy

Roman emperor by Pope Clement. As much as the emperor's fortunes
had risen, the pope's had drooped. In fact, when Charles's troops had
sacked Rome in 1527, Clement had to go into hiding in a castle for six
months, emerging disguised as a beggar in order to escape with his life.
And now, in a further humiliation, he must crown the man who had
defeated him.

Still, the emperor was required by custom to kiss Clement's big toe,
which would be formally humiliating. This was at least something. And
the pope would also demand that the emperor promise to wipe out the
evangelical heresy once and for all. Because Rome was still smoking from
its recent torching by imperial soldiers, Bologna was chosen to take its
place as the site of the coronation. But Bologna was gaudily tricked out
to look like Rome, in its way, which was an indignity the proud Bolog-
nese sincerely resented.

So after Charles was crowned by the pope, he could finally turn his
attention to the rebellious Reformers, who were growing and now consisted of both the Lutherans in Germany and the Zwinglians in Switzerland. The subsequent imperial diet was held at Speyer, sixty miles
south of Frankfurt and right next to Heidelberg, in the spring of 1529,
and it was there decided that the Edict of Worms would finally be
reinstated—after a nice three-year hiatus—and would be enforced. So
the question was, what would Luther and the Reformation leaders
now do? What they did at Speyer was to lodge a formal protest, and
it was because of this protest that the name "Protestant" first came
into the world. But it has to be said that the protest of these newly
named Protestants was duly shot down by the emperor and the other
Catholics in charge, so things ended in a stalemate. Now what should
they do?

The Marburg Colloquy

Landgrave Philip of Hesse had some ideas what might be done. He was
no political naïf and had been thinking about this eventuality for some
time. He concluded that unless the Lutheran Wittenberg branch of the
Reformation could unite politically with the Zwinglian Swiss branch,
the emperor and the Catholic powers would have the upper hand, and
the Reformation would be lost. But if the two Reformation parties did

unite—at least politically—they could bargain much more effectively. So Philip thought he would summon both parties to a colloquy at his castle in Marburg.

Luther was not at all interested in going, however, knowing that what Zwingli had written on the subject of the Sacrament said everything that needed to be said, and there was no conceivable way that Luther would be willing to compromise with any of it. Luther also felt that Zwingli was the one pushing for this meeting, hoping that seeming to desire peace between them would give him an advantage with Landgrave Philip, who would himself push Luther to make some theological accommodation he knew he could never make. Melanchthon didn't want to attend either. For his part, he somewhat amazingly believed it would still be possible to find some compromise with the Catholics and to be reunited with them. So if the Lutherans went a step further toward Zwingli's excesses, that would scotch those hopes irrevocably. But Elector John knew they must make an effort, and at last he succeeded in twisting Luther's arm into an agreement to go. Nonetheless, Luther wrote to Philip beforehand. "I know I cannot give an inch," he said, "and, after reading their arguments, I remain certain they are wrong."[1]

And there were further problems. Not only would Luther not compromise on the issue of whether the Real Presence of Christ—meaning the actual body of Christ—was present in the Eucharist, but he could not even consent to the fundamental idea behind the meeting. He knew that Philip wanted them all to come together for the specific purposes of a political—and therefore military—alliance against the emperor, but Luther's understanding of Scripture did not give him permission to disobey the governmental authorities whom God had placed over him. He could disagree with them, as he had already done, and could be willing to die for what he believed. He could let them kill him, but he could not take up arms against them. That was simply something outside what was possible. He also realized that to create such an alliance as was being proposed would be hopelessly provocative:

> We cannot in conscience approve such a league inasmuch as bloodshed or other disaster may be the outcome, and we may find ourselves so involved that we cannot withdraw even though we would. Better be ten times dead than that our consciences should be burdened with the insufferable weight of such disaster and that our gospel should be the cause of

bloodshed, when we ought rather to be as sheep for the slaughter and not avenge or defend ourselves.[2]

So we see that here Luther sounds as much like a pacifist as any who ever lived, and although trying to square that with the man who exhorted the nobles to "stab and kill" the uprising peasants may seem difficult, we see that Luther's theology held that we must obey the governmental authorities set over us, even if they should wish to kill us. If we take up arms against them, as the peasants had, then Luther sided with the government and did not counsel them to put up their swords at all; on the contrary, they must use them in their proper sphere to restore order. In any event the idea of some kind of common theological confession was itself not objectionable to Luther, so at the end of July he and Melanchthon agreed that they would go. The meeting was set for October 1–4.

Luther left with Melanchthon and Justus Jonas on September 14 or 15. They were joined by their younger colleague Kaspar Crüciger and by George Rörer. Luther's assistant during this time was Veit Dietrich, who might have been along as well. They traveled through Torgau, where they met with Elector John, and then through Gotha and Eisenach, where two more Lutheran ministers joined them. In Altenburg, Spalatin greeted them, and then they continued on to Marburg. The city and castle of Marburg itself were begun in the eleventh century as a fort overlooking the Lahn River, which lay almost a thousand feet below the castle's ramparts. When Luther and his team arrived in their several wagons on the morning of the thirtieth, they discovered that Zwingli, Oecolampadius, and others were already there, including Martin Bucer, whom Luther rather good-naturedly called a "rascal" for siding with the Zwinglians on the issue of the Real Presence. Andrew Osiander from Nuremberg and Johannes Agricola from Augsburg would arrive the next day. All in all, it was the largest gathering of Protestant theologians ever assembled.

On the first day, two separate discussions were held, one between Luther and Oecolampadius and another between Zwingli and Melanchthon. As Luther fully expected, nothing at all new was said by anyone. Oecolampadius and Zwingli reiterated their position that while it was true that Jesus was by faith spiritually present in the Communion elements, nonetheless he could not be bodily present in any way. Their prequantum understanding of the physical universe made it difficult for them to imagine that somehow Jesus could be seated at the right hand of the Father in heaven and simultaneously somehow in the body and blood of the Lord's Supper. Luther again contended that God could do many things we could not understand and if the Scripture said "This is my body" we need not worry about the details. We had enough in those words to have what we needed. The words were not fuzzy or complicated in any way, and to pretend they were was a simple lack of faith or worse.

In Zwingli's meeting with Melanchthon, which was predictably less combative than the meeting between Luther and Oecolampadius, Zwingli wrote everything down and then invited Melanchthon to read it, to be sure they understood each other and what they had agreed upon. Zwingli wrote to a colleague to explain why he did this:

> Because Melanchthon is extremely slippery and, like Proteus, can transform himself into anything imaginable, he forced me—aided by a penholder instead of salt—to arm and dry my hand the better to hold on to this man who bares his teeth while searching for who-knows-what kind of ways to escape or slip through.[3]

But the general slipperiness of the entire debate reveals itself when we learn that Melanchthon is supposed to have agreed to Zwingli's idea that "words can no more than signify." But who was debating the meaning of meaning—or the idea that words were symbols that signified things? Was not the debate over whether when Jesus said "This is my body" he meant that the bread actually was his body or that bread (and not the *word* "bread") merely signified his body? No one was debating whether words themselves were signifiers, which very obviously they were and must be. They were debating whether Jesus's use of the word "is" was literal or merely metaphorical.

The next morning before they gathered, Luther sneakily chalked the words *Hoc est corpus meum* (This is my body) onto the table in the middle of the room and then covered it with a velvet cloth. At some point during their conversations, when Zwingli asked for proof that Jesus's body was present in the Communion bread, Luther saw his magic moment. Like some prestidigitating magus who had cleverly drawn his audience into his outspread net, Luther now dramatically whisked the tablecloth away and with an authoritative flourish indicated the stark words there

written. It was all as if to say that the proof you have sought is here—
only look—and the answer you seek is as self-evident as these four short
and simple words, and who but a willful churl would refuse to see that?

It didn't seem that anyone had moved or would move, but all Philip
was hoping for was that on this single sticking point they would agree to
disagree and not let it hamper them from uniting in a common Protestant front against the emperor. Surely they agreed on so much else that
to allow this single disagreement to scuttle everything was unwise. And
perhaps it was, but essentially that was what now happened. When they
ended their discussion, Zwingli was visibly moved, even saying that he
had deeply desired Luther's friendship and that he had looked forward to
meeting Luther more than any other person in all of France or Germany.
But Luther was no more moved by this Swiss olive branch than by the
Italian kiss of Miltitz eleven years before. His response to Zwingli was as
cold as ice. "Pray God," he said, "that you may come to a right understanding of this matter."[4]

But why was Luther behaving this way? When Bucer, trying to get an
answer, asked what it was that Luther did not like about the position of
their Swiss friends, Luther replied,

> Our spirit is different from yours; it is clear that we do not possess the
> same spirit, for it cannot be the same spirit when in one place the words
> of Christ are simply believed and in another place the same faith is cen-
> sured, resisted, regarded as false, and attacked with all kinds of malicious
> and blasphemous words. Therefore, as I have previously said, we com-
> mend you to the judgment of God.[5]

Again he had brought up the dubious and ironically unbiblical idea of
"the spirits." And that was that. So Luther effectively showed the back of
his hand to this man, who was on the verge of tears. As a result, Zwingli
now actually wept. But it seems that Luther would not even allow himself to lean in Zwingli's direction, much less share in his warm desire for
friendship.

Luther's dismissively resorting to this language of different "spirits"
was precisely the same as when he had spoken with Karlstadt about
whether Karlstadt possessed "the spirit of Allstedt," which was a murderous and wild spirit that he knew to be in Müntzer. What led Luther
to think that he saw such things so clearly, that they might have the same

"spirit"—which is to say the Holy Spirit of God—while differing in good faith on some details, however important those details might be? But Luther was not interested in discussing this. That he categorized Zwingli's good faith attempts to explain himself as in any way "malicious" or "blasphemous" is patently strange, for who else would have characterized them that way? Certainly not anyone else in the room, including all those on Luther's side. So the question remains: Was Luther being insufferably, abominably, perversely bullheaded, or was he being a divinely inspired and immovable outpost of truth?

The Augsburg Diet, *Aetatis* 46

Psalm 118: "I shall not die, but live, and proclaim the works of the Lord."[6]

The Holy Roman Emperor Charles V convened an imperial diet in the city of Augsburg in 1530 and would himself attend. It had been nine years since he was in Germany at the diet at Worms in 1521. The Augsburg Diet was slated to begin on April 8, and because the emperor would be in Bologna for his coronation by the pope in late February, he would thereafter proceed directly to Augsburg from Italy.

But Luther himself would not be able to go. Charles had provided safe passage to Augsburg for all of the other Protestants—who were technically outlaws—but not for Martin Luther himself. It was not merely disdain for the arch outlaw Luther that influenced him in this decision. He rightly believed that Luther's presence at the diet would be unavoidably incendiary. So Luther's plan was to travel as far as Nuremberg and stay there during the proceedings. That was only seventy-five miles away, and messages and updates on what was happening could be delivered to him, and he could weigh in on what he thought best and then send his advice back to the diet. But as it happened, Nuremberg would not have him. Protecting a known heretic and imperial criminal was further than they were willing to go. So although they genially wished Luther well, they would not be able to accommodate him. So in his plans concerning the diet, Luther must now retreat all the way to Coburg. Although it is today within the borders of Bavaria, Coburg was during that time the southernmost castle outpost in Saxony and would therefore be safe. But alas it was 150 miles from Augsburg, so getting news to Luther, and getting

Luther's response to that news, would be precisely twice as difficult. His opinions and advice would be vital, but there was nothing to be done about it, and much to prepare in the meantime.

With the emperor in attendance, this diet might serve as something like a church council, where ecclesiastical matters and doctrinal differences were debated and resolved. This was something the pope deeply resented. The very idea of an emperor meddling in such things was a clear case of imperial state overreach in the affairs of the church. But the lines between what constituted church and state had never been fuzzier. Besides, there was little Pope Clement could do about it.

Luther, Melanchthon, Bugenhagen, and Jonas began preparing a statement of their evangelical faith that they would present at the diet. It seems likely that Luther wrote the accompanying letter in which he clarified that their faith was not "seditious" and did not therefore rise to the level in which the governing authorities must step in. Luther was trying to establish what the lines between church and state should be from a biblical viewpoint. He rightly believed that the Scriptures had much to say on this subject, and what they seemed to say was that the sphere of the empire and state did not extend as far as a person's religious beliefs, provided those beliefs were not openly seditious. If the believer complied with the rules and laws of the empire and lesser governmental authorities—if he rendered unto Caesar the things that were Caesar's—then "Caesar" or "Tsar" or "Kaiser"* must allow him to "render unto God the things that are God's." So Luther was from the Gospels themselves establishing what would become the future idea of religious liberty that the American founders would enshrine in the U.S. Constitution.

Luther wished to be clear that his faith was never meant to be a threat to the peace and the order either of Saxony or of the empire. Therefore they should be allowed to practice that faith without the governmental authorities taking offense or action against it. In making this case, Luther always had difficulty separating himself from such as Müntzer, who had been more than a threat to the peace and order of Germany, and it is one of the reasons he so hated Müntzer and his ilk: they made it only more difficult for genuine Christians to live out their faith. Nonetheless, Luther consistently maintained that the Bible he read ordered him to

* "Tsar" and "Kaiser" are derivations of "Caesar."

respect the governing authorities—as per Romans 13:1–7—so any kind of rebellion was not possible. This was also why Luther was willing to die for his faith and why he exhorted other Christians to be willing to die for their faith too; it was not something for which they could take up arms. Luther had done all he could to make this case to Elector John and to Philip of Hesse, saying that the time for them all to rebel against the Catholic forces—to take up arms, even in self-defense—was not yet near. But Luther was not clear on whether that time would ever come or, theologically, whether it ever could.

So this statement of faith that Luther and the others now presented at the diet was in essence a listing of those items they felt immutable and that differed from the Roman church's teaching. This list included marriage of the clergy, rejection of the idea of the Mass as a sacrifice, the Lord's Supper in both kinds to everyone, and the end of monastic communities. There were a few additional things, as well as a clear statement that the "Sacramentarians"—meaning those who did not believe in the Real Presence as Luther did—were not of the evangelical party. On April 4, they left Wittenberg. Luther, Jonas, and Melanchthon traveled first to Torgau, where the elector, Spalatin, Agricola, and others joined them. The journey then carried them through Grimma, Altenburg, Eisenberg, Jena, and Weimar. They stopped in Weimar for four days, where on Palm Sunday Luther preached. He preached there on the following two days as well, and then they proceeded to Coburg. They arrived on Easter Eve in time for Luther to preach there too.

When Luther arrived at the high Coburg Castle—and was abandoned by all his friends, who continued on to the diet—he must have felt very much as though he were again at the Wartburg. And perhaps in homage to that previous season in his life, he once again disguised himself somewhat by sprouting the second of two beards separated by nine years. He wrote:

> The loftiest dwelling that towers over the castle is completely ours. Besides, to us have been entrusted the keys to every sort of conclave. More than thirty men, they say, are fed here. Twelve of them are the night watch, and two trumpeters are lookouts on the several towers. So what? Alas, I have nothing else to write about. Tonight, I hope, the warden or the marksman will come by and maybe I'll pick up some news.

We have finally arrived at our Sinai, dearest Philip, but we shall make a Zion out of this Sinai and construct here three huts:* one for the Psalter, one for the Prophets, and one for Aesop. . . . To be sure, the place is extremely pleasant and most suitable for study, except that your absence makes it a sad spot.[7]

With his mention of the "three huts," Luther was referring to the three things he planned to work on while here. Luther had always had a fondness for Aesop's fables, but many editions included things that were unsuitable for children, and so he planned his own translation, hoping it would be used by families together in the evenings. Luther was less concerned with the morals of the stories than with the realistic pictures they gave of the fallen world in which we lived. He thought it a good way to help children to understand the world, with its various kinds of sinners and sins to be dealt with, "so that you can live wisely and peacefully among wicked people in the treacherous, evil world."[8] Luther obviously wasn't of that tribe that felt children must be restricted to reading Bible stories, nor of that tribe that insists on stories being used as bludgeons toward moral lessons. Just as in his letters from the Wartburg, Luther now entertained his friends with wry observations on the birds all around him:

> Here you might see proud kings, dukes, and other noblemen of the kingdom who seriously care for their belongings and offspring and who with untiring voice proclaim their decisions and dogmas through the air. Finally, they do not live, or rather they are not locked up in, such holes and caves as you people call (with but little reason) palaces. Rather, they live under the open sky, so that the sky itself serves them as a paneled ceiling, the green trees as a floor of limitless variety, and the walls [of their palaces] are identical with the ends of the earth.[9]

Luther dragged the joke forward, never stopping. "I have not yet seen nor heard their emperor," he writes. And then, "Like knights they preen themselves, wipe their bill, and flap their wings, as if anticipating victory and honor [in their raids] against grain and malted barley."[10]

On the wall, Luther painted or chalked the words of Psalm 118: "I

---

* Luther is referencing the New Testament passage in which Jesus is on the Mount of Transfiguration. Peter is awestruck by Jesus's appearance and says that they should construct three huts (usually translated "booths" or "tabernacles") so that they could stay there.

shall not die, but live, and proclaim the works of the Lord."[11] These words had particular meaning for Luther and were even at some point set to music by his friend Ludwig Senfl, at Luther's request

As happened a decade earlier in the Wartburg, Luther turned his silence to writing productively.

One of his first projects was a pamphlet self-explanatorily titled *Exhortation to All Clergy Assembled at Augsburg for the Imperial Diet of 1530.* Though he might not be at the diet in person, his thoughts would not long be absent. He finished the manuscript on May 12 and immediately sent it back the four-day, 150-mile journey to Wittenberg, where it was quickly printed and the five hundred copies promptly taken the 300 miles to Augsburg, where they quickly sold out.

As ever, it was strong tea:

> Have you forgotten that at Worms the German nobility presented His Imperial Majesty with about four hundred grievances against the clergy and declared openly that if His Imperial Majesty did not wish to abolish such abuses, they would do so themselves, for they could not long endure them?[12]

He reminded them that much he had said—and especially his original attacks on indulgences and monasticism—had been met with great approval by the common people, who knew the truth of them and were glad someone was pointing them out.

> But who among all of you would ever have repented for such frightful abomination, would ever have sighed or would ever have moistened an eye? Yes, now like hardened, unrepentant men you want to pretend that you never did any evil. Now you have come to Augsburg and want to persuade us that the Holy Spirit is with you and will accomplish great things through you (although in your whole lifetime you have done Christendom nothing but harm) and that he will thereafter lead you straight to heaven with all such abominations, unrepented and defended besides, as though he had to rejoice over you who have served your god-belly so gloriously and laid waste his church so miserably. For this reason you have no success and also shall have none until you repent and mend your ways.[13]

One cannot help but wonder whether such strong language pushed these recipients away from what Luther said or indeed succeeded in bringing any of them to reconsider their views, which might have led to conviction and repentance. In any case, Jonas was hugely pleased with it and told Luther so, calling the work "unexpected, wonderful, and powerful."[14] But when one reads the details, one can see how the corruption and hypocrisy must have been enraging to anyone with a soul. Luther talks, for example, of the particular outrageousness of the "butter-letters," which were letters of indulgence that granted the purchaser the privilege of eating an unlimited amount of foods otherwise forbidden during Lent.

On and on he thundered, aiming particular fire at the single lie that lay at the rotten black heart of it all, that men and women could themselves "make satisfaction" for their own sins, that the free gift of God's grace did not exist, and that Jesus had therefore suffered and died in vain. "This doctrine," he wrote, "has filled hell and has troubled the kingdom of Christ more horribly than the Turk or the whole world could ever do. . . . Alas, where are the tongues and voices that can say enough about this?"[15]

His ending is a chilling imprecation, and one wonders who reading it could fail at least to see that here was a man who believed in something, for whom life was more than a search for comfort:

> Your blood be on your own head! We are and want to be innocent of your blood and damnation, since we pointed out to you sufficiently your wrongs, faithfully admonished to repentance, prayed sincerely, and offered to the uttermost all that could serve the cause of peace, seeking and desiring nothing else than the one comfort for our souls, the free, pure gospel. Therefore we may boast with a good conscience that the fault has not been ours. But may the God of peace and comfort give you his Spirit, to direct and lead you to all truth through our Lord Jesus Christ.[16]

One night while at the Coburg, Luther had a powerful dream in which he lost a tooth, but the size of the tooth filled him with amazement. Such dreams were generally taken as portents of an impending death, and indeed two days later Luther was staggered to receive word of his own father's death.

The letter informing him arrived on June 5 and was from his lifelong Mansfeld friend Hans Reinecke. According to Veit Dietrich, who was staying with him at the Coburg, as soon as he read it, he took his Psalter, went into his bedchamber, and "crie[d] so much that he could not think clearly the next day."[17]

Luther wrote to Melanchthon:

> Even though it comforts me that my father, strong in faith in Christ, fell gently asleep, yet sadness of heart and the memory of the most loving dealings with him have shaken me in the innermost parts of my being, so that seldom if ever have I despised death as much as I do now. . . . Since I am now too sad, I am writing no more, for it is right and God-pleasing for me as a son to mourn such a father, from whom the Father of mercies has brought me forth and through whose sweat [the Creator] has fed and raised me to whatever I am. I rejoice that he has lived until now so that he could see the light of truth.[18]

Not long thereafter, Luther wrote a letter to his four-year-old son, Hänschen. Luther had deputized Hieronymus Weller, one of the students living with them at the Black Cloister, to be the boy's tutor, and when Weller let Luther know that Hans had been doing well, Luther felt moved to write him:

> I know of a pretty, beautiful, and cheerful garden where there are many children wearing little golden coats. They pick up fine apples, pears, cherries, and yellow and blue plums under the trees; they sing, jump, and are merry. They also have nice ponies with golden reins and saddles. I asked the owner of the garden whose children they were. He replied: "These are children who like to pray, study, and be good." Then I said: "Dear sir, I also have a son, whose name is Hänschen Luther. Might he also be permitted to enter the garden, so that he too could eat such fine apples and pears, and ride on these pretty ponies, and play with these children?" Then the man answered: "If he likes to pray, study, and be good, he too may enter the garden along with Lippus and Jost."[19]

Because Veit was with Luther during much of his time at the Coburg, his loneliness was not nearly as pronounced as it had been at the Wartburg nine years before. But Veit wrote to Kathie Luther,

> Dear and gracious Mrs. Luther:
> Rest assured that your lord and we are hale and hearty by God's grace. You did well to send the doctor the portrait [of his daughter,

Magdalena], for it diverts him from his worries. He has nailed it on the wall opposite the table where we eat in the elector's apartment. At first he could not quite recognize her. "Dear me," said he, "Lenchen is too dark." But he likes the picture now, and more and more comes to see that it is Lenchen. She is strikingly like Hans in the mouth, eyes, and nose, and in fact in the whole face, and will come to look even more like him. I just had to write you this.[20]

Luther's physical problems continued to plague him, and not a little. In May, he again suffered from headaches and ringing in his ears, which sometimes was so severe it seemed to him like roaring thunder. And there was more *Anfechtungen*. Luther knew that the devil was behind it and often said as much in his letters. "All right," he wrote, "if [the devil] devours me he shall devour a laxative (God willing) which will make his bowels and anus too tight for him. Do you want to bet? One has to suffer if he wants to possess Christ."[21]

Luther welcomed many visitors during this time, so many in fact that he was worried someone would give his location away. In May, he received Wenceslas Linck and others. Hans Reinecke visited too. Then Argula von Grumbach paid a visit. Among other things, she had advice about weaning their new daughter, Magdalena (Lenchen), which Luther passed along in a letter to Kathie. At the end of June, a few weeks after their father's death, Luther's younger brother Jakob stopped by. In September, Luther was visited by the crown prince John Frederick, who was Duke John's son, and who would become the elector upon his father's death. But Luther's beard baffled the young John Frederick, so much so that at first he didn't recognize Luther at all. Luther sometimes wore glasses now too, to help him read. From Wittenberg, Christian Döring had sent him a new pair of them, which he crankily reckoned "the worst of them all."

It was not until June 15 that the emperor finally arrived at the diet he had called. The procession with which he traveled was like a small city unto itself, flaunting no fewer than one thousand infantry and a phalanx of personal bodyguards. In the rear marched a retinue of "cooks, apothecaries, falconers," and finally—befitting a Spaniard—a monstrous pack of two hundred Spanish dogs. The emperor himself sat astride a milk-white horse under a golden canopy and was arrayed all in gold and carrying a golden sword. It was transfixing and sobering to witness the majesty—and both the implicit and the explicit might—of the empire in this grandest of grand displays. Those in the small group of Protestants attending who saw it understood what it was they dared to defy. If God was not with them, they were certainly in trouble. A few days hence, Jonas would write, "The emperor is surrounded by cardinals . . . they are in his palace every day, and there is a swarm of priests like bees around him, who burn with hatred against us."[22] But now that Charles and his thousands had at last arrived at Augsburg, the real business of the diet would be attended to with all alacrity.

Melanchthon had written what has come to be known as the *Augsburg Confession*, which was to be and indeed has been the official summation of what all Lutherans believe. On June 23, the Lutheran theologians and princes gathered for a final reading of the document and signatures, although only the princes, other nobles, and those who officially represented territories and cities were to sign. It most likely was presented to the emperor on the following day, and on the afternoon of the twenty-fifth the German translation was read aloud with everyone in attendance, including the emperor himself, who understood German, but poorly, so that the profusion of meaningless Teutonic syllables—like the wordless lullaby of a bird's song—soon lured him deep into the forest of a well-documented snooze.

Luther soon received a report of the event from Melanchthon, in which Melanchthon asked Luther what he thought might still be conceded, to which Luther unsurprisingly answered: nothing. Luther praised Melanchthon's great work and did not suggest that anything be changed, although he did wish that the *Confession* had more fulsomely rejected the authority of the pope. To be sure, this would have made it impossible for the emperor to accept the document, and Melanchthon very much hoped to craft something that would make it possible for the Lutherans to go about their business. Luther was just as inclined to go to war—or rather, to offend who would be offended and accept whatever consequences should follow, including his own martyrdom. Melanchthon was of a different view.

On July 15, Luther wrote to Jonas, Spalatin, Melanchthon, and Agricola, counseling them to fold up their tents and return home to Wittenberg:

> I believe that by now you have the answer of the opponents, which,
> as you write, you were expecting; that is, you will have to hear
> "fathers, fathers, fathers, church, church, church, usage, custom."*

---

* A proper contemporary translation capturing the flavor of Luther's sarcasm might better read, "Yada yada yada church fathers yada yada yada church yada yada yada tradition."

Moreover you will hear nothing taken from Scripture. Based on these arbiters and witnesses, the Emperor will pronounce a verdict against you. Then will follow threats and boasting. . . .[23]

Luther went on to say they had already done more than should be expected: they had "rendered unto Caesar" by appearing at the diet and faithfully doing all they had done, and they had "rendered unto God" by preparing the *Augsburg Confession,* in which they had made clear what they believed, which also had the effect of exposing those on the other side to the truth. Thus "those who do not believe are without excuse."[24] "Therefore," Luther wrote, "in the name of the Lord I free you from this diet. Home, and again, home!" In other words, Luther was fed up with the haggling he knew was going on and suspected that Melanchthon was all too eager to continue in the vain hopes of some agreement Luther knew he would never get. Campeggio, the papal legate, had told Melanchthon that he himself had the authority to make some concessions regarding the issue of priests getting married and the issue of "communion in both kinds," but Luther knew this all to be a sickening waste of time: "To Campeggio's boast that he has the power to grant dispensations, I reply with Amsdorf's words: 'I shit on the legate and his lord's [the pope's] dispensations; we shall find sufficient dispensations [elsewhere].'" He concluded the letter with "Home, home! May the Lord Jesus preserve and comfort you, who for his name's sake have worked hard, and have been sufficiently afflicted. Amen." And in a final playful fillip—because he never in these letters revealed his location in print—he teasingly listed his location as "Gruboc"—which was simply the name of his location spelled backward.[25]

But Luther's team was not nearly ready to depart the diet, and he would himself not be free to leave the Coburg Castle until the first days of October. By August 3, the twenty Catholic theologians were required to formulate a response to the *Confession,* which they did, and this was read to the diet on that day. It was called the *Confutation,* and it seemed to concede that much of what was in the *Confession* was from Scripture and therefore unassailable, but of course it did not agree that what the Lutherans termed "abuses"—such as required celibacy for clergy and Communion taken only in one kind for laity—were indeed abuses. Melanchthon now set to work writing a rebuttal to the *Confutation,* which he titled the *Apology,* of course using the word in the ancient Greek and Socratic sense, and not in our modern sense of expressing regrets and contrition.

On September 8, Luther wrote one of many letters to Kathie:

> I am really amazed that someone has told you I am ill, [because]
> you [can] see with your own eyes the books I am writing. For I
> have finished [translating all] the prophets, except for Ezekiel; I
> am working on [that] now, and [also] on a sermon on the
> sacrament, not to speak of the writing of letters and whatever
> more there is to be done.
>
> I could not write any more now because of the hurry. Greet
> everyone and all! I have for Hansen Luther a big fine piece of
> sugar which Cyriac has brought from Nürnberg.[26]

It is staggering to think that he had been as productive as indeed he
had during this time, given all of his interruptions from visitors and his
ongoing maladies. The translation of the Bible moved forward apace, and
the entire extraordinary work would be published in a single volume in
1534. In the letter's last line, Luther was referring to his nephew Cyriac
Kaufmann, who was staying with him during this time but who he
thought would appreciate being able to see the great pomp and circumstance of the diet, so he sent him there. And finally, making a joke of his
literary productivity, he literally used the phrase "big fine book of sugar."

The *Confutation* was ready by September 22, when the emperor invited the delegates to the bishop's palace, where he would give the final
verdict on the Lutherans' *Confession*. The document was indeed ready on
time and given to the emperor, who read it and was obviously unmoved.
When they were all gathered, he announced that the *Confutation* had
indeed confuted—which is to say, refuted—the *Confession*, and that was
all there was to be said.

The Lutherans were now informed that they had until April of the
following year to decide whether they would return to the papal fold. But
they immediately and officially rejected the imperial verdict. One of the
Saxon counselors, George Brück, was the one to speak and say so. And
he then proffered a copy of Melanchthon's answer to the *Confutation*—
his *Apology*—to the emperor. But as the emperor put his hand out to
take it, someone—likely his brother, the Archduke Ferdinand—pulled
the imperial hand back and whispered into his ear. And so it was refused.

This was another deadlock, so perhaps the can would once more be
kicked down history's road to a church council. Still, there was a simple

political question to be discussed. Would the emperor and all of the Catholic princes in the next year attempt to strike against the Lutheran princes and at last end the rebellion by force as promised in the Edict of Worms in 1521? Would they do this after April 15, when the Lutheran princes officially gave their answer to Charles's ultimatum? Again Philip of Hesse proposed an alliance of the Reformation factions so that they would be prepared for this eventuality, and Duke John agreed that something must be done.

Duke John and Spalatin, along with Melanchthon, Jonas, and the rest of the Wittenbergers, arrived at Coburg on October 1, and three days later they left with Luther for Torgau and Wittenberg. But Duke John summoned them all back to Torgau later in the month to discuss Philip of Hesse's proposal for a league to be formed—an alliance—in anticipation of a military attack from Charles's forces.

At this meeting, Luther was able to come around on the question of whether it was possible to form an alliance whose purpose was potential armed resistance to the emperor. But what had changed for him on this? One statement of his gives us a clue: "If princes as princes are permitted to resist the emperor, let it be a matter of their judgement and their conscience. Such resistance is certainly not permitted to a Christian who has died to the world." The problem with this logic is that it seems to contradict Luther's larger formulation, that there are no classes of Christians as in the Catholic world, where priests form a certain superior class, along with monks and nuns, and all outside that circle are second-class laymen. To be a Christian, for Luther, was to subscribe to universal ideas and to be part of a "royal priesthood" that was the "priesthood of all believers." How was it that the princes, whom he knew to be serious Christians, should be allowed to step outside the rules of other Christians, like himself? Luther's theology never pushed forward on this issue of the precise boundaries between church and state, so those who belonged to the church—which is to say all true Christians—were not given clear parameters on when they were permitted to take up arms against the state. Dietrich Bonhoeffer would four centuries later bump up against this again and would do his best to resolve the dilemma and formulate a solution, but by then he was so far ahead of the Lutheran ministers in Germany that they could not follow him, and the National Socialists had no resistance from the churches and were able to do as they liked.

On the last day of 1530, the league was officially formed in the town of

Schmalkalden—and thenceforth unpleasantly dubbed the Schmalkaldic League—and that next February Duke John and Philip of Hesse signed the actual documents. But as April drew near and the answer from the German princes came due, Luther wrote his *Warning to His Dear German People*. But again, the circumstances of imperial politics served up an unexpected boon to the Lutherans. Archbishop Albrecht of Mainz and another Catholic elector had approached Charles, asking him whether they could have further negotiations with the Protestants. Charles would have preferred not to do this, but he needed their two votes to guarantee that his brother, Archduke Ferdinand, would be elected the next king of Germany. He also continued to need their help in fighting the Turks, so he complied, and yet again the threat was lifted from the Protestant princes. Now it was the Edict of Augsburg that had hung over their heads rather than the Edict of Worms, but with these new negotiations to come, they were free to do as they had done and the Reformation was given still more room to grow.

CHAPTER TWENTY-ONE

Confronting Death

Do not be disturbed by people to whom Christ is just
a joke and a laughingstock . . . they live on, certain of
everything and untroubled by the devil. Why should
he bother them? They already belong to him.

—Martin Luther

IN 1531, WHEN he heard from his brother Jakob that his mother was
quite ill, Luther on May 20 sent her a letter, quite like the one he had
written to his father a year earlier. It is a particular measure of the
man to see Luther comfort his mother as he does:

My dearly beloved [from the heart] Mother! I have received my
brother [Jakob's] letter concerning your illness. Of course this
grieves me deeply, especially because I cannot be with you in
person, as I certainly would like to be.

He went on to preach to her in his way, saying that she well knows
that this sickness is God's "fatherly, gracious chastisement" and that she
should know it is a small one that he allows, and then he reminds her to
seek comfort in "Jesus Christ, the cornerstone," writing, "He will not
waver or fail us nor allow us to sink or perish." And then he confronted
death directly:

Let us therefore now rejoice with all assurance and gladness, and
should any thought of sin or death frighten us, let us in opposition
to this lift up our hearts and say: "Behold, dear soul, what are you
doing? Dear death, dear sin, how is it that you are alive and terrify
me? Do you not know that you have been overcome? Do you,

death, not know that you are quite dead? Do you not know the
One who says of you: "I have overcome the world?"[1]

Not long after receiving this letter, Luther's mother died. And then
on November 9, Kathie gave birth to a fourth child, a son whom they
named Martin junior, presumably because he was born a day before his
father's birthday. It is also likely that he was baptized two days later, on
St. Martin's Day too.

In August 1532, Duke John was at his hunting lodge in Schweinitz
when he suffered a stroke. Luther and Melanchthon heard of it and hastened the twenty miles from Wittenberg to be with him. They prayed
with him and consoled him, but the next morning he lay dead. It was
usual to use balsam for embalming—indeed the word "embalm" comes
from "balm" and "balsam," an aromatic resinous tree—and because none
could be had in Schweinitz, the body was speedily carried to Wittenberg.*

Then, in 1534, Pope Clement died, but his successor, Paul III, put
forth plans for a church council in Mantua in 1537, although it would
never actually happen. But already in 1535, plans for it were moving ahead,
and the papal nuncio Paolo Vergerio traveled to Wittenberg to meet
with Luther to discuss it. Luther was so tickled that a papal legate had
dragged his Roman corpus all the way to Wittenberg to meet him that
he knew he must be properly outfitted for the occasion. Thus he had
himself barbered to a dandy fare-thee-well, as he sometimes did before
important sermons. He was trimmed, shaved, and bathed and then be-
decked himself in a doublet decorated with fur and a robe sumptuously
lined with fur, and he wore the fine hose of a nobleman. He loaded his
fingers with borrowed rings and punctuated the gaudy costume with a
gold pendant so eye-poppingly large that even the barber made bold to
tut-tut his disapproval. And rather than walking the short distance to
the city gate to meet Vergerio, as he might typically have done, Luther
rode there grandly in a carriage with Bugenhagen. Vergerio himself arrived with twenty horsemen.

In a January 1536 letter to Caspar Müller, Luther referenced a document (drafted by Melanchthon) that was the Schmalkaldic League's response to a question from Vergerio about whether the proposed church
council might be held outside Germany. The answer was a flat negative,

---

* His son, John Frederick, who succeeded Duke John, soon after his father's death bequeathed to Luther and Kathie the entirety of the Black Cloister.

because they knew that were the council held on their ground, it would be far less likely that the pope would have undue influence in what transpired. Luther wrote that he could not put his hand to a copy of the document—which he would like to send along to Müller—because at that very moment he was suffering from a coughing fit. He then joked that if Müller would only pray for him, he was sure the coughing would stop and he could find the document.

Three months later, Luther wrote to Thomas Cromwell, at that time the most powerful man in England—save the king—and one of the chief architects of the English Reformation. Cromwell hoped to bring England into the Schmalkaldic League so that England could stand with it against the pope and the emperor, but this was not to be. But Robert Barnes, who had just left Wittenberg, had raised Luther's hopes along these lines and had sent greetings from Cromwell, which Luther now returned:

> Doctor Barnes has . . . made me extraordinarily happy in telling
> me of Your Lordship's earnest and determined will regarding the
> cause of Christ, especially since because of your prestige, by
> which you are capable of accomplishing very many things
> through the whole kingdom and with the Most Serene Lord
> King, you can do much good. I do pray and I shall pray to the
> Lord to strengthen abundantly his work, begun in Your
> Lordship, to his glory and the salvation of many. Amen.[2]

It was soon decided that the Schmalkaldic League would not send a delegation to England—which would have included Melanchthon. In June, when the shocking news of Anne Boleyn's trial and subsequent beheading made its way to Wittenberg, which Luther called "that absolutely monstrous tragedy in England,"[3] it served to confirm them in their decision.

In that same year of 1536, Erasmus died. He was sixty-nine years old. And in Antwerp, the English Reformer William Tyndale was imprisoned and questioned by the same man—Jacob van Hoogstraten—who had questioned and murdered the Lutheran priests so many years before. Tyndale was then sentenced to be burned, but for some reason, while bound to the stake, he was first strangled to death before his body was burned. He had dared to write against Cardinal Wolsey and against King Henry VIII's marriage to Anne Boleyn. Cardinal Wolsey had condemned him as a heretic. But before his death he had translated the Bible into English and smuggled many copies into England and Scotland, spreading the Reformation there.

By the late 1530s, Luther's health continued to decline to the point that his body had become a bright constellation of pains and difficulties. The rich diet he had been eating most of his life had caused an accretion in his joints of uric acid—the condition commonly known as gout—and at one point the pain in his large toe was such that he loudly threatened to cut it off. But in 1537, his gout was the worst it had ever been. Nor did kidney stones cease to plague him, and he passed an especially large one on February 8, causing much bleeding. Ten days later, another one made it impossible for him to urinate, and he nearly died. The situation was dangerously exacerbated when the elector's doctor curiously prescribed large amounts of water, which Luther dutifully drank. Afterward, he was dosed with a fresh concoction of garlic and pure manure. The pain soon became so excruciating that Luther prayed for death, and he was soon put on a wagon to return to Wittenberg to die. But the terrible jostling and jangling of the wagon on the bumpy winter roads somehow must have caused the stone blocking his urinary functioning to be jarred free and as with the fabled rock struck by Moses at Horeb, the dammed-up waters at last found egress. Luther now urinated with spirited abandon. No fewer than four quarts gushed forth, and Luther survived. That night in Wittenberg he proclaimed, "Luther lives!"

As the Reformation continued to spread, Luther sometimes now found himself being honored in various ways, as when a book was published in 1539 containing all of his German writings. Luther was asked to write a preface to it and in it made fun of himself and all authors, who he well knew were tempted to take overweening pride in their great works. Here is a famous passage from that preface:

> If, however, you feel you have made it, flattering yourself with your own little books, teaching, or writing, because you have done beautifully and preached excellently . . . if you perhaps look for praise, you are of that stripe, dear friend then take yourself by the ears, and if you do this in the right way you will find a beautiful pair of big, long, shaggy donkey ears. Then do not spare any expense! Decorate them with golden bells, so that people will be able to hear you wherever you go, point their fingers at you, and say, "See, See! There goes that clever beast, who can write such

exquisite books and preach so remarkably well." That very moment you will be blessed and blessed beyond measure in the kingdom of heaven.[4]

The Death of Lenchen, *Aetatis* 58

In late August 1542, Luther sent his sixteen-year-old son, Johannes—whom they called Hans—to the Latin school in Torgau, twenty-two miles away. There he was to study grammar and music. Along with him came his cousin Florian, who was Kathie's nephew and who had been living with them in Wittenberg for some time. But a few weeks later, Luther's thirteen-year-old daughter, Magdalena, fell ill quite suddenly with a high fever. She was otherwise perfectly healthy, but the illness was so severe that they sensed she was dying. They immediately summoned Hans to come home from Torgau. Luther sent a carriage to fetch him.

Magdalena—whom they called Lenchen—was especially dear to Luther and Kathie, not least because she had been born not long after the death of their first daughter, Elisabeth. Luther went to his beloved Lenchen's bedside and asked her, "You would like to stay here with me, your father, but are you also willing to go to that other father, or not?" Her reply was that she wanted whatever her earthly father wished. While at his daughter's bedside, Luther reportedly said,

> The spirit is willing but the flesh is weak. I love her very much.... In the last thousand years God has given to no bishop such great gifts as God has given me (for one should boast of God's gifts). I am angry with myself that I am unable to rejoice from my heart and be thankful to God, though I do at times sing a little song and give thanks. Whether we live or die, we belong to God.[5]

Here was the very wound at the heart of human existence: even when we know as much as or more than anyone else of the truth of God, we are nonetheless sufficiently mired in the fallenness of this world so that we are unable fully to comprehend what we know to be true. Lenchen died in her father's arms at 9:00 a.m. It was September 20. Melanchthon was there, as was Kathie, who reportedly sobbed uncontrollably for days. And young Hans was likely there, as was George Rörer.

When Lenchen was placed into her coffin, Luther said, "Go ahead and close it! She will rise again on the last day!" And when the coffin was carried out of their home, he said to those in attendance, "Do not be sorrowful! I have sent a saint to heaven!" Then he recalled their infant Elisabeth, who had died fourteen years before, and said, "In fact, I have now sent two of them!" Luther composed a poem for her epitaph:

> I, Lenchen, Luther's beloved girl
> Sleep among the saints of the world
> And lie here at peace and rest,
> For now I am our God's own guest.

> A child of death I was, 'tis true
> From mortal seed my mother bore me through;
> Now I live and am rich with God.
> And so I thank Christ's death and blood.[6]

Earlier that year, Luther had revised his will and decided to buck convention by leaving everything he had not to his eldest son but to his dear Kathie, whom he esteemed tremendously. This is yet another example of how Luther valued women more than most men of his time did, and how he especially esteemed his beloved Kathie. It was around this time that he quipped, "I would not give up my Kathie for France or for Venice." Luther also wrote in his commentary on Genesis, "With the woman who has been joined to me by God I may jest, have fun, and converse more pleasantly." But in revising his will, Luther made clear that he believed a mother should be honored by her children as the Bible commanded, and for her to be financially dependent upon them, as was usually the case, went against this. "A mother," he declared, "is the best guardian for children."

But it was always around death that Luther's faith shone brightest. From an account in one of the *Table Talk* volumes, we have Luther's words as he consoles a man on his deathbed:

> God will not forsake you. He is not a tyrant who holds a good, crude blunder against you either, not even blasphemy when you are in distress, or denial of God, such as Peter committed and Paul too. Do not be disturbed by people to whom Christ is just a joke and a laughingstock . . . they live on, certain of everything and untroubled by the devil. Why

should he bother them? They already belong to him. You and I are the
ones he would like to seize. Now how will he do that? He will continue
attacking you with small things until he gets to your substance. But resist
him. He who is with us is greater than he who is in the world.[7]

Luther and the Jews

Without question, one of the most bizarre episodes of Luther's life concerns his writings at the very end of his life on the subject of the Jews. No
scholar in five centuries has been able to make sense of the worst of what
he said, mainly because it flatly contradicts much of what he had written
on the subject earlier in his life. In fact, early in life Luther hoped that the
Reformation would help many of the European Jews see that the Christians who had so mistreated and reviled them were not actual Christians
at all, but were merely Gentile hypocrites. In 1519, he wondered why Jews
would ever consider converting to the Christian faith given the "cruelty
and enmity we wreak on them—that in our behavior towards them we
less resemble Christians than beasts." In 1523, he wrote a treatise titled
"That Jesus Christ Was Born a Jew" in which he wrote,

> If I had been a Jew and had seen such dolts and blockheads govern and
> teach the Christian faith, I would sooner have become a hog than a Chris-
> tian. They have dealt with the Jews as if they were dogs rather than hu-
> man beings, they have done little else than deride them and seize their
> property.[8]

But the perplexing irony is that in his bilious later years, Luther
seemed to be advocating precisely this and worse. In his superlatively
intemperate and vile *On the Jews and Their Lies*, he angrily advocates setting fire to their synagogues, destroying their houses, and even confiscat-
ing their prayer books and money. Whatever leanings Luther had toward
religious liberty are here flushed into the sea, and we are left to wonder
how it could be possible that the same person could write things that not
only are different from but seem violently to contradict each other.

If it hadn't been for the Nazis, almost no one would ever have heard of
these writings. When Luther wrote them, he had little idea that four
centuries in the future a political malevolence would rise up in his

beloved Germany and that its most diabolical proponents would ferret out from the mountains of his writings those few passages of his most injudicious writings to aid their cause. Or that that diabolical cause would end with the murder of six million Jewish noncombatants in as cold-blooded and calculated a manner as anything in the history of the world. That the Nazis' cynical master of propaganda would find the few vile words Luther had written against Jews and broadcast them to the world, ignoring the 110 volumes of Luther's other writings, is of course fathomlessly cynical. Even at the time, those who knew Luther's other works very well either were unaware of this pamphlet or simply ignored it, feeling that it was such a strange outlier it could hardly be understood rationally.

Still, the main question remains: How is it that someone so very focused on the love and grace of God for so much of his life could come to say things that seem to contradict what he said earlier in life? It almost beggars belief, but because we have the texts and cannot avoid them, these writings force us to ask whether a person's life can be seen as a whole or must be taken in parts, as though we were not one person who can be perceived as a single person throughout our lives, but can be some concatenation of persons spread throughout our lifetimes. If the devil was at work in Luther's weaknesses—in his body and mind and soul—in tempting Luther to write such things, he could never have been more effective. If he had bided his time those many years only to tempt Luther to give in to his basest emotions, he was successful, for what he accomplished not merely would help the Nazis justify what they did to the Jews, which is itself the standard by which we measure human evil, but also would cause millions to read with a jaundiced eye every good thing Luther had ever written before. It is all a disorienting Möbius strip of contradictions.

Thus making sense of his late statements against the Jews seems impossible. Half of what Luther wrote in that lamentable pamphlet was based on things he obviously earnestly believed, but which we now know to be untrue. For example, much of what he wrote took its lead from books such as *Victory over the Godless Hebrews*, written by a Carthusian monk named Salvagus Porchetus around 1300. According to this and other books, Jews blasphemed against Jesus and Mary, which Luther felt must not be tolerated. Modern shibboleths regarding freedoms of speech and religion were unthinkable in his day, and Luther felt that not to expel the Jews from Saxony was in some way to aid and abet such blasphemies. The Porchetus book catalogs one of the blasphemies against Jesus as the accusation that he had used kabbalistic magic to perform his miracles—until he was at last exposed and executed. In these writings, Mary was called a "whore" or a "dung heap" and was said to have given birth to Jesus while menstruating. Porchetus—and therefore Luther—believed that all Jews hoped their true Messiah would come and slay all the Christians. Luther also believed that Jews really did poison wells and abduct children for ritual murders and that they would lead others away from Christ with these terrible lies, which for him was the worst thing imaginable.

And for some final context, we recall that Luther said as vile things about many other groups too. We know that he said extremely foul things about the Muslim Turks, saying for example that their marriages had "all the chastity of a soldier's relations with a prostitute." He accused them of being practitioners of "such Latin and sodomitical unchastity that it is not to be mentioned in front of respectable people," and he called the Koran a "cursed, shameful, desperate" book filled with "dreadful abominations." And what he said of the papists we already know.

If there is the slimmest silver lining in all of this, it might be that we are because of these vilest writings less inclined to make a hagiographic idol out of Luther. We may also take the slight comfort in knowing that a year later he would double back on himself once more and seemingly contradict the gist of what he had written in *The Jews and Their Lies*. In 1544, he rewrote a hymn titled "O, You Poor Judas, What Did You Do?" and added this verse:

> T'was our great sins and misdeeds gross
> Nailed Jesus, God's true Son, to the cross.
> Thus you, poor Judas, we dare not blame,
> Nor the band of Jews; ours is the shame.[9]

So if people wish to see Luther as any kind of run-of-the-mill anti-Semite, they must be disappointed. He rightly lays the blame for Jesus's Crucifixion not on the Jews but on every one of us and on himself, as well he should.

Before we leave this grimmest of subjects, we must realize that our horror at it comes from the deep irony of it, not just the surface irony that a man so dedicated to worship of the Jewish rabbi Jesus should speak in this way of his ethnic children, but the deeper irony that the man who brought the idea of religious liberty and pluralism into the world within his own lifetime did not recognize these as the natural and inevitable and important outworkings of his own discoveries and teachings.

As horrible as all he wrote against the Jews and others can be, perhaps his most execrable fireworks toward the end of his apoplectic life were reserved for the pope, as one might well have expected. In 1545, Luther outdid himself when he wrote *Against the Papacy in Rome*, from which we pluck this choicest morsel:

> The pope is not and cannot be the head of the Christian church. Instead, he is the head of the accursed church of all the worst scoundrels on earth, a vicar of the devil, an enemy of God, and adversary of Christ, a destroyer of Christ's churches; a teacher of lies, blasphemies, and idolatries; an arch church-thief and church robber of the keys and all the goods of both the church and the temporal lords; a murderer of kings and inciter to all kinds of bloodshed; a brothel-keeper over all brothel-keepers and all vermin, even that which cannot be named; an Antichrist, a man of sin and a genuine werewolf.[10]

But to drive this point home yet further—if that were possible—Luther commissioned Cranach to create a dozen woodcuts depicting the extraordinarily vulgar and disgusting things Luther had written about. The horrific images rival Hieronymus Bosch's worst, and some of them have an almost emetic power. In one a brindle-haired grinning demon with tail and breasts defecates half a dozen cardinals, while nearby the pope is suckled by a naked hag with Medusa-like hair. In another, a demon sitting with two confreres atop a gallows defecates a diarrhea of tonsured monks who lie in a jumbled pile, one of whom displays his genitals. In making fun of clerical celibacy, Luther even refers to Pope Paul III as "Her Sodomitical Hellishness Paula III." For anyone interested in such writings, Luther has produced a hatful.

The endless comments recorded in his *Table Talk* conversations offer a smorgasbord of conversational delights, thankfully all infinitely milder. Many of them are undeniably funny, revealing the late-in-life irascibility for which he has, alas, become known. Here are two:

> Someone sent to know whether it was permissible to use warm water in baptism? The Doctor replied: "Tell the blockhead that water, warm or cold, is water."[11]

When one asked, where God was before heaven was created? St Augustin answered: He was in himself. When another asked me the same question, I said: He was building hell for such idle, presumptuous, fluttering, and inquisitive spirits as you.[12]

At this last part of Luther's life, his larger personality came out in almost everything he wrote or said. Here is a Christmas sermon he wrote in his last months. In it he is very much himself, hectoring and scolding the ancient Bethlehem and then browbeating his own Christmas congregation and shaming them:

> The inn was full. No one would release a room to this pregnant woman. She had to go to a cow stall and there bring forth the Maker of all creatures because nobody would give way. Shame on you, wretched Bethlehem! The inn ought to have been burned with brimstone, for even though Mary had been a beggar maid or unwed, anybody at such a time should have been glad to give her a hand. There are many of you in this congregation who think to yourselves: "If only I had been there! How quick I would have been to help the baby! I would have washed his linen! How happy I would have been to go with the shepherds to see the Lord lying in the manger!" Yes you would! You say that because you know how great Christ is, but if you had been there at that time you would have done no better than the people of Bethlehem. Childish and silly thoughts are these! Why don't you do it now? You have Christ in your neighbor. You ought to serve him, for what you do to your neighbor in need you do to the Lord Christ himself.[13]

CHAPTER TWENTY-TWO

"We Are Beggars. This Is True."

The charioteer of Israel has fallen!

—Melanchthon

1546, *Aetatis* 62

LUTHER'S CONNECTION TO Mansfeld was a lifelong one. His mother and father had lived there until their relatively recent deaths, and his brother and sister lived there, both having married and raised families. Luther's connections in Mansfeld and in nearby Eisleben, where he had been born, had always remained strong. So whatever happened there concerned him, and over the years he had had to intercede a number of times with Count Albrecht of Mansfeld. Albrecht himself was an evangelical and had a close relationship with Luther, but in 1536 he had tried to bring the copper-mining industry under his control. Luther's brother Jakob and his brother-in-law Paul Mackenrot both objected to Albrecht's actions, because they had followed in Luther's father's footsteps as mining entrepreneurs. Several times Luther interceded on their behalf, pulling no punches with Albrecht in telling him that his greed in these things would cause him to forfeit God's blessings. He also asked the Mansfeld pastor Coeleus to speak to the count similarly, and in 1542 he sent Albrecht an especially stern pastoral letter. It seems to have so infuriated Albrecht that he threw it to the ground and stomped on it. Later Luther asked one of the Saxon nobles to intervene with Albrecht over a case involving Bartholomew Drachstedt, one of the Eisleben mining entrepreneurs. And then there was a tremendous to-do between Albrecht and his brother Gebhard. It seems that this was the worst of the difficulties, and Luther felt obliged to travel to Eisleben to help them sort out their troubles. He went there with Melanchthon in October 1545 but knew that a return trip would be necessary.

So at the beginning of 1546, Luther decided to make the trip, though this time Melanchthon was unable to join him because of illness. In fact, it was Luther who suggested Melanchthon stay home, fearing that the strain of such a journey could be too much for him, whose health had been poor for a few years. If Melanchthon's life were to end, Luther feared the university would never recover. The journey from Wittenberg was one of more than sixty miles, and Luther—knowing he might be there for two weeks or more—decided to take his three boys with him. He was sixty-two years old. His eldest, Hans, was nineteen; Martin was fourteen; and Paul was thirteen. Because Luther's brother and sister lived in Mansfeld, only nine miles from Eisleben, we may assume the plan was for the boys to spend some time there with their cousins. A week before his departure, on January 17, Luther preached what would be his last sermon from the pulpit at the *Schlosskirche* in Wittenberg. That same day he confessed in a letter to his friend Jakob Propst that he felt "like an old man, decrepit, sluggish, tired, cold, and now also one-eyed." He half joked that he should therefore now be reckoned already dead and said he longed for "the highly deserved rest."[1] But he was not quite finished. On January 23, Luther said good-bye to Kathie and their remaining daughter, Margaret, who was then eleven, and with his boys began the trip to Eisleben.

Luther was also traveling with Johannes Aurifaber, his assistant at that time. When they arrived at Halle on the twenty-fourth, Luther met Justus Jonas, who would join him on the final leg of the trip. While at Halle, Luther preached at the Market Church of Our Lady, not neglecting to take the opportunity to criticize Archbishop Albrecht's formerly vast collection of relics that were here, although the archbishop had himself passed away four months earlier. The following day they decided to leave for Eisleben, but the Saale River was so swollen and the water rushing and boiling so powerfully—with numerous pitching ice floes—that it was unsafe to cross. On the twenty-sixth, still waiting for the waters to subside, Luther preached a second sermon in the church at Halle, but the next day the river was still reckoned unsafe. So at last on the twenty-eighth, the Mansfeld counts sent a troop of sixty horsemen to escort Luther and his party. Once they arrived safely at Eisleben, his three boys were to continue the nine miles to Mansfeld. But just before they entered Eisleben, Luther became quite ill. He wrote about it two days later in his letter to Melanchthon.

"You know that I am an old man, and a man who ought to be retired," he wrote.

> During the trip both a loss of consciousness and that illness which you usually call humor ventriculi [heart palpitations] caught me. For I went on foot, but this was beyond my strength, so that I perspired. Afterwards in the carriage when my shirt also had gotten cold from the sweat, the cold grabbed a muscle in my left arm. From this came that tightness of the heart and something like shortness of breath. It is my own stupid fault. But now I am quite well again, how long—well that of course I do not know, since one cannot trust old age.

It seems that he fell unconscious and was ultimately revived with warm towels. In the same letter, he told Melanchthon of his progress in the negotiations thus far: "With God's help we have slain today the most bristly of all the porcupines . . . though not without a fight."[2]

But in his letter to Kathie the same day, he mentioned only the dizziness. He knew she was worried about him, and with good reasons. During this time, Luther's leg abscess healed, but according to his personal physician, Matthias Ratzenberger, this abscess was in fact a "fontanelle"—meaning it was a place where the bodily humors may escape, which was thought a good thing, and so Ratzenberger advised Luther to keep it perpetually open. But he hadn't brought along the medicine he used for this, and so it began to heal closed, something he was convinced was bad for his overall health. Luther did tell Kathie that he was enjoying the Naumburg beer, which he volunteered afforded him about three excellent bowel movements each morning. He also mentioned in the letter that the dizziness that struck him before entering Eisleben might well have been caused by "the Jews" because just before it happened he had passed through a town in which many Jews were said to live. Luther believed in "spiritual warfare" and demonic attacks, as we have well established, and seemed to think that this might have been an attack of witchcraft on the part of the Jews, who had cursed him, or perhaps a general satanic attack that the Jews' presence might have exacerbated. According to those who had been in the carriage with him at the time of the health issues, he said, "The devil does this to me every time I intend and ought to undertake something important. He . . . attacks me with such a *tentatio* [trial]."[3]

Luther knew that spiritually speaking, he was a marked man and that the devil often harassed him. He said as much in his February 3 letter to Melanchthon, citing the difficulty of the negotiations and then a bizarre event:

> Satan lets loose all his forces. Thus far we have resisted him by prayer. Yesterday after my sermon the chimney of my quarters was set on fire,* no doubt by Satan himself who has very much frightened my poor hosts. I suspect Satan of ridiculing our efforts, or of threatening [us with] something else.[4]

On February 10, Luther wrote to Kathie again, making the chimney fire sound more dangerous than in his previous communication and then telling her that a huge and heavy stone almost brained him during one of his celebrated bowel movements. He explained that mortar in the wall above the toilet had been dripping down, and when someone had come to fix it, he merely touched the wall with two fingers, and the stone—about three feet long and six inches thick—had immediately fallen. Had it fallen of its own accord while Luther was on the toilet, it might well have struck him dead—and right in the cloaca.

Kathie had made it clear in her letters that her worries over her husband at this time were so severe that she was losing sleep over them. Whether these were premonitions of his death, no one can say, but one doesn't get the impression that this sort of thing was typical of her. She knew her husband's health was poor, that this had been an especially bitter winter, and that owing to a recent sudden thaw, causing serious flooding along the route Luther and his sons had to travel, his trip had been perilous. Luther was indeed not well, but he nonetheless never ceased teasing his Kathie about her concerns, although behind the teasing lay a pastor's and husband's concern for his beloved wife:

> To my dear wife, Katherine Luther, doctoress and self-tormentor at Wittenberg, my gracious lady,

---

* Chimney fires, which typically occur when the buildup of creosote in the flue itself catches fire, make a loud roaring sound and can be very dangerous due to the tremendous heat of burning creosote, sometimes even causing the house itself to catch fire.

Grace and peace in the Lord! Read, dear Kathie [the Gospel of] John and [my] Small Catechism, of which you once said: Indeed, everything in this book is said about me. For you want to assume the cares of your God, just as if He were not almighty and were unable to create ten Dr. Martins if this old one were drowned in the Saale or suffocated in a stove.... Leave me in peace with your worrying! I have a better Caretaker than you and all the angels. He it is who lies in a manger and nurses at a virgin's breast, but at the same time sits at the right hand of God, the almighty Father. Therefore be at rest. Amen.[5]

Luther wrote his last letters to Kathie and Melanchthon on the fourteenth. He told Kathie that all was well and that God willing he would begin his return journey that week. He also sent along the gift of some trout he received from the wife of Count Albrecht. He said that his boys were still in Mansfeld with his brother, Jakob, who was taking good care of them.

It seems that it was on this day or the next that he made his famous remark: "If I get back home to Wittenberg, I'll lie down in a coffin and give the maggots a fat doctor to eat." What would be his final sermon was preached either on the fourteenth or the fifteenth of February. He had preached many millions of words from pulpits over the decades, but his final words would be preached sitting down, for sometime during this last sermon his ill health overtook him. He even ended the sermon earlier than he had wished, saying, "This and much more might be said concerning this Gospel, but I am too weak and we shall let it go at that."[6] This was his final sentence from a pulpit.*

Luther had preached four sermons during this time in Eisleben, all at St. Andrew's Church. In each of them, he had emphasized what for him was the central message of his entire life, and the central message at the heart of humanity, that God in Christ offers himself freely to us while we are still sinners. So if we do not understand that we are incorrigible sinners who need his help—and allow him to come into our lives to save us from ourselves—we cannot be saved. In these sermons, he contrasted this idea with the faith of the papists and the Jews and the Turks, in which one must earn God's favor and make one's way to heaven through one's own efforts. He preached these sermons on January 31, February 2, February 7,

---

* During a lifetime in the pulpit—roughly from 1510 until his death—Luther preached roughly seven thousand sermons. About twenty-three hundred have survived.

and then his final sermon on the fourteenth or fifteenth. And every second or third day that he was in Eisleben, he attended the meetings with the counts and their lawyers for which he had come, though his health didn't permit him to remain much longer than an hour or hour and a half at each session. There could have been no doubt that his health was not good by any who were around him. He was at one of these sessions on the sixteenth, but on the seventeenth his health would not permit it. But he did have dinner with his companions that evening. It had been his habit to do this every night and then to retire at eight for his personal prayers.

During dinner on that night—in what would be his last meal—the conversation rather macabrely and presciently turned to whether friends would be able to recognize each other in the next life. Luther held that they would. Following dinner, he retired to his chamber to pray at the window and this time brought his two younger sons to join him. But very soon thereafter, he experienced serious chest pains and coldness. Pastor Coeleus and Jonas quickly went to him and, knowing this was serious, rubbed him with hot towels. Meanwhile, Aurifaber went to find Count Albrecht and his wife, Anna, who arrived quickly, bearing what was believed to be a unicorn's horn, which at that time was associated with divine salvation and with the purity of Mary. In fact, it was the horn of a narwhal, which in those days was still taken for the actual horn of a unicorn. Count Albrecht grated some of the horn into a glass of wine, for it was thought to be a particularly powerful restorative, and one of his councillors, Conrad von Wolfframsdorf, took a spoonful of it, perhaps to allay Luther's fears that it did not contain poison, for his fears of being poisoned were now with him always. The wine and narwhal horn were administered to him, and then Luther rested, sleeping for an hour or so on a daybed in the sitting room.

When he awoke, he was surprised to see that he was not alone and that others were still sitting up, although of course they were doing so only because of their concern for him. He arose and walked unaided to the bathroom, saying, "Into your hands I commit my spirit. You have redeemed me, God of truth." This prayer from Psalm 31:5 was often spoken by those who believed themselves to be dying, not least because these were the last words Jesus himself spoke from the cross before he died (Luke 23:46). After this he shook everyone's hands and bade them goodnight, returning to his bedchamber. But Jonas and Luther's sons Martin and Paul sat in the room with him, as did his servant Ambrosius Rutfelt.

Word had gotten out that Luther was dying, and more people came to stand vigil. Pastor Coeleus remained there, as did Aurifaber, but two doctors had arrived, along with the house's owner and the Eisleben city clerk, Johann Albrecht, and his wife. At about 1:00 a.m., another pang of pain in his chest woke Luther. He told those present of it and also complained again of a feeling of coldness. He woke his servant Ambrosius and asked him to make a fire, but the room was already quite warm. Luther believed he was dying and with an irrepressible wink even now told Jonas, "I think I will stay here at Eisleben where I was born and baptized." He then again arose from his bed and again went to the bathroom, again repeating the words from Psalm 31. When he returned, he was once again rubbed with hot towels.

At some point, Luther began to sweat, and he understood it to be a sign of his impending death. "This is a cold death sweat," he said. "I am going to give up the ghost, for I am getting worse." The two physicians were quickly summoned, and Luther prayed aloud to God, "the God of all comfort, the Father of Jesus Christ," thanking him that he had revealed to him his son, "whom I have believed, whom I have loved, whom I have preached, confessed, and praised, whom the pope and all the godless revile and blaspheme." Luther had confidence that he was going to be with God and did not fear as others did in their moments of death that he might now be slipping into the hands of devils to be dragged to hell. He prayed the words of Simeon from Luke 2:29: "Lord, now lettest thou thy servant depart in peace. Amen." And then he prayed three times more the words from Psalm 31:5 and then fell silent. They shook him, but he did not respond. Then Countess Anna rubbed his nostrils with a solution of rose vinegar and aqua vitae, but still he was not revived.[7]

But Jonas and Coeleus were both keenly aware that the manner of Luther's death would soon be known all across Europe, and how he died was vitally important. To die ignobly or in terrible agony was always taken as a sign that the dead had gone not to his reward but to everlasting punishment. So for the historical record, they both shouted loudly, so that even someone on the very verge of eternity might hear: "Revered father! Are you ready to die trusting in your Lord Jesus Christ and to confess the doctrine which you have taught in his name?"[8] Luther had heard them, for out of his mouth now came his last spoken word, a loud and distinct *Ja.* He then turned over onto his right side, which made them think perhaps he would recover, but then he slipped into a sleep and was from that point unresponsive. Fifteen or so minutes later, at about a quarter to three, he was observed to take a final especially deep breath, and then he gave up the ghost. It was obvious to all that he had died peacefully.

But the apothecary, Johann Landau, had by now entered the scene, and in a final, vain attempt to revive Luther—one that amounted to a bizarrely fitting scatological postscript—he administered an enema to the lifeless body. It was unsuccessful. But in its way it can be seen as the kind of gallows humor that Luther was himself unable to suppress. He laughed at corporeality and celebrated it too. We could not be ethereal sprites unmoored from this earth or our own earthiness, literally or figuratively. From the ground we were made and back to the ground we would go, but God had seen fit in filling us creatures of earth with the very breath of heaven, with the wind of eternity. So it was not the devil who had the last laugh but us—and God. We who were made from the mud of Eden and who would be devoured by maggots as we returned to the soil would be resurrected on the Last Day, would fly in the air to meet with the loving Lord and King who made us, and both of us would have bodies, young and fresh—eternally young and beautiful. *That* is redemption: to make from these fleshly containers of blood and bile and excrement something so extraordinary that we could never ourselves be so free as to truly imagine it and appreciate it. But Luther would get closer than anyone before and would draw millions in his happy wake.

Hoc Est Corpus Lutherum

Those around him knew that the man who lay before them had many years ago made it clear that the last rites practiced by the Catholics were not in his eyes a sacrament, so he was not given those rites, nor now anointed with oil. At 4:00 a.m., people who had received word of his death began arriving to view the body. For five hours, many citizens of the town came to view it, and many of them sobbed to see him there, dead but a few yards from the very spot where he had come into the world sixty-two years before. Jonas early that morning dispatched word to Elector John Frederick and Melanchthon of his death. At some point that morning, Luther was dressed in a white "Swabian smock," much like the smocks worn by the farmers of that time, and moved from his bed into a pewter coffin. There visited many noble persons who had known him and many ordinary townspeople too. Some had known him his whole life.

Early on the morning of the nineteenth in Wittenberg, a messenger rode into the town with the news of Luther's death. The funeral procession bearing Luther's body would not arrive for three more days. Philip Melanchthon was at that early hour about to lecture his students on Saint Paul's epistle to the Romans. But when the messenger gave him Justus Jonas's letter, he was overcome. When he stood behind the lectern at 9:00 a.m., he was not able to speak on the subject of Romans. He explained to his students that he would not be able to discharge his duties in speaking on that subject because "I have this day received a sad letter which troubles me so much that I doubt whether I shall be able in the future to discharge my duties in the University. What this is I will now relate to you so that you may not believe other persons who may circulate false reports in regard to the matter."[9] And he then related the details of Luther's death, as described by Jonas.

Toward the end of his speech, he said, "Alas, obiit auriga et currus Israel!"—meaning "The charioteer of Israel has fallen!" It was a paraphrase of the words Elisha speaks after the death of Elijah from 2 Kings 2:12.

Back in Eisleben, the Mansfeld counts predictably insisted that Luther be buried there, where he had been born—and now where God had ordained that he should die too. So that day, the nineteenth, at two in the afternoon, Luther's coffin was carried into St. Andrew's Church, literally across the street, some fifty feet from where he had died. Justus Jonas preached the funeral sermon. Lukas Fortennagel of Halle was commissioned to paint Luther as he now was. That night in the church, ten citizens stood vigil over the body. On the morning of the next day—the twentieth—another service was held at which the Eisleben pastor Coeleus preached. But Luther would not be buried here in Eisleben after all. This was because the Mansfeld counts had been outranked and overruled by the elector, who insisted that Luther be brought back home to Wittenberg and buried there, in the Castle Church, on whose doors he had posted his theses nearly three decades before.

So the afternoon of the twentieth, Luther's coffin was set in a wagon, and the church bells tolled as the wagon—accompanied by fifty horsemen—bore Luther's body from the city of his birth, and now his death too. Around five that afternoon, the procession reached Halle, where a tremendous crowd was gathered at the city gate, waiting. The church bells tolled upon his arrival, and the crowd was so vast and packed so tightly that in the Halle main square and even on the side streets one could hardly move. The body was then carried into St. Mary's Church, but it was too late for a worship service. At some point during this period in Halle, a death mask was prepared. Death masks were at that time traditional for figures of Luther's stature, but what was not traditional was what the casters did next: they made casts of his hands,* which in their own way are more affecting to see than the face. It is first of all extraordinary that we have the perfectly detailed cast of a face and hands from five hundred years ago. In their way, these are better than photographs in their exquisite detail. There are several copies of the death mask, but staring at the hands, one of which is slightly curved in as hands naturally fall and the other of which is straight, and upon which we see the smallest finger ever so slightly crooked, is as close as we can come to being in Luther's physical presence. These are the hands that five hundred years ago would have held the mallet, and that wrote those infinite words in all of those books, and that caressed his Kathie and his Hänschen and his Elisabeth and his Martin and his Paul and his Margaret and his Lenchen.

On the twenty-first, the procession traveled to Bitterfeld, where the local dignitaries came to pay their respects and then accompanied the procession for the next twenty miles to Kemberg. And then on the morning of the twenty-second, at around 9:00, the procession reached Wittenberg. At the Elster gate, it was welcomed by a great host of Wittenbergers, who formed a procession and went through the city toward the Castle Church. At the head of the procession were schoolboys and the clergy. Behind them were Elector John Frederick's representatives as well as two of the Mansfeld counts and sixty-five horsemen. Next came the wagon that bore the coffin. It was drawn by four horses and covered with a black cloth upon which a cross of white had been embroidered. Just behind this wagon was a smaller, lower wagon carrying Kathie Luther and her daughter Margaret, as well as some other local women. And walking behind this wagon were Luther's three boys and their uncle Jakob, as well as Luther's sister's sons and other family members. Next were the university rector and a number of Wittenberg students from the ranks of the nobility. Then came the university chancellor, and then Jonas, Bugenhagen,

---

* The copy of this death mask that is currently in Halle is a modified copy, such that Luther's eyes are open. The casts of his hands have been placed in a corresponding position on the plum-colored velvet background, which, along with Luther's staring eyes, lends an unnerving luridness to the whole.

and Melanchthon. And with them Hieronymus Schurff and some other doctors of the university. Behind them were more doctors and some masters of the university too. Finally, there was the city council of Wittenberg and then the University of Wittenberg students, followed by the many male citizens of Wittenberg and then many more women and children of the city.

The coffin was carried into the *Schlosskirche* and placed in the aisle, perpendicular to the chancel. A grave had been dug, aptly almost underneath the pulpit from which Luther had so many times preached the Gospel.

That day Bugenhagen preached the sermon but because of his emotions had great difficulty in delivering it. The text was 1 Thessalonians 4:13–14 ("Brothers and sisters, we do not want you to be uninformed about those who sleep in death, so that you do not grieve like the rest of mankind, who have no hope. For we believe that Jesus died and rose again, and so we believe that God will bring with Jesus those who have fallen asleep in him"). And then Melanchthon gave the eulogy, lifting Luther up as one of the greatest figures in history:

> Luther brought to light the true and necessary doctrine. He showed what true repentance is, and what is the refuge and the sure comfort of the soul which quails under the sense of the wrath of God. He expounded Paul's doctrine, which says that man is justified by faith. . . . Many of us witnessed the struggles through which he passed in establishing the principle that by faith are we received and heard of God. Hence throughout eternity pious souls will magnify the benefits which God has bestowed on the Church through Luther.

But even now, Melanchthon did not shy from mentioning Luther's shortcomings:

> Some have complained that Luther displayed too much severity. I will not deny this. But I answer in the language of Erasmus: "Because of the magnitude of the disorders, God gave this age a violent physician." . . . I do not deny that the more ardent characters sometimes make mistakes, for amid the weakness of human nature no one is without fault. But we may say of such a one, "rough indeed, but worthy of all praise!" If he was severe, it was the severity of zeal for the truth, not the love of strife, or of harshness. . . . God was his anchor, and faith never failed him.[10]

Kathie was devastated by her husband's death. She grieved that she had been unable to care for him in his final hours and to be there for her sons, who must have suffered to see their father dying. A few weeks after Luther's death, Kathie wrote to her sister-in-law, Christina von Bora:

> For who would not be sad and afflicted at the loss of such a precious man as my dear lord was? He did great things not just for a city or a single land, but for the whole world. Therefore I am truly so deeply grieved that I cannot tell a single person of the great pain that is in my heart. And I do not understand how I can cope with this. I cannot eat or drink, nor can I sleep. And if I had had a principality or an empire and lost it, it would not have been as painful as it is now that the dear Lord God has taken from me this precious and beloved man, and not from me alone, but from the whole world.[11]

Final Words

The day Luther died, a piece of paper was found in his pocket with the following written upon it:

> Nobody can understand Vergil in his Bucolics and Georgics unless he has first been a shepherd or a farmer for five years. Nobody understands Cicero in his letters unless he has been engaged in public affairs of some consequence for twenty years. Let nobody suppose that he has tasted the Holy Scriptures sufficiently unless he has ruled over the churches with the prophets for a hundred years. Therefore there is something wonderful, first about John the Baptist; second, about Christ, third, about the apostles. "Lay not your hand on this divine Aeneid, but bow in reverence before its footprints!"*[12]

And below this were what must be his last written words, aptly macaronic and profound: "*Wir sind Pettler. Hoc est verum.*"†

---

* This is a quotation from the poet Statius about Virgil's actual *Aeneid*.
† "We are beggars. This is true."

The Man Who Created the Future

I N THE YEAR after Luther's death, Emperor Charles V rode his horse into the Wittenberg Castle Church and guided his mount toward the pulpit, the fountain of heresy from which Luther had so often preached. From that imperious height, the emperor was able to gaze down at the grave of the superlatively pesky fellow whose legacy now lay in ruins. This was because a month earlier, in April 1547, Charles had finally been able to break free from his other military duties and deal decisively with the Schmalkaldic League, at long last bringing these wayward Protestant children to heel. Joining with his brother, Ferdinand, their Catholic armies at Mühlberg soundly defeated Saxony's John Frederick and Philip of Hesse. Protestant Germany no longer existed on any maps. Both leaders were arrested and imprisoned, and it seemed the Protestant revolution was at an end. As he sat on his horse overlooking the place where Luther's mortal remains lay, Charles weighed whether to exhume his posthumously humiliated opponent and have his decomposed remains publicly burned, as befit every heretic. The most reliable stories say it was Charles's hot-blooded Spanish soldiers who demanded this but that the noble and cooler-headed Hapsburg declined the suggestion, declaring, "I do not make war on dead men!" Thus the emperor let the arch heretic lie where he lay and lies at this very moment, then rode out of the great stone edifice and out of the troublemaking city of Wittenberg, never again to return.

It was a fact that the imperial forces won the Schmalkaldic War and laid waste to much of Saxony, but by 1547 Luther's ideas had spread too wide and sunk too deep into the lives of too many for the Reformation to be thus defeated. What might have sufficed a decade or two earlier did not suffice now. There followed resistance and more resistance until at last in 1555 the emperor was forced to accept the Protestant territories as such. He capitulated when that year he signed the Peace of Augsburg, formally granting status to the Protestant territories. Europe would never be a united Catholic territory again, and the next year Charles V abdicated his throne.

Luther's Family

Because of the Schmalkaldic War and the battles following, Kathie and her children were twice forced to abandon Wittenberg, and when they returned, the Black Cloister and much that was theirs had been laid waste. Even livestock had been stolen or simply killed. Her late husband's refusal to take payment for his voluminous writings had left the family essentially bereft and at the mercy of the elector and others, who were not as kind to Kathie as her husband would have hoped. In 1552, the plague again returned to Wittenberg, forcing the "Mother of the Reformation" and her youngest children to flee to Torgau. But at the very gates of that city, her wagon crashed, hurling her into a ditch filled with icy water. The fall and the cold would be the death of her. Three months later, at age fifty-three, she breathed her last and was buried at Torgau, where her remains lie today. Her final words are supposed to have been "I will stick to Christ as a burr sticks to a topcoat."

In 1564, Martin and Kathie's grown children sold the Black Cloister back to the university. Hans, the eldest, went into the study of law and came to be an adviser to the elector. Martin, like his father and namesake, studied theology, although he never found a pastorate and died at age thirty-three. The third son, Paul, became a renowned doctor. The male line of the family continued until 1759, but through the line of Luther's surviving daughter, Margaret, who married a nobleman, the family line continues to the present day. In fact, the German national hero President Paul von Hindenburg proudly claimed to be a direct descendant of Martin Luther. Alas, Hitler made great use of this in co-opting Hindenburg and Luther to his own diabolical purposes, something that has stained Luther's legacy more than anything else.

The People's Hero and the Vox Populi

When one considers Luther's legacy, his encouragement of the budding democratic movements of his time takes an important place. No one before him had given voice to the concerns of the working classes in the way that he had. Previous figures who might have done this lived before the printing press existed, so even if someone had possessed his outsized talents as a communicator, there was simply no medium in which to express oneself and find a wide audience. Luther had an uncanny and unparalleled ear for communicating with those of other social castes. He was able to write to emperors and popes with perfect fluency and to argue academic points in Latin with Erasmus and others, but he was unmatched in speaking directly to those whose knowledge of their own German language was primitive. In this capacity, he was able with ease to run blurred circles around less capable opponents.

In turning to the new medium of pamphlets written in German instead of Latin, Luther opened a direct vein to the people themselves, many of whom had never read before and who had never heard from someone who shared and gave voice to their concerns. In doing this, Luther almost single-handedly created the vox populi, or voice of the people. He was their voice and became their hero, and so adept was he at channeling their concerns that he crushed his oversized opponents through his widely printed pamphlets. No one—whether on his side of the issues or against him—could compete. In doing this, he rode the free market to broader and broader audiences, at the same time creating a desperate desire for more of what he had to say. His humbler readers had never previously thought of themselves as worthy of entering the conversation about their futures. That conversation had always taken place previously without anyone speaking for them. Luther became their champion and their voice. He appeared fearlessly before papal legates and before the emperor himself. This was not some rural buffoon or pot-stirring maniac. Anyone interested could read any of the many other things he had written. And they did. By raising the voices of the people to a level that must be heard by their leaders, Luther brought the people themselves into the wider conversation in history. That the people might know better than their betters is as modern an idea as any, and not until Martin Luther did it burst once and for all onto history's stage.

Luther's Legacy in the Catholic Church

Recently, I attended the funeral of my beloved father-in-law, Joseph Schiavone. It was held at St. Mary's-by-the-Sea on the New Jersey seashore. In the midst of the wonderful ceremony, I noticed a handful of things no one but I would have thought remarkable, because I had been thinking about Luther and the Catholic church. For one thing, I and other lay-people in the service were asked to do readings from Scriptures. This would have been unthinkable in Luther's day, and much more recently too. More dramatically, none who read the Scriptures were baptized Catholics. We also sang beautiful hymns during the service. Congregational singing is today considered de rigueur in many Catholic services, but that is the result of Luther's having brought it into the Lutheran churches of the sixteenth century and its eventually finding its way over the subsequent centuries into the Catholic churches themselves. I then further noticed that all but one of the hymns were written by Protestants.

To be sure, some Catholic traditionalists continue to see Martin Luther as an implacable foe, as the man who ruined the world forever and fractured things into the splintered pile of cultural rubble in which we have ever since strained to exist. But most Catholics wittingly or unwittingly enjoy many of the reforms that over time have come into the church and that have mirrored the very reforms Luther was advocating. For example, the ideas that the congregation ought to be more involved in worship and that the Mass might be performed in a language the people understood must be traced back to the persona non grata named Martin Luther. It was the church council called Vatican II that incorporated many of these reforms.

Luther's Larger Legacy and the Advent of the Future

The far-reaching results of Martin Luther's life and work are unprecedented, touching nearly every aspect of modern life in the West, and these values continue to grow beyond the West. The world of Luther's youth was a single reality, an unyielding plinth of Western Christendom, in which hairline cracks were neither permitted nor existent. And then that changed forever. The world after Luther was a world of variegated pluralism—of dissent, of religious wars, of the advent of religious freedom, of egalitarianism, and then of democracy and self-government and liberty, and of much else. And all of these things are still with us today as history dances along the horizon toward its unknown telos. Therefore many see Luther's legendary hammer blows upon the door of the Schlosskirche as the prime movers in creating the complicated and free future in which we live. Those first concussions pushed the world beyond its medieval stasis and set us on our current course. But the first place to begin in considering Luther's legacy is with the simple idea of pluralism.

The Roman Catholic Church before Luther had nearly infinite power and authority, and after Luther that changed. Luther opened the door to innumerable possibilities counter to the Roman church. Of course this was never his intention. His idée fixe was simply to mend what was broken, to save the foundering ship of the church, to steer it from the rocks ahead, and to be used by God as a savior and reformer of the institution that Luther loved and had served as faithfully as any before him. But we know this was not to be and that in his zeal to do this one thing he instead unintentionally did quite another.

What he did was open the door to a second church—what we today call the Lutheran church—but more important, by doing this he did something else again: he opened the door to a veritable infinity of churches, and to much else. This is because the door Luther dared to open was not merely one through which the truth could come but was a door through which anything at all could come. It was a door through which Luther hoped to welcome Jesus back into Christendom, but it was this same door through which many demons would come too. Luther's critics were right in seeing this, and it is the most compelling reason for their efforts to stop him.

Prominent churchmen of this time—Erasmus and the Dutch pope Adrian VI among them—well understood that the church had tremendous problems. Correcting them was vital, and they hoped to do just that. But what they opposed was Luther's seemingly mad idea of blasting away at the church's very foundations. That could surely end in toppling the whole edifice and, God forbid, might cause many to fall away from Rome altogether and perhaps even start a new, false church.

Luther's critics correctly saw that once the pope and the church's authority was openly challenged, lies and confusion would be given a free hearing along with the truth. How then would the truth prevail and order be maintained? What guarantees would there be toward these ends? Once this extremely dangerous step was taken, couldn't any fool establish his own interpretation of things and create his own religion and delude millions—leading them all to eternal perdition? In the centuries since Luther, we have seen precisely that, and many times over. Innumerable heresies and cults and false churches have arisen and led millions away from the truth.

The Free Market of Ideas

We must ask then, why did Luther not fear these things as others did?

For one thing, he firmly believed that the devil's horse was already out of the barn. In his view, the Catholic church, which of course he felt was not being Catholic at all, was already leading many to everlasting perdition. This troubled him so much that he felt almost anything must be risked. So for him the only way forward was a scorched-earth policy to fight for the truth, come what may. He hadn't thought much about how this would open the door to every other competing ideology. That is indeed the problem of pluralism, and it is a very real problem. But these initial steps toward our modern world of pluralism form the principal and foundational part of Luther's legacy.

Another reason for his fearlessness in moving forward was that around 1520 Luther became convinced that God himself was compelling him to continue on this bold—and some thought reckless—path. Luther believed that as much harm as might be caused, in the end the truth nonetheless must prevail. He understood it was all a wild gamble, but Luther's confidence that the truth would win in the end was clear. He seemed to intuit that free competition and freedom itself were not only healthy but somehow a necessary part of the nature of God's truth. But we should ask, on what basis might someone five hundred years ago think competition should tilt in a truthward direction?

One argument is that if the universe was indeed created and is now sustained by the God of truth, then perhaps if it is given a level playing field of competition, the truth will always prevail. In other words, God has stacked the deck. Perhaps if we do not risk losing, we cannot actually win. Perhaps freedom is our only chance to find truth. If so, then we must allow argument and dissent and debate. Our modern era surely believes this, and less than a century after Luther's death one of his spiritual descendants, John Milton, eloquently argued along these lines in his landmark essay *Areopagitica*. Today we take this for granted, as we take so much of what Luther dared; indeed, so for granted do we take them that we certainly don't remember with whom they originated.

Problems with Pluralism

Luther knew that an open debate on indulgences would be a good thing for the church and society. So he pushed for it with everything he had, although of course he never got that debate, which led to all the troubles that followed. But it seems clear that Luther never thought much past this initial battle. What would happen when others rebelled against church teaching in ways Luther himself disagreed with? This was the question he had not anticipated.

So he was surprised and very upset at having to deal with Karlstadt and Müntzer and then with Zwingli and all the others. He had never anticipated that his ideas would lead not merely away from falsehoods and back to truth but to pluralism, and from within his own ranks too. But this was the door he had opened.

How Luther dealt with these dissents on his other flank is much of the story of this book. How should one judge among competing ideas? It was one thing to criticize those in Rome for how they dealt with his own dissent, but was Luther up to establishing a general standard by which everyone should deal with dissent? Did how one debated and battled for truth matter, or was the thing that mattered only that the right view won? Clearly Luther didn't believe the latter. But he had been too busy to think through the details and essentially made up his responses to this as he went along.

Whether Luther had thought about it much or hadn't, once he broke away from the theological lockstep of Rome, he had broken away not only from what it believed but from the deeper and larger idea that one could force another's beliefs. This was an astounding development. He had opened the door to what we today call conscience and dissent. He had therefore also opened the door to the idea that truth and power were inevitably at odds with each other. This was an immeasurably significant moment, and most of what we take for granted in the West, especially with regard to democracy and human rights, began with this crucial idea. Once this brightest of all ideas took hold, who could believe that a forced conversion to another religion was a real conversion? Brute power itself had been vanquished by the human right to believe as one wished.

Conscience and Dissent

It is this, more than his theological views, that makes Martin Luther such an outsized figure in history. Anyone could dissent from theological views, and others had done so. Many had agitated for reform in the church. But to succeed such that one created a new world in which dissent was genuinely possible—in which it was even important and almost encouraged—was something new and shocking. What door had Luther opened? No one knew, including Luther himself. It was both wonderful and terrible. And it led directly to the world in which we have lived ever since.

Luther had begun by arguing for a view of the truth, but in so doing, he had dragged with him the brand-new idea of truthful argument. Perhaps this is the greatest part of his legacy, that in fighting with Rome, he semi-wittingly discovered that truth had a nature that was, as it were, both noun and verb. The world had always understood the idea that truth was what was right and true, but suddenly now how one sought the truth and whether and how one argued for the truth were on the table as well.

Thus, because of Luther, truth had become two things, had burst into another dimension. It had overnight been doubled, or perhaps squared. There was first what was true, and now suddenly there was also the process of how one determined what was true. And this second thing mattered as much as what was true. How one arrived at and argued for truth must itself partake of truth. Thus the means and the end had become inextricably and forevermore intertwined. This certainly followed from what one finds in the Bible, but never before had it come into history as it had with Luther. In this he had unwittingly been the vessel for what was the greatest revolution in history, the one that would lead to all the others.

It followed, for example, that if how one discovered truth and fought for truth had to partake of truth itself, then torturing or executing someone to prevent his speaking lies itself took part in a greater lie. It followed that the idea of human rights must soon come onto history's docket. Luther had not worked all of this out, but by suggesting that there was something called the truth and that this truth might be discovered and embraced outside the worldly institution of the church, he had inadvertently linked the facts of the truth with the way one approached the search for truth. This was itself a revolution, one that is still being fought today and will likely always be fought, as long as human history continues. But it is this that has changed everything, and this that is Luther's principal legacy in the world.

Truth Divorced from Power

Luther had dared to say that just because the Roman church had the power to crush dissent did not mean that it represented the truth and probably even indicated that it didn't. For one thing, crushing dissent violently and cruelly was itself anathema to the life of Jesus, who had not killed to protect the truth but on the contrary had freely died for the truth. He might well have forced those who crucified him to accept his teachings. That would have seemed the practical path. But he did not. Instead, Jesus freely suffered and died, and in doing so, he illustrated as eloquently as may be done that naked power was not the most powerful thing in the universe. On the contrary, truth itself was more powerful. But this revolutionary act and the world-changing idea that it represented had to wait fifteen centuries until Martin Luther could bring it into Western culture forever. The idea that an all-powerful God does not use that power to compel us to believe in him or in truth had to wait until the death of Jesus to be illustrated in history, but that same idea needed to wait until Luther to be introduced into the actual workings of history, where it has lived ever since.

So the events that Luther forced into being by his unwillingness to recant implied that if one must burn heretics to kill heresy, perhaps this was a clue that one feared open debate. As time passed, this idea of power being inherently suspect gained purchase throughout Europe and the growing West. The limits of power and a way of seeing the limits of power had been born. Power had to be leavened with truth and with grace and freedom. This was something fresh and green in history. It was God's idea, and it was therefore an ancient idea, but it must sprout through the world's turf now; it must be born into the world through the rough-hewn former Augustinian monk named Martin Luther.

Luther did not discover any especially new ideas. Nor did he discover the God behind these ideas. But what he did was rediscover the ideas, and pull them out from under centuries of accreted neglect. To see that this last idea is an ancient one, we need only read the Old Testament story of Solomon and the baby, which prefigures it.

In that hoary and still startling story, two women claim to be the mother of a baby boy; unable to solve the dilemma, they come before the great and wise king Solomon, who devises a frightening solution. Cut the baby in two, he says. That way each of the women claiming to be the boy's mother may have an equal share. But of course this bisection will not happen, and what does happen shows the unfathomable wisdom of Solomon, because it quickly reveals the identity of the baby's true mother. One of the women says, "No, don't cut the baby! Give it to her. As long as the child lives I will be happy." The other woman says, "Cut the baby in half! That way neither of us will have him." Solomon of course knows that the woman willing to give the baby to the other woman must be the baby's true mother. This extraordinary story, which must be read in full, presages the principle at work once the world entered the door that Luther opened. The willingness on the part of the child's mother to lose what is dear to her is a picture of God and his love. It is not enough simply to be right. That was the way of the Pharisee. The law of love and freedom was now in play too.

What that story and what Luther did so many years later showed was that there was something deeper and more important than merely being right or merely winning. If I must win by the sword—or by any kind of force—then my victory is Pyrrhic and worthless. I must not only win but win the right way. I must not only aver the truth but do so in a way that itself honors truth. This marked a new epoch, and it is happily that epoch in which we live today. Although it is the job of the state to forcefully protect the innocent and its citizens, it is never the state's job to enforce truth or morality or to "establish" any religion above another. That it can never and must never do.

So when Luther himself got the upper hand—theologically speaking and in terms of governmental power too—how would he deal with dissent? We see that Luther still had one foot in the medieval world, because when writing on the subject of the Jews in 1543, he was not arguing that they should be able to live freely, even with their (to him) flawed ideas. He feared greatly that they would be able to convince Christians of the falseness of the Christian view, and rather than be willing to deal with the consequences of this, he argued that their dissent must be crushed, which is precisely what he had experienced himself from the powers at Rome in his own dissent.

But the willingness to tolerate dissent, which is the true nature of freedom and of love, like the good leaven of which Jesus spoke, could not be stopped in spreading throughout the whole lump of Western civilization, despite Luther's late-in-life abrogation of what he had set in motion. Luther virtually single-handedly had put the leaven into history's dough, and his most grievous sins had little effect on the process of the eventual rising of the whole.

In the past, we lived in a world where might actually made right, where truth was the power of the sword. Or where there was no actual right, so that the appearance that might made right held sway completely. The Catholic church was in those days the Christian church, and in those days the church much like the Turks and the Ottoman caliphate battled with guns, not with competing truth claims. So just as today radical Islamists may believe there is no truth but the sword—that they can enforce their views through torture and death—the church once did this too. But today we live in a world where even if someone can do that, there are voices that will rise up and say that it is wrong. We live in a world where even though someone might be right and know he is right, he also knows that to try to force his views is as bad as holding the wrong views. That is the revolution that is the father and mother of all other revolutions.

Democracy and Freedom

Thus, despite his grievous failings and contradictions, once Luther sided with a view of the Bible that was different from Rome's, our modern idea of freedom had been born.

What follows is, in a word, everything. First there was a plurality of churches. The Reformation spread beyond Germany to England and to many other countries. But then this phenomenon metastasized as aspects of this new way of seeing things raised their heads even against these newly established Protestant churches. Still more churches broke out everywhere, but not without skirmishes and horrible bloodshed. But hope had been born, and from that point on the momentum once and for all lay with the thing with feathers that Luther had hatched.

In 1644, in the midst of the English Civil War, John Milton published

Areopagitica, his landmark defense of the freedom of expression. In 1689, England decided that it would tolerate religions other than the established Church of England. In the first years of that century, those men and women we today call the Pilgrims were being persecuted by King James in England. But emboldened by their faith, they would flee first to Holland and then in a famous ship cross the Atlantic to what is today Massachusetts. Hard on their heels were John Winthrop and what came to be called the Massachusetts Bay Colony in Boston. Religious tolerance certainly was not yet enshrined in their way of thinking. The stories of Anne Hutchinson and Roger Williams are two infamous examples.

But in part because in the American colonies different faiths found themselves living cheek by jowl, tolerance of other views became a growing trend. During the Great Awakening of the eighteenth century, George Whitefield preached the Gospel up and down the thirteen American colonies so often that by the time of his death in 1770 not less than 80 percent of all Americans had heard him preach in person at least once. What he preached was a kind of ecumenical Christianity that underscored the profoundly Lutheran idea that conscience and fealty to God preceded fealty to any church or government. It therefore followed that those who did violence to the teachings of Jesus must be disobeyed. This played a huge role in emboldening the American colonists to move toward self-government. When England forced their hand, as Rome had forced Luther's, they would vote with their feet and rebel against their mother country, just as Luther had rebelled against Mother Church.

The new nation in 1776 enshrined the idea of religious liberty in its laws, such that every citizen must be free to follow his own conscience and his own religion. This stands as another of the high-water marks of Luther's legacy. The government of the new country was specifically forbidden to establish a religion in any state or throughout the country and was obliged to trust the free market of ideas—regulated by the democratic government of the people—to make such decisions as the people themselves thought best. It is this so-called wall of separation that allowed the genius of the free market of ideas to flourish.

Social Reforms

Around this same time in England, a group of Methodists led by John Wesley were frowned upon by the official Church of England. But they and the Quakers were nonetheless now allowed to exist, and because of the greater devotion of these dissenters to the ideals of the New Testament they led the battle for the end of the slave trade in the British Empire. Without the respect for dissent and the free market of ideas that Luther introduced, this could never have occurred. The champion in Parliament of these evangelicals was William Wilberforce, who cannily never officially separated from the Church of England but who led the battle to end the slave trade—and then slavery—throughout the British Empire. He also led the way for its end throughout Europe, and of course it ended in America too, with such as Abraham Lincoln and Frederick Douglass looking back to Wilberforce as their hero and the great pioneer of the movement.

Abolition was only the first and most important of the innumerable social reforms that took place in England in the nineteenth century. Evangelicals—led by Wilberforce—pushed forward reforms in helping the poor, in child labor laws, in animal cruelty laws, in penal reform, and much else. Wilberforce and his spiritual heirs took Luther's ideas that next step into the world of culture and government in a way Luther himself could never have done but that Luther had nonetheless made possible, and these ideas leaped the borders of Wilberforce's England and ran rampant throughout the West. By freeing truth and the ideas of the Bible from the institution of the church, Luther enabled these things to enter the entirety of the secular world, such that every good agnostic and atheist today knows that caring for the poor and the marginalized is a measure of our humanity.

The End of History

In the end, what Luther did was not merely to open a door in which people were free to rebel against their leaders but to open a door in which people were obliged by God to take responsibility for themselves and free to help those around them who could not help themselves. No longer could we complain that we were forced to accept the poor spiritual or governmental leadership of those in authority over us. On the contrary, we now had not only the freedom but the responsibility to take these things into our own hands, trusting only in God. So what Luther did was usher the West into its maturity. What this further did—as Luther foresaw and passionately hoped—was encourage people to depend the more on God, to deepen their relationship with him personally, and to increase their knowledge of his Scriptures; else how could they justify their dissent? This was how Luther had done it. He knew there was no substitute for this and that it was far better that someone try to understand God and truth with the possibility of getting some things wrong than to depend on others to understand these things. Freedom with God, with the possibility of growth and death, was better than the safe fetters of childhood.

So here we stand. We face the serious questions history continues to ask of us and do our best to answer them, knowing the stakes are high: When does liberty become license and oppression? When does freedom bleed across the invisible border into forced ideology? When does pluralism become its own oppressive monolithic ideology? And so we go forward, sometimes still getting things wrong, and yet this great dance between truth and freedom continues as it has done and as it must and will. It may sometimes seem more a battle than a dance; nonetheless, in the end these two parts of a larger whole keep going round and round, in the process circling inexorably toward that happy day when the two will be one—and not just in the mind of God but in history too.

Maranatha.

ACKNOWLEDGMENTS

Creating a book such as the one you are this moment reading* requires significantly more than mere researching and writing, both of which I am generally able to do without any help, thank you very much. It is a here-and-now documented fact that this book would not exist without the sparkling editorial efforts of my team at Viking, led by their own *capo di tutt' i capi*, Brian Tart, whom I must (and here do) thank for his inestimable encouragement and sensitive editorial and publishing guidance, not to mention (though I do) his oversight of the eminently capable Amy Sun and others, including (but not limited to) Ryan Boyle, Colin Webber, Amy Hill, and Rebecca Marsh. Though I would never say so publicly, it is a fixed certainty that had Brian and his team been at Viking in the early seventies, *Gravity's Rainbow* might well be (readable and) still selling briskly. *Quelle domage.*

I would also (but refuse to) be gravely and inexcusably remiss in failing to thank my own crackerjack team, led by HRH Elisa Leberis, whose various efforts on my behalf are so encyclopaedic as to beggar description here, and without which I'm sure I might not only lack the tremendous boon of this finished book, but shelter, shoes, and teeth too. I am particularly grateful to Ruthie Totheroh and Brandon Santulli for helping me track down the source citations to some of the more wriggly quotations herein; thus any and all errors along those lines I here must also—and alas—lay at their young feet.†

I am everlastingly grateful to my wife, Susanne, and our daughter, Annerose, for their love and grace toward me, not least in bearing up under such jiggy idiosyncrasies as sometimes attend the messy birth of manuscripts. Finally, I wish to thank my dearest friends, Markus Spieker and

---

* Yes, I can see you.

† In the interests of full legal disclosure, this statement is itself erroneous; in fact, all errors—this one included—must be charged to my own account, though I remain peevishly disinclined to admit such things in point sizes any larger than this.

Greg Thornbury, to whom I have very generously dedicated this book (and all ancillary products proceeding herefrom); the former for strongly suggesting this book to me in an afternoon phone call from Berlin (I was at the Arctic Club Hotel in Seattle, before dawn) in 2012; the latter for convincing me, during a more recent dinner conversation at Orsay restaurant here in Manhattan, that Luther's was an extraordinary story I really must tell, preferably before the happy quincentenary in October 2017 had passed us. To have such friends as I—and to know it—is to horselaugh at the wealth of poor Croesus. And I do.

APPENDIX

FREDERICK'S DREAM

The following account of a dream supposedly dreamt by Frederick the Wise the night before October 31, 1517, forms a large part of the legend surrounding Martin Luther. Whether there is some root of authenticity to this remains unknown, but it has been very widely circulated and is worth recording here.

We step a moment out of the domain of history to narrate a dream that the elector Frederick of Saxony had on the night preceding the memorable day on which Luther affixed his theses to the door of the Castle Church.

The elector told it the next morning to his brother Duke John, who was then residing with him at his palace of Schweinitz, six leagues* from Wittenberg. The dream is recorded by all the chroniclers of the time. Of its truth there is no doubt, however we may interpret it. We cite it here as a compendious and dramatic epitome of the affair of the theses and the movement that grew out of them:

On the morning of the 31st October, 1517, the elector said to Duke John, "Brother, I must tell you a dream which I had last night, and the meaning of which I should like much to know. It is so deeply impressed on my mind, that I will never forget it, were I to live a thousand years. For I dreamed it thrice, and each time with new circumstances."

DUKE JOHN: Is it a good or a bad dream?

THE ELECTOR: I know not; God knows.

DUKE JOHN: Don't be uneasy at it; but be so good as tell it to me.

THE ELECTOR: Having gone to bed last night, fatigued and out of spirits, I fell asleep shortly after my prayer, and slept calmly for about two hours and a half; I then awoke, and continued awake to midnight, all sorts of thoughts passing through my mind. Among other things, I thought how I

* A league is approximately three miles.

was to observe the Feast of All Saints. I prayed for the poor souls in purgatory; and supplicated God to guide me, my counsels, and my people according to truth. I again fell asleep, and then dreamed that Almighty God sent me a monk, who was a true son of the Apostle Paul. All the saints accompanied him by order of God, in order to bear testimony before me, and to declare that he did not come to contrive any plot, but that all that he did was according to the will of God. They asked me to have the goodness graciously to permit him to write something on the door of the church of the Castle of Wittenberg. This I granted through my chancellor. Thereupon the monk went to the church, and began to write in such large characters that I could read the writing at Schweinitz. [Eighteen miles away.] The pen which he used was so large that its end reached as far as Rome, where it pierced the ears of a lion that was crouching there, and caused the triple crown upon the head of the Pope to shake. All the cardinals and princes, running hastily up, tried to prevent it from falling. You and I, brother, wished also to assist, and I stretched out my arm;—but at this moment I awoke, with my arm in the air, quite amazed, and very much enraged at the monk for not managing his pen better. I recollected myself a little; it was only a dream.

I was still half asleep, and once more closed my eyes. The dream returned. The lion, still annoyed by the pen, began to roar with all his might, so much so that the whole city of Rome, and all the States of the Holy Empire, ran to see what the matter was. The Pope requested them to oppose this monk, and applied particularly to me, on account of his being in my country. I again awoke, repeated the Lord's prayer, entreated God to preserve his Holiness, and once more fell asleep.

Then I dreamed that all the princes of the Empire, and we among them, hastened to Rome, and strove, one after another, to break the pen; but the more we tried the stiffer it became, sounding as if it had been made of iron. We at length desisted. I then asked the monk (for I was sometimes at Rome, and sometimes at Wittenberg) where he got this pen, and why it was so strong. "The pen," replied he, "belonged to an old goose of Bohemia, a hundred years old.* I got it from one of my old schoolmasters. As to its strength, it is owing to the impossibility of depriving it of its pith or marrow; and I am quite astonished at it myself." Suddenly I heard a loud noise—a large number of other pens had sprung out of the long pen of the monk. I awoke a third time: it was daylight.

* This is a reference to Jan Hus, whose surname means "goose" in Bohemian.

DUKE JOHN: Chancellor, what is your opinion? Would we had a Joseph, or a Daniel, enlightened by God!

CHANCELLOR: Your highness knows the common proverb, that the dreams of young girls, learned men, and great lords have usually some hidden meaning. The meaning of this dream, however, we shall not be able to know for some time—not till the things to which it relates have taken place. Wherefore, leave the accomplishment to God, and place it fully in his hand.

DUKE JOHN: I am of your opinion, Chancellor; 'tis not fit for us to annoy ourselves in attempting to discover the meaning. God will overrule all for his glory.

THE ELECTOR: May our faithful God do so; yet I shall never forget, this dream. I have, indeed, thought of an interpretation, but I keep it to myself. Time, perhaps, will show if I have been a good diviner.

So passed the morning of the 31st October, 1517, in the royal castle of Schweinitz. The events of the evening at Wittenberg we have already detailed. The elector has hardly made an end of telling his dream when the monk comes with his hammer to interpret it.

NOTES

CHAPTER ONE: Beyond the Myths

1. Translated by Alexander Roberts, in *Nicene and Post-Nicene Fathers, Second Series*, Vol. 11, ed. Philip Schaff and Henry Wace (Buffalo, N.Y.: Christian Literature, 1894). Revised and edited for New Advent by Kevin Knight, http://www.newadvent.org/fathers/3501.htm.
2. Sproul and Nichols, *Legacy of Luther*, 16.
3. Andreas Stahl and Björn Schlenker, "Luther in Mansfeld: Excavations and Accompanying Architectural Research on Martin Luther's Parents' Home," *Martin Luther and the Reformation: Essays*, ed. Gotha Stiftung Schloss Friedenstein (Dresden: Sandstein Verlag, 2016).
4. Ibid.
5. Ibid., 68–69.
6. Luther to Philip Melanchthon, June 5, 1530, in WA Br 5:351, 20–27; Martin Luther, *Luther's Works* (*LW*), American Edition, 55 vols., ed. Jaroslav Pelikan and Helmut T. Lehman (Philadelphia: Muehlenberg and Fortress, and St. Louis: Concordia, 1955–86), 49:318–19.
7. *LW*, 46:250.
8. Hendrix, *Martin Luther*, 25.
9. Brecht, *His Road to Reformation*, 18.
10. Quoted in ibid., 19.
11. Quoted in Tuchman, *March of Folly*, 60.
12. Quoted in ibid., 56.
13. Julius Koestlin, *Life of Luther* (Charleston: BiblioBazaar, 2008), 31.
14. Oberman, *Luther*, 113.
15. John Milton, *Paradise Lost*, bk. 1, line 63.
16. William Styron, *Darkness Visible: A Memoir of Madness* (New York: Random House, 1990).
17. Dante Alighieri, *Inferno*, in *The Divine Comedy*, trans. Henry F. Cary (New York: P. F. Collier & Son, 1909), canto 3, line 9.
18. Brecht, *His Road to Reformation*, 45.

CHAPTER TWO: Lightning Strikes

1. Luke 10:18, New International Version.
2. Quoted in Bainton, *Here I Stand*, 20.
3. Ibid.
4. Ibid., 21–22.
5. *LW*, 48:4.
6. Stahl and Schlenker, "Luther in Mansfeld," *Martin Luther and the Reformation*, 68–69.
7. Quoted in Bainton, 25.
8. Philippians 2:12, New International Version.
9. *LW*, 31:129.

Chapter Three: The Great Change

1. Oberman, *Luther*, 59.
2. Brecht, *His Road to Reformation*.
3. Ibid., 94.
4. Ibid., 87.
5. Luke 23:21, New International Version.
6. Matthew 6:9–13.
7. Quoted in Oberman, *Luther*, 149.
8. Quoted in Hendrix, *Martin Luther*, 7.

Chapter Four: A Monk at Wittenberg

1. *LW*, 54:.
2. Brecht, *His Road to Reformation*, 107.
3. Bainton, *Here I Stand*, 57.
4. *LW*, 48:27–28.
5. Quoted in Oberman, *Luther*, 252.
6. Quoted in ibid., 71.
7. Ozment, *The Serpent and the Lamb*, 70.
8. Ibid., 90–92.
9. *LW*, 48:10.
10. Lewis William Spitz, *Luther and German Humanism* (Aldershot, U.K.: Variorum, 1996), 85.
11. Kenneth Scott Latourette, *A History of Christianity* (New York: Harper & Brothers, 1953), 661.
12. Quoted in Carlos Eire, *Reformations: The Early Modern World, 1450–1660* (New Haven, Conn.: Yale University Press, 2016), 65.
13. Quoted in ibid., 112.
14. Tuchman, *March of Folly*, 112.
15. Bedini, *Pope's Elephant*, 92.
16. Allusion to Milton, *Paradise Lost*, bk. 12, line 648.

Chapter Five: The "Cloaca" Experience

1. *LW*, 25:409.
2. *LW*, 48:37–38.
3. *LW*, 48:42.
4. Ibid.; 34:336–37.
5. *LW*, 34:337.
6. Volker Leppin, "Becoming a Reformer," *Martin Luther and the Reformation*: Essays (Dresden: Sandstein Verlag, 2016), 87.
7. Quoted in Bainton, *Here I Stand*, 64–65.
8. Pettegree, *Brand Luther*, 56.

Chapter Six: The Theses Are Posted

1. Brecht, *His Road to Reformation*, 201.
2. "Luther's Posting of His Theses: Much Ado About Nothing?" *Martin Luther and the Reformation: Essays*.
3. *LW*, 48:45–47.
4. Brecht, *His Road to Reformation*, 206.
5. Martin Luther's Ninety-five Theses, with the pertinent documents from the history of the Reformation, from *Martin Luther, 1483–1546*, ed. Kurt Aland (St. Louis: Concordia Pub. House, 1967).
6. Smith, *The Life and Letters of Martin Luther*, 43–44.

7. Kittelson, *Luther the Reformer*, 23.

8. Brecht, *His Road to Reformation*, 210.

9. Ibid.

10. Ibid., 211.

11. Ibid., 212.

12. Quoted in ibid., 213.

13. American King James Version.

14. Quoted in Brecht, *His Road to Reformation*, 217.

15. Bainton, *Here I Stand*, 77.

16. Quoted in Oberman, *Luther*, 194.

17. Quoted in Bainton, *Here I Stand*, 77.

18. LW, 48:72.

19. LW, 48:74.

20. Quoted in Manschreck, *Melanchthon*, 42.

21. LW, 48:78.

22. LW, 48:83.

CHAPTER SEVEN: The Diet at Augsburg

1. Quoted in Bainton, *Here I Stand*, 75.

2. Quoted in ibid.

3. Ibid., 76.

4. Quoted in ibid., 81.

5. Quoted in ibid., 73.

6. New International Version.

7. Robert E. McNally, "The Ninety-five Theses of Martin Luther: 1517–1967," *Theological Studies* 28, issue 3 (1967): 475, doi:10.1177/004056396702800301.

8. LW, 48:94.

9. Quoted in Bainton, *Here I Stand*, 88.

10. James M. Kittelson, *Luther the Reformer: The Story of the Man and His Career*, 2nd ed. (Minneapolis: Fortress Press, 2016), 97.

11. Brecht, *His Road to Reformation*, 265.

12. Quoted in Bainton, *Here I Stand*, 89.

13. Quoted in ibid.

14. Quoted in ibid., 94.

15. LW, 48:98.

16. LW, 48:100–102.

17. LW, 34:332.

CHAPTER EIGHT: The Leipzig Debate

1. Bainton, *Here I Stand*, 98.

2. Hendrix, *Martin Luther*, 78.

3. LW, 48:107.

4. Quoted in Brecht, *His Road to Reformation*, 303.

5. Ibid., 304.

6. Kittelson, *Luther the Reformer*, 99.

7. LW, 48:114. Parenthetical is per the original.

8. Ibid., 311.

9. Quoted in Bainton, *Here I Stand*, 102.

10. Ibid.

11. Kittelson, *Luther the Reformer*, 101.

12. Quoted in Gene Edward Veith, *A Place to Stand: The Word of God in the Life of Martin Luther*, ed. David J. Vaughan (Nashville: Cumberland House, 2005), 62.
13. Bainton, *Here I Stand*, 103.
14. Brecht, *His Road to Reformation*, 315.
15. Ibid., 297.
16. Matthew 16:18, New International Version.
17. Kittelson, *Luther the Reformer*, 102.
18. Roper, *Martin Luther*, 135.
19. Bainton, *Here I Stand*, 104.
20. Ibid., 105.
21. Ibid., 107.
22. LW, 48:153.
23. Desiderius Erasmus, *The Correspondence of Erasmus: Letters 1122–1251, 1520–1521* (Toronto: University of Toronto Press, 1974), 8:210.
24. LW, 48:210.
25. Oberman, *Luther*, 42.
26. LW, 48:160.
27. Quoted in Oberman, *Luther*, 43.
28. Quoted in Roper, *Martin Luther*, 146.
29. Quoted in ibid., 159.
30. Quoted in Kittelson, *Luther the Reformer*, 112.
31. LW, 48:170.
32. Reston, *Luther's Fortress*, 13.
33. Kittelson, *Luther the Reformer*, 110.
34. Quoted in Bainton, *Here I Stand*, 126.
35. Quoted in ibid.
36. LW, 48:178.
37. Quoted in Kittelson, *Luther the Reformer*, 115.
38. Bainton, *Here I Stand*, 230.

Chapter Nine: The Bull Against Luther

1. Kittelson, *Luther the Reformer*, 110.
2. Bainton, *Here I Stand*, 140.
3. Murphy, *Pope's Daughter*.
4. Bainton, *Here I Stand*, 140.
5. Hendrix, *Martin Luther*, 94.
6. Bainton, *Here I Stand*, 152–53.
7. Pettegree, *Brand Luther*, 131.
8. Brecht, *His Road to Reformation*, 424.
9. Quoted in Reston, *Luther's Fortress*, 18.
10. Quoted in ibid.
11. Quoted in ibid., 20–21.
12. Quoted in ibid., 21–22.
13. Quoted in ibid., 22.
14. LW, 48:188.

Chapter Ten: The Diet of Worms

1. Pettegree, *Brand Luther*, 180.
2. Quoted in Roper, *Martin Luther*, 179.
3. LW, 48:198.
4. Quoted in Oberman, *Luther*, 197.

5. Quoted in Hendrix, *Martin Luther*, 103.
6. Quoted in Pettegree, *Brand Luther*, 135.
7. Quoted in Oberman, *Luther*, 198–99.
8. Brecht, His *Road to Reformation*, 453.
9. Quoted in Oberman, *Luther*, 199.
10. Quoted in Brecht, *His Road to Reformation*, 453.
11. Bainton, *Here I Stand*, 178.
12. Quoted in ibid.
13. *LW*, 32:107.
14. Quoted in Oberman, *Luther*, 199.
15. *LW*, 48:200.
16. Quoted in Bainton, *Here I Stand*, 181.
17. *LW*, 32:109–13.
18. Quoted in Bainton, *Here I Stand*, 182.
19. Quoted in Brecht, *His Road to Reformation*, 451.
20. Quoted in Bainton, *Here I Stand*, 182.

Chapter Eleven: An Enemy of the Empire

1. Quoted in Oberman, *Luther*, 203.
2. *LW*, 32:114.
3. Charles Beard, *Martin Luther and the Reformation in Germany Until the Close of the Diet of Worms* (London: Philip Green, 1896), 444–45.
4. Brecht, *His Road to Reformation*, 467.
5. Acts 5:38–39, New International Version.
6. Quoted in Brecht, *His Road to Reformation*, 470.
7. Bainton, *Here I Stand*, 185.
8. Oberman, *Luther*, 203.
9. *LW*, 48:201.
10. Ibid., 201–2.
11. John 19:10–11.
12. *LW*, 48:225.
13. Quoted in Bainton, *Here I Stand*, 189.

Chapter Twelve: The Wartburg

1. Bornkamm, *Luther in Mid-career*, 2.
2. Revelation 1:9, New International Version.
3. *LW*, 48:212.
4. Ibid., 213.
5. Ibid., 214.
6. Ibid., 233.
7. Bornkamm, *Luther in Mid-career*, 3.
8. *LW*, 48:215.
9. Ibid., 217.
10. Ibid., 219.
11. Ibid., 255.
12. Ibid., 268.
13. Ibid., 276.
14. Erikson, *Young Man Luther*, 176.
15. *LW*, 48:255.
16. Ibid., 21:356–57.
17. Ibid., 48:306–7.

18. Ibid., 319.
19. Ibid., 217, 222, 236.
20. Ibid., 283–84.
21. Genesis 3:15, New American Standard Bible.
22. *LW*, 48:293–94.
23. Ibid., 295.
24. Ibid., 307.
25. Ibid., 316.
26. Ibid., 282.
27. Ibid., 308–9.
28. Bainton, *Here I Stand*, 195.

Chapter Thirteen: The Revolution Is Near

1. *LW*, 48: 350–51.
2. Ibid., 354.
3. Ibid., 354–55.
4. Ibid., 45:63.
5. Bornkamm, *Luther in Mid-career*, 40.
6. Quoted in Brecht, *Shaping and Defining*, 32.
7. Bornkamm, *Luther in Mid-career*, 57.
8. Quoted in Bainton, *Here I Stand*, 207.
9. *LW*, 48:363.
10. Exodus 20:4.
11. Quoted in Roper, *Martin Luther*, 226.
12. Quoted in Bainton, *Here I Stand*, 206.
13. Quoted in ibid., 208.
14. Quoted in ibid.
15. Quoted in ibid., 209.
16. Bornkamm, *Luther in Mid-career*, 50.
17. Quoted in ibid., 49.
18. *LW*, 48:387.

Chapter Fourteen: Luther Returns

1. Brecht, *Shaping and Defining*, 43.
2. Quoted in Bainton, *Here I Stand*, 210–11.
3. Mullett, *Martin Luther*, 180.
4. *LW*, 51:70.
5. Bornkamm, *Luther in Mid-career*, 74.
6. Quoted in ibid.
7. Quoted in Brecht, *Shaping and Defining*, 57.
8. Roper, *Martin Luther*, 233.
9. Quoted in Bainton, *Here I Stand*, 213.
10. Quoted in Kittelson, *Luther the Reformer*, 182.
11. Bornkamm, *Luther in Mid-career*, 79.
12. *LW*, 36:262.
13. Kittelson, *Luther the Reformer*, 143.
14. Quoted in Hendrix, *Martin Luther*, 131.
15. Veith, *A Place to Stand*, 84–85.
16. Quoted in Bornkamm, *Luther in Mid-career*, 77.
17. Quoted in Hendrix, *Martin Luther*, 139.
18. *LW*, 51:109.

19. Ibid., 49:11–12.

20. Ozment, *The Serpent and the Lamb*, 107.

21. *LW*, 35:362.

22. 2 Timothy 4:14, New American Standard Bible.

23. *LW*, 49:19.

24. Acts 8:30–31, Berean Study Bible.

25. *LW*, 35:371.

26. Fred Sanders, *Wesley on the Christian Life: The Heart Renewed in Love* (Wheaton, Ill.: Crossway, 2013), 33.

CHAPTER FIFTEEN: Monsters, Nuns, and Martyrs

1. Brecht, *Shaping and Defining*, 100.

2. Bornkamm, *Luther in Mid-career*, 101.

3. *LW*, 49:21.

4. Brecht, *Shaping and Defining*, 103.

5. Luther, *Spiritual Songs of Martin Luther*, 68.

6. Ibid., 72.

7. *Luther's Correspondence and Other Contemporary Letters*, vol. 2, ed. Preserved Smith and Charles Michael Jacobs (Philadelphia: Lutheran Publication Society, 1918), 2:213–14.

8. *LW*, 32:265–66.

9. Ernst Kroker, *The Mother of the Reformation: The Amazing Life and Story of Katharine Luther*, trans. Mark E. DeGarmeaux (St. Louis: Concordia, 2013), 34.

10. Ibid., 39.

CHAPTER SIXTEEN: Fanaticism and Violence

1. *LW*, 40:130.

2. Quoted in Tom Scott, *Thomas Müntzer: Theology and Revolution in the German Reformation* (New York: St. Martin's Press, 1989), 73.

3. Brecht, *Shaping and Defining*, 148.

4. Roper, *Martin Luther*, 250.

5. Bornkamm, *Luther in Mid-career*, 147.

6. Brecht, *Shaping and Defining*, 150.

7. Quoted in Bornkamm, *Luther in Mid-career*, 160. Parenthetical per original.

8. Quoted in ibid., 161.

9. Luke 19:27, English Standard Version.

10. Brecht, *Shaping and Defining*, 153.

11. Quoted in Bornkamm, *Luther in Mid-career*, 160.

12. Quoted in Bainton, *Here I Stand*, 282.

13. Quoted in Roper, *Martin Luther*, 242.

14. Quoted in Bornkamm, *Luther in Mid-career*, 165.

15. Quoted in ibid., 166.

16. Brecht, *Shaping and Defining*, 161.

17. *LW*, 40:52–57.

18. Ibid., 128.

19. Ibid., 223.

20. Quoted in Bornkamm, *Luther in Mid-career*, 356.

21. James Harvey Robinson, *Readings in European History*, vol. 2, *From the Opening of the Protestant Revolt to the Present Day* (Boston: Ginn, 1906), 94–96.

22. Quoted in Bornkamm, *Luther in Mid-career*, 365.

23. Martin Luther, *Selected Writings of Martin Luther*, ed. Theodore G. Tappert (Minneapolis: Fortress Press, 2007), 3:335.

24. Ibid., 329–31.

25. Bornkamm, *Luther in Mid-career*, 380.

26. Martin Luther, "An Open Letter on the Harsh Booklet Against the Peasants," in *Luther: Selected Political Writings*, ed. J. M. Porter (Philadelphia: Fortress Press, 1974), 88.

27. Bornkamm, *Luther in Mid-career*, 380.

28. Ibid., 381.

29. Roper, *Martin Luther*, 264.

30. Bornkamm, *Luther in Mid-career*, 382.

31. Brecht, *Shaping and Defining*, 186.

Chapter Seventeen: Love and Marriage

1. *LW*, 3:210.

2. Quoted in Bainton, *Here I Stand*, 283.

3. Quoted in Roper, *Martin Luther*, 271.

4. Hendrix, *Visionary Reformer*, 164.

5. *LW*, 49:93.

6. Ibid., 49:104–5.

7. Ibid., 49:111.

8. Quoted in Oberman, *Luther*, 273.

9. Quoted in ibid., 275.

10. Quoted in Bainton, *Here I Stand*, 225.

11. Quoted in Oberman, *Luther*, 282.

12. Smith and Jacobs, *Luther's Correspondence*, 2:326–27.

13. Brecht, *Shaping and Defining*, 199.

14. *LW*, 49:117.

15. Quoted in Herbert David Rix, *Martin Luther: The Man and the Image* (New York: Irvington, 1983), 187.

16. Quoted in ibid.

17. Roper, *Martin Luther*, 269.

18. Smith and Jacobs, *Luther's Correspondence*, 2: 364.

19. *LW*, 54:191.

20. Ibid., 432.

21. Quoted in Bainton, *Here I Stand*, 298.

22. Quoted in ibid., 298–99.

23. *LW*, 49:152–53.

Chapter Eighteen: Erasmus, Controversy, Music

1. Bainton, *Here I Stand*, 116.

2. Quoted in ibid., 116–17.

3. *LW*, 44:22.

4. Quoted in Brecht, *Shaping and Defining*, 217.

5. Quoted in ibid., 218.

6. Manschreck, *Melanchthon*, 115.

7. Preserved Smith, *The Life and Letters of Martin Luther* (Boston: Houghton Mifflin, 1911), 209.

8. Martin Luther, *On the Bondage of the Will: A New Translation of "De Servo Arbitrio"* (1525), *Martin Luther's Reply to Erasmus of Rotterdam*, ed. J. I. Packer and O. R. Johnston (London: James Clarke, 1957), 42.

9. Ibid., 174.
10. Mark 14:22–24; Luke 22:18–20.
11. *LW,* 37:305.
12. Ibid., 300.
13. 2 Corinthians 3:6, King James Version.
14. John 6:63, King James Version.
15. Bornkamm, *Luther in Mid-career,* 171.
16. *LW,* 40:63.
17. Ibid., 214.
18. Quoted in Bainton, *Here I Stand,* 352.
19. Abraham Kuyper, "Sphere Sovereignty," in *Abraham Kuyper: A Centennial Reader,* ed. James D. Bratt (Grand Rapids: W. B. Eerdmans, 1998), 488.
20. *LW,* 49:68–69.

Chapter Nineteen: The Plague and *Anfechtungen* Return
1. Quoted in Hendrix, *Martin Luther,* 181.
2. Ibid., 182.
3. *LW,* 43:160.
4. Quoted in ibid., 181.
5. Quoted in Bornkamm, *Luther in Mid-career,* 556.
6. *LW,* 49:174.
7. John S. Stamp, John Foxe, and William Harris Rule, *Martyrologia; or, Records of Religious Persecution, Being a New and Comprehensive Book of Martyrs* (London: John Mason, 1851), 118.
8. Quoted in Brecht, *Shaping and Defining,* 209.
9. Quoted in ibid.
10. Denis R. Janz, ed., *A Reformation Reader* (Minneapolis: Fortress Press, 2008), 118.
11. Martin Luther, *The Large Catechism of Martin Luther* (Philadelphia: Fortress Press, 1959), 9.
12. Bornkamm, *Luther in Mid-career,* 564.

Chapter Twenty: The Reformation Comes of Age
1. Quoted in Hendrix, *Martin Luther,* 205.
2. Quoted in Bainton, *Here I Stand,* 327.
3. Quoted in Bornkamm, *Luther in Mid-career,* 637.
4. *LW,* 38:35.
5. Ibid., 70–71.
6. Psalm 118:17, King James Version.
7. *LW,* 49:288.
8. Quoted in Brecht, *Shaping and Defining,* 380.
9. Quoted in Bornkamm, *Luther in Mid-career,* 668.
10. Quoted in ibid.
11. Psalm 118:17, King James Version.
12. *LW,* 34:14.
13. Ibid., 18.
14. Quoted in Bornkamm, *Luther in Mid-career,* 669.
15. *LW,* 34:19–20.
16. Ibid., 60–61.
17. Oberman, *Luther,* 311.
18. Quoted in Hendrix, *Martin Luther,* 216.

19. Quoted in ibid., 217.
20. Quoted in Bainton, *Here I Stand*, 332.
21. *LW*, 49:329.
22. Roper, *Martin Luther*, 327.
23. *LW*, 49:375.
24. Romans 1:20.
25. *LW*, 49:377.
26. Ibid., 418–19.

CHAPTER TWENTY-ONE: Confronting Death

1. *LW*, 50:18–19.
2. Ibid., 138.
3. Ibid., 142.
4. *LW*, 34:288.
5. *LW*, 54:430.
6. Quoted in Lull and Nelson, *Resilient Reformer*, 343.
7. Quoted in Kittelson, *Luther the Reformer*, 238.
8. *LW*, 45:200.
9. Quoted in Brecht, *Preservation of the Church*, 349.
10. *LW*, 41:357.
11. Martin Luther, *The Table Talk or Familiar Discourse of Martin Luther*, trans. William Hazlitt (Oxford: Oxford University, 1848), 165.
12. Ibid., 30.
13. Quoted in Bainton, *Here I Stand*, 365.

CHAPTER TWENTY-TWO: "We Are Beggars. This Is True."

1. *LW*, 50:284.
2. Ibid., 292.
3. Ibid., 291.
4. Ibid., 295.
5. Ibid., 302.
6. Ibid., 51:392.
7. Quoted in Brecht, *Preservation of the Church*, 376.
8. Quoted in ibid.
9. Manschreck, *Melanchthon*, 274.
10. Ibid., 275–76.
11. Quoted in Brecht, *Preservation of the Church*, 377–78.
12. *LW*, 54:476.

BIBLIOGRAPHY

Bainton, Roland. *Here I Stand*. Nashville: Abingdon Press, 2013.

Bedini, Silvio A. *The Pope's Elephant*. Nashville: J. S. Sanders, 1998.

Bornkamm, Heinrich. *Luther in Mid-career, 1521–1530*. Philadelphia: Fortress Press, 1983.

Brecht, Martin. *Martin Luther: His Road to Reformation, 1483–1521*. Philadelphia: Fortress Press, 1985.

———. *Martin Luther: The Preservation of the Church, 1532–1546*. Minneapolis: Fortress Press, 1993.

———. *Martin Luther: Shaping and Defining the Reformation, 1521–1532*. Minneapolis: Fortress Press, 1990.

Erikson, Erik H. *Young Man Luther: A Study in Psychoanalysis and History*. New York: W. W. Norton, 1958.

Friedenstein, Gotha Stiftung Schloss, ed. *Martin Luther and the Reformation: Essays*. Dresden: Sandstein Verlag, 2016.

Hendrix, Scott H. *Martin Luther: Visionary Reformer*. New Haven, Conn.: Yale University Press, 2015.

Kittelson, James M. *Luther the Reformer: The Story of the Man and His Career*. 2nd ed. Minneapolis: Fortress Press, 2016.

Lull, Timothy F., and Derek R. Nelson. *Resilient Reformer: The Life and Thought of Martin Luther*. Minneapolis: Fortress Press, 2015.

Luther, Martin. *The Spiritual Songs of Martin Luther, from the German by J. Hunt*. London: Hamilton, Adams, 1853.

Manschreck, Clyde L. *Melanchthon: The Quiet Reformer*. New York: Abingdon Press, 1958.

Marty, Martin E. *Martin Luther: A Life*. New York: Penguin, 2004.

———. *October 31, 1517: Martin Luther and the Day That Changed the World*. Brewster, Mass.: Paraclete Press, 2016.

Mullett, Michael A. *Martin Luther*. New York: Routledge, 2015.

Murphy, Caroline. *The Pope's Daughter*. New York: Oxford University Press, 2005.

Nichols, Stephen J. *Martin Luther: A Guided Tour of His Life and Thought*. Phillipsburg, N.J.: P&R, 2002.

Oberman, Heiko A. *Luther: Man Between God and the Devil*. New York: Image Books, 1992.

Ozment, Steven. *The Serpent and the Lamb: Cranach, Luther, and the Making of the Reformation*. New Haven, Conn.: Yale University Press, 2011.

Pettegree, Andrew. *Brand Luther: How an Unheralded Monk Turned His Small Town into a Center of Publishing, Made Himself the Most Famous Man in Europe—and Started the Protestant Reformation*. New York: Penguin Books, 2015.

Reston, James, Jr. *Luther's Fortress: Martin Luther and His Reformation Under Siege.* New York: Basic Books, 2015.

Roper, Lyndal. *Martin Luther: Renegade and Prophet.* London: Bodley Head, 2016.

Ryrie, Alec. *Protestants: The Faith That Made the Modern World.* New York: Viking Press, 2017.

Sproul, R. C., and Stephen J. Nichols, eds. *The Legacy of Luther.* Orlando, Fla.: Reformation Trust, 2016.

Tuchman, Barbara W. *The March of Folly: From Troy to Vietnam.* New York: Random House, 2011.

INDEX

Page numbers in italics refer to illustrations.

PHOTOGRAPH AND ILLUSTRATION SOURCES AND CREDITS

BLACK-AND-WHITE IMAGES

49. Unknown, *Johann von Staupitz*, ca. 1600. Austrian National Library, Vienna
72. Albrecht Dürer, *Frederick the Wise, Elector of Saxony*, 1524. The Metropolitan Museum of Art, New York
91. Unknown, *Hanno with Baraballo on the Back*, sixteenth century. Via Wikimedia Commons
100. Graf Hans Moritz von Bruhl, *Johann Tetzel*, 1717. Via Wikimedia Commons
102. Lucas Cranach the Elder, *Cardinal Albrecht of Brandenburg*, 1520. The Metropolitan Museum of Art, New York
105. Unknown, title page for *On Aplas von Rom kan man wol selig werden*, Augsburg, 1521. Courtesy of the Bavarian State Library, Munich
114. Martin Luther, *Amore et studio elucidande veritatis*, Nuremberg: [Höltzel], 1517. Berlin State Library, Berlin
139. Lucas Cranach the Younger, *Philip Melanchthon, Full-Length Towards the Right*, 1561. The Metropolitan Museum of Art, New York
165. Unknown, *Portrait of Andreas Carlstadius*, eighteenth century. Via Wikimedia Commons
184. Lucas Cranach the Elder, *Martin Luther as an Augustinian Monk*, 1520. The Metropolitan Museum of Art, New York
203. Lucas Cranach the Elder, *Luther as an Augustinian Friar, with Cap*, ca. 1521. The Metropolitan Museum of Art, New York
238. Lucas Cranach the Elder, *Luther as "Junker Jörg,"* 1522. Klassik Stiftung Weimar, Weimar. Via Wikimedia Commons
291. Lucas Cranach the Elder, *The Whore of Babylon*, in *Das Newe Testament Deutzsch*, translated by Martin Luther (Wittenberg: Melchior Lotther, [September] 1522)
334. Christoph van Sichem, *Contemporary Portrait of Thomas Müntzer*, sixteenth or seventeenth century. Via Wikimedia Commons

FIRST INSERT

1. Lucas Cranach the Elder, *Luther as Junker Jörg*, 1522. Klassik Stiftung Weimar, Weimar. Via Wikimedia Commons
2. Lucas Cranach the Elder, *Portrait of Hans Luther, Luther's Father / Portrait of Margaretha Luther, Luther's Mother*, 1527. Wartburg-Stiftung, Eisenach. Via Wikimedia Commons
3. Lucas Cranach the Elder, *Portrait of Hans Luther, Luther's Father / Portrait of Margaretha Luther, Luther's Mother*, 1527. Wartburg-Stiftung, Eisenach. Via Wikimedia Commons
4. Decoration from the Martinická Bible, ca. 1429. Academy of Sciences of the Czech Republic, Prague. Via Wikimedia Commons
5. (bottom, left): Via Wikipedia Commons. Photograph: BrThomas
5. (top): Photograph courtesy of the author

5. (bottom, right): Photograph courtesy of the author
6. Barend van Orley, *Portrait of Charles V,* 1519. Museum of Fine Arts, Budapest. Via Wikimedia Commons
7. Raphael, *Portrait of Pope Leo X and His Cousins, Cardinals Giulio de' Medici and Luigi de' Rossi,* 1518–19. Uffizi Gallery, Florence. Via Wikimedia Commons
8. Lucas Cranach the Elder, *Friedrich III (1463–1525), the Wise, Elector of Saxony,* 1533. The Metropolitan Museum of Art, New York

SECOND INSERT

1. Lucas Cranach the Elder, *Luther as Junker Jörg,* 1522. Klassik Stiftung Weimar, Weimar. Via Wikimedia Commons
2. (top): Lucas Cranach the Elder, *Portrait of Katharina von Bora,* 1526. Private collection. Via Wikimedia Commons
2. (bottom): Lucas Cranach the Elder, *Portrait of Philipp Melanchthon,* 1537. Staatliche Kunsthalle, Karlsruhe. Via Wikimedia Commons
3. (top): Via Wikipedia Commons. Photograph: Robert Scarth
3. (bottom): Photograph courtesy of the author
4. Lucas Cranach the Elder, *The Sky Car and Hell Car of Andreas Bodenstein of Karlstadt,* 1519. Via Zeno.org
5. (top): Lucas Cranach the Elder, *Portrait of Georg Spalatin,* 1509. Museum der bildenden Künste, Leipzig. Via Wikimedia Commons
5. (bottom): Lucas Cranach the Elder, *Portrait of Georg Spalatin,* 1537. Staatliche Kunsthalle, Karlsruhe. Via Wikimedia Commons
6. (top): Lucas Cranach the Elder, *Self-Portrait,* 1531. Herzogliche Museum Gotha, Gotha. Via Wikimedia Commons
6. (bottom): Hans Holbein the Younger, *Erasmus of Rotterdam,* ca. 1532. The Metropolitan Museum of Art, New York
7. Via Wikimedia Commons. Photograph: Paul T. McCain

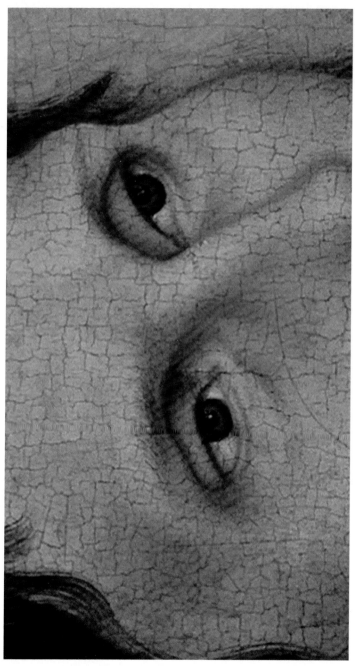

A close-up of Lucas Cranach the Elder's December 1521
portrait of Luther as "Junker George."

ANNO·1530·AM·29·TAG·IVNII·IST·HANS·LVTH
·D·MARTINVS· ·VATER·INN·GOTT
·VERSCHIE DENN·

Cranach's portrait of Luther's parents, Hans (*left*) and

Margarethe (*right*), painted during their visit to Wittenberg in 1527.

The oldest known rendering of Jan Hus being burned at the stake. It is featured in an illuminated bible from 1429, only fourteen years after Hus's death.

The very spot at which Luther took his historic stand at Worms.
The German reads: "Here stood Martin Luther before emperor and state."

The German reads: "In this house, Dr. Martin Luther was born the tenth of November, 1483."

A stone memorializing the place outside the village of Stotternheim where Martin Luther vowed to become a monk in 1505.

A portrait of Emperor Charles V
by Barend van Orley.

Raphael's official portrait of Pope Leo X, whose indifference to the ample troubles of the church led to the irrevocable sundering of Christendom in western Europe. The portrait is dated 1518–19 and hangs in the Uffizi Gallery in Florence, Italy.

A portrait of Frederich III (1463–1525).

When Luther snuck back to Wittenberg incognito in December 1521,
Lucas Cranach the Elder seized the opportunity to memorialize him in
his bearded, untonsured guise as "Junker George." Luther grew two beards
in his life, the second sprouting in similar conditions to the first during his
sequestration atop the Coburg during the Diet of Augsburg in 1530.

EFFIGIES PHIL: MELANCHTHONIS·ANN·AET·
XXX C̄Z LVCA CRONACHIO PICTORE·
·M·D·XXXVII·

Cranach's 1537 portrait of Philip Melanchthon.

Cranach's 1526 portrait of Katharina Luther.

The Wartburg Castle where Luther lived as "Junker George" after the Diet of Worms. It is here that in the spring of 1521 he translated the New Testament into German.

Luther's quarters at the Wartburg. The whale vertebra is the only item original to Luther's occupancy.

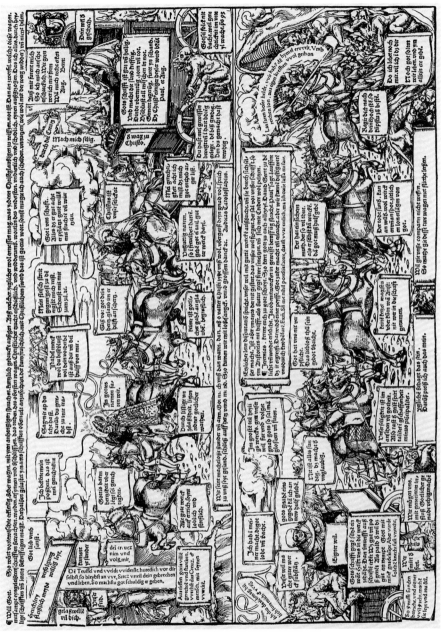

Andreas Karlstadt von Bodenstein's cartoon (created with Cranach) is an example of the earliest print propaganda, and amply illustrates his theological differences with Johannes Eck. The cartoon was published as a way to advertise their debate in Leipzig, and to influence the subsequent thinking about it.

Cranach's 1509 portrait of the twenty-five-year-old Georg Spalatin.

Cranach's 1537 portrait of the fifty-three-year-old Spalatin.

A self-portrait of Lucas Cranach
the Elder from 1531.

Hans Holbein's famous
portrait of Erasmus, the
"prince of the humanists."
In the end, Luther decried
him as "an eel" for his
slippery unwillingness
to commit to any single
position. *On the Bondage
of the Will*, Luther's
response to Erasmus's
writing on free will, is
widely regarded as his
best theological work.

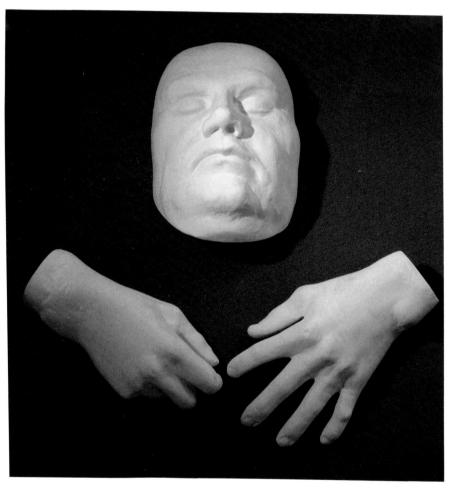

The plaster cast death mask and hands of Luther.